W9-BJN-506

THE INDISPENSABLE PILL BOOK

The Pill Book gives you the answers to the questions millions of Americans are asking about the pills their physicians are prescribing for them and their families.

This newly revised, updated and expanded 2nd edition—bigger and better than ever—gives you the essentials about all the revolutionary new drugs and drug types.

Now, thanks to *The Pill Book*, the general public can easily understand and accurately identify the medicines their doctors prescribe. *The Pill Book* describes practically everything you should know about over 1300 prescription drugs, including generic and brand names, usual dosages, side effects, adverse effects, cautions and warnings, overdose potential, and much more. It includes new, vital information on drugs considered ineffective by the U.S. government.

It is based on the same information your physician and pharmacist rely on—information seldom available to patients—*The Pill Book* synthesizes the most important facts about each drug in a concise, readable entry. Warnings about drug use are given special prominence.

THE PILL BOOK
2nd Edition

NO HOME SHOULD BE WITHOUT IT!

The purpose of this book is to provide educational information to the public concerning the majority of various types of prescription drugs which are presently utilized by physicians. It is not intended to be complete or exhaustive or in any respect a substitute for personal medical care. *Only a physician may prescribe these drugs and the exact dosage which should be taken.*

While every effort has been made to reproduce products on the cover and insert of this book in an exact fashion, certain variations of size or color may be expected as a result of the photographic process. Furthermore, pictures identified as brand name drugs should not be confused with their generic counterparts, and vice versa. *In any event, the reader should not rely upon the photographic image to identify any pills depicted herein, but should rely solely upon the physician's prescription as dispensed by the pharmacist.*

THE PILL BOOK

2nd EDITION

BERT STERN

Producer

LAWRENCE D. CHILNICK

Editor-in-Chief

Text By

HAROLD M. SILVERMAN,

Pharm. D.

GILBERT I. SIMON,

D.Sc.

Introduction by
DR. FRANK FIELD

Additional Text
LAWRENCE D. CHILNICK

Art Direction
MILTON GLASER

Photography
**BERT STERN
BURT COHEN**

Production Assistant
JOY Z. DERMANJIAN

BANTAM BOOKS
TORONTO · NEW YORK · LONDON · SYDNEY

QUANTITY PURCHASES

Companies, professional groups, churches, clubs and other organizations may qualify for special terms when ordering 24 or more copies of this title. For information, contact the Direct Response Department, Bantam Books, 666 Fifth Avenue, New York, N.Y. 10103. Phone (212) 765-6500.

THE PILL BOOK

A Bantam Book / June 1979

2nd printing......June 1979	*9th printing ..January 1980*
3rd printing ......June 1979	*10th printing .....April 1980*
4th printing .....June 1979	*11th printing......May 1980*
5th printing.......July 1979	*12th printing ..October 1980*
6th printing September 1979	*13th printing December 1980*
7th printing ...October 1979	*14th printing .....April 1981*
8th printing .November 1979	*15th printing September 1981*

Bantam Revised edition / October 1982

This revised edition was published simultaneously in hardcover, trade paperback, and mass market paperback by Bantam, October 1982

Library of Congress Catalog Card No.: 82-90322

ISBN 0-553-22527-8

Published simultaneously in the United States and Canada

PRINTED IN THE UNITED STATES OF AMERICA

O   0 9 8 7 6 5 4 3 2 1

Contents

ACKNOWLEDGMENTS

The staff of the 2nd Edition of *The Pill Book* wish to acknowledge the following people whose help and dedication has contributed to the value of this book: Richard Berman, Toni Burbank, Janet S. Chilnick, Bryan Colmer, John DeLorenzo R.Ph., Kenneth Gilberg, Maime Harris, Maggie Jakobson, Judy Knipe, Jeffrey Levine, James Miglino, Nick Miglino, Jeff Packer and Dave Phillips—Carlyle Chemists, N.Y.C., Richard Roemer, Barry Secunda, Noel Silverman, Trista Stern, Rosemarie Vitrano.

Introduction
to the Revised Edition

If you've never swallowed a pill and don't ever intend to, stop reading this book, put it down, and save yourself the purchase price. But if you're like most of us who occasionally do take pills when we're ill, then read on. Because what's in the following pages may increase your awareness about the drugs you are taking and may even be instrumental in saving your life.

How? Well, let's say you're not feeling well and you decide to visit your family doctor. Predictably, his waiting room is filled with patients, some sitting quietly, others coughing, sneezing, wheezing, and worse. To benefit from the visit, you have to stay alive. And to do that, you must breathe. But the air you're inhaling is the same air that others have exhaled in the form of those coughs, sneezes, wheezes, and worse. And the waiting time seems to crawl along.

So the scene is set. When you're finally ushered into the doctor's office, you're not only ill but tense and impatient.

Yes, the doctor tells you after his examination, there's a pill to help you. And as he hands you the prescription, he says something about meals and times-a-day. But by then you're already stuffing the prescription into your pocket and eagerly waiting to pay the fee and make your exit.

Once on your way, you breathe a sigh of relief—until those nagging doubts start to creep in: What did he say about those pills? Take them before or after meals? How many a day? Oh, I forgot to tell him I'm allergic to egg yolks. I didn't mention that my stomach gets upset easily. What shall I do?

If you've asked yourself such questions or feel that someday you might, then let me suggest that the following pages contain just the type of information to assist your memory and avoid the danger of not having listened closely or asked enough questions about the pills prescribed by your doctor.

This book has been designed for use by you, the consumer.

Among its many features, *The Pill Book*, Second Edition, has almost 700 frequently prescribed pills, pictured by color, each with its brand or generic name, dosage strength and reference to more information on other pages. Think of the value of accurate, life-sized, color pictures of pills if, for example, you are in an emergency situation with an elderly relative whose various pills are mixed together in an unmarked pillbox.

This is only one of the many reasons that no home should be without this book.

The Pill Book profiles the most commonly prescribed drugs in the United States, alphabetically, by both brand name and generic name. It tells you the reasons they're prescribed, their possible side effects, adverse effects, benefits and dangers. It spells out the usual dosage and what to do if you overdose. There's a summary of how various drugs work—among them, antibiotics, high blood pressure pills, the new heart drugs, anticancer agents and tranquilizers. Questions are answered on how the food you eat affects drug therapy and how the drugs you take affect diet and nutrition. The book contains a handy list of important questions and points to remember to raise with your doctor. (In fact, why not carry the list with you when you visit him?) There are pages of charts telling which drugs may interact with one another and what may happen as a result. In addition, *The Pill Book*, Second Edition, fully explains the effects of drugs on the elderly, children, pregnant women and even tells you which drugs the U.S. government says are not effective.

Let me emphasize that this book is not meant to substitute for the professional care of a trained physician. Nor is it designed to be the final word on whether a particular pill is dangerous or safe for your body. Only a doctor should advise conclusively on that.

But this book will provide the kind of information that either can set your mind at ease because it confirms what you thought you heard the doctor say, or can point you in the right direction if you discover or even suspect that your body may not be suited to a certain drug.

If you're faced with such a situation, you never know when, as a lawyer friend of mine would say, time is of the essence. And just then, an inexpensive ready-reference book

like this, sitting within reach by the medicine chest, can
suddenly be worth all the money in the world and maybe
more.

—Dr. Frank Field,
Science Editor,
WNBC TV, New York

In an Emergency!

Each year some 1.5 million people are poisoned in the United States; about 70,000 of the poisonings are drug-related. In fact, drug overdose is a leading cause of fatal poisoning in this country, with about 7,000 deaths recorded each year. Sedatives, barbiturates, benzodiazepine tranquilizers, and topically applied medicines are responsible for the bulk of the drug-related poisonings or overdoses.

Although each of the product information descriptions in the new revised edition of *The Pill Book* has specific information on overdose management, there are also some general rules to remember if you are confronted with someone who has been poisoned.

Do the following:

1. Make sure the victim is breathing—call for medical help immediately.
2. When calling for help, the place to call is your local poison control center. The telephone number can be obtained from information; just ask for "poison control." When you call, be prepared to tell the person who answers:

   • What was taken and how much.
   • What the victim is doing (conscious or sleeping, vomiting, having convulsions, etc.).
   • The approximate age and weight of the victim.
   • Any chronic medical problems of the victim (such as diabetes, epilepsy, or high blood pressure), if you know them.
   • What medicines, if any, the victim takes regularly.

3. Remove anything that could interfere with breathing. A person who has poor oxygen supply will turn blue (the fingernails or tongue change color first). If this happens, lay the victim on his back, open the collar, place one hand

under the neck, and lift, pull, or push the victim's jaw so that it juts outward. This will open the airway between the mouth and lungs as wide as possible. If the victim is not breathing, begin mouth-to-mouth resuscitation.

4. If the victim is unconscious or having convulsions, call for medical help immediately. While waiting for the ambulance, lay the victim on the stomach and turn the head to one side. This will prevent inhalation of vomit should the victim throw up. Do not give an unconscious victim anything by mouth. Keep the victim warm.

5. If the victim is conscious, call for medical help and give the victim an 8-ounce glass of water to drink. This will dilute the poison.

Only a small percent of poisoning victims require hospitalization. Most can be treated with simple actions or need no treatment at all.

Depending on what was taken, you may be instructed to make the patient vomit. The best way to do this is to use syrup of ipecac, which can be purchased without a prescription at any pharmacy. Specific instructions on how much to give infants, children, or adults are printed on the label and will also be given by your poison control center. Remember, *do not* make the victim vomit unless you have been instructed to do so. Never make the victim vomit if the victim is unconscious, is having a convulsion, has a painful, burning feeling in the mouth or throat, or has swallowed a corrosive poison. (Corrosive poisons include bleach—liquid or powder—washing soda, drain cleaner, lye, oven cleaner, toilet bowl cleaner, and dishwasher detergent.) If a corrosive poison has been taken and the victim can still swallow, give milk or water to dilute the poison. The poison control center will give you further instructions.

If the victim has swallowed a petroleum derivative such as gasoline, kerosene, machine oil, lighter fluid, furniture polish, or cleaning fluids, do not do anything. Call the poison control center for instructions.

If the poison or chemical has spilled onto the skin, remove any clothing or jewelry that has been contaminated and wash the area with plenty of warm water for at least 15 minutes. Then wash the area thoroughly with soap and water. The poison control center will give you more instructions.

Be Prepared

The best way to deal with a poisoning is to be ready for it. Do the following *now*:

1. Get the telephone number of your local poison control center and write it down with your other emergency phone numbers.
2. Decide which hospital you will go to, if necessary, and how you will get there.
3. Buy 1 ounce of syrup of ipecac from your pharmacy. The pharmacist will explain how to use it, if needed. Remember, this is a potent drug to be used only if directed.
4. Learn to give mouth-to-mouth resuscitation. You may have to use this on a victim of poisoning.

In order to reduce the possibility of poisoning, do the following:

- Keep all medicine, household cleaners, disinfectants, insecticides, gardening products, and similar products out of the reach of young children, in a locked place.
- Do not store poisonous materials in containers that have contained food.
- Do not remove the labels from bottles so that the contents cannot be read.
- Discard all medicines after you no longer need them.
- Do not operate a car engine or other gasoline engine in an unventilated space. Do not use a propane heater indoors.
- If you smell gas, call the gas company immediately.

Poison prevention is best achieved by common sense. If you follow the simple advice given in this chapter, you will have taken a giant step toward assuring household safety for you and your family members.

How to Use This Book

The Pill Book, like pills themselves, should be used with caution. Used properly, this book can save you money and perhaps your life.

Our book contains a section of life-sized pictures of the drugs most often prescribed in the United States. New drugs that have had an important impact on medical care, such as cancer chemotherapy and heart drugs, are included in this edition.

The Pill Book's product identification system is designed to help you check that the drug you're about to take is the right drug. Included are the most prescribed brand-name drugs and some of the more frequently prescribed generic versions of those drugs. Although many dosage forms are included, not all dosage forms of a certain drug have been shown.

Organized by color, each drug has been as faithfully reproduced as possible. While every effort has been made to depict the products accurately, certain variations of size or color may be expected as a result of the photographic process. In any event, readers should not rely solely upon the photographic image to identify any pills, but should check with their pharmacist if they have any questions about identification.

Most, although not all drugs, in the color section can be matched with the pill you have by checking to see if:
* the imprinted company logos (e.g. "Lilly," "Roche,") are the same;
* the product strengths (e.g. "250 mg.," "10 mg.,") which are frequently printed on the pills are the same;
* and if any product code numbers, which may be imprinted, are the same.

Note: Because many generic drugs look the same as their

brand-name counterparts, some manufacturers have begun to print the product name on a drug.

To find out more about the drugs depicted, check the descriptive material in the text (page numbers are given). The pill profiles provide a complete description of over 1,300 generic and brand-name drugs. These are the drugs most often prescribed to Americans. The descriptions should give you a detailed explanation of what your doctor and pharmacist have told you about your prescription. Most drugs are listed alphabetically under their generic classification; however, when a drug is a combination of two or more active ingredients, the listing is under the major brand name. Every brand and generic name is cross-referenced in the Index beginning on page 605.

Each drug profile contains the following information:

Generic or **Brand Name:** The generic name, the common name or chemical description of the drug approved by the Food and Drug Administration, is listed along with the current brand names available for each generic drug.

Most prescription drugs are sold in more than one strength. Some, such as the oral contraceptive drugs, come in packages containing different numbers of pills. A few manufacturers reflect this fact by adding letters and/or numbers to the basic drug name; others do not. An example: Norlestrin 21 1/50, Norlestrin 21 2.5/50, Norlestrin 28 1/50, Norlestrin 28 2.5/50. (The numbers here refer to the number of tablets in each monthly supply—28 or 21—and the strength of medication found in the tablets.) Other drugs come in different strengths: this is often indicated by a notation such as "DS" (double strength) or "Forte" (stronger).

The Pill Book lists only the generic or brand names (e.g., Norlestrin) where there are no differences in the basic ingredients, only in amounts of ingredients.

Type of Drug: Describes the general pharmacologic use of each drug: "antidepressant," "tranquilizer," "decongestant," "expectorant," and so on. A separate index begins on page 618 and gives page references for all the pills of a particular type.

Prescribed for: The reasons for which a drug is most often prescribed. Most drugs are given for certain symptoms, but often a drug may be prescribed in combination with another for a quite different reason. Check with your doctor if you are not sure why you have been given a certain pill.

Cautions and Warnings: Any drug can be harmful if the patient is sensitive to any of its actions. The information given alerts you to possible allergic reactions and to certain personal physical conditions such as pregnancy and heart disease which should be taken into consideration if the drug is prescribed for you.

Possible Side Effects: These are the more common side effects to be expected from a drug.

Possible Adverse Drug Effects: More uncommon effects of a pill that can be cause for concern. If you are not sure whether you are experiencing an adverse reaction, ALWAYS call your doctor.

Drug Interactions: This section tells you what other drugs should not be taken at the same time as the drug under discussion. This important information is also summarized in a general interaction chart. Drug interactions with other pills, alcohol, food, or other substances can cause death. Interactions are more common than overdoses. Obviously, it is important to be careful when taking alcohol with any medication or when taking several medications at the same time. Be sure to inform your doctor of any medication that you have been taking. Your pharmacist should also keep a record of all your prescription and nonprescription medicines. This listing, generally called a Patient Drug Profile, is used to review your record for any potential problems. You may want to keep your own drug profile and bring it to your pharmacist for review whenever a new medicine is added to it.

Usual Dose: The maximum and minimum amounts of a drug usually prescribed; however, you may be given different dosage instructions by your doctor. It is important to check with your doctor if you are confused about how often to take a pill and when, or why a different dosage than indicated in the book has been prescribed. You should not change the prescribed dosages for a drug you are taking without first calling your doctor. Dosages differ for different age groups, and this information is also given.

Overdosage: Symptoms of an overdose of drugs and the immediate steps to take in that event.

Special Information: Facts to help you take your medicine more safely, symptoms to watch for, and special instructions.

The Pill Book also describes how some of the most common drug types work. It suggests some questions you may want to ask your doctor or pharmacist about your medicine.

This book is a unique visual reference tool. Its use, however, is only intended to amplify the information given by your doctor and pharmacist.

If you read something in *The Pill Book* which does not jibe with your instructions, call your doctor. Any drug can have serious side effects if abused or used improperly.

The Most Commonly Prescribed Drugs in the United States, Generic and Brand Names, with Complete Descriptions of Drugs and Their Effects

Acetaminophen

Brand Names

A'Cenol	Neopap Supprettes
Aceta	Oraphen-PD
Actamin	Panex
Amphenol	Pedric Wafers
Anuphen	Phenaphen
APAP	SK-APAP
Bromo Seltzer	Sudoprin
Dapa	Tapar
Datril	Tempra
Dolanex	Tenol
Febrigesic	Tylenol
Febrinol	Tylenol Extra Strength
G-1	Valadol
Liquiprin	Valorin

Type of Drug

Antipyretic analgesic

Prescribed for

Symptomatic relief of pain and fever for people who cannot take Aspirin.

General Information

Acetaminophen is generally used to provide symptomatic relief from pain and fever associated with the common cold, flu, viral infections, or other disorders where pain or fever may be a problem. It is also used to relieve pain in people with an Aspirin allergy or those who cannot take Aspirin because of potential interactions with other drugs such as oral anticoagulants. It can be used to relieve pain from a variety of sources including arthritis, headache, and tooth and periodontic pain. People taking Acetaminophen for long periods of time experience restlessness and excitement when the drug is stopped.

Cautions and Warnings

Do not take Acetaminophen if you are allergic or sensitive to it. Do not take Acetaminophen for more than 10 consecutive days unless directed by your doctor. Do not take more than is prescribed for you or recommended on the package.

Possible Side Effects

This drug is relatively free from side effects. For this reason it has become extremely popular, especially among those who cannot take Aspirin.

Possible Adverse Drug Effects

Taking large doses of Acetaminophen for a long time may cause rash, itching, fever, lowered blood sugar, stimulation, and/or yellowing of the skin or whites of the eyes. Other effects of overuse may be a change in the composition of your blood.

Usual Dose

Adult: 325 to 650 milligrams 3 to 4 times per day. Do not take more than 2.6 grams (8 of the 325-milligram tablets) per day.

Child (age 7 to 12): 162 to 325 milligrams 3 to 4 times per day. Do not take more than 1.3 grams per day.

Child (age 3 to 6): 120 milligrams 3 to 4 times per day. Do not take more than 480 milligrams per day.

Child (age 1 to 3): 80 milligrams 3 times per day.

Child (under age 1): 60 milligrams 3 to 4 times per day.

Overdosage

Symptoms are development of bluish color of the lips, fingertips, etc., rash, fever, stimulation, excitement, delirium, depression, nausea and vomiting, abdominal pain, diarrhea, yellowing of the skin and/or eyes, convulsions, and coma. The patient should be taken to a hospital emergency room immediately. ALWAYS bring the medicine bottle.

Special Information

Unless abused, Acetaminophen is a beneficial, effective, and relatively nontoxic drug.

Generic Name

Acetaminophen with Codeine

Brand Name

Tylenol with Codeine

Ingredients

Acetaminophen
Codeine Phosphate

Other Brand Names

Aceta with Codeine	Panelex
Bayapap with Codeine	Papa-Deine
Capital with Codeine	Pavadon Elixir
Coastaldyne	Phenaphen with Codeine
Codap	Proval
Empracet with Codeine	SK-APAP with Codeine
Liquix-C	

Type of Drug

Narcotic analgesic combination.

Prescribed for

Relief of mild to moderate pain.

General Information

Acetaminophen with Codeine is generally prescribed for the patient who is in pain but is allergic to Aspirin. Acetaminophen with Codeine is probably not effective for arthritis or other pain caused by inflammation because the ingredient Acetaminophen does not reduce inflammation. Aspirin with Codeine will produce an anti-inflammatory effect, and this is the major difference between these two products.

Cautions and Warnings

Do not take Acetaminophen with Codeine if you know you are allergic or sensitive to it. Use this drug with extreme caution if you suffer from asthma or other breathing problems. Long-term use of Acetaminophen with Codeine may cause drug dependence or addiction. Codeine is a respiratory depressant and affects the central nervous system, producing sleepiness, tiredness, and/or inability to concentrate. Be careful if you are driving, operating machinery, or performing other functions requiring concentration. If you are pregnant or suspect that you are pregnant do not take this drug.

Possible Side Effects

Most frequent: light-headedness, dizziness, sleepiness, nausea, vomiting, loss of appetite, sweating. If these effects occur, consider calling your doctor and asking him about lowering the dose of Codeine you are taking. Usually the side effects disappear if you simply lie down.

More serious side effects of Acetaminophen with Codeine are shallow breathing or difficulty in breathing.

Possible Adverse Drug Effects

Euphoria (feeling high), weakness, sleepiness, headache, agitation, uncoordinated muscle movement, minor hallucinations, disorientation and visual disturbances, dry mouth, loss of appetite, constipation, flushing of the face, rapid heartbeat, palpitations, faintness, urinary difficulties or hesitancy, reduced sex drive and/or potency, itching, rashes, anemia, lowered blood sugar, yellowing of the skin and/or whites of the eyes. Narcotic analgesics may aggravate convulsions in those who have had convulsions in the past.

Drug Interactions

Because of its depressant effect and potential effect on breathing, Acetaminophen with Codeine should be taken with extreme care in combination with alcohol, sleeping medicine, tranquilizers, or other depressant drugs.

Usual Dose

Adult: 1 to 2 tablets every 4 hours.
Child: not recommended for children.

Overdosage

Symptoms are depression of respiration (breathing), extreme tiredness progressing to stupor and then coma, pinpointed pupils of the eyes, no response to stimulation such as a pin stick, cold and clammy skin, slowing down of the heart rate, lowering of blood pressure, yellowing of the skin and/or whites of the eyes, bluish color in skin of hands and feet, fever, excitement, delirium, convulsions, cardiac arrest, and liver toxicity (shown by nausea, vomiting, pain in the abdomen, and diarrhea). The patient should be taken to a hospital emergency room immediately. ALWAYS bring the medicine bottle.

Special Information

Acetaminophen with Codeine is best taken with food or at least ½ glass of water to prevent stomach upset.

Generic Name

Acetazolamide

Brand Names

AK-Zol
Diamox

Type of Drug

Carbonic anhydrase inhibitor.

Prescribed for

General elimination of excess body water. Treatment of glaucoma where it is desirable to lower the pressure inside the eye.

Different brands of this drug may not be absorbed into the body in exactly the same amounts. According to some studies these (bioequivalence) problems can be serious enough to alter the drug's effect on your body. Do not indiscriminately switch brands.

General Information

Acetazolamide inhibits an enzyme in the body called carbonic anhydrase. This effect allows the drug to be used as a weak diuretic, and as part of the treatment of glaucoma by helping to reduce pressure inside the eye. The same effect on carbonic anhydrase is thought to make Acetazolamide a useful drug in treating certain epileptic seizure disorders. The exact way in which the effect is produced is not understood.

Cautions and Warnings

Do not take Acetazolamide if you are pregnant. If you become pregnant and are taking Acetazolamide, discuss it with your doctor.

Do not take Acetazolamide if you have serious kidney, liver, or Addison's disease. This drug should not be used by people with low blood sodium or potassium.

Possible Side Effects

Side effects of short-term Acetazolamide therapy are usually minimal. Those which have been noted include tingling feeling in the arms or legs or at lips, mouth, or anus, loss of appetite, increased frequency in urination (to be expected, since this drug has a weak diuretic effect), occasional drowsiness and/or convulsion. Transient myopia has been reported.

Since this drug is chemically considered to be a sulfa drug it can cause all of the side effects of the sulfa drugs: fever, rash, the formation of drug crystals in the urine, and adverse effects of the drug.

Possible Adverse Drug Effects

Infrequent: itching, rash, blood in stool or urine, increased blood sugar, convulsions, diarrhea, loss of weight, nausea, vomiting, constipation, weakness, nervousness, depression, dizziness, dry mouth, disorientation, muscle spasms, ringing in the ears, loss of taste or smell, not feeling well.

Drug Interactions

Avoid over-the-counter drug products which contain stimulants or anticholinergics, which tend to aggravate glaucoma or cardiac disease. Ask your pharmacist about ingredients contained in the over-the-counter drugs.

Usual Dose

250 milligrams to 1 gram per day, according to disease and patient's condition.

Special Information

Acetazolamide may cause minor drowsiness and confusion, particularly during the first 2 weeks of therapy. Take care while performing tasks which require concentration, such as driving or operating appliances or machinery.

May be taken with food to minimize stomach upset. Call your doctor if you develop sore throat, fever, unusual bleeding or bruises, tingling in the hands or feet, rash, or unusual pains. These can be signs of important drug side effects.

Brand Name

Actifed-C Expectorant

Ingredients

Codeine Phosphate
Guaifenesin
Pseudoephedrine Hydrochloride
Triprolidine Hydrochloride

Type of Drug

Decongestant; expectorant.

Prescribed for

Relief of cough, nasal congestion, runny nose, and other symptoms associated with the common cold, viruses, or other upper respiratory diseases. The drug may also be used to treat allergies, asthma, ear infections, or sinus infections.

General Information

Actifed-C is one of almost 100 products marketed to relieve the symptoms of the common cold and other upper respiratory infections. These products contain ingredients to relieve congestion, act as an antihistamine, relieve or suppress cough, and help cough up mucus. They may contain medicine for each purpose, or may contain a combination of medicines. Some combinations leave out the antihistamine, the decongestant, or the expectorant. You must realize while taking Actifed-C or similar products that these drugs are good only for the relief of symptoms and do not treat the underlying problem, such as a cold virus or other infections.

Cautions and Warnings

Can cause excessive tiredness or drowsiness.

Possible Side Effects

Dry mouth, blurred vision, difficulty passing urine, (possibly) constipation, nervousness, restlessness or inability to sleep.

Drug Interactions

Taking Actifed-C with an MAO inhibitor can produce severe interaction. Consult your doctor first.

Do not take this drug with sedatives, tranquilizers, antihistamines, sleeping pills, thyroid medicine, or antihypertensive drugs such as Reserpine or Guanethidine.

Since Actifed-C contains ingredients which may cause sleepiness or difficulty in concentration, do not drink alcoholic beverages while taking this drug. The combination can cause excessive drowsiness or sleepiness, and result in inability to concentrate and carry out activities requiring extra concentration and coordination.

Usual Dose

1 to 2 teaspoons 4 times per day.

Special Information

Take with a full glass of water to remove excessive mucus from the throat and reduce stomach upset.

Brand Name
Actifed Tablets

Ingredients

Pseudoephedrine Hydrochloride
Triprolidine

Other Brand Names

Actamine Tablets
Eldafed Tablets
Suhist Tablets

Type of Drug

Antihistamine-decongestant.

Prescribed for

Relief of sneezing, runny nose, and nasal congestion associated with the common cold, allergy, or other upper respiratory condition.

General Information

Actifed is one of many products marketed to relieve the symptoms of the common cold. Most of these products contain ingredients to relieve nasal congestion or to dry up runny noses or relieve a scratchy throat; and several of them may contain ingredients to suppress cough, or to help eliminate unwanted mucus. All these products are good only for the relief of symptoms and do not treat the underlying problem, such as a cold virus or other infections.

Cautions and Warnings

Can cause excessive tiredness or drowsiness, restlessness, nervousness with an inability to sleep. If you are pregnant you should not take this drug.

Possible Side Effects

Tremor, headache, palpitations, elevation of blood pressure, sweating, sleeplessness, loss of appetite, nausea, vomiting, dizziness, constipation.

Drug Interactions

Interaction with alcoholic beverages may cause excessive drowsiness and/or sleepiness, or inability to concentrate. Do not take this drug with alcohol, sedatives, tranquilizers, antihistamines, sleeping pills, thyroid medicine, or antihypertensive drugs such as Reserpine or Guanethidine.

Do not self-medicate with over-the-counter drugs for the relief of cold symptoms: taking Actifed with such drugs may aggravate high blood pressure, heart disease, diabetes, or thyroid disease.

Do not take Actifed if you are taking or suspect you may be taking a monoamine oxidase (MAO) inhibitor; severe elevation in blood pressure may result.

Usual Dose

Adult: 1 tablet 2 to 3 times per day. Syrup preparation, 1 to 2 teaspoons 3 times per day.

Child (over age 6): 1 tablet 3 times per day. Syrup preparation, 2 teaspoons 3 times per day.

Child (age 4 months to 6 years): 1 teaspoon 3 times per day.

Child (under age 4 months): ½ teaspoon 3 times per day.

Special Information

Since drowsiness may occur during use of Actifed Tablets, be cautious while performing mechanical tasks requiring concentration and alertness.

If this drug upsets your stomach it should be taken with food.

Generic Name

Acyclovir

Brand Name

Zovirax

Type of Drug

Antiviral.

Prescribed for

Herpes simplex virus infections of the genital areas.

General Information

This is the first antiviral drug which has a specific effect against Herpes simplex virus and other viruses, including the virus associated with shingles, a painful condition. When applied to Herpes infections of the genital areas, Acyclovir decreases the number of new lesions, shortens the time required for healing, may decrease the pain associated with genital Herpes infections and may decrease the period during which an infected patient can transmit the disease; but it does not prevent recurrence of the infection. Treatment with Acyclovir should begin as soon as possible after the infection begins.

Cautions and Warnings

Do not use this drug if you are allergic to it. Do not use this drug if you are pregnant since there may be some risks to the unborn child. This drug should not be used by breast feeding women, as it may pass into mother's milk.

Possible Side Effects

The most common reaction to this drug is local burning and stinging. Other common reactions are genital itching and rash. However, these effects may also be experienced after local application of a plain, non-medicated ointment.

Drug Interactions

None known.

Usual Dose

Apply to Herpes lesions every 3 hours, 6 times per day for 1 week.

Special Information

Use a finger cot or rubber glove when applying Acyclovir to prevent infecting other parts of the body. It is possible for Herpes to become resistant to Acyclovir. Therefore, this drug should only be used when specifically prescribed by your doctor.

Brand Name

Aldactazide

Ingredients

Hydrochlorothiazide
Spironolactone

Other Brand Names

Spiractazide
Spironazide
Spironolactone with Hydrochlorothiazide

Type of Drug

Diuretic.

Prescribed for

High blood pressure or any condition where it is desirable to eliminate excess fluid from the body.

General Information

Aldactazide is a combination of two diuretics and is a convenient, effective approach for the treatment of diseases where the elimination of excess fluids is required. One of the ingredients in Aldactazide has the ability to hold potassium in the body while producing a diuretic effect. This balances off the other ingredient, Hydrochlorothiazide, which normally causes a loss of potassium from outside sources.

Combination drugs such as Aldactazide should only be used when you need the exact amount of ingredients contained in the product and when your doctor feels you would benefit from taking one dose per day.

Cautions and Warnings

Do not use Aldactazide if you have nonfunctioning kidneys, if you may be allergic to this drug or any sulfa drug, or if you have a history of allergy or bronchial asthma. Aldactazide may be used to treat specific conditions in pregnant women, but the decision to use this medication by pregnant women should be weighed carefully because the drug may cross the placental barrier into the blood of the unborn child. Aldactazide may appear in the breast milk of nursing mothers. Do not take any potassium supplements together with Aldactazide unless specifically directed to do so by your doctor.

Possible Side Effects

Drowsiness, lethargy, headache, gastrointestinal upset, cramping and diarrhea, rash, mental confusion, fever, feeling of ill health, enlargement of the breasts, inability to achieve or maintain erection in males, irregular menstrual cycles or deepening of the voice in females.

Possible Adverse Drug Effects

Loss of appetite, headache, tingling in the toes and fingers, restlessness, anemias or other effects on components of the blood, unusual sensitivity to sunlight, dizziness when rising quickly from a sitting position. Aldactazide can also produce muscle spasms, gout, weakness, and blurred vision.

Drug Interactions

Aldactazide will increase (potentiate) the action of other blood-pressure-lowering drugs. This is beneficial, and is frequently used to help lower blood pressure in patients with hypertension.

The possibility of developing imbalances in body fluids (electrolytes) is increased if you take other medications such as Digitalis and adrenal corticosteroids while you are taking Aldactazide.

If you are taking an oral antidiabetic drug and begin taking Aldactazide, the antidiabetic dose may have to be altered.

Lithium Carbonate should not be taken with Aldactazide because the combination may increase the risk of lithium toxicity.

Avoid over-the-counter cough, cold, or allergy remedies containing stimulant drugs which can aggravate your condition.

Aldactazide may interfere with the oral blood-thinning drugs (like Warfarin) by making the blood more concentrated (thicker).

Usual Dose

2 to 4 tablets per day, adjusted by your doctor until the desired therapeutic effect is achieved.

Special Information

This drug may cause drowsiness or sleepiness. Do not drive or operate machinery. Call your doctor if you develop muscle or stomach cramps, dizziness, nausea, diarrhea, unusual thirst, headache, rash, voice changes, breast enlargement, or unusual menstrual period. This drug may be taken with food to reduce stomach upset.

Brand Name

Aldoril

Ingredients

Hydrochlorothiazide
Methyldopa

Type of Drug

Antihypertensive combination.

Prescribed for

High blood pressure.

General Information

Be sure to take this medicine exactly as prescribed: if you
don't, it cannot exert its maximum effect.

An ingredient in this drug can cause loss of potassium.
Potassium loss leads to a condition known as hypokalemia.
Warning signs of hypokalemia or other electrolyte imbalances that can be due to Aldoril are dryness of the mouth,
excessive thirst, weakness, drowsiness, restlessness, muscle
pains or cramps, muscular fatigue, lack of urination, abnormal heart rhythms, and upset stomach. If this happens, call
your doctor. You may have to take extra potassium to supplement loss due to Aldoril. This may be taken as a potassium supplement (tablet, powder, liquid) or as a high
concentration of foods in your diet which contain potassium.
Some of these foods are bananas, citrus fruits, melons, and
tomatoes.

Cautions and Warnings

Do not take Aldoril if you are allergic to either of its ingredients,
if you have any liver diseases such as hepatitis or active
cirrhosis (liver disease), or if previous therapy with Methyldopa has been associated with signs of liver reaction (jaundice or unexplained fever).

This drug will pass into the unborn child and can be found
in mother's milk. Pregnant women should use this drug only
if it is absolutely necessary. Women taking Aldoril should
not breast-feed their infants.

Possible Side Effects

Loss of appetite, stomach upset, nausea, vomiting, cramps, diarrhea, constipation, dizziness, headache, tingling in the extremities, restlessness, chest pains, abnormal heart rhythms, drowsiness during the first few days of therapy.

Possible Adverse Drug Effects

Aldoril can cause abnormal liver function in the first 2 to 3 months of therapy. Watch for jaundice (yellowing of the skin or whites of the eyes), with or without fever. If you are taking Aldoril for the first time, be sure the doctor checks your liver function, particularly during the first 6 to 12 weeks of therapy. If fever or jaundice appears, notify your doctor immediately and discontinue therapy. Other adverse effects: stuffed nose, breast enlargement lactation (in females), impotence or decreased sex drive, mild arthritis, skin reactions such as mild eczema, stomach gas, dry mouth, sore or black tongue, fever.

Drug Interactions

Interaction with Digitalis or Quinidine can result in the development of abnormal heart rhythms.

Interaction with lithium products can lead to lithium toxicity unless appropriate dose adjustments are made.

Do not self-medicate with over-the-counter cough, cold, or allergy remedies containing stimulant drugs which may raise your blood pressure. If you are not sure which over-the-counter drugs are safe for you, ask your pharmacist.

Usual Dose

Individualized to suit the patient. The usual starting dose, 1 tablet 2 to 3 times per day for the first 2 days, is adjusted up or down as needed.

Special Information

Aldoril may cause temporary mild sedation. Contact your doctor if your normal urine output is dropping or you are less hungry or nauseated.

Be aware that Aldoril can cause orthostatic hypotension (dizziness when rising from a sitting or lying position). Alcohol will worsen this effect, so avoid alcohol at the beginning of Aldoril therapy.

You may take this drug with food to reduce upset stomach. Call your doctor if you develop muscle weakness, cramps, nausea, dizziness, fever, or tiredness.

Generic Name

Allopurinol

Brand Names

Lopurin
Zyloprim

Type of Drug

Anti-gout, anti-uric medication.

Prescribed for

Prevention of the formation of uric acid by the body.

General Information

Unlike other anti-gout drugs which affect the elimination of uric acid from the body, Allopurinol acts on the system that manufactures uric acid in your body. A high level of uric acid can mean that you have gout or that you have one of many other diseases, including various cancers and malignancies, or psoriasis. High uric acid levels can be caused by taking some drugs, including diuretic medicines. The fact that you have a high blood level of uric acid does not point to a specific disease.

Cautions and Warnings

Do not take this medication if you have ever developed a severe reaction to it. If you develop a rash or any other adverse effects while taking Allopurinol, stop taking the medication immediately and contact your doctor. Allopurinol should be used by children only if they have high uric acid levels due to neoplastic disease. A nursing mother should not take this medication, since it will pass through the mother's milk into the child. Allopurinol can affect the development of the unborn child if taken through pregnancy; pregnant women should not use this medication without specifically discussing this with a doctor.

Possible Side Effects

You may develop rash. Such rashes have been associated with severe, allergic, or sensitivity reactions to Allopurinol. If you develop an unusual rash or other sign of drug toxicity, stop taking this medication and contact your doctor. Other side effects: nausea, vomiting, diarrhea, intermittent stomach pains, effects on blood components, drowsiness or lack of ability to concentrate, and, rarely, effects on the eyes.

Possible Adverse Drug Effects

Loss of hair, fever, chills, arthritislike symptoms, itching.

Drug Interactions

Avoid interaction with iron tablets or vitamins with iron: Allopurinol can cause iron to concentrate in your liver. Megadoses of Vitamin C may increase the possibility of kidney stone formation.

Interaction with drugs used to treat cancer is important and should be taken into account by your physician.

Allopurinol may interact with anticoagulant (blood-thinning) medication such as Dicoumarol. The importance of this interaction is not yet known.

Usual Dose

Adult: 200 to 600 milligrams per day, depending on disease and patient's response.

Child (age 6 to 10): 300 milligrams per day.

Child (under age 6): 150 milligrams per day.

The dose should be reviewed periodically by your doctor to be sure that it is producing the desired therapeutic effect.

Special Information

Drink large amounts of water, juices, soda, or other liquids to avoid the formation of crystals in your urine and/or kidneys.

Allopurinol can make you sleepy or make it difficult for you to concentrate: take care while driving a car or using other equipment or machinery.

This drug may be taken with food to reduce upset stom-

ach. Take each dose with a full glass of water. While taking
this drug, drink 10 to 12 glasses of fluid each day. Call your
doctor if you develop a rash.

Generic Name

Alprazolam

Trade Name

Xanax

Type of drug

Tranquilizer.

Prescribed for

Relief of symptoms of anxiety, tension, fatigue and agitation.

General Information

Alprazolam is a member of the chemical group of drugs
known as benzodiazepines. These drugs are used either as
antianxiety agents, anticonvulsants, or sedatives (sleeping
pills). They exert their effects by relaxing the large skeletal
muscles and by a direct effect on the brain. In doing so, they
can relax you and make you either more tranquil or sleepier,
depending upon which drug you use and how much you
take. Many doctors prefer the benzodiazepines to other drugs
that can be used for the same effects because benzodiazepines
tend to be safer, have fewer side effects, and are usually as,
if not more, effective. The benzodiazepines are generally
prescribed in any situation where they can be a useful adjunct.

The benzodiazepines, including Alprazolam, can be abused
if taken for long periods of time, and it is possible to experience withdrawal symptoms if you stop taking the drug abruptly. Withdrawal symptoms include tremor, muscle cramp,
stomach cramps, vomiting, insomnia, and convulsions.

Cautions and Warnings

Do not take Alprazolam if you know you are sensitive or
allergic to this drug or other benzodiazepines such as Diaze-

pam, Oxazepam, Chlorazepate, Halazepam, Lorazepam, Prazepam, Flurazepam, and Clonazepam. Alprazolam and other members of this group can aggravate narrow angle glaucoma, but if you have open angle glaucoma you may take the drug. In any case, check with your doctor. Alprazolam can cause tiredness, drowsiness, inability to concentrate, or similar symptoms. Be careful if you are driving, operating machinery, or performing other activities which require concentration. Avoid taking this drug during the first 3 months of pregnancy, except under the strict supervision of your doctor.

Possible Side Effects

Most common: mild drowsiness during the first few days of therapy, especially in the elderly or debilitated. If drowsiness persists, contact your doctor.

Possible Adverse Drug Effects

Major adverse effects: confusion, depression, lethargy, disorientation, headache, inactivity, slurred speech, stupor, dizziness, tremor, constipation, dry mouth, nausea, inability to control urination, sexual difficulties, irregular menstrual cycle, changes in heart rhythm, lowered blood pressure, fluid retention, blurred or double vision, itching, rash, hiccups, nervousness, inability to fall asleep, and occasional liver dysfunction. If you experience any of these symptoms, stop taking the medicine and contact your doctor immediately.

Drug Interactions

Alprazolam is a central nervous system depressant. Avoid alcohol, other tranquilizers, narcotics, barbiturates, MAO inhibitors, antihistamines, and medicine used to relieve depression. Taking Alprazolam with these drugs may result in excessive depression, tiredness, sleepiness, difficulty breathing, or similar symptoms. Smoking may reduce the effectiveness of Alprazolam by increasing the rate at which it is broken down by the body. The effects of Alprazolam may be prolonged when taken together with Cimetidine.

Usual Dose

0.75 to 4 milligrams per day. The dose must be tailored to the individual needs of the patient. Elderly or debilitated

patients will require less of the drug to control anxiety or
tension. This drug should not be used in children.

Overdosage

Symptoms are: confusion, sleepiness, lack of response to
pain such as a pin stick, shallow breathing, lowered blood
pressure, and coma. The patient should be taken to a hospital emergency room for treatment. ALWAYS bring the medicine bottle with you.

Special Information

Do not drink alcoholic beverages while taking Alprazolam.
Sleeping pills, narcotics, barbiturates, other tranquilizers, or
any other drug which produces central nervous depression
should be used with caution while taking Alprazolam. Tell
your doctor if you become pregnant or are nursing an infant.

Brand Name

Ambenyl Expectorant

Ingredients

Ammonium Chloride
Bromodiphenhydramine Hydrochloride
Codeine Sulfate
Diphenhydramine
Potassium Guaiacolsulfonate

Type of Drug

Cough suppressant and expectorant combination.

Prescribed for

Coughs.

General Information

Ambenyl Expectorant may make you tired or drowsy. Avoid
other drugs which may have the same effect, since they will
add to the drowsiness.

Cautions and Warnings

Do not take this medicine if you are allergic to any of its
ingredients.

Possible Side Effects

Drowsiness, dry mouth, blurred vision, difficulty in urination,
constipation.

Possible Adverse Drug Effects

Palpitations—pounding of the heart.

Drug Interactions

Avoid alcohol, sedatives, tranquilizers, antihistamines, and
other medications which can cause tiredness and/or drowsiness.

  Taking Ambenyl Expectorant with Isocarboxazid (Marplan),
Tranylcypromine Sulfate (Parnate), Phenelzine Sulfate (Nardil),
or other MAO inhibitor drugs can produce a severe interaction. Consult your doctor first.

Usual Dose

  Adult: 2 teaspoons 4 times per day.
  Child (over age 1): ½ to 1 teaspoon 3 to 4 times per day.
  Take with a full glass of water. This will help the expecto-
rant effect of the drug and may reduce stomach upset.

Special Information

Be aware of the potential depressive effects of Ambenyl
Expectorant; be careful when driving or operating heavy or
dangerous machinery.

Generic Name

Amitriptyline

Brand Names

Amitril
Elavil
Endep
SK-Amitriptyline

Type of Drug

Antidepressant.

Prescribed for

Depression with or without symptoms of anxiety.

General Information

Amitriptyline and other members of this group are effective in treating symptoms of depression. They can elevate your mood, increase physical activity and mental alertness, improve appetite and sleep patterns. These drugs are mild sedatives' and therefore useful in treating mild forms of depression associated with anxiety. You should not expect instant results with this medicine: results are usually seen after 1 to 4 weeks. If symptoms are not affected after 6 to 8 weeks, contact your doctor. Occasionally this drug and other members of the group of drugs have been used in treating night-time bed-wetting in the young child, but they do not produce long-lasting relief and therapy with one of them for night-time bed-wetting is of questionable value.

Cautions and Warnings

Do not take Amitriptyline if you are allergic or sensitive to this or other members of this class of drug: Doxepin, Nortriptyline, Imipramine, Desipramine, and Protriptyline. The drugs should not be used if you are recovering from a heart attack. Amitriptyline may be taken with caution if you have a history of epilepsy or other convulsive disorders, difficulty in urination, glaucoma, heart disease, or thyroid disease. Amitriptyline can interfere with your ability to perform tasks which require concentration, such as driving or operating machinery. Do not stop taking this medicine without first discussing it with your doctor, since stopping may cause you to become nauseated, weak, and headachy. Amitriptyline will pass from mother to unborn child: consult your doctor before taking this medicine if you are pregnant.

Possible Side Effects

Changes in blood pressure (both high and low), abnormal heart rates, heart attack, confusion, especially in elderly patients, hallucinations, disorientation, delusions, anxiety, restlessness, excitement, numbness and tingling in the extremities, lack of coordination, muscle spasms or tremors, seizures and/or convulsions, dry mouth, blurred vision, constipation, inability to urinate, rash, itching, sensitivity to bright light or sunlight, retention of fluids, fever, allergy, changes in composition of blood, nausea, vomiting, loss of appetite, stomach upset, diarrhea, enlargement of the breasts in males and females, increased or decreased sex drive, increased or decreased blood sugar.

Possible Adverse Drug Effects

Infrequent: agitation, inability to sleep, nightmares, feeling of panic, a peculiar taste in the mouth, stomach cramps, black coloration of the tongue, yellowing eyes and/or skin, changes in liver function, increased or decreased weight, excessive perspiration, flushing, frequent urination, drowsiness, dizziness, weakness, headache, loss of hair, nausea, not feeling well.

Drug Interactions

Interaction with monoamine oxidase (MAO) inhibitors can cause high fevers, convulsions, and occasionally death. Don't take MAO inhibitors until at least 2 weeks after Amitriptyline has been discontinued.

Amitriptyline interacts with Guanethidine and Clonidine, drugs used to treat high blood pressure: if your doctor prescribes Amitriptyline and you are taking medicine for high blood pressure, be sure to discuss this with him.

Amitriptyline increases the effects of barbiturates, tranquilizers, other depressive drugs, and alcohol. Don't drink alcoholic beverages if you take this medicine.

Taking Amitriptyline and thyroid medicine will enhance the effects of the thyroid medicine. The combination can cause abnormal heart rhythms. The combination of Amitriptyline and Reserpine may cause overstimulation.

Large doses of Vitamin C (Ascorbic Acid), oral contraceptives, or smoking can reduce the effect of Amitriptyline. Drugs such as Bicarbonate of Soda, Acetazolamide, Quinidine, or Procainamide will increase the effect of Amitriptyline. Ritalin and phenothiazine drugs such as Thorazine and Compazine block the metabolism of Amitriptyline, causing it to stay in the body longer. This can cause possible overdose.

The combination of Amitriptyline with large doses of the sleeping pill Ethchlorvynol has caused patients to experience passing delirium.

Usual Dose

25 milligrams 3 times per day, which may be increased to 150 milligrams per day if necessary. The medication must be tailored to the needs of the patient.

Adolescent or elderly: lower doses are recommended—generally, 30 to 50 milligrams per day.

Overdosage

Symptoms are confusion, inability to concentrate, hallucinations, drowsiness, lowered body temperature, abnormal heart rate, heart failure, enlarged pupils of the eyes, convulsions, severely lowered blood pressure, stupor, and coma (as well as agitation, stiffening of body muscles, vomiting, and high fever). The patient should be taken to a hospital emergency room immediately. ALWAYS bring the medicine bottle.

Generic Name

Amobarbital

Brand Name

Sodium Amytal

Type of Drug

Hypnotic; sedative; anticonvulsive.

Prescribed for

Daytime sedation, sedation before surgery, sleeping medication, control of convulsive disorders.

General Information

Amobarbital, like the other barbiturates, appear to act by interfering with nerve impulses to the brain. When used as an anticonvulsive, Amobarbital is not very effective by itself; but when used with anticonvulsive agents such as Phenytoin, the combined action of Amobarbital and Phenytoin is dra-

matic. This combination has been used very successfully to
control epileptic seizures.

Cautions and Warnings

Amobarbital may slow down your physical and mental
reflexes; be extremely careful when operating machinery,
driving an automobile, or performing other potentially dangerous tasks. Amobarbital is classified as a barbiturate; long-
term or unsupervised use may cause addiction. Elderly people
on Amobarbital may exhibit nervousness and confusion at
times. Barbiturates are neutralized in the liver and eliminated from the body through the kidneys; consequently,
people who have liver or kidney disorders—namely, difficulty in forming or excreting urine—should be carefully monitored by their doctor when taking Amobarbital.

   If you have known sensitivities or allergies to barbiturates,
or if you have previously been addicted to sedatives or
hypnotics, or if you have a disease affecting the respiratory
system, you should not take Amobarbital.

Possible Side Effects

Difficulty in breathing, rash, and general allergic reaction
such as running nose, watering eyes, and scratchy throat.

Possible Adverse Drug Effects

Drowsiness, lethargy, dizziness, hangover, nausea, vomiting,
diarrhea. More severe adverse reactions may include anemia and yellowing of the skin and eyes.

Drug Interactions

Interaction with alcohol, tranquilizers, or other sedatives
increases the effect of Amobarbital.

   Interaction with anticoagulants (blood-thinning agents) can
reduce their effect. This is also true of muscle relaxants and
painkillers.

Usual Dose

Daytime sedative: up to 150 milligrams per day.
Sleeping medication: up to 200 milligrams at bedtime.
Anticonvulsant: 65 milligrams 2 to 4 times a day.
Sedation before surgery: 200 milligrams 1 to 2 hours before
surgery.

Overdosage

Symptoms are difficulty in breathing, decrease in size of the pupils of the eyes, lowered body temperature progressing to fever as time passes, fluid in the lungs, and eventually coma.

Anyone suspected of having taken an overdose must be taken to the hospital for immediate care. ALWAYS bring the medicine bottle to the emergency room physician so he can quickly and correctly identify the medicine and start treatment. Severe overdosage of this medication can kill; the drug has been used many times in suicide attempts.

Generic Name

Amoxapine

Brand Name

Asendin

Type of Drug

Antidepressant.

Prescribed for

Depression with or without symptoms of anxiety.

General Information

Amoxapine and other members of this group are effective in treating symptoms of depression. They can elevate your mood, increase physical activity and mental alertness, improve appetite and sleep patterns. These drugs are mild sedatives and therefore useful in treating mild forms of depression associated with anxiety. You should not expect instant results with this medicine: results are usually seen after 1 to 4 weeks. If symptoms are not affected after 6 to 8 weeks, contact your doctor. Occasionally this drug and other members of the group of drugs have been used in treating nighttime bed-wetting in the young child, but they do not produce long-lasting relief, and therapy with one of them for nighttime bed-wetting is of questionable value.

Cautions and Warnings

Do not take Amoxapine if you are allergic or sensitive to this or other members of this class of drug: Doxepin, Nortriptyline, Imipramine, Desipramine, and Amitriptyline. The drugs should not be used if you are recovering from a heart attack. Amoxapine may be taken with caution if you have a history of epilepsy or other convulsive disorders, difficulty in urination, glaucoma, heart disease, or thyroid disease. Amoxapine can interfere with your ability to perform tasks which require concentration, such as driving or operating machinery. Amoxapine will pass from mother to unborn child: consult your doctor before taking this medicine if you are pregnant.

Possible Side Effects

Changes in blood pressure (both high and low), abnormal heart rates, heart attack, confusion, especially in elderly patients, hallucinations, disorientation, delusions, anxiety, restlessness, excitement, numbness and tingling in the extremities, lack of coordination, muscle spasms or tremors, seizures and/or convulsions, dry mouth, blurred vision, constipation, inability to urinate, rash, itching, sensitivity to bright light or sunlight, retention of fluids, fever, allergy, changes in composition of blood, nausea, vomiting, loss of appetite, stomach upset, diarrhea, enlargement of the breasts in males and females, increased or decreased sex drive, increased or decreased blood sugar.

Possible Adverse Drug Effects

Infrequent: agitation, inability to sleep, nightmares, feeling of panic, a peculiar taste in the mouth, stomach cramps, black coloration of the tongue, yellowing eyes and/or skin, changes in liver function, increased or decreased weight, perspiration, flushing, frequent urination, drowsiness, dizziness, weakness, headache, loss of hair, nausea, not feeling well.

Drug Interactions

Interaction with monoamine oxidase (MAO) inhibitors can cause high fevers, convulsions, and occasionally death. Don't take MAO inhibitors until at least 2 weeks after Amoxapine has been discontinued.

Amoxapine interacts with Guanethidine, a drug used to treat high blood pressure: if your doctor prescribes Amoxapine and you are taking medicine for high blood pressure, be sure to discuss this with him.

Amoxapine increases the effects of barbiturates, tranquilizers, other depressive drugs, and alcohol. Don't drink alcoholic beverages if you take this medicine.

Taking Amoxapine and thyroid medicine will enhance the effects of the thyroid medicine. The combination can cause abnormal heart rhythms.

Large doses of Vitamin C (Ascorbic Acid) can reduce the effect of Amoxapine. Drugs such as Bicarbonate of Soda or Acetazolamide will increase the effect of Amoxapine.

Usual Dose

Adult: 150 to 400 milligrams per day. Hospitalized patients may need up to 600 milligrams per day. The dose of this drug must be tailored to patient's need.

Elderly: lower doses are recommended; for people over 60 years of age, usually 75 to 300 milligrams per day.

This drug should not be given to patients under age 16.

Overdosage

Symptoms are confusion, inability to concentrate, hallucinations, drowsiness, lowered body temperature, abnormal heart rate, heart failure, large pupils of the eyes, convulsions, severely lowered blood pressure, stupor, and coma (as well as agitation, stiffening of body muscles, vomiting, and high fever). The patient should be taken to a hospital emergency room immediately. ALWAYS bring the medicine bottle.

Generic Name

Amoxicillin

Brand Names

Amoxil	Sumox
Larotid	Trimox
Polymox	Wymox
Robamox	

Type of Drug

Broad-spectrum antibiotic.

Prescribed for

Gram-positive bacterial infections. Gram-positive bacteria (pneumococci, streptococci, and staphylococci) are organisms which usually cause diseases such as pneumonia, infections of the tonsils and throat, venereal disease, meningitis (infection of the spinal column), and septicemia (general infection of the bloodstream).

Infections of the urinary tract and some infections of the gastrointestinal tract can also be treated with Amoxicillin.

General Information

Amoxicillin is manufactured in the laboratory by fermentation and by general chemical reaction and is classified as a semisynthetic antibiotic. Because the effectiveness of the antibiotic is determined by the drug's ability to destroy the cell wall of the invading bacteria, it is very important that the patient completely follow the doctor's prescribing directions. These directions include spacing of doses as well as the number of days the patient should continue taking the medicine. If they are not followed, the effect of the antibiotic is severely reduced. To ensure the maximum effect of this drug, you should take the medication on an empty stomach, either 1 hour before or 2 hours after meals.

Cautions and Warnings

If you have a known history of allergy to Penicillin you should avoid taking Amoxicillin, since the drugs are chemically very similar. The most common allergic reaction to Amoxicillin, as well as to the other penicillins, is a hivelike rash over the body with itching and redness. It is important to tell your doctor if you have ever taken this drug or penicillins before and if you have experienced any adverse reaction to the drug such as rash, itching, or difficulty in breathing.

Possible Side Effects

Common: stomach upset, nausea, vomiting, diarrhea, and possible rash. Less common: hairy tongue, itching or irritation around the anus and/or vagina. If these symptoms occur, you should contact your doctor immediately.

Drug Interactions

The effect of Amoxicillin can be significantly reduced when it is taken with other antibiotics. Consult your doctor if you are taking both. Otherwise, Amoxicillin is generally free of interaction with other medications.

Usual Dose

Adult: 250 milligrams every 8 hours.

Child: 9 milligrams per pound of body weight per day in 3 divided doses (every 8 hours). Amoxicillin pediatric drops (under 3 pounds), 1 milliliter every 8 hours; (3 to 4 pounds), 2 milliliters every 8 hours. Dose may be halved for less serious infections or doubled for severe infections.

Storage

Amoxicillin can be stored at room temperature.

Special Information

Do not take Amoxicillin after the expiration date on the label.

The safety of the drug in pregnancy has not been established.

Generic Name

Ampicillin

Brand Names

Amcil	Polycillin
Ampico	Principen
Omnipen	SK-Ampicillin
Penbritin	Supen
Pensyn	Totacillin
Pfizerpen A	

Type of Drug

Broad-spectrum antibiotic.

Prescribed for

Gram-positive bacterial infections. Gram-positive bacteria

(pneumococci, streptococci, and staphylococci) are organisms which usually cause diseases such as pneumonia, infections of the tonsils and throat, venereal disease, meningitis (infection of the spinal column), and septicemia (general infection of the bloodstream).

Infections of the urinary tract and some infections of the gastrointestinal tract can also be treated with Ampicillin.

General Information

Ampicillin is manufactured in the laboratory by the process known as fermentation and by general chemical reaction and is classified as a semisynthetic antibiotic. Because the effectiveness of the antibiotic is determined by the drug's ability to destroy the cell wall of the invading bacteria, it is very important that the patient completely follow the doctor's prescribing directions. These directions include spacing of doses as well as the number of days the patient should continue taking the medicine. If they are not followed, the effect of the antibiotic is severely reduced. To ensure the maximum effect of this drug, you should take the medication on an empty stomach, either 1 hour before or 2 hours after meals.

Cautions and Warnings

If you have a known history of allergy to Penicillin you should avoid taking Ampicillin, since the drugs are chemically very similar. The most common allergic reaction to Ampicillin, as well as to the other penicillins, is a hivelike rash over the body with itching and redness. It is important to tell your doctor if you have ever taken this drug or penicillins before and if you have experienced any adverse reaction to the drug such as skin rash, itching, or difficulty in breathing.

Possible Side Effects

Common: stomach upset, nausea, vomiting, diarrhea, and possible rash. Less common: hairy tongue, itching or irritation around the anus and/or vagina. If these symptoms occur, you should contact your doctor immediately.

Drug Interactions

The effect of Ampicillin can be significantly reduced when taken with other antibiotics. Consult your doctor if you are

taking both. Otherwise, Ampicillin is generally free of interaction with other medications.

Usual Dose

Adult: 250 to 500 milligrams every 6 hours.
Child (44 pounds and over): same as adult.
Child (under 44 pounds): 25 to 50 milligrams per pound
per day.

Storage

Ampicillin can be stored at room temperature.

Special Information

Do not take Ampicillin after the expiration date on the label.
The safety of the drug in pregnancy has not been established.

Type of Drug
Antacids

Brand Names

Aluminum Antacids

Aluminum Hydroxide Gel	Dialume
AlternaGel	Nephrox
Alu-Cap	Phosphaljel
Alu-Tab	Robalate
Amphojel	Rolaids
Basaljel	

Calcium Antacids

Alka-2	Equilet
Alkets	Gustalac
Amitone	Macalbis
Calcilac	Mallamint
Calcium Carbonate	P.H. Tablets
Calglycine	Titralac
Chooz	Trialka Tablets
Dicarbosil	Tums
El-Da-Mint	

Magnesium Antacids

Magnesium Carbonate
Magnesium Oxide
Magnesium Trisilicate
Mag-Ox 400
Maox

Milk of Magnesia
Mint-o-Mag
Oxabid
Par-Mag
Ur-Omag

Sodium Bicarbonate Antacids

Bell/ans
Soda Mint

Sodium Bicarbonate

Aluminum + Calcium Antacid

Bisodol

Aluminum + Magnesium Antacids

Algenic Alka
Algimate
Algitab
Alka-Med
Alma-Mag
Aludrox
Alumid
Alurex
Aluscop
Alusil
A-M-T
Creamalin
Delcid
Estomul-M
Gaviscon
Kolantyl
Kudrox
Maalox

Magmalin
Magnagel
Magnalum
Magnatril
Maxamag
Neutracomp
Neutralox
PAMA
Riopan
Rolox
Rulox
Spenox
Syntrogel
Tralmag
Trialka Liquid
Trimagel
Trisogel
WinGel

Calcium + Magnesium Antacids

Krem
Ratio
Spastosed

Aluminum + Calcium + Magnesium Antacids

Camalox

Co-Gel
Eugel
Glycogel

Aluminum + Magnesium + Simethicone (an antigas ingredient) Antacids

Almacone	Gelusil-M
Alumid Plus	Maalox Plus
Antar	Mylanta
Digel	Silain Gel
Flacid	Simaal
Gelusil	Simeco

Effervescent powders or tablets Antacids

Alka-Seltzer without aspirin
Bisodol Powder
Bromo Seltzer
Citrocarbonate
ENO

Type of Drug

Gastrointestinal acid antagonist.

Prescribed for

Relief of heartburn, acid indigestion, sour stomach, or other conditions related to an upset stomach. These drugs are also prescribed for excess acid in the stomach or intestine associated with ulcer, gastritis, esophagitis, and hiatal hernia. Antacid therapy will help these conditions to heal more quickly. Aluminum antacids are prescribed for kidney failure patients to prevent phosphate from being absorbed into the body. Only Aluminum Hydroxide Gel (any brand) and Basalgel have been shown to be useful as phosphate binders.

General Information

In spite of the large number of antacid products available on the market, there are basically only a few different kinds. All antacids work against stomach acid in the same way—by neutralizing the acid through a chemical reaction. The choice of an antacid is based upon its "neutralizing capacity," that is, how much acid is neutralized by a given amount of antacid. Sodium and calcium have the greatest capacity but should not be used for long-term or ulcer therapy because of the effects large amounts of sodium and calcium can have on your body. Of the other products, Magnesium Hydroxide has the greatest capacity. Next come mixtures of magnesium and aluminum compounds, Magnesium Trisilicate, Aluminum Hydroxide, and Aluminum Phosphates, in that order. The neutralizing capacity of an antacid product also depends upon how it is formulated, how much antacid is put in the mixture, and what the form of the mixture is. Antacid suspensions have greater neutralizing capacity than powders or tablets. Antacid tablets should be thoroughly chewed before they are swallowed.

In most cases, the choice of an antacid product is based purely upon advertising, packaging, convenience, taste, or price. The similarity among so many products accounts for the vast amounts of advertising and promotion put behind antacid products.

Cautions and Warnings

People with high blood pressure or heart failure, and those on low sodium diets, must avoid antacids with a high sodium content. Riopan has the lowest sodium content of all antacids.

Sodium Bicarbonate is easily absorbed and may result in a condition called systemic alkalosis if it is taken for a long period of time. Magnesium antacids must be used with caution by patients with kidney disease.

Possible Side Effects

Diarrhea (magnesium products); constipation (aluminum and calcium products). Aluminum/magnesium combinations are usually used to avoid affecting the bowel.

Kidney failure patients who take magnesium antacids may develop magnesium toxicity.

Calcium and sodium antacids may cause a rebound effect, with more acid produced after the antacid is stopped than before it was started.

Magnesium trisilicate antacids used over long periods may result in the development of silicate renal stones.

Drug Interactions

Antacids can interfere with the absorption of most drugs

into the body. Intake of antacids should be separated from that of other oral drugs by 1 to 2 hours. Those drugs with which antacids are definitely known to interfere are anticholinergic drugs, phenothiazines, Digoxin, Phenytoin, Isoniazid, Quinidine, Warfarin, iron-containing products, and tetracycline-type antibiotics.

Usual Dose

The dose of antacids must be individualized to the patient's requirement. For ulcers, antacids are given every hour for the first 2 weeks (during waking hours) and 1 to 3 hours after meals and at bedtime thereafter.

Special Information

If you are using antacid tablets, be sure they are completely chewed. Swallow with milk or water.

   Aluminum antacids may cause speckling or add a whitish coloration to the stool.

Brand Name

Anusol-HC

Ingredients

Balsam Peru
Benzyl Benzoate
Bismuth Resorcin Compound
Bismuth Subgallate
Hydrocortisone Acetate
Zinc Oxide

Type of Drug

Hemorrhoid relief compound.

Prescribed for

Relief of rectal pain and itching due to hemorrhoids or local itching.

General Information

Although its ingredients are unique, Anusol-HC is one of

many products available for the relief of rectal pain and itching. The bismuth compounds and Zinc Oxide act to help shrink hemorrhoids, and the Hydrocortisone acts to reduce inflammation throughout the general area. This and similar products provide effective relief but do not treat the underlying cause of the problem.

Cautions and Warnings

Do not use if the area is infected or if you have herpes cold sores, tuberculosis of the skin or other generalized skin infections, or glaucoma. Use with caution if you experience urinary difficulties, are elderly, or suffer from prostate disease.

Possible Side Effects

Local irritation, aggravation of glaucoma, or infection.

Possible Adverse Drug Effects

A lot of the Hydrocortisone in this drug will be absorbed into the bloodstream and it is possible to experience the adverse effects seen when a corticosteroid drug is taken by mouth. This will not become a serious problem except in cases where the medicine is used for too long or when it is used by someone also taking corticosteroids by mouth.

Usual Dose

Children: should be used with caution by children under age 6.

Cream: apply locally twice a day for up to 7 days.

Suppository: 1 suppository twice a day for up to 7 days.

Storage

Keep away from excessive heat.

Special Information

Do not use for more than 7 days unless specifically directed to do so. Stop taking or call your doctor if you experience dry mouth, blurred vision, eye pain, or dizziness.

Generic Name

A.P.C. with Codeine

Ingredients

Aspirin
Caffeine
Codeine Sulfate
Phenacetin

Brand Names

Monacet with Codeine
P-A-C Compound with Codeine
Papa-Deine Tablets
Salatin with Codeine
Tabloid APC with Codeine

*Combinations containing
only Aspirin and Codeine:*
A.S.A. and Codeine
Emprin w/Codeine

Type of Drug

Narcotic analgesic and cough suppressant.

Prescribed for

Relief of mild to moderate pain.

General Information

A.P.C. with Codeine is one of many combination products
containing narcotics and analgesics. These products often
also contain barbiturates or tranquilizers, and Acetaminophen may be substituted for Aspirin, or Phenacetin and/or
Caffeine may be omitted.

Cautions and Warnings

Do not take Codeine if you know you are allergic or sensitive
to it. Use this drug with extreme caution if you suffer from
asthma or other breathing problems. Long-term use of this
drug may cause drug dependence or addiction. Codeine is a
respiratory depressant and affects the central nervous system, producing sleepiness, tiredness, and/or inability to concentrate. If you are pregnant or suspect that you are pregnant
do not take this drug.

Possible Side Effects

Most frequent: light-headedness, dizziness, sleepiness, nausea, vomiting, loss of appetite, sweating. If these occur, consider calling your doctor and asking him about lowering the dose of Codeine you are taking. Usually the side effects disappear if you simply lie down.

More serious side effects of A.P.C. with Codeine are shallow breathing or difficulty in breathing.

Possible Adverse Drug Effects

Euphoria (feeling high), weakness, sleepiness, headache, agitation, uncoordinated muscle movement, minor hallucinations, disorientation and visual disturbances, dry mouth, loss of appetite, constipation, flushing of the face, rapid heartbeat, palpitations, faintness, urinary difficulties or hesitancy, reduced sex drive and/or potency, itching, rashes, anemia, lowered blood sugar, yellowing of the skin and/or whites of the eyes. Narcotic analgesics may aggravate convulsions in those who have had convulsions in the past.

Drug Interactions

Interaction with alcohol, tranquilizers, barbiturates, or sleeping pills produces tiredness, sleepiness, or inability to concentrate, and seriously increases the depressive effect of A.P.C. with Codeine.

The Aspirin component of A.P.C. with Codeine can affect anticoagulant (blood-thinning) therapy. Be sure to discuss this with your doctor so that the proper dosage adjustment can be made.

Interaction with adrenal cortical steroids, Phenylbutazone, or alcohol can cause severe stomach irritation with possible bleeding.

Usual Dose

1 to 2 tablets 3 to 4 times per day.

Overdosage

Symptoms are depression of respiration (breathing), extreme tiredness progressing to stupor and then coma, pinpointed pupils of the eyes, no response to stimulation such as a pin stick, cold and clammy skin, slowing down of the heartbeat, lowering of blood pressure, convulsions, and cardiac arrest. The patient should be taken to a hospital emergency room immediately.

REMEMBER: ALWAYS bring the medicine bottle.

Special Information

Drowsiness may occur: be careful when driving or operating hazardous machinery.

Take with food or ½ glass of water to prevent stomach upset.

The Phenacetin ingredient of A.P.C. with Codeine may be toxic to your kidneys: do not take this medication for longer than 10 days unless so directed by your doctor.

Brand Name

Apresazide

Ingredients

Hydralazine
Hydrochlorothiazide

Type of Drug

Antihypertensive combination.

Prescribed for

High blood pressure.

General Information

This is a combination of two drugs used for the treatment of high blood pressure. Together, they are more effective than either drug taken alone. Since many people take the individual ingredients for high blood pressure, the combination may be a more convenient way to take their medicine.

This is a good example of a drug which takes advantage of a drug interaction. Both of the drugs work by different mechanisms to lower blood pressure. Hydrochlorothiazide is a diuretic which works through its effects on muscles in the walls of the blood vessels and its effect on lowering fluid levels in the body. As the volume of blood decreases so does the pressure exerted on the walls of the blood vessels. Hydralazine works by affecting the muscles in the walls of the arteries and lowers blood pressure by dilating, or widening, these blood vessels.

Cautions and Warnings

Do not take Apresazide if you are allergic to either of the ingredients or to sulfa drugs. It should not be used if you have certain kinds of heart disease, including rheumatic heart, or severe kidney disease. It must be used with care in patients who have severe liver disease.

This drug, in a few patients, may produce symptoms of a serious disease called lupus erythematosus. The symptoms of this are aching muscles and joints, skin rash and other complications, fever, anemia, and spleen enlargement. If these occur, the drug must be stopped immediately.

Apresazide must be used with caution by women who are pregnant or breast-feeding, and only when absolutely necessary.

Possible Side Effects

One of the ingredients in this drug can cause the lowering of potassium levels in the body. Signs of this are dryness of the mouth, thirst, weakness, lethargy, drowsiness, restlessness, muscle pains or cramps, muscle tiredness, low blood pressure, decreased frequency of urination, abnormal heart rate, and stomach upset, including nausea and vomiting. To prevent this, potassium supplements are given in the form of tablets, liquid, or powders, or by increasing consumption of high-potassium foods such as bananas, citrus fruits, melons, and tomatoes. This drug can also cause loss of appetite, diarrhea, rapid heartbeat, and chest pain.

Possible Adverse Drug Effects

Stuffed nose, flushing, tearing, itching, and redness of the eyes, numbness and tingling in the hands or feet, dizziness, tremors, muscle cramps, depression, disorientation, anxiety. The drug can also cause nausea, vomiting, cramps and diarrhea, constipation, dizziness, headache, tingling in the arms, hands, legs, or toes, changes in blood composition, sensitivity to the sun, rash, itching, fever, drug allergy, difficulty in breathing, blurred vision, weakness, and dizziness when rising from a sitting or lying position.

Drug Interactions

This combination should be used with caution by people taking an MAO inhibitor drug.

The possibility of developing imbalances in body fluids is increased if you take medicines like the digitalis drugs or adrenal corticosteroids with Apresazide. This problem can be avoided by periodic laboratory monitoring of the blood.

One of the ingredients in Apresazide will affect oral antidiabetic drugs. If you are already taking an oral drug for diabetes and start taking Apresazide, your dose of diabetes medicine may have to be changed.

Lithium drugs should not be given together with Apresazide because of the increased possibility of lithium toxicity.

Usual Dose

1 to 2 tablets per day. The exact dose must be tailored to your needs. This drug comes in several different dosage strengths.

Overdosage

Symptoms: very low blood pressure, rapid heartbeat, headache, flushing of the skin, chest pain, abnormal heart rhythms, fatigue, and coma may develop. In case of an overdose take the patient to a hospital emergency room immediately. ALWAYS bring the medicine bottle.

Special Information

Always take your medicine exactly as directed.

Avoid over-the-counter drugs containing stimulants; most of these are for colds and allergies. If you are in doubt, ask your pharmacist.

You may develop headache or heart palpitations, especially during the first few days of therapy with Apresazide.

If you develop weakness, muscle cramps, nausea, dizziness, or other signs of potassium loss, or if you develop fever or muscle aches or chest pains, call your doctor.

This drug may be taken with meals if it causes upset stomach.

Generic Name

Aspirin, Buffered Aspirin

Brand Names

A.S.A.	Children's Aspirin
A.S.A. Enseals	Ecotrin
Aspergum	Empirin Analgesic
Bayer Timed-Release Aspirin	Measurin

Alka-Seltzer	Bufferin
Antalgesic	Buffex
Arthritis Strength Bufferin	Buffinol
Ascriptin	Buf-Tabs
Ascriptin A/D	Cama Inlay-Tabs
Asperbuf	Midrin
Buff-A	Wesprin Buffered
Buffaprin	

Type of Drug

Analgesic, anti-inflammatory.

Prescribed for

Mild to moderate pain; fever; inflammation of bones, joints, or other body tissues; reducing the probability that men who have had a stroke or TIA (oxygen shortage to the brain) because of a problem with blood coagulation will have another such attack. Aspirin may also be prescribed as an anticoagulant (blood-thinning) drug, although it has not been approved by the government for this purpose.

General Information

Aspirin is probably the closest thing we have to a wonder drug. It has been used for more than a century as a pain and fever remedy but is now used for its effect on the blood as well.

Aspirin is the standard against which all other drugs are compared for pain relief. Chemically, Aspirin is a member of the group called Salicylates. Other salicylates include Sodium Salicylate, Sodium Thiosalicylate, Choline Salicylate, and Magnesium Salicylate (Trilisate). These drugs are no more effective than regular Aspirin, although two of them (Choline Salicylate and Magnesium Salicylate) may be a little less irritating to the stomach. They are all more expensive than Aspirin.

Scientists think that they have finally discovered how Aspirin works. It reduces fever by causing the blood vessels in the skin to open, thereby allowing heat from our body to leave more rapidly. Its effects on pain and inflammation are thought to be related to its ability to prevent the manufacture of complex body hormones called prostaglandins. Of all the salicylates, Aspirin has the greatest effect on prostaglandin production.

Many people find that they can take Buffered Aspirin but not regular Aspirin. This is because in the buffered product, antacids have been added to the Aspirin. The addition of antacid makes the drug less irritating to the stomach and gastrointestinal tract. Otherwise, there is no difference between Aspirin and Buffered Aspirin. The addition of antacids to aspirin can be important to patients who must take large doses of aspirin for chronic arthritis or other conditions. In many cases, Aspirin is the only effective drug and it can be tolerated only with the antacids present.

Cautions and Warnings

People with liver damage should avoid Aspirin. People who are allergic to Aspirin may also be allergic to drugs such as Indomethacin, Sulindac, Ibuprofen, Fenoprofen, Naproxen, Tolmetin, and Meclofenamate Sodium, or to products containing tartrazine (a commonly used orange dye and food coloring). People with asthma and/or nasal polyps are more likely to be allergic to Aspirin.

Aspirin may be associated with the development of Reyes Syndrome, a serious, potentially life-threatening disease in children with virus infections. If you suspect a virus infection, do not use Aspirin for any purpose; use a product with Acetaminophen instead.

Aspirin can interfere with normal blood coagulation and should be avoided for 1 week before surgery for this reason.

Possible Side Effects

Nausea, upset stomach, heartburn, loss of appetite, and loss of small amounts of blood in the stool. Aspirin may contribute to the formation of a stomach ulcer and bleeding.

Drug Interactions

People taking anticoagulants (blood-thinning drugs) should avoid Aspirin. The effect of the anticoagulant will be increased.

Aspirin may increase the possibility of stomach ulcer when taken together with adrenal corticosteroids, Phenylbutazone, or alcoholic beverages. Aspirin will counteract the uric acid eliminating effect of Probenecid and Sulfinpyrazone.

Usual Dose

Child: 30 milligrams per pound per day.

Adult: aches, pains, and fever, 325 to 650 milligrams every 4 hours; arthritis and rheumatic conditions, up to 5200 milligrams (16 325-milligram tablets) per day; rheumatic fever, up to 7800 milligrams (24 325-milligram tablets) per day; to prevent recurrence of stroke or TIA in men, 325 milligrams 4 times per day.

Overdosage

Symptoms of mild overdosage are rapid and deep breathing, nausea, vomiting, dizziness, ringing or buzzing in the ears, flushing, sweating, thirst, headache, drowsiness, diarrhea, and rapid heartbeat.

Severe overdosage may cause fever, excitement, confusion, convulsions, coma, or bleeding.

The initial treatment of Aspirin overdose involves making the patient vomit to remove any Aspirin remaining in the stomach. Further therapy depends on how the situation develops and what must be done to maintain the patient. DO NOT INDUCE VOMITING UNTIL YOU HAVE SPOKEN WITH YOUR DOCTOR OR POISON CONTROL CENTER. If in doubt, go to a hospital emergency room.

Special Information

Since Aspirin can cause upset stomach or bleeding, take each dose with food, milk, or a glass of water.

Contact your doctor if you develop a continuous stomach pain or a ringing or buzzing in the ears.

Generic Name

Atenolol

Brand Name

Tenormin

Type of Drug

Beta-adrenergic blocking agent.

Prescribed for

High blood pressure.

General Information

This drug is very much like Metoprolol, another beta-adrenergic blocker with specific effects on the heart and less specific effects on receptors in the blood vessels and respiratory tract than Propranolol, the first beta-adrenergic blocker marketed in the United States. The exact way that these drugs lower blood pressure is not known, but it is thought to be the result of their effect on the heart and body hormone systems. Atenolol and Metoprolol cause fewer side effects than Propranolol because of their specificity on receptors in the heart.

Cautions and Warnings

Atenolol should be used with care if you have a history of asthma or upper respiratory disease, seasonal allergies, or other respiratory conditions which may be worsened by this drug. Do not take this drug if you are allergic to any of the beta-adrenergic blocking drugs.

Possible Side Effects

Coldness in the hands or feet, dizziness, tiredness, depression, decreased heart rate, dizziness on rising quickly from a sitting or lying position, leg pains, light-headedness, lethargy, drowsiness, unusual dream patterns, diarrhea, nausea, difficulty breathing, wheezing, tingling in the extremities, visual disturbances, hallucinations, short-term memory loss, or abdominal cramps. Atenolol may aggravate or worsen an existing condition of congestive heart failure. It may induce spasms in the bronchial muscles, which will make any existing asthmatic or respiratory condition worse.

Possible Adverse Drug Effects

Atenolol can cause adverse effects on the blood system, drug allergy (fever, aching, sore throat, and difficulty breathing), emotional instability or personality changes, hair loss (reversible when the drug is stopped), rash.

Drug Interactions

Atenolol will interact with any psychotropic drug, including the MAO inhibitors. If you are taking a psychotropic or psychiatric drug, discuss this potential problem with your doctor. Atenolol may increase the effectiveness of Insulin or the oral antidiabetic drugs and may require a reduction in the dose of the antidiabetic medicine. Atenolol may reduce the effectiveness of digitalis drugs on your heart. Any dose of digitalis medication will have to be altered. If you are taking Digitalis for a purpose other than congestive heart failure, the effectiveness of the Digitalis may be increased by Atenolol, and the Digitalis dose reduced. Atenolol will interact with other blood pressure lowering drugs to yield an enhanced effect. This is an interaction with positive results and is used in treating patients for high blood pressure.

Do not self medicate with over-the-counter cold, cough, or allergy remedies which may contain stimulant drugs that will aggravate certain types of heart disease and high blood pressure, or other ingredients that may antagonize the effects of Atenolol. Check with your pharmacist before taking an over-the-counter medication.

Usual Dose

50 to 100 milligrams given once a day. Patients with kidney disease may need only 50 milligrams every other day. The dosage must be tailored to individual patient need.

Overdosage

Symptoms are: slowed heart rate, heart failure, lowered blood pressure, and spasms of the bronchial muscles which make it difficult to breathe. The patient should be taken to a hospital emergency room for treatment. ALWAYS bring the medicine bottle with you.

Special Information

This drug may make you tired, so take care while driving or doing anything that requires coordination. Call your doctor if you become dizzy or develop diarrhea. Do not stop taking this medicine abruptly. The dose should be reduced gradually over a period of time. Serious heart pain may develop if you do not taper the dosage.

Brand Name

Auralgan

Ingredients

Antipyrine
Glycerin

Other Brand Names

Aurasol
Eardro

Other products with the same ingredients in different concentrations:

Auromid
OTO (also contains Chlorobutanol)
Spenaural

Type of Drug

Analgesic.

Prescribed for

Earache.

General Information

This drug is a combination product containing a local anesthetic to deaden nerves inside the ear which transmit painful impulses, an analgesic to provide additional pain relief, and Glycerin to remove any water present in the ear. This drug is often used to treat painful conditions where water is present in the ear canal, such as "swimmer's ear." This drug does not contain any antibiotics and will not treat any infection.

Cautions and Warnings

Do not use Auralgan if you are allergic to any of its ingredients.

Possible Side Effects

Local irritation.

Possible Adverse Drug Effects

None.

Drug Interactions

None.

Usual Dose

Place drops of Auralgan in the ear canal until it is filled. Saturate a piece of cotton with Auralgan and put it in the ear canal to keep the drug from leaking out. Leave the drug in the ear for several minutes. Repeat 3 to 4 times per day.

Special Information

Before using, warm the bottle of eardrops to body temperature by holding it in your hand for several minutes. Do not warm the bottle to a temperature above normal body temperature.

Call your doctor if you develop a burning or itching feeling or if the pain does not go away.

Brand Name

AVC Cream

Ingredients

Allantoin
Aminacrine
Sulfanilamide

Other Brand Names

Amide-VC	Triconol
Cervex	Vagidine
Par	Vagimine
Sufamal	Vagi-Nil
Tricholon	Vagitrol

Type of Drug

Vaginal anti-infective.

Prescribed for

Relief of vaginal infection.

General Information

AVC Cream should only be used to treat vaginal irritation due to an infection. In such cases there may be relief within a few days, but the drug should be used through an entire menstrual cycle. If no relief occurs within a few days, or if the symptoms return, do not continue this drug. Consult your doctor, as a new medication may be required.

Cautions and Warnings

Do not use if you are allergic to sulfa drugs. If a rash develops, stop using the drug and consult your doctor.

Possible Side Effects

Most frequent: vaginal burning or discomfort. Less frequent: rash or other side effects associated with sulfa drug toxicity.

Usual Dose

1 applicator full of cream inserted into the vagina once or twice per day.

Generic Name

Azatidine Maleate

Brand Name

Optimine

Type of Drug

Antihistamine.

Prescribed for

Seasonal allergy, stuffed and runny nose, itching of the eyes, scratching of the throat caused by allergy, and other allergic symptoms such as itching, rash, or hives.

General Information

Antihistamines generally, and Azatidine Maleate specifically, act by blocking the release of the chemical stubstance histamine from the cell. Antihistamines work by drying up the secretions of the nose, throat, and eyes.

Cautions and Warnings

Azatidine Maleate should not be used if you are allergic to this drug. It should be avoided or used with extreme care if you have narrow angle glaucoma (pressure in the eye), stomach ulcer or other stomach problems, enlarged prostate, or problems passing urine. It should not be used by people who have deep-breathing problems such as asthma.

Azatidine Maleate can cause dizziness, drowsiness, and lowering of blood pressure, particularly in the elderly patient. Young children can show signs of nervousness, increased tension, and anxiety.

Possible Side Effects

Occasionally seen: itching, rash, sensitivity to light, excessive perspiration, chills, dryness of the mouth, nose, and throat, lowering of blood pressure, headache, rapid heartbeat, sleeplessness, dizziness, disturbed coordination, confusion, restlessness, nervousness, irritability, euphoria (feeling high), tingling of the hands and feet, blurred vision, double vision, ringing in the ears, stomach upset, loss of appetite, nausea, vomiting, constipation, diarrhea, difficulty in urination, tightness of the chest, wheezing, nasal stuffiness.

Possible Adverse Drug Effects

Use with care if you have a history of asthma, glaucoma, thyroid disease, heart disease, high blood pressure, or diabetes.

Drug Interactions

Azatidine Maleate should not be taken with the MAO inhibitors.

Interactions with tranquilizers, sedatives, and sleeping medication will increase the effect of these drugs; it is extremely important that you discuss this with your doctor so that doses of these drugs can be properly adjusted.

Be extremely cautious when drinking alcohol while taking Azatidine Maleate, which will enhance the intoxicating effect of alcohol. Alcohol also has a sedative effect.

Usual Dose

1 to 2 milligrams twice per day.

Overdosage

Symptoms are depression or stimulation (especially in children), dry mouth, fixed or dilated pupils, flushing of the skin, and stomach upset. Take the patient to a hospital emergency room immediately, if you cannot make him vomit. ALWAYS bring the medicine bottle.

Special Information

Antihistamines produce a depressing effect: be extremely cautious when driving or operating heavy equipment.

The safety of Azatidine Maleate in pregnancy has not been established. A breast-feeding mother should avoid taking this medication, since it is known to pass from the mother to the baby through the milk.

Brand Name

Azo Gantrisin

Ingredients

Phenazopyridine
Sulfisoxazole

Other Brand Names

Ameri-EZP   Azo-Sulfizin
Azo-Sulfisoxazole   Suldiazo

Type of Drug

Urinary anti-infective.

Prescribed for

Urinary tract infections.

General Information

Azo Gantrisin is one of many combination products used to treat urinary tract infections. The primary active ingredient is Sulfisoxazole. The other ingredient, Phenazopyridine, is added as a pain reliever.

Cautions and Warnings

Do not take Azo Gantrisin if you know you are allergic to sulfa drugs, salicylates, or similar agents or if you have the disease porphyria. Do not take this drug if you are pregnant or nursing a young child, since the drug can pass from the mother into the unborn child. Azo Gantrisin should not be considered if you have advanced kidney disease.

Possible Side Effects

Headache, itching, rash, sensitivity to strong sunlight, nausea, vomiting, abdominal pains, feeling of tiredness or lassitude, hallucinations, dizziness, ringing in the ears, chills, feeling of ill health.

Possible Adverse Drug Effects

Blood diseases or alterations of normal blood components, itching of the eyes, arthritis-type pain, diarrhea, loss of appetite, stomach cramps or pains, hearing loss, drowsiness, fever, chills, hair loss, yellowing of the skin and/or eyes, reduction in sperm count.

Drug Interactions

When Azo Gantrisin is taken with an anticoagulant (blood-thinning) drug, any drug used to treat diabetes, Methotrexate, Phenylbutazone, salicylates (Aspirin-like drugs), Phenytoin, or Probenecid, it will cause unusually large amounts of these drugs to be released into the bloodstream, producing symptoms of overdosage. If you are going to take Azo Gantrisin for an extended period, your physician should reduce the dosage of these interactive drugs. Also, avoid large doses of Vitamin C.

Usual Dose

Adult: first dose, 4 to 6 tablets, then 2 tablets every 4 hours. Take each dose with a full glass of water.

Overdosage

Induce vomiting and give a rectal enema; then take the patient to a hospital emergency room. ALWAYS bring the medicine bottle.

Special Information

Azo Gantrisin can cause photosensitivity—a severe reaction to strong sunlight. Avoid prolonged exposure to strong sunlight while taking it.

Sore throat, fever, unusual bleeding or bruising, rash, and feeling tired are early signs of serious blood disorders and should be reported to your doctor immediately.

The Phenazopyridine ingredient in Azo Gantrisin is an orange-red dye and will color the urine. Do not be worried, since this is a normal effect of the drug; but note that if you are diabetic, the dye may interfere with testing your urine for sugar.

Generic Name

Beclomethasone

Brand Names

Beclovent
Vanceril

Type of Drug

Adrenal cortical steroid.

Prescribed for

Treatment of chronic asthma.

General Information

Beclomethasone is used as an inhalor to relieve symptoms associated with seasonal allergy. It works by reducing inflammation of the mucosal lining within the nose, thereby making it easier to breathe. This drug should not be used more than three weeks if it has not worked within that time. Beclomethasone will not work immediately, as a decongestant would; it may take several days to exert its effect.

Cautions and Warnings

Do not use this drug if you are allergic to Beclomethasone. This drug cannot be used as the primary treatment of severe asthma. It is only for people who usually take Prednisone, or another adrenal cortical steroid, by mouth and those who are taking other asthma drugs but are still having asthmatic attacks.

Even though this drug is taken by inhaling directly into the lungs, it should be considered a potent adrenal corticosteriod drug. During periods of severe stress, you may have to go back to taking steroid drugs by mouth if Beclomethasone does not control your asthma. This drug should be used by women who are pregnant or breast-feeding only if absolutely necessary.

Possible Side Effects

Dry mouth, hoarseness.

Possible Adverse Drug Effects

Deaths have occurred in patients taking adrenal corticosteroid tablets or syrup and being switched to Beclomethasone by inhalation due to failure of the adrenal gland. This is a rare complication and usually results from stopping the liquid or tablets too quickly. They must be stopped gradually over a long period of time.

This drug can also cause rash or spasm of the bronchial muscles.

Usual Dose

Adult and child (over age 12): 6 to 20 inhalations per day.

Child (age 6 to 12): 3 to 10 inhalations per day.

Special Information

People using both Beclomethasone and a bronchodilator by inhalation should use the bronchodilator first, wait a few minutes, then use the Beclomethasone. This will allow more Beclomethasone to be absorbed.

This drug is for preventive therapy only and will not affect an asthma attack. Beclomethasone must be inhaled regularly, as directed. Wait at least 1 minute between inhalations.

Dry mouth or hoarseness may be reduced by rinsing the mouth after each use of the inhaler.

Brand Name

Bendectin

Ingredients

Doxylamine Succinate
Pyridoxine Hydrochloride

Other Brand Names

Doxylamine Succinate with Peridoxine Hydrochloride

Type of Drug

Antivomiting, antidizziness combination.

Prescribed for

Control of nausea, vomiting, and morning sickness.

General Information

Bendectin is often used to control the symptoms of morning sickness because of its relative safety for pregnant women. However, there is no proof that Pyridoxine Hydrochloride adds anything to the effectiveness of the combination. Doxylamine Succinate, the primary ingredient, is an antihistamine with antiemetic properties. It works by antagonizing any histamine present as a result of any sort of allergic or sensitivity reaction.

Cautions and Warnings

Bendectin should be avoided or used with extreme caution

if you have glaucoma or certain types of stomach ulcer. Bendectin can reduce the body's ability to produce or excrete urine, but this is mostly seen in elderly or debilitated patients. Pregnant women and nursing mothers should use this drug only if nothing else has worked for them.

Possible Side Effects

Difficulty in urination, blurred vision, change in heartbeat, sensitivity to light, headache, flushing of the skin, nervousness, dizziness, weakness, drowsiness, nausea, inability to sleep, vomiting, fever, nasal stuffiness, heartburn, constipation, feeling of being bloated, and occasionally, drug allergy.

Drug Interactions

The drug should be used with caution with alcoholic beverages, depressants such as sleeping medicines, sedatives, tranquilizers, or other drugs which may cause drowsiness or other signs of depression.

Do not take Bendectin if you are taking monoamine oxidase (MAO) inhibitor drugs.

Usual Dose

2 tablets at bedtime. If nausea occurs during the day, 1 tablet may be taken in the morning and afternoon if needed.

Special Information

Bendectin may produce tiredness or inability to concentrate. Be very careful when driving an automobile or operating other machinery.

Brand Name

Bentyl with Phenobarbital

Ingredients

Dicyclomine Hydrochloride
Phenobarbital

Other Brand Names

Dibent-PB
Dicyclomine with Phenobarbital

Type of Drug

Gastrointestinal anticholinergic agent.

Prescribed for

Symptomatic relief of stomach upset and spasms.

General Information

Bentyl with Phenobarbital works by reducing spasms in muscles of the stomach and other parts of the gastrointestinal tract. In doing so, it helps relieve some of the uncomfortable symptoms associated with peptic ulcer, irritable bowel and/or colon, spastic colon, and other gastrointestinal disorders. It only relieves symptoms. It does not cure the underlying disease.

Cautions and Warnings

Bentyl with Phenobarbital should not be used if you know you are sensitive or allergic to Dicyclomine Hydrochloride. Do not use this medicine if you have glaucoma, asthma, obstructive disease of the gastrointestinal tract, or other serious gastrointestinal disease. Because this drug reduces your ability to sweat, its use in hot climates may cause heat exhaustion.

Possible Side Effects

Occasional: difficulty in urination, blurred vision, rapid heartbeat, palpitations, sensitivity to light, headache, flushing, nervousness, dizziness, weakness, drowsiness, inability to sleep, nausea, vomiting, fever, nasal congestion, heartburn, constipation, feeling of being bloated. There is also occasionally drug allergy or a drug idiosyncratic reaction, which may include itching or other skin manifestations.

Possible Adverse Drug Effects

Use of this drug in elderly patients may be associated with some degree of mental confusion and/or excitement.

Drug Interactions

Interaction with antihistamines, phenothiazines, tranquilizers, antidepressants, and some narcotic painkillers may cause blurred vision, dry mouth, or drowsiness.

Do not use with Tranylcypromine Sulfate (Parnate), Isocar-boxazid (Marplan), Phenelzine Sulfate (Nardil), or other MAO inhibitor drugs, which will tend to prevent excretion of Bentyl with Phenobarbital from the body and thus potentiate it (increase its effects).

Usual Dose

1 capsule or 1 tablet every 3 to 4 hours as needed for relief of symptoms. If necessary, capsules may be given up to 8 times per day, tablets up to 4 times per day.

Syrup: 1 teaspoon 3 to 4 times per day, but as many as 8 teaspoons per day may be required.

Special Information

Dry mouth produced by Bentyl with Phenobarbital can be relieved by chewing gum or sucking hard candy; constipation can be treated with a stool softener (rather than a harsh cathartic).

Brand Name

Benylin Cough Syrup

Ingredients

Ammonium Chloride
Diphenhydramine Hydrochloride
Sodium Citrate

Other Brand Names

Benachlor Cough Syrup	Eldadryl
Diphenadril	Noradryl Cough Syrup
Diphenallin Cough Syrup	Tusstat
Diphen-Ex	Valdrene
Diphenhydramine Hydro- chloride Cough Syrup	

Type of Drug

Cough syrup expectorant.

Prescribed for

Coughs associated with the common cold and other upper respiratory infections.

General Information

Benylin Cough Syrup is one of many products marketed for the relief of coughs. Its major active ingredient is an antihistamine; therefore, the drug is most effective in relieving the symptoms of excess histamine product. Basically, Benylin Cough Syrup is only able to help you feel well. It cannot help you recover more quickly, only more comfortably.

Cautions and Warnings

Do not use Benylin Cough Syrup if you have glaucoma (increased pressure in the eye).

Possible Side Effects

Tiredness, inability to concentrate, blurred vision, dry mouth, difficulty in urination, constipation.

Drug Interactions

Benylin Cough Syrup contains an antihistamine and may produce some depression, drowsiness, or inability to concentrate. Don't drink large quantities of alcoholic beverages, which can increase this depressant effect.

Usual Dose

1 to 2 teaspoons 4 times per day.

Special Information

Take with a full glass of water to reduce stomach upset and help loosen mucus that may be present in the breathing passages.

Generic Name

Benztropine Mesylate

Brand Name

Cogentin

Type of Drug

Anticholinergic.

Prescribed for

Treatment of Parkinson's disease or prevention or control of muscle spasms caused by other drugs, particularly phenothiazine drugs.

General Information

Benztropine Mesylate has an action on the body similar to that of Atropine Sulfate (see page 177), but side effects are less frequent and less severe. It is an anticholinergic and has the ability to reduce muscle spasms. This property makes the drug useful in treating Parkinson's disease and other diseases associated with spasms of skeletal muscles.

Cautions and Warnings

Benztropine Mesylate should be used with caution if you have narrow angle glaucoma, stomach ulcers, obstructions in the gastrointestinal tract, prostatitis, or myasthenia gravis.

Possible Side Effects

The same as with any other anticholinergic drug: difficulty in urination, constipation, blurred vision, and increased sensitivity to strong light. The effects may increase if Benztropine Mesylate is taken with antihistamines, phenothiazines, antidepressants, or other anticholinergic drugs.

Drug Interactions

Interaction with other anticholinergic drugs, including tricyclic antidepressants or phenothiazine drugs, may cause severe stomach upset or unusual abdominal pain. If this happens, contact your doctor. Avoid over-the-counter remedies which contain Atropine or similar drugs. Your pharmacist can tell you the ingredients of over-the-counter drugs.

This drug should be used with caution by people taking barbiturates. Use alcoholic beverages with care while taking this drug.

Usual Dose

0.5 to 6 milligrams per day, depending upon the disease being treated and patient's response.

Special Information

Side effects of dry mouth, constipation, and increased sensitivity to strong light may be relieved by, respectively, chewing gum or sucking on hard candy, taking a stool softener, and wearing sunglasses. Such side effects are easily tolerated in the absence of undesirable drug interaction.

Generic Name

Betamethasone Topical Ointment/ Cream/Lotion/Gel/Aerosol

Brand Names

Benisone Cream/Gel
Celestone Cream
Diprosone Dipropionate
    Ointment/Cream/Lotion/
    Aerosol

Uticort Gel
Valisone Ointment/Cream/
Lotion/Aerosol

Type of Drug

Corticosteroid.

Prescribed for

Relief of skin inflammation, itching, or other skin problems in a localized area.

General Information

Betamethasone is one of many adrenal cortical steroids used today. The major differences between Betamethasone and other adrenal cortical steroids are potency of medication and variation in some secondary effects. In most cases the choice of adrenal cortical steroids to be used in a specific disease is a matter of doctor preference and past experience. Other adrenal cortical steroids include Cortisone, Hydrocortisone, Prednisone, Prednisolone, Triamcinolone, Methylprednisolone, Meprednisone, Paramethasone, Fluprednisolone, Dexamethasone, and Fludrocortisone.

Cautions and Warnings

Betamethasone should not be used if you have viral diseases of the skin (herpes), fungal infections of the skin (athlete's foot), or tuberculosis of the skin, nor should it be used in the ear if the eardrum is perforated. People with a history of allergies to any of the components of the ointment, cream, or gel should not use this drug.

Possible Side Effects

Burning sensations, itching, irritation, dryness, and redness of the skin, secondary infection.

Special Information

Clean the skin before applying Betamethasone, to prevent secondary infection. Apply in a very thin film (effectiveness is based on contact area and not on the thickness of the layer applied).

Generic Name

Benzphetamine Hydrochloride

Brand Name

Didrex

Type of Drug

Central nervous system stimulant.

Prescribed for

Short-term (2 to 3 weeks) aid to diet control, minimal brain dysfunction in children, narcolepsy (uncontrollable and unpredictable desire to sleep).

General Information

When taking this medicine as part of a weight control program it is usual to experience *less* appetite reduction as time goes on. This is because your body is breaking down the drug faster. Do not increase the amount of drug you are taking: simply stop taking the medicine.

The use of Benzphetamine Hydrochloride (as well as other drugs) in the treatment of minimal brain dysfunction in children is extremely controversial and must be undertaken only on the advice of a physician qualified to treat the disorder. Children whose problems are judged to have been produced by their surroundings or by primary psychiatric disorders may not be helped by Benzphetamine Hydrochloride.

Cautions and Warnings

Benzphetamine Hydrochloride is highly abusable and addictive. It must be used with extreme caution. People with hardening of the arteries (arteriosclerosis), heart disease, high blood pressure, thyroid disease, or glaucoma, or who are sensitive or allergic to any amphetamine, should not take this medication. Benzphetamine Hydrochloride should not be used by pregnant women (it may cause birth defects).

Possible Side Effects

Palpitations, restlessness, overstimulation, dizziness, sleeplessness, increased blood pressure, rapid heartbeat.

Possible Adverse Drug Effects

Euphoria, hallucinations, muscle spasms and tremors, headache, dryness of the mouth, unpleasant taste, diarrhea, constipation, stomach upset, itching, loss of sex drive, (rarely) psychotic drug reactions.

Drug Interactions

Benzphetamine Hydrochloride should not be given at the same time or within 14 days following the use of MAO inhibitors. To do so may cause severe lowering of blood pressure.

Benzphetamine Hydrochloride may also decrease the effectiveness of Guanethidine Sulfate.

Usual Dose

25 to 150 milligrams per day.

Overdosage

Symptoms are tremors, muscle spasms, restlessness, exaggerated reflexes, rapid breathing, hallucinations, confusion, panic, and overaggressive behavior, followed by depression and exhaustion after the central nervous system stimulation wears off, as well as abnormal heart rhythms, changes in blood pressure, nausea, vomiting, diarrhea, convulsions, and coma. The patient should be taken to a hospital emergency room immediately. ALWAYS bring the medicine container.

Special Information

Do not take this medicine after 6 to 8 hours before you plan to go to sleep, or it will interfere with a sound and restful night's sleep.

Generic Name

Brompheniramine Maleate

Brand Names

Bromamine	Midatane
Bromatane	Puretane
Bromphen	Spentane
Dimetane	Symptom 3
Disophrol	Veltane

Type of Drug

Antihistamine.

Prescribed for

Seasonal allergy, stuffed and runny nose, itching of the eyes, scratchy throat caused by allergy, and other allergic symptoms such as itching, rash, or hives.

General Information

Antihistamines generally, and Brompheniramine Maleate specifically, act by blocking the release of the chemical substance histamine from the cell. Antihistamines work by drying up the secretions of the nose, throat, and eyes.

Cautions and Warnings

Brompheniramine Maleate should not be used if you are allergic to this drug. It should be avoided or used with extreme care if you have glaucoma (pressure in the eye), stomach ulcer or other stomach problems, enlarged prostate, or problems passing urine. It should not be used by people who have deep-breathing problems such as asthma.

Brompheniramine Maleate can cause dizziness, drowsiness, and lowering of blood pressure, particularly in the elderly patient. Young children can show signs of nervousness, increased tension, and anxiety.

Possible Side Effects

Occasionally seen: itching, rash, sensitivity to light, perspiration, chills, dryness of the mouth, nose, and throat, lowering of blood pressure, headache, rapid heartbeat, sleeplessness, dizziness, disturbed coordination, confusion, restlessness, nervousness, irritability, euphoria (feeling high), tingling of the hands and feet, blurred vision, double vision, ringing in the ears, stomach upset, loss of appetite, nausea, vomiting, constipation, diarrhea, difficulty in urination, tightness of the chest, wheezing, nasal stuffiness.

Possible Adverse Drug Effects

Use with care if you have a history of asthma, glaucoma, thyroid disease, heart disease, high blood pressure, or diabetes.

Drug Interactions

Brompheniramine Maleate should not be taken with MAO inhibitors.

Interaction with tranquilizers, sedatives, and sleeping medication will increase the effects of these drugs; it is extremely important that you discuss this with your doctor so that doses of these drugs can be properly adjusted.

Be extremely cautious when drinking while taking Brompheniramine Maleate, which will enhance the intoxicating effect of the alcohol. Alcohol also has a sedative effect.

Usual Dose

Adult: 4 milligrams 3 to 4 times per day.
Child (age 6 to 12): 2 to 4 milligrams 3 to 4 times per day.
Child (under age 6): ¼ milligram per pound per day in divided doses.

Time-release doses are as follows.

Adult: 8 to 12 milligrams at bedtime or every 8 to 12 hours during the day.

Child (age 6 to 12): 8 milligrams during the day or at bedtime.

Overdosage

Symptoms are depression or stimulation (especially in children), dry mouth, fixed or dilated pupils, flushing of the skin, and stomach upset. Take the patient to a hospital emergency room immediately, if you cannot make him vomit. ALWAYS bring the medicine bottle.

Special Information

Antihistamines produce a depressing effect: be extremely cautious when driving or operating heavy equipment.

The safety of Brompheniramine Maleate in pregnancy has not been established. A breast-feeding mother should avoid taking this medication, since it is known to pass from the mother to the baby through the milk.

Generic Name

Butabarbital

Brand Names

Butal	Buticaps
Butalan	Butisol Sodium
Butatran	Sarisol
Butazem	Soduben

Type of Drug

Hypnotic; sedative; anticonvulsive.

Prescribed for

Epileptic seizures, convulsions: as an anticonvulsive or a daytime sedative; as a mild hypnotic (sleeping medication); and for eclampsia (toxemia in pregnancy).

General Information

Butabarbital, like the other barbiturates, appears to act by interfering with nerve impulses to the brain. When used as an anticonvulsive, Butabarbital is not very effective by itself, but when used with anticonvulsive agents such as Phenytoin, the combined action of Butabarbital and Phenytoin is dramatic. This combination has been used very successfully to control epileptic seizures.

Cautions and Warnings

Butabarbital may slow down your physical and mental reflexes, so you must be extremely careful when operating machinery, driving an automobile, or performing other potentially dangerous tasks. Elderly patients on Butabarbital exhibit nervousness and confusion at times. Barbiturates are neutralized in the liver and eliminated from the body through the kidneys; consequently, people who have liver or kidney disorders—namely, difficulty in forming or excreting urine— should be monitored by their doctor when taking Butabarbital. Butabarbital is classified as a barbiturate; long-term or unsupervised use may cause addiction.

If you have known sensitivities or allergies to barbiturates, or if you have previously been addicted to sedatives or hypnotics, or if you have a disease affecting the respiratory system, you should not take Butabarbital.

This drug should not be taken by pregnant women, since it can pass to the baby, which could cause birth defects.

Possible Side Effects

Difficulty in breathing, rash, and general allergic reaction such as running nose, watering eyes, and scratchy throat.

Possible Adverse Drug Effects

Drowsiness, lethargy, dizziness, hangover, nausea, vomiting, diarrhea. More severe adverse reactions may include anemia and yellowing of the skin and eyes.

Drug Interactions

Interaction with alcohol, tranquilizers, or other sedatives increases the sedative effect of Butabarbital.

Interaction with anticoagulants (blood-thinning agents) can reduce their effect. This is also true of muscle relaxants and painkillers.

Usual Dose

Adult: daytime sedative, 15 to 30 milligrams 3 to 4 times per day: hypnotic sleep, 50 to 100 milligrams at bedtime.

Child: 7½ to 30 milligrams as determined by age, weight, and degree of sedation desired.

Overdosage

Symptoms are difficulty in breathing, decrease in size of the pupils of the eyes, lowered body temperature progressing to fever as time passes, fluid in the lungs, and eventually coma.

Anyone suspected of having taken an overdose must be taken to the hospital for immediate care. ALWAYS bring the medicine bottle to the emergency room physician so he can quickly and correctly identify the medication and start treatment. Severe overdosage of this medication can kill; the drug has been used many times in suicide attempts.

Generic Name

Captopril

Brand Name

Capoten

Type of Drug

Antihypertensive.

Prescribed for

Patients who have high blood pressure which cannot be controlled with other drugs or who suffer from unacceptable side effects of other drugs. Captopril should be used together with a diuretic drug.

General Information

This drug is the first member of a new class of drugs which work by preventing the conversion of a potent hormone called Angiotensin I. This directly affects the production of other hormones and enzymes which participate in the regulation of blood pressure. The effect is to lower blood pressure relatively quickly, within 1 to 1½ hours after taking the medicine.

The drug can cause serious side effects and so should be used only by patients who really need a potent antihypertensive drug.

Cautions and Warnings

This drug can cause kidney disease, especially loss of protein in the urine. Patients should have the amount of protein in their urine measured during the first month and monthly for a few months afterward. The drug can also cause reduction in the white blood cell count, and this can result in increased susceptibility to infection. Captopril should be used with caution by people who have kidney disease or diseases of the immune/collagen system (particularly lupus erythematosus), or who have taken other drugs which affect the white blood cell count. The use of this drug by women who are pregnant or breast-feeding or by children is recommended only when absolutely necessary.

Possible Side Effects

Rash (usually mild), itching, fever, loss of taste perception (usually returns in 2 to 3 months).

Possible Adverse Drug Effects

Adverse effects on the kidney including protein in the urine, kidney failure, excessive or frequent urination, reduction in the amount of urine produced; adverse effect on the blood system, especially white blood cells; swelling of the face, mucous membranes of the mouth, or arms and legs, flushing or pale color of skin. Captopril may also cause low blood pressure, adverse effects on the heart (chest pain, abnormal heartbeats, spasms of blood vessels, heart failure).

Drug Interactions

The blood pressure effect of Captopril is additive with diuretic drugs. Some other hypertensive drugs can cause severe blood pressure drops when used with Captopril. They should be used with extreme caution. Beta-adrenergic blocking drugs may add some blood-pressure-lowering effect to Captopril.

Usual Dose

75 milligrams per day to start. Dose may be increased up to 450 milligrams per day, if needed. The dose of this medicine must be tailored to your needs.

Overdosage

The primary effect of Captopril overdosage is very low blood pressure. A person who has taken a Captopril overdose must be taken to a hospital emergency room for treatment. ALWAYS bring the medicine bottle with you.

Special Information

Do not take this medicine with food or meals. It must be taken at least 1 hour before or 2 hours after meals.

Call your doctor if you develop fever, sore throat, mouth sores, abnormal heart beat, or chest pain, or if you have persistent rash or loss of taste perception.

This drug may cause dizziness when you rise quickly from sitting or lying down.

Avoid strenuous exercise and/or very hot weather as heavy sweating and/or dehydration can cause a rapid drop in blood pressure.

Generic Name

Carisoprodol

Brand Names

Rela
Soma

Type of Drug

Skeletal muscle relaxant.

Prescribed for

Partial treatment for the relief of pain and other discomforts associated with acute conditions such as sprains, strains, or bad backs.

General Information

Carisoprodol is one of several drugs available for the relief of pain caused by spasms of large skeletal muscles. These drugs give symptomatic relief only. They should not be the only form of therapy used. If you are taking Carisoprodol, follow any other instructions given by your doctor about rest, physical therapy, or other measures to help relieve your problem.

Cautions and Warnings

The effect of Carisoprodol on the pregnant female has not been studied. It may have an effect on the unborn child: if you are pregnant, you should not use this medicine unless it is absolutely necessary and this problem has been considered by your physician. Do not use this drug if you are allergic to it or to Meprobamate, Mebutamate, or Tybamate. This drug should not be used if you have the disease porphyria.

This drug may cause a rare, unusual reaction within minutes or hours after taking the first dose. The reaction consists of extreme weakness, momentary loss of control over arms and legs, dizziness, double vision or temporary loss of vision, agitation, confusion, a "high" feeling, and loss of orientation. Although the reaction usually goes away within a few hours, hospitalization may be necessary.

Possible Side Effects

Most common: light-headedness, dizziness, drowsiness, loss of muscle control, tremors, agitation, headache, depression, sleeplessness, rash, itching, fever, weakness, difficulty in breathing, low blood pressure. If one of these occurs, call your doctor immediately.

Possible Adverse Drug Effects

Rapid heartbeat, flushing of the face, dizziness when rising quickly from a sitting or lying position, nausea, vomiting, upset stomach, hiccups. This drug may cause adverse effects on the blood system.

Drug Interactions

Other drugs which, like Carisoprodol, may cause drowsiness,

sleepiness, or lack of ability to concentrate must be taken
with extreme caution: sleeping pills, tranquilizers, barbiturates, narcotics, and alcoholic beverages.

Usual Dose

350 milligrams 4 times per day.

Overdosage

Symptoms are central nervous system depression, desire to
sleep, weakness, lassitude, and difficulty in breathing. The
patient should be taken to a hospital immediately. ALWAYS
bring the medicine bottle.

Special Information

Carisoprodol may cause drowsiness, sleepiness, and inability to concentrate: this can affect you if you drive or operate
any sort of appliance, equipment, or machinery.

Generic Name

Cefaclor

Brand Name

Ceclor

Type of Drug

Cephalosporin antibiotic.

Prescribed for

Bacterial infections susceptible to this medication. Cefaclor
is generally prescribed for respiratory tract infections, infections of the middle ear, infections of the skin and other soft
tissues, bone infections, and infections of the urinary tract.

General Information

Cefaclor is manufactured in the laboratory by the process
known as fermentation and by general chemical reaction,
and is classified as a semisynthetic antibiotic. Because the
effectiveness of the antibiotic is determined by the drug's
ability to destroy the cell wall of the invading bacteria, it is

very important that the patient completely follow the doctor's prescribing directions. These directions include spacing of doses as well as the number of days the patient should continue taking the medicine. If directions are not followed, the effect of the antibiotic is severely reduced.

Cefaclor is a member of the group of antibiotics known as cephalosporins. All the members of this group have the same basic effects and are excellent drugs. Most experts consider the forms of these drugs that are taken by mouth to be equivalent in effectiveness for most infections. The cephalosporins are chemical cousins of Penicillin.

Cautions and Warnings

If you know that you are allergic or feel that you might be allergic to Penicillin, you should avoid taking Cefaclor because of the chance that you will be allergic to it too. The most common allergic effect experienced with any of the antibiotics similar to Penicillin is a hivelike rash over large areas of the body, with itching and redness. It is extremely important that you tell your doctor if you have ever taken this drug or any of the penicillins before, and if you have experienced any adverse effects to the drug such as rash, itching, or difficulty in breathing. The safe use of Cefaclor in pregnant females has not been definitely established and it should be used only if there is a specific need for it, since it is possible that this drug may cross the blood barrier into the unborn child. These drugs will also pass into the milk of a nursing mother.

Possible Side Effects

If you are taking Cefaclor you may experience one or more of the following allergic reactions ranging from mild to life-threatening. Most often, however, reactions are quite mild: itching, rashes, occasional fever, chills, and reactions of one or more of the components of the blood. Serious reactions are called anaphylactic reactions; although they are quite rare, some deaths have been reported from anaphylactic reactions to this or another member of the cephalosporin class.

Possible Adverse Drug Effects

Cefaclor and other cephalosporin antibiotics have been known to induce adverse effects on the blood system; it is the other antibiotics in this group that have been more definitely associated with decrease in kidney function. Taking Cefaclor induces nausea, vomiting, or diarrhea in about one-third of patients. Less frequent adverse effects: cramps in the abdomen, upset stomach, headache, not feeling well, dizziness, difficulty in breathing, tingling in the extremities, and (occasional) enlargement of the liver.

Drug Interactions

Cefaclor, which works by killing microorganisms which cause infections, may be inhibited by antibiotics, such as Erythromycin and Tetracycline, which do not kill but simply stop the growth of microorganisms. The two types should not be taken together.

Usual Dose

Adult: 250 to 1000 milligrams every 8 hours.

Child: up to 9 milligrams per pound per day; maximum dose is 1000 milligrams per day.

Doses may be doubled for severe infections.

Special Information

Cefaclor, to be effective, must be taken continuously for 7 to 10 days; so take it exactly as prescribed.

The drug has maximum effect if taken 1 hour before or 2 hours after meals, but if upset stomach occurs the drug can be taken with meals.

Generic Name

Cephalexin

Brand Name

Keflex

Type of Drug

Cephalosporin antibiotic.

Prescribed for

Bacterial infections susceptible to this medication. Cephalexin is generally prescribed for respiratory tract infections, infections of the middle ear, infections of the skin and other soft tissues, bone infections, and infections of the urinary tract.

General Information

Cephalexin is manufactured in the laboratory by the process known as fermentation and by general chemical reaction, and is classified as a semisynthetic antibiotic. Because the effectiveness of the antibiotic is determined by the drug's ability to destroy the cell wall of the invading bacteria, it is very important that the patient completely follow the doctor's prescribing directions. These directions include spacing of doses as well as the number of days the patient should continue taking the medicine. If they are not followed, the effect of the antibiotic is severely reduced.

Cautions and Warnings

If you know that you are allergic or feel that you might be allergic to Penicillin, you should avoid taking Cephalexin because of the chance that you will be allergic to it too. The most common allergic effect experienced with any of the antibiotics similar to Penicillin is a hivelike rash over large areas of the body with itching and redness. It is extremely important that you tell your doctor if you have ever taken this drug or any of the penicillins before, and if you have experienced any adverse effects to the drug such as rash, itching, or difficulty in breathing. The safe use of Cephalexin in pregnant females has not been definitely established and it should be used only if there is a specific need for it, since it is possible that this drug may cross the blood barrier into the unborn child. These drugs will also pass into the milk of a nursing mother.

Possible Side Effects

If you are taking Cephalexin you may experience one or more of the following allergic reactions ranging from mild to life-threatening. Most often, however, reactions are quite mild: itching, rashes, occasional fever, chills, and reactions of one or more of the components of the blood. Serious reactions are called anaphylactic reactions; although they are quite rare, some deaths have been reported from anaphylactic reactions to this or another member of the cephalosporin class.

Possible Adverse Drug Effects

Cephalexin and other cephalosporin antibiotics have been known to induce adverse effects on the blood system; it is the others that have been more definitely associated with decrease in kidney function. Taking Cephalexin induces nausea, vomiting, or diarrhea in about one-third of patients. Less frequent adverse effects: cramps in the abdomen, upset stomach, headache, not feeling well, dizziness, difficulty in breathing, tingling in the extremities, and (occasional) enlargement of the liver.

Drug Interactions

Cephalexin, which works by killing microorganisms which cause infections, may be inhibited by antibiotics, such as Erythromycin and Tetracycline, which do not kill but simply stop the growth of microorganisms. The two types should not be taken together. Probenecid will slow down the excretion rate of cephalosporins.

Usual Dose

Adult: 1 to 4 grams per day in divided doses.

Child: 12½ to 25 milligrams per pound of body weight per day in 4 divided doses.

Doses may be doubled for severe infections.

Special Information

Cephalexin, to be effective, must be taken continuously for 7 to 10 days; so take it exactly as prescribed.

The drug has maximum effect if taken 1 hour before or 2 hours after meals, but if upset stomach occurs the drug can be taken with meals.

Generic Name

Cephradine

Brand Names

Anspor
Velosef

Type of Drug

Cephalosporin antibiotic.

Prescribed for

Bacterial infections susceptible to this medication. Cephradine is generally prescribed for respiratory tract infections, infections of the middle ear, infections of the skin and other soft tissues, bone infections, and infections of the urinary tract.

General Information

Cephradine is manufactured in the laboratory by the process known as fermentation and by general chemical reaction, and is classified as a semisynthetic antibiotic. Because the effectiveness of the antibiotic is determined by the drug's ability to destroy the cell wall of the invading bacteria, it is very important that the patient completely follow the doctor's prescribing directions. These directions include spacing of doses as well as the number of days the patient should continue taking the medicine. If they are not followed, the effect of the antibiotic is severely reduced.

Cephradine is a member of the group of antibiotics known as cephalosporins. All the members of this group have the same basic effects and are excellent drugs. Most experts consider the forms of these drugs that are taken by mouth to be equivalent in effectiveness for most infections. The cephalosporins are chemical cousins of Penicillin.

Cautions and Warnings

If you know that you are allergic or feel that you might be allergic to Penicillin, you should avoid taking Cephradine because of the chance that you will be allergic to it too. The most common allergic effect experienced with any of the antibiotics similar to Penicillin is a hivelike rash over large areas of the body, with itching and redness. It is extremely important that you tell your doctor if you have ever taken this drug or any of the penicillins before, and if you have experienced any adverse effects to the drug such as rash, itching, or difficulty in breathing. The safe use of Cephradine in pregnant females has not been definitely established and it should be used only if there is a specific need for it, since it is possible that this drug may cross the blood barrier into the unborn child. These drugs will also pass into the milk of a nursing mother.

Possible Side Effects

If you are taking Cephradine you may experience one or more of the following allergic reactions ranging from mild to life-threatening. Most often, however, reactions are quite mild: itching, rashes, occasional fever, chills, and reactions of one or more of the components of the blood. Serious reactions are called anaphylactic reactions; although they are quite rare, some deaths have been reported from ana-phylactic reactions to this or another member of the cepha-losporin class.

Possible Adverse Drug Effects

Cephradine and other cephalosporin antibiotics have been known to induce adverse effects on the blood system; it is the others that have been more definitely associated with decrease in kidney function. Taking Cephradine induces nau-sea, vomiting, or diarrhea in about one-third of patients. Less frequent adverse effects: cramps in the abdomen, upset stomach, headache, not feeling well, dizziness, difficulty in breathing, tingling in the extremities, and (occasional) enlargement of the liver.

Drug Interactions

Cephradine, which works by killing microorganisms which cause infections, may be inhibited by antibiotics, such as Erythromycin and Tetracycline, which do not kill but simply stop the growth of microorganisms. The two types should not be taken together. Probenicid will slow down the excretion rate of cephalosporins.

Usual Dose

Adult: 250 milligrams every 6 hours.

Child: 11 to 9 milligrams per pound per day; maximum dose is 4000 milligrams per day.

Doses may be doubled for severe infections.

Special Information

Cephradine, to be effective, must be taken continuously for 7 to 10 days; so take it exactly as prescribed.

The drug has maximum effect if taken 1 hour before or 2 hours after meals, but if upset stomach occurs the drug can be taken with meals.

Generic Name

Chloral Hydrate

Brand Names

Aquachloral Supprettes (suppositories)	Noctec
	Oradrate
Cohidrate	SK-Chloral Hydrate

Type of Drug

Sedative-hypnotic.

Prescribed for

Insomnia, or as a daytime sedative.

General Information

Chloral Hydrate is very effective in producing sleep. Most people will fall asleep within an hour after taking this medicine. This drug usually does not cause the morning "hangover" seen with other sleeping pills.

Cautions and Warnings

Do not take Chloral Hydrate if you have liver or kidney disease, severe heart disease, or stomach problems, or if you are sensitive or allergic to this or similar drugs. The drug passes through the bloodstream of pregnant women into the unborn child and into the breast milk of nursing mothers; it should not be taken by women who are pregnant or nursing. Chloral Hydrate may be habit-forming or addictive. It should only be taken when absolutely necessary and only in the amounts prescribed.

Possible Side Effects

Most common: reduction in alertness. If you plan to drive a car or operate other machinery, do so with extreme caution.

Possible Adverse Drug Effects

Headache, hangover, hallucinations, drowsiness, stomach upset, nausea, vomiting, difficulty in walking, bad taste in the mouth, feeling of excitement, itching, light-headedness, dizziness, nightmares, feeling unwell, changes in the composition of the blood.

Drug Interactions

Taking Chloral Hydrate with blood-thinning drugs may require a change of dosage of the latter: consult your doctor. Chloral Hydrate is a potent depressant, so avoid drinking alcohol or taking other drugs with depressant properties such as tranquilizers, barbiturates, or sleeping pills.

Usual Dose

Adult: sleeping medicine, 500 milligrams to 1 gram ½ hour before sleep. Daytime sedative, 250 milligrams 3 times per day after meals. Daily dose should not exceed 2 grams.

Child: sleeping medicine, 20 milligrams per pound of body weight (maximum of 1 gram). Daytime sedative, half the dose for sleeping, divided into 3 equal doses.

Overdosage

Symptoms are listed in "Possible Adverse Drug Effects" above. The patient should be taken to a hospital emergency room immediately. ALWAYS bring the medicine bottle.

Storage

Store at room temperature in a night table drawer, not in an area that is hot and/or humid, such as a bathroom.

Special Information

The combination of Chloral Hydrate and alcohol is notorious as the Mickey Finn. Avoid it.

Stomach upset can be minimized if you take Chloral Hydrate with a full glass of water, juice, or other liquid and never chew or break the capsule.

Generic Name

Chlordiazepoxide

Brand Names

A-poxide	Sereen
Chlordiazachel	SK-Lygen
Libritabs	Tenax
Librium	Zetran
Murcil	

Type of Drug

Tranquilizer.

Prescribed for

Relief of symptoms of anxiety, tension, fatigue, or agitation.

General Information

Chlordiazepoxide is a member of the chemical group of drugs known as benzodiazepines. These drugs are used as either antianxiety agents, anticonvulsants, or sedatives (sleeping pills). They exert their effects by relaxing the large skeletal muscles and by a direct effect on the brain. In doing so, they can relax you and make you either more tranquil or sleepier, depending on the drug and how much you use. Many doctors prefer Chlordiazepoxide and the other members of this class to other drugs that can be used for the same effect. Their reason is that the benzodiazepines tend to be safer, have fewer side effects, and are usually as, if not more, effective.

These drugs are generally used in any situation where they can be a useful adjunct.

Benzodiazepine tranquilizing drugs can be abused if taken

for long periods of time and it is possible to develop withdrawal symptoms if you discontinue the therapy abruptly. Withdrawal symptoms include tremor, muscle cramps, stomach cramps, vomiting, insomnia, agitation, sweating, and even convulsions.

Cautions and Warnings

Do not take Chlordiazepoxide if you know you are sensitive or allergic to this drug or to other benzodiazepines such as Diazepam, Oxazepam, Clorazepate, Lorazepam, Prazepam, Flurazepam, and Clonazepam.

Chlordiazepoxide and other members of this drug group may aggravate narrow angle glaucoma, but if you have open angle glaucoma you may take the drugs. In any case, check this information with your doctor. Chlordiazepoxide can cause tiredness, drowsiness, inability to concentrate, or similar symptoms. Be careful if you are driving, operating machinery, or performing other activities which require concentration. Avoid taking this drug during the first 3 months of pregnancy except under strict supervision of your doctor.

Possible Side Effects

Most common: mild drowsiness during the first few days of therapy, especially in the elderly or debilitated. If drowsiness persists, contact your doctor.

Possible Adverse Drug Effects

Major adverse reactions: confusion, depression, lethargy, disorientation, headache, inactivity, slurred speech, stupor, dizziness, tremor, constipation, dry mouth, nausea, inability to control urination, changes in sex drive, irregular menstrual cycle, changes in heart rhythm, lowered blood pressure, retention of fluids, blurred or double vision, itching, rash, hiccups, nervousness, inability to fall asleep, (occasional) liver dysfunction. If you experience any of these reactions stop taking the medicine and contact your doctor immediately.

Drug Interactions

Chlordiazepoxide is a central nervous system depressant. Avoid alcohol, tranquilizers, narcotics, barbiturates, MAO inhibitors, antihistamines, and other medicines used to relieve depression. Smoking may reduce the effectiveness of Chlordiazepoxide. The effects of Chlordiazepoxide may be prolonged when taken together with Cimetidine.

Usual Dose

Adult: 5 to 100 milligrams per day. This tremendous range in dosage exists because of varying response of individuals, related to age, weight, severity of disease, and other characteristics.

Child (over age 6): may be given this drug if it is deemed appropriate by the physician. Initial dose, lowest available (5 milligrams 2 to 4 times per day). Later, may increase in some children to 30 to 40 milligrams per day. The dose must be individualized to obtain maximum benefit.

Overdosage

Symptoms are confusion, sleep or sleepiness, lack of response to pain such as a pin stick, shallow breathing, lowered blood pressure, and coma. The patient should be taken to a hospital emergency room immediately. ALWAYS bring the medicine bottle.

Generic Name

Chlorothiazide

Brand Names

Diuril
SK-Chlorothiazide

Type of Drug

Diuretic.

Prescribed for

Congestive heart failure, cirrhosis of the liver, kidney malfunction, high blood pressure, and other conditions where it is necessary to rid the body of excess fluid.

General Information

This drug is a member of the class known as thiazide diuretics. Thiazides act on the kidneys to stimulate the production

of large amounts of urine. They also cause you to lose
bicarbonate, chloride, and potassium ions from the body.
They are used as part of the treatment of any disease where
it is desirable to eliminate large quantities of body water.
These diseases include heart failure, some kidney diseases,
and liver disease.

Cautions and Warnings

Do not take Chlorothiazide if you are allergic or sensitive to
this drug, similar drugs of this group, or sulfa drugs. If you
have a history of allergy or bronchial asthma, you may also
have a sensitivity or allergy to Chlorothiazide. Although the
drug has been used to treat specific conditions in pregnancy,
unsupervised use by pregnant women should be avoided.
Chlorothiazide will cross the placenta and pass into the unborn
child, possibly causing problems. The drug will also pass
into the breast milk of nursing mothers.

Possible Side Effects

Chlorothiazide will cause a lowering of potassium in the
body. Signs of low potassium levels are dryness of the
mouth, thirst, weakness, lethargy, drowsiness, restlessness,
muscle pains or cramps, gout, muscular tiredness, low blood
pressure, decreased frequency of urination and decreased
amount of urine produced, abnormal heart rate, and stomach upset including nausea and vomiting.

To treat this, potassium supplements are given in the form
of tablets, liquids, or powders, or by increased consumption
of foods such as bananas, citrus fruits, melons, and tomatoes.

Possible Adverse Drug Effects

Loss of appetite, stomach upset, nausea, vomiting, cramping, diarrhea, constipation, dizziness, headache, tingling of
the toes and fingers, restlessness, changes in blood composition, sensitivity to sunlight, rash, itching, fever, difficulty in
breathing, allergic reactions, dizziness when rising quickly
from a sitting or lying position, muscle spasms, weakness,
blurred vision.

Drug Interactions

Chlorothiazide will increase (potentiate) the action of other
blood-pressure-lowering drugs. This is beneficial, and is fre-

quently used to help lower blood pressure in patients with hypertension.

The possibility of developing imbalances in body fluids (electrolytes) is increased if you take medication such as Digitalis and adrenal corticosteroids while you take Chlorothiazide.

If you are taking an oral antidiabetic drug and begin taking Chlorothiazide, the antidiabetic dose may have to be altered.

Lithium Carbonate should not be taken with Chlorothiazide because the combination may increase the risk of lithium toxicity.

If you are taking Chlorothiazide for the treatment of high blood pressure or congestive heart failure, avoid over-the-counter medicines for the treatment of coughs, colds, and allergies: such medicines may contain stimulants. If you are unsure about them, ask your pharmacist.

Usual Dose

Adult: ½ to 1 gram 1 to 2 times per day. Often people respond to intermittent therapy; that is, getting the drug on alternate days or 3 to 5 days per week. This reduces side effects.

Child: 10 milligrams per pound of body weight each day in 2 equal doses.

Infant (under age 6 months): up to 15 milligrams per pound per day in 2 equal doses.

Overdosage

Symptoms are large amount of urination, fatigue, and coma. The patient should be taken to a hospital emergency room immediately. ALWAYS bring the medicine bottle.

Generic Name

Chlorphenesin Carbomate

Brand Name

Maolate

Type of Drug

Skeletal muscle relaxant.

Prescribed for

A part of the treatment for pain and discomfort of skeletal muscle disorders and spasms.

General Information

This drug should always be used together with rest, physical therapy, and other measures designed to treat lower back and other musculoskeletal disorders. The exact way this drug works is not known, but its results may be associated with the sedative effects it exerts.

Cautions and Warnings

This drug may interfere wtih normal concentration and usual day-to-day tasks. It should not be taken by pregnant or breast-feeding women unless absolutely necessary. Do not take this drug if you are allergic to it. The safe use of Chlorphenesin Carbomate beyond 8 weeks has not been definitely established. Patients with liver disease should use this drug with caution.

Possible Side Effects

Drowsiness, dizziness, nausea, confusion, upset stomach, sleeplessness, stimulation, rash, itching, fever, low blood pressure.

Possible Adverse Drug Effects

May cause adverse effects on the blood system.

Drug Interactions

Other drugs which, like Chlorphenesin Carbomate, may cause drowsinesss, sleepiness, or lack of ability to concentrate must be taken with extreme caution: sleeping pills, tranquilizers, barbiturates, narcotics, and alcoholic beverages.

Usual Dose

800 milligrams 3 times per day to start. Dose may be reduced to 400 milligrams 4 times per day after desired effect is obtained.

Overdosage

Symptoms are central nervous system depression, desire to

sleep, weakness, lassitude, and difficulty in breathing. The patient should be taken to a hospital immediately. ALWAYS bring the medicine bottle.

Special Information

Take care while driving or performing other activities requiring concentration: avoid alcohol and other depressant drugs.

Generic Name

Chlorpheniramine Maleate

Brand Names

Alermine	Hal Chlor
Chlo-Amine	Histaspan
Chloramate Unicelles	Histex
Chlor-Mal	Histrey
Chlor-Niramine	Isoclor Timesule
Chlorophen	Panahist
Chlorspan	Phenetron
Chlortab	T.D. Alermine
Chlor-Trimeton	Teldrin Spansules
Ciramine	Trymegen

Type of Drug

Antihistamine.

Prescribed for

Seasonal allergy, stuffed and runny nose, itching of the eyes, scratching of the throat caused by allergy, and other allergic symptoms such as itching, rash, or hives.

General Information

Antihistamines generally, and Chlorpheniramine Maleate specifically, act by blocking the release of the chemical substance histamine from the cell. Antihistamines work by drying up the secretions of the nose, throat, and eyes.

Cautions and Warnings

Chlorpheniramine Maleate should not be used if you are

allergic to this drug. It should be avoided or used with extreme care if you have narrow angle glaucoma (pressure in the eye), stomach ulcer or other stomach problems, enlarged prostate, or problems passing urine. It should not be used by people who have deep-breathing problems such as asthma.

Chlorpheniramine Maleate can cause dizziness, drowsiness, and lowering of blood pressure, particularly in the elderly patient. Young children can show signs of nervousness, increased tension, and anxiety.

Possible Side Effects

Occasionally seen: itching, rash, sensitivity to light, perspiration, chills, dryness of the mouth, nose, and throat, lowering of blood pressure, headache, rapid heartbeat, sleeplessness, dizziness, disturbed coordination, confusion, restlessness, nervousness, irritability, euphoria (feeling high), tingling of the hands and feet, blurred vision, double vision, ringing in the ears, stomach upset, loss of appetite, nausea, vomiting, constipation, diarrhea, difficulty in urination, tightness of the chest, wheezing, nasal stuffiness.

Possible Adverse Drug Effects

Use with care if you have a history of asthma, glaucoma, thyroid disease, heart disease, high blood pressure, or diabetes.

Drug Interactions

Chlorpheniramine Maleate should not be taken with MAO inhibitors.

Interaction with tranquilizers, sedatives, and sleeping medication will increase the effect of these drugs; it is extremely important that you discuss this with your doctor so that doses of these drugs can be properly adjusted.

Be extremely cautious when drinking alcohol while taking Chlorpheniramine Maleate, which will enhance the intoxicating effect of alcohol. Alcohol also has a sedative effect.

Usual Dose

Adult: 4-milligram tablet 3 to 4 times per day.
Child (age 6 to 12): 2-milligram tablet 3 to 4 times per day.
Time-release doses (capsules or tablets) are as follows.

Adult: 8 to 12 milligrams at bedtime or every 8 to 10 hours during the day.

Child (age 6 to 12): 8 milligrams during the day or at bedtime.

Overdosage

Symptoms are depression or stimulation (especially in children), dry mouth, fixed or dilated pupils, flushing of the skin, and stomach upset. Take the patient to a hospital emergency room immediately, if you cannot make him vomit. ALWAYS bring the medicine bottle.

Special Information

Antihistamines produce a depressing effect: be extremely cautious when driving or operating heavy equipment.

The safety of Chlorpheniramine Maleate in pregnancy has not been established. A breast-feeding mother should avoid taking this medication, since it is known to pass from the mother to the baby through the milk.

Generic Name

Chlorpromazine

Brand Names

Chloramead
Clorazine
Foypromazine
Ormazine

Promapar
Promaz
Psychozine
Thorazine

Type of Drug

Phenothiazine antipsychotic.

Prescribed for

Psychotic disorders, moderate to severe depression with anxiety, control of agitation or aggressiveness of disturbed children, alcohol withdrawal symptoms, intractable pain, and senility. Chlorpromazine may also be used to relieve nausea, vomiting, hiccups, and restlessness, and/or apprehension before surgery or other special therapy.

General Information

Chlorpromazine and other members of the phenothiazine group act on a portion of the brain called the hypothalamus. They affect parts of the hypothalamus that control metabolism, body temperature, alertness, muscle tone, hormone balance, and vomiting, and may be used to treat problems related to any of these functions.

Cautions and Warnings

Chlorpromazine should not be taken if you are allergic to one of the drugs in the broad classification known as phenothiazine drugs. Do not take Chlorpromazine if you have any blood, liver, kidney, or heart disease, very low blood pressure, or Parkinson's disease. This medication is a tranquilizer and can have a depressive effect, especially during the first few days of therapy. Care should be taken when performing activities requiring a high degree of concentration, such as driving. If you are taking this medication and become pregnant contact your doctor immediately.

This drug should be used with caution and under strict supervision of your doctor if you have glaucoma, epilepsy, ulcers, or difficulty passing urine.

Avoid insecticides and extreme exposure to heat.

Possible Side Effects

Most common: drowsiness, especially during the first or second week of therapy. If the drowsiness becomes troublesome, contact your doctor.

Possible Adverse Drug Effects

Chlorpromazine can cause jaundice (yellowing of the whites of the eyes or skin), usually in 2 to 4 weeks. The jaundice usually goes away when the drug is discontinued, but there have been cases when it did not. If you notice this effect or if you develop symptoms such as fever and generally not feeling well, contact your doctor immediately. Less frequent: changes in components of the blood including anemias, raised or lowered blood pressure, abnormal heart rates, heart attack, feeling faint or dizzy.

Phenothiazines can produce "extrapyramidal effects," such as spasm of the neck muscles, rolling back of the eyes, convulsions, difficulty in swallowing, and symptoms associated with Parkinson's disease. These effects look very serious but disappear after the drug has been withdrawn; however, symptoms of the face, tongue, and jaw may persist for as long as several years, especially in the elderly with a history of brain damage. If you experience extrapyramidal effects contact your doctor immediately.

Chlorpromazine may cause an unusual increase in psychotic symptoms or may cause paranoid reactions, tiredness, lethargy, restlessness, hyperactivity, confusion at night, bizarre dreams, inability to sleep, depression, and euphoria. Other reactions are itching, swelling, unusual sensitivity to bright lights, red skin, and rash. There have been cases of breast enlargement, false positive pregnancy tests, changes in menstrual flow in females, and impotence and changes in sex drive in males, as well as stuffy nose, headache, nausea, vomiting, loss of appetite, change in body temperature, loss of facial color, excessive salivation, excessive perspiration, constipation, diarrhea, changes in urine and stool habits, worsening of glaucoma, blurred vision, weakening of eyelid muscles, spasms in bronchial and other muscles, increased appetite, excessive thirst, and changes in the coloration of skin, particularly in exposed areas.

Drug Interactions

Chlorpromazine should be taken with caution in combination with barbiturates, sleeping pills, narcotics, other tranquilizers, or any other medication which may produce a depressive effect. Avoid alcohol.

Usual Dose

Adult: 30 to 1000 milligrams or more per day, individualized according to disease and patient's response.

Child: 0.25 milligram per pound of body weight every 4 to 6 hours up to 200 milligrams or more per day (by various routes including rectal suppositories), depending on disease, age, and response to therapy.

This drug may turn the color of your urine pink or reddish brown.

Overdosage

Symptoms are depression, extreme weakness, tiredness,

desire to go to sleep, coma, lowered blood pressure, uncontrolled muscle spasms, agitation, restlessness, convulsions, fever, dry mouth, and abnormal heart rhythms. The patient should be taken to a hospital emergency room immediately. ALWAYS bring the medicine bottle.

Generic Name

Chlorpropamide

Brand Name

Diabinese

Type of Drug

Oral antidiabetic.

Prescribed for

Diabetes mellitus (sugar in the urine).

General Information

Chlorpropamide is one of several oral antidiabetic drugs that work by stimulating the production and release of insulin from the pancreas. The primary difference between these drugs lies in the duration of action. Because they do not lower blood sugar directly, they require some function of pancreas cells.

Cautions and Warnings

Mild stress such as infection, minor surgery, or emotional upset reduces the effectiveness of Chlorpropamide. Remember that while you are taking this drug you should be under your doctor's continuous care.

Chlorpropamide is an aid to, not a substitute for, a diet. Diet remains of primary importance in the treatment of your diabetes. Follow the diet plan your doctor has prescribed for you.

Chlorpropamide and similar drugs are not oral Insulin, nor are they a substitute for Insulin. They do not lower blood sugar by themselves.

This drug should not be used if you have serious liver, kidney or endocrine disease.

The safety of this drug during pregnancy has not been established.

Possible Side Effects

Common: loss of appetite, nausea, vomiting, stomach upset. At times, you may experience weakness or tingling in the hands and feet. These effects can be eliminated by reducing the daily dose of Chlorpropamide or, if necessary, by switching to a different oral antidiabetic drug. This decision must be made by your doctor.

Possible Adverse Drug Effects

Chlorpropamide may produce abnormally low levels of blood sugar when too much is taken for your immediate requirements. (Other factors which may cause lowering of blood sugar are liver or kidney disease, malnutrition, age, drinking alcohol, and diseases of the glands.)

Chlorpropamide may cause a yellowing of the whites of the eyes or skin, itching, rash, or changes in the results of laboratory tests made by your doctor. Usually these reactions will disappear in time. If they persist you should contact your doctor.

Drug Interactions

Thiazide diuretics may lessen the effect of Chlorpropamide, while Insulin, sulfa drugs, Oxyphenbutazone, Phenylbutazone, and MAO inhibitor drugs prolong and enhance the action of Chlorpropamide.

Interaction with alcoholic beverages will cause flushing of the face and body, throbbing pain in the head and neck, difficult breathing, nausea, vomiting, sweating, thirst, chest pains, palpitations, lowered blood pressure, weakness, dizziness, blurred vision, and confusion. If you experience these reactions, contact your doctor immediately.

Because of the stimulant ingredients in many over-the-counter drug products for the relief of coughs, colds, and allergies, avoid them unless your doctor advises otherwise.

Usual Dose

Adult: 250 milligrams daily.

Elderly: 100 to 250 milligrams daily.
For severe cases: 500 milligrams daily.

Overdosage

A mild overdose of Chlorpropamide lowers the blood sugar, which can be treated by consuming sugar in such forms as candy and orange juice. A patient with a more serious overdose should be taken to a hospital emergency room immediately. ALWAYS bring the medicine bottle.

Special Information

The treatment of diabetes is your responsibility. You should follow all instructions about diet, body weight, exercise, personal hygiene, and all measures to avoid infection. If you are not feeling well, or if you have symptoms such as itching, rash, yellowing of the skin or eyes, abnormally light-colored stools, a low-grade fever, sore throat, or diarrhea—contact your doctor immediately.

Generic Name

Chlorthalidone

Brand Name

Hygroton

Type of Drug

Diuretic.

Prescribed for

Congestive heart failure, cirrhosis of the liver, kidney malfunction, high blood pressure, and other conditions where it is necessary to rid the body of excess fluid.

General Information

This drug is a member of the class known as thiazide diuretics. Thiazides act on the kidneys to stimulate the production of large amounts of urine. They also cause you to lose bicarbonate, chloride, and potassium ions from the body.

They are used as a part of the treatment of any disease where it is desirable to eliminate large quantities of body water. These diseases include heart failure, some kidney diseases, and liver diseases.

Cautions and Warnings

Do not take Chlorthalidone if you are allergic or sensitive to this drug, similar drugs of this group, or sulfa drugs. If you have a history of allergy or bronchial asthma, you may also have a sensitivity or allergy to Chlorthalidone. Although this drug has been used to treat specific conditions in pregnancy, unsupervised use by pregnant patients should be avoided. Chlorthalidone will cross the placenta and pass into the unborn child, possibly causing problems. The drug will pass into the breast milk of nursing mothers.

Possible Side Effects

Chlorthalidone will cause a lowering of potassium in the body. Signs of low potassium are dryness of the mouth, thirst, weakness, lethargy, drowsiness, restlessness, muscle pains or cramps, muscular tiredness, low blood pressure, gout, decreased frequency of urination and decreased amount of urine produced, abnormal heart rate, and stomach upset including nausea and vomiting.

To treat this, potassium supplements are given in the form of tablets, liquids, or powders, or by increased consumption of foods such as bananas, citrus fruits, melons, and tomatoes.

Possible Adverse Drug Effects

Loss of appetite, stomach upset, nausea, vomiting, cramping, diarrhea, constipation, dizziness, headache, tingling of the toes and fingers, restlessness, changes in blood composition, sensitivity to sunlight, rash, itching, fever, difficulty in breathing, allergic reactions, dizziness when rising quickly from a sitting or lying position, muscle spasms, weakness, blurred vision.

Drug Interactions

Chlorthalidone will add to (potentiate) the action of other blood-pressure-lowering drugs. This is beneficial, and is frequently used to help lower blood pressure in patients with hypertension.

The possibility of developing imbalances in body fluids (electrolytes) is increased if you take medications such as Digitalis and adrenal corticosteroids while you take Chlorthalidone.

If you are taking an oral antidiabetic drug and begin taking Chlorthalidone, the antidiabetic dose may have to be altered.

Lithium Carbonate should not be taken with Chlorthalidone because the combination may increase the risk of lithium toxicity.

If you are taking this drug for the treatment of high blood pressure or congestive heart failure, avoid over-the-counter medicines for the treatment of coughs, colds, and allergies: such medicines may contain stimulants. If you are unsure about them, ask your pharmacist.

Usual Dose

50 to 100 milligrams per day; or 100 milligrams on alternate days or 3 days per week.

Some patients may require 150 or 200 milligrams per day; doses of more than 200 milligrams per day generally do not produce greater response. A single dose is taken with food in the morning. Dose often declines from the initial dose, according to patient's need.

Overdosage

Symptoms are excessive urination, fatigue, and coma. The patient should be taken to a hospital emergency room immediately. ALWAYS bring the medicine bottle.

Generic Name
Cimetidine

Brand Name

Tagamet

Type of Drug

First member of a new class of drugs available in the U.S. known as histamine H_2 antagonists.

Prescribed for

Part of the treatment of ulcers. Also used in the treatment of other conditions characterized by secretions of large amounts of gastrointestinal fluids.

Cautions and Warnings

Do not take Cimetidine if you know you are allergic to it. This drug should be used with extreme caution if you are pregnant or if you might become pregnant while taking it. Cimetidine should not be used by nursing mothers.

Possible Side Effects

Most frequent: mild diarrhea, muscle pains and cramps, dizziness, rash, nausea, vomiting, headache, mental confusion, drowsiness.

Possible Adverse Drug Effects

Changes in heart rhythm, adverse effects on the blood system, hepatitis, kidney disorders, impotence, hair loss, hallucinations, double vision. A few patients have reported breast enlargement.

Drug Interactions

Cimetidine may increase the effects of blood-thinning drugs like Warfarin, tranquilizers of the benzodiazepine group, and Theophylline.

Usual Dose

300 milligrams 4 times per day, with meals and at bedtime.

Overdosage

Symptoms: rapid heart beat, difficulty breathing. The patient should be taken to a hospital emergency room immediately. ALWAYS bring the medicine bottle.

Because this is a new drug, there have been few Cimetidine overdoses. Doses of as much as 10 grams (approximately 33 tablets) have been taken, though, without any unusual effects.

Special Information

Many doctors believe that Cimetidine, properly used, will decrease the amount of ulcer surgery because the drug reduces the amount of irritating secretions produced by stomach glands. Report any unusual side effects of this drug to your doctor immediately.

Generic Name

Clindamycin

Brand Name
Cleocin

Type of Drug
Antibiotic.

Prescribed for
Serious infections caused by bacteria which are generally found to be susceptible to this drug.

General Information
This is one of the few drugs, given by mouth, which is effective against anaerobic organisms: bacteria which grow only in the absence of oxygen and are frequently found in infected wounds, lung abscesses, abdominal infections, and infections of the female genital tract. It is also effective against the organisms usually treated by Penicillin or Erythromycin.

Cautions and Warnings
Do not take Clindamycin if you are allergic to it or to Lincomycin, another antibiotic drug. It may cause a severe intestinal irritation called colitis, which may be fatal. Because of this, Clindamycin should be reserved for serious infections due to organisms known to be affected by it. It should not be taken for the casual treatment of colds or other moderate infections, or for infections which can be successfully treated with other drugs. If you develop severe diarrhea or stomach pains, call your doctor at once.

Possible Side Effects
Stomach pain, nausea, vomiting, diarrhea, pain when swallowing.

Possible Adverse Drug Effects

Itching and rash or more serious signs of drug sensitivity, such as difficulty in breathing; also yellowing of the skin or whites of the eyes, occasional effects on components of the blood, and joint pain.

Drug Interactions

Clindamycin may antagonize Erythromycin; these drugs should not be taken together.

Usual Dose

Adult: 150 to 450 milligrams every 6 hours.

Child: 2 to 11 milligrams per pound of body weight per day in divided doses. No child should be given less than 37 ½ milligrams 3 times per day, regardless of weight.

Special Information

Safety in pregnant women has not been established. Since this drug is transferred to the breast milk of nursing mothers, its use by them should be carefully considered. Unsupervised use of this drug or other antibiotics can cause secondary infections from susceptible organisms such as fungi.

Generic Name

Clofibrate

Brand Name

Atromid-S

Type of Drug

Antihyperlipidemic.

Prescribed for

Reduction of high blood levels of cholesterol and/or triglycerides, in patients not responding to diet, weight control, and exercise measures to control their diabetes.

General Information

Although we don't know exactly how Clofibrate works, we
know that it works on blood cholesterol and triglycerides.
The lowering of blood levels of these fatty materials may be
beneficial, and may have an effect on the development of
heart disease. No one knows for sure. However, it is generally considered better to have low levels of cholesterol and
triglycerides in the blood. Clofibrate is only part of the therapy for high blood levels of cholesterol and/or triglycerides.
Diet and weight control are also very important. You must
remember that taking this medicine is not a substitute for
other activities or dietary restrictions which have been prescribed for you by your doctor.

Cautions and Warnings

Clofibrate should not be used if you have severe liver or
kidney disease, are pregnant, or are a nursing mother. There
is the possibility that this medication may pass from you
into your baby and cause an adverse effect.

Clofibrate causes liver cancer in rats and may do the same
to human patients. Its use has not been definitely associated
with reductions in death from heart disease; therefore, this
drug should be used only by patients whose diets and other
activities have not solved their triglyceride or cholesterol
problems. Some studies have reported a large increase in
death rates and drug side effects when people have taken
Clofibrate over a long term.

Possible Side Effects

The most frequent side effect of Clofibrate is nausea. Other
gastrointestinal reactions may be experienced: loose stools,
stomach upset, stomach gas, abdominal pain. Less frequent:
headache, dizziness, tiredness, cramped muscles, aching and
weakness, rash, itching, brittle hair and loss of hair.

Possible Adverse Drug Effects

Abnormal heart rhythms, blood clots in the lungs or veins,
enlargement of the liver, gallstones (especially in patients
who have taken Clofibrate for a long time), decreased sex
drive, sexual impotence. If you suffer from angina pectoris, a
specific type of chest pain, Clofibrate may either increase or

decrease this pain. It may cause you to produce smaller amounts of urine than usual, and has been associated with blood in the urine, tiredness, weakness, drowsiness, dizziness, headache, and increased appetite. Clofibrate has been accused of causing stomach ulcers, stomach bleeding, arthritislike symptoms, uncontrollable muscle spasms, increased perspiration, blurred vision, breast enlargement, and some effects on the blood.

Drug Interactions

If you are taking an anticoagulant and get a new prescription for Clofibrate, your anticoagulant dose will have to be reduced by as much as a third to a half. It is absolutely essential that your doctor knows you are taking these drugs in combination so that the proper dose adjustments can be made.

Usual Dose

4 capsules per day in divided doses.

Storage

Clofibrate capsules are covered with soft gelatin that must be protected from heat and moisture. They should not be stored in the refrigerator, or in a bathroom medicine chest where there may be a lot of heat or moisture in the air, but in a dresser or night table where room temperature is normal.

Special Information

This drug may be taken with food or milk if it causes upset stomach. Call your doctor if you develop chest pains, difficulty in breathing, abnormal heart rates, severe stomach pains with nausea and vomiting, fever and chills, sore throat, blood in the urine, swelling of the legs, weight gain, or change in urine habits.

Follow your diet and limit your intake of alcoholic beverages.

Generic Name

Clonidine

Brand Name

Catapres

Type of Drug

Antihypertensive.

Prescribed for

High blood pressure.

General Information

Clonidine acts in the brain by causing the dilation of certain blood vessels, thereby decreasing blood pressure. The drug produces its effect very quickly, causing a decline in blood pressure within 1 hour. If you abruptly stop taking Clonidine you may experience an unusual increase in blood pressure with symptoms of agitation, headache, and nervousness. These effects can be reversed by simply resuming therapy or by taking another drug to lower the blood pressure. Under no circumstances should you stop taking Clonidine without your doctor's knowledge. People who abruptly stop taking this medication may suffer severe reactions and even die. Be sure you always have an adequate supply on hand.

Cautions and Warnings

Some people develop a tolerance to their usual dose of Clonidine. If this happens to you your blood pressure may increase, and you will require a change in the Clonidine dose. Clonidine is not recommended for use by women who are pregnant or who feel they may become pregnant.

Possible Side Effects

Most common: dry mouth, drowsiness, sedation, constipation, dizziness, headache, fatigue. These effects tend to diminish as you continue taking the drug.

Possible Adverse Drug Effects

Infrequent: loss of appetite, not feeling well, nausea, vomiting, weight gain, breast enlargement, various effects on the heart, changes in dream patterns, nightmares, difficulty sleeping, nervousness, restlessness, anxiety, mental depression, rash, hives, itching, thinning or loss of scalp hair, difficulty urinating, impotence, dryness and burning of the eyes.

Drug Interactions

Clonidine has a depressive effect and will increase the depressive effects of alcohol, barbiturates, sedatives, and tranquil-izers. Avoid them.

Usual Dose

Starting dose of 0.1 milligram twice per day may be raised by 0.1 to 0.2 milligram per day until maximum control is achieved. The dose must be tailored to your individual needs. It is recommended that no one should take more than 2.4 milligrams per day.

Overdosage

Symptoms are severe lowering of blood pressure, weakness, and vomiting. The patient should be taken to a hospital emergency room immediately. ALWAYS bring the medicine bottle.

Special Information

Clonidine causes drowsiness in about 35 percent of those who take it: be extremely careful while driving or operating any sort of appliance or machinery. The effect is prominent during the first few weeks of therapy, then tends to decrease.

Avoid taking nonprescription cough and cold medicine unless so directed by your doctor.

Generic Name

Clorazepate

Brand Names

Azene
Tranxene
Tranxene-SD

Type of Drug

Tranquilizer.

Prescribed for

Relief of symptoms of anxiety, tension, fatigue, or agitation.

General Information

Clorazepate is a member of the chemical group of drugs

known as benzodiazepines. These drugs are used as either antianxiety agents, anticonvulsants, or sedatives (sleeping pills). They exert their effects by relaxing the large skeletal muscles and by a direct effect on the brain. In doing so, they can relax you and make you either more tranquil or sleepier, depending on the drug and how much you use. Many doctors prefer Clorazepate and the other members of this class to other drugs that can be used for the same effect. Their reason is that the benzodiazepines tend to be safer, have fewer side effects, and are usually as, if not more, effective.

These drugs are generally used in any situation where they can be a useful adjunct.

Benzodiazepine tranquilizing drugs can be abused if taken for long periods of time, and it is possible to develop withdrawal symptoms if you discontinue the therapy abruptly. Withdrawal symptoms include tremor, muscle cramps, stomach cramps, vomiting, insomnia, agitation, sweating, and even convulsions.

Cautions and Warnings

Do not take Clorazepate if you know you are sensitive or allergic to this drug or other benzodiazepines such as Diazepam, Chlordiazepoxide, Oxazepam, Lorazepam, Prazepam, Flurazepam, and Clonazepam.

Clorazepate and other members of this drug group may aggravate narrow angle glaucoma, but if you have open angle glaucoma you may take the drugs. In any case, check this information with your doctor. Clorazepate can cause tiredness, drowsiness, inability to concentrate, or similar symptoms. Be careful if you are driving, operating machinery, or performing other activities which require concentration. Avoid taking this drug during the first 3 months of pregnancy except under strict supervision of your doctor.

Possible Side Effects

Most common: mild drowsiness during the first few days of therapy, especially in the elderly or debilitated. If drowsiness persists, contact your doctor.

Possible Adverse Drug Effects

Major adverse reactions: confusion, depression, lethargy, disorientation, headache, inactivity, slurred speech, stupor, dizziness, tremor, constipation, dry mouth, nausea, inability to control urination, changes in sex drive, irregular menstrual cycle, changes in heart rhythm, lowered blood pressure, retention of fluids, blurred or double vision, itching, rash, hiccups, nervousness, inability to fall asleep, (occasional) liver dysfunction. If you experience any of these reactions stop taking the medicine and contact your doctor immediately.

Drug Interactions

Clorazepate is a central nervous system depressant. Avoid alcohol, tranquilizers, narcotics, barbiturates, MAO inhibitors, antihistamines, and other medicines used to relieve depression. Smoking may reduce the effectiveness of Clorazepate. The effects of Clorazepate may be prolonged when taken together with Cimetidine.

Usual Dose

15 to 60 milligrams daily; average dose, 30 milligrams in divided quantities. Must be adjusted to individual response for patient to receive maximum effect.

    Tranxene-SD, a long-acting form of Clorazepate, may be given as a single dose, either 11.25 or 22.5 milligrams once every 24 hours. The daily dose of Azene, another brand name, is slightly different, from 12 to 52 milligrams per day according to patient's response. The drug may be given as a single daily dose at bedtime; usual starting dose for helping patients go to sleep is 13 milligrams.

Overdosage

Symptoms are confusion, sleep or sleepiness, lack of response to pain such as a pin stick, shallow breathing, lowered blood pressure, and coma. The patient should be taken to a hospital emergency room immediately. ALWAYS bring the medicine bottle.

Generic Name

Clotrimazole

Brand Names

Gyne-Lotrimin
Lotrimin
Mycelex

Type of Drug

Antifungal.

Prescribed for

Fungus infections of the skin and vaginal tract.

General Information

Clotrimazole is one of the newer antifungal drugs in the U.S., although it has been available in other parts of the world for some time. This drug is especially useful against a wide variety of fungus organisms which other drugs do not affect.

Cautions and Warnings

If Clotrimazole causes local itching and/or irritation, stop using it. Do not use in the eyes. Women who are in the first three months of pregnancy should only use this drug after specific direction from their doctor.

Possible Side Effects

Side effects do not occur very often and are usually mild. Cream or solution: redness, stinging, blistering, peeling, itching and swelling of local areas. Vaginal tablets: mild burning, skin rash, mild cramps, frequent urination, and burning or itching in a sexual partner.

Usual Dose

Cream or solution: apply to affected areas, morning and night.

Vaginal cream: one applicatorful at bedtime for 7 to 14 days.

Vaginal tablets: 1 tablet inserted into the vagina at bedtime for 7 days, or 2 tablets a day for 3 days.

Special Information

If treating a vaginal infection, you should refrain from sexual activity or be sure that your partner wears a condom until the treatment is finished. Call your doctor if burning or itching develop or if the condition does not show improvement in 7 days.

Generic Name

Codeine

Type of Drug

Narcotic analgesic and cough suppressant.

Prescribed for

Relief of moderate to moderately severe pain, and as a cough suppressant.

General Information

Codeine is a narcotic drug with some pain-relieving and cough-suppressing activity. As an analgesic it is useful for mild to moderate pain. 30 to 60 milligrams of Codeine is approximately equal in pain-relieving effect to 2 Aspirin tablets (650 milligrams). Codeine may be less active than Aspirin for types of pain associated with inflammation, since Aspirin reduces inflammation and Codeine does not. Codeine suppresses the cough reflex but does not cure the underlying cause of the cough. In fact, sometimes it may not be desirable to overly suppress a cough, because cough suppression reduces your ability to naturally eliminate excess mucus produced during a cold or allergy attack. Other narcotic cough suppressants are stronger than Codeine, but Codeine remains the best cough medicine available today.

Cautions and Warnings

Do not take Codeine if you know you are allergic or sensitive to it. Use this drug with extreme caution if you suffer from asthma or other breathing problems. Long-term use of this drug may cause drug dependence or addiction. Codeine is a respiratory depressant and affects the central nervous system, producing sleepiness, tiredness, and/or inability to concentrate. Be careful if you are driving, operating machinery, or performing other functions requiring concentration. If you are pregnant or suspect that you are pregnant do not take this drug.

Possible Side Effects

Most frequent: light-headedness, dizziness, sleepiness, nausea, vomiting, loss of appetite, sweating. If these occur, consider calling your doctor and asking him about lowering the dose of Codeine you are taking. Usually the side effects disappear if you simply lie down.

More serious side effects of Codeine are shallow breathing or difficulty in breathing.

Possible Adverse Drug Effects

Euphoria (feeling high), sleepiness, headache, agitation, uncoordinated muscle movement, minor hallucinations, disorientation and visual disturbances, dry mouth, loss of appetite, constipation, flushing of the face, rapid heartbeat, palpitations, faintness, urinary difficulties or hesitancy, reduced sex drive and/or potency, itching, rashes, anemia, lowered blood sugar, yellowing of the skin and/or whites of the eyes. Narcotic analgesics may aggravate convulsions in those who have had convulsions in the past.

Drug Interactions

Because of its depressant effect and potential effect on breathing, Codeine should be taken with extreme care in combination with alcohol, sleeping medicine, tranquilizers, or other depressant drugs.

Usual Dose

Adult: 15 to 60 milligrams 4 times per day for relief of pain; 10 to 20 milligrams every few hours as needed to suppress cough.

Child: 1 to 2 milligrams per pound of body weight in divided doses for relief of pain; ½ to ¾ milligram per pound of body weight in divided doses to suppress cough.

Overdosage

Symptoms are depression of respiration (breathing), extreme tiredness progressing to stupor and then coma, pinpointed pupils of the eyes, no response to stimulation such as a pin stick, cold and clammy skin, slowing down of the heartbeat, lowering of blood pressure, convulsions, and cardiac arrest. The patient should be taken to a hospital emergency room immediately.

REMEMBER: ALWAYS bring the medicine bottle.

Special Information

Avoid alcohol while taking Codeine. Call your doctor if you develop constipation or dry mouth. Codeine may be taken with food to reduce stomach upset.

Brand Name

Combid

Ingredients

Isopropamide
Prochlorperazine

Type of Drug

Gastrointestinal anticholinergic agent.

Prescribed for

Excess acid in the stomach, spasms of the stomach and small intestine, and relief of anxiety and tension or nausea and vomiting associated with gastrointestinal disease.

General Information

The antinauseant in Combid works to relieve and prevent nausea and vomiting and the anticholinergic works to prevent and treat stomach and intestinal spasms. By relieving these spasms, Combid can prevent or treat stomach or intestinal pains. Combid spansules release their ingredients over an 8-to-12-hour period; only 2 capsules per day are usually required.

Cautions and Warnings

Do not take Combid if you have glaucoma. Other disorders where an anticholinergic drug such as Combid may be damaging are prostatic hypertrophy, pyloric obstruction, bladder-neck obstruction, and obstructive lesions of the intestine. Nausea and vomiting may be a drug side effect or a sign of disease: if you have this medication at home, do not self-medicate for nausea and vomiting until you have checked with your doctor. The safety of this drug for pregnant or nursing women has not been established.

Possible Side Effects

Primary: sleepiness or drowsiness, dry mouth, blurred vision, increased sensitivity to strong light, difficulty in urination, loss of sense of taste.

Possible Adverse Drug Effects

Rare: sore throat, fever, unusual bleeding or bruising, rash, yellowing of the skin or whites of the eyes. If you experience any of these, contact your doctor immediately.

Drug Interactions

Combid can cause sleepiness, tiredness, or difficulty in concentration. Do not aggravate the problem by taking alcoholic beverages, tranquilizers, sedatives, and other drugs that cause tiredness.

Usual Dose

1 capsule every 12 to 24 hours.

Overdosage

Symptoms (from either ingredient in Combid) are central nervous system depression possibly to the point of coma, lowered blood pressure, agitation, restlessness, convulsions, fever, dry mouth, severe stomach cramps, abnormal heart rhythms, difficulty in swallowing, extreme thirst, blurred vision, sensitivity to bright light, flushed, hot dry skin, rash, high blood pressure, confusion, and delirium. The patient should be taken to a hospital emergency room immediately. ALWAYS bring the medicine bottle.

Brand Name

Combipres

Ingredients

Chlorthalidone
Clonidine

Type of Drug

Antihypertensive.

Prescribed for

High blood pressure.

General Information

This drug is a combination of two effective antihypertensive drugs. One of them works by causing the dilation of certain blood vessels. The other is a diuretic which lowers blood pressure through its effect on body ions (sodium and potassium). Although it is convenient to take the two drugs in one tablet, it may not be in your best interest. If you need more or less of one of the ingredients than are available in the Combipres tablets, you must take the drugs as separate pills. Often, doctors are able to lower your blood pressure most effectively by manipulating the doses of one drug or the other.

Cautions and Warnings

Do not take Combipres if you are allergic to either of the ingredients or to sulfa-type drugs. This drug should not be taken by pregnant women or nursing mothers. Some people develop a tolerance to the effect of one of the ingredients in this product. If this happens, your blood pressure may increase and you may require a change of dose or medicine.

Possible Side Effects

One of the ingredients in this drug can cause loss of potassium from the body (hypokalemia). The signs of this problem are dryness of the mouth, weakness, lethargy, drowsiness, restlessness, muscle pains or cramps, muscular tiredness, stomach upset, nausea and vomiting, and abnormal heart rhythms. To prevent or treat hypokalemia, potassium supplements, in the form of tablets, powders, or liquids, are given every day. You may increase your potassium intake naturally by eating more bananas, citrus fruits, melons, or tomatoes.

Combipres may also cause constipation or headache.

Possible Adverse Drug Effects

Loss of appetite, feeling of ill health, nausea, vomiting, weight gain, breast enlargement, adverse effects on the heart, changes in dream patterns, nightmares, difficulty sleeping, anxiety, depression, rash, hives, itching, thinning or loss of hair, dryness or burning of the eyes, sexual impotence. Other possible adverse effects from this combination are tingling of the toes or fingers, changes in blood composition, sensitivity to sunlight, difficulty in breathing, drug allergy, dizziness when rising quickly from a sitting or lying position, muscle spasms, weariness, blurred vision.

Drug Interactions

May interact with Digitalis to cause abnormal heart rhythms. The effect of an oral antidiabetic medicine may be altered by Combipres. People taking lithium drugs should be careful about also taking Combipres since the combination may lead to lithium toxicity. Avoid alcohol, barbiturates, sedatives, and tranquilizers while taking Combipres. Their action may be increased by one of the ingredients in Combipres.

Usual Dose

2 tablets per day (of either strength). The dose of this drug must be tailored to your individual needs for maximum effectiveness.

Overdosage

Symptoms are excessive urination, fatigue, and extreme lowering of blood pressure. The patient should be taken immediately to a hospital emergency room. ALWAYS bring the medicine bottle.

Special Information

Avoid over-the-counter drugs containing stimulant drugs. If you are unsure which ones to avoid, ask your pharmacist.

One of the ingredients in Combipres causes drowsiness in about 35 percent of those who take it. Be extremely careful while driving or operating any equipment. This effect is most prominent during the first few weeks of therapy.

Generic Name

Conjugated Estrogens

Brand Names

Conjugated Estrogenic Substances	Evestrone
	Premarin
Estroate	Sodestrin-H

Type of Drug

Estrogen.

Prescribed for

Moderate to severe symptoms associated with menopause. There is no evidence that this drug is effective for nervous symptoms or depression occurring during menopause: it should not be used to treat this condition. Conjugated Estrogens may also be used to treat various types of cancer in selected patients; and other conditions where supplementation of normal estrogenic substances is required.

General Information

Because of the potential development of secondary disease after a long period of taking Conjugated Estrogens, the decision to take this medication chronically should be made cautiously by you and your doctor.

Cautions and Warnings

Estrogens have been reported to increase the risk of certain types of cancer in postmenopausal women taking this type of drug for prolonged periods of time: this risk tends to depend upon the duration of treatment and the dose of the estrogen being taken. When long-term estrogen therapy is indicated for the treatment of menopausal symptoms, the lowest effective dose should be used. If you have to take Conjugated Estrogens for extended periods of time, you should see your doctor at least twice a year so that he can assess your current condition and your need to continue the drug therapy. If you are taking an estrogenic product and experience vaginal bleeding of a recurrent, abnormal, or persistent nature, contact your doctor immediately. If you are pregnant you should not use this or any other estrogenic substance, since these drugs, if used during the earlier stages of pregnancy, may seriously damage the offspring. If you have active thrombophlebitis or any other disorder associated with the formation of blood clots, you probably should not take this drug. If you feel that you have a disorder associated with blood clots and you have been taking Conjugated Estrogens or a similar product, you should contact your doctor immediately so that he can evaluate your situation and decide about stopping the drug therapy.

Prolonged continuous administration of estrogenic substances to certain animal species has increased the frequency of cancer in these animals, and there is evidence that these drugs may increase the risk of various cancers in humans. This drug should be taken with caution by women with a strong family history of breast cancer or those who have breast nodules, fibrocystic disease of the breast, or abnormal mammogram. Furthermore, long-term taking of Conjugated Estrogens may expose a woman to a two- to threefold increase in chance of developing gallbladder disease. It is possible that women taking Conjugated Estrogens for extended periods of time may experience some of the same development of long-term adverse effects as women who have taken oral contraceptives for extended periods of time. These long-term problems may include thromboembolic disease or the development of various disorders associated with the development of blood clots, liver cancer or other liver tumors, high blood pressure, glucose intolerance or a development of a symptom similar to diabetes or the aggravation of diabetes in patients who had this disease before they started the estrogen, and high blood levels of calcium in certain classes of patients.

Possible Side Effects

Breakthrough bleeding, spotting, changes in menstrual flow, dysmenorrhea, premenstrual-type syndrome, amenorrhea, vaginal infection with candida, cystitislike syndrome, enlargement or tenderness of the breasts, nausea, vomiting, abdominal cramps, feeling of bloatedness, jaundice or yellowing of the skin or whites of the eyes, rash, loss of scalp hair, development of new hairy areas. Lesions of the eye have been associated with estrogen therapy. If you wear contact lenses and are taking estrogens, it is possible that you will become intolerant to the lenses. You may also experience headache—possibly migraine headache—dizziness, depression, weight changes, retention of water, and changes in sex drive.

Usual Dose

0.3 to 3.75 milligrams per day, depending on the disease and patient's response.

Overdosage

Overdosage may cause nausea and withdrawal bleeding in adult females. Accidental overdosage in children has not resulted in serious adverse effects.

Special Information

This drug may be taken with food to reduce upset stomach. Call your doctor if you develop chest pain, difficulty breathing, pain in the groin or calves, unusual vaginal bleeding, missed menstrual period, lumps in the breast, sudden severe headaches, dizziness or fainting, disturbances in speech or vision, weakness or numbness in the arms or legs, abdominal pains, depression, yellowing of the skin or whites of the eyes. Call your doctor if you think you are pregnant.

Brand Name

Cortisporin Otic

Other Brand Name

Otobione

Ingredients

Hydrocortisone
Neomycin Sulfate
Polymyxin-B

Type of Drug

Steroid antibiotic combination product.

Prescribed for

Superficial infections, inflammation, itching, and other problems involving the outer ear.

General Information

Cortisporin Otic contains a steroid drug to reduce inflammation and two antibiotics to treat local infections. This combination can be quite useful for local infections and inflammations of the ear because of its dual method of action and its relatively broad, nonspecific applicability.

Possible Side Effects

Local irritation such as itching or burning can occur if you are sensitive or allergic to one of the ingredients in this drug.

Usual Dose

2 to 4 drops in the affected ear 3 to 4 times per day.

Special Information

Use only when specifically prescribed by a physician. Overuse of this or similar products can result in the growth of other organisms such as fungi. If new infections or new problems appear during the time you are using this medication, stop using the drug and contact your doctor.

Generic Name

Cyclandelate

Brand Names

Cyclospasmol
Cydel
Cyvaso

Type of Drug

Vasodilator.

Prescribed for

Nighttime leg cramps. Also prescribed to dilate large blood

vessels in the brain so that more blood can be delivered to it.

General Information

Cyclandelate relaxes various smooth muscles: it slows their normal degree of responsiveness but does not paralyze muscle cells. Cyclandelate may directly widen blood vessels in the brain and other areas, increasing the flow of blood and oxygen to these areas.

Cautions and Warnings

Do not take Cyclandelate if you are allergic or sensitive to it. Do not take Cyclandelate if you have a history of glaucoma, or of heart or other disease in which major blood vessels have been partly or completely blocked. Safe use of this drug by pregnant women has not been established.

Possible Side Effects

The most common side effect of Cyclandelate is mild stomach upset, but this can be avoided by taking the medicine with food or antacid. Cyclandelate can produce mild flushing, particularly in the face and extremities. It can also cause headache, feeling of weakness, and rapid heartbeat, especially during the first few weeks of therapy.

Possible Adverse Drug Effects

Cyclandelate can make you feel weak, dizzy, or faint when you rise quickly from a lying or sitting position: this is called orthostatic hypotension and is caused by a sudden drop in the amount of blood being supplied to your brain. You can usually avoid orthostatic hypotension by getting up slowly. If the symptom becomes a problem, contact your doctor so that he can adjust your dose or prescribe a different medicine for you.

Drug Interactions

Avoid taking over-the-counter drugs for cough, cold, or allergy as some of these drugs can aggravate heart disease or other diseases related to blocked blood vessels. Contact your doctor or pharmacist for more specific information about over-the-counter products which could be a problem.

Usual Dose

Starting dose: 1200 to 1600 milligrams per day in divided doses before meals and at bedtime. As you begin to respond to the medication, the dose may be reduced to a lowest effective level of, usually, 400 to 800 milligrams per day given in 2 to 4 divided doses. Improvement takes several weeks to appear; do not look for immediate benefits. Use of this medication for less than several weeks is usually of little or no value and certainly of no permanent value.

Special Information

This drug may be taken with food or antacids to reduce stomach upset.

Generic Name

Cyclobenzaprine

Brand Name

Flexeril

Type of Drug

Skeletal muscle relaxant.

Prescribed for

Painful muscle spasm associated with certain conditions.

General Information

This drug can relieve painful muscle spasm and does not interfere with muscle function. It should be used for only 2 to 3 weeks because the kind of conditions for which the drug is used generally do not last longer and it has not been studied in depth for any longer period of use. It should be used until muscle spasm and pain have been relieved, the patient has regained full movement, and complete daily activities have been restored. This drug is a chemical cousin to tricyclic antidepressant drugs.

Cautions and Warnings

Do not use if you are allergic to this drug, are taking MAO

inhibitor drugs (or have been taking them within the last 2 weeks), are just recovering from a heart attack, or have abnormal heart rhythms, heart failure, or an overactive thyroid. Pregnant women, nursing mothers, and children under age 15 should avoid this drug.

Possible Side Effects

Drowsiness occurs in 40 percent of people taking this drug. It can also cause dry mouth, dizziness, increased heart rate, and weakness.

Possible Adverse Drug Effects

Sweating, muscle aches, difficulty in breathing, abdominal pain, constipation, coated tongue, tremors, poor muscle control, nervousness, feeling of euphoria, disorientation, confusion, headache, difficulty in urination, depression, hallucination, rash, itching, swelling of the face or tongue.

Drug Interactions

Cyclobenzaprine may interact with MAO inhibitors to produce high fever and convulsions. It may increase the depressive effect of alcohol, sleeping pills, tranquilizers, or other depressant drugs. It may block the effect of Guanethidine and other blood-pressure-lowering drugs. It may interact with Atropine or atropinelike (anticholinergic) drugs to produce symptoms of anticholinergic overdose (dry mouth, difficult urination, thirst).

Usual Dose

20 to 60 milligrams per day.

Overdosage

Symptoms of overdose include temporary confusion, stiff muscles, vomiting, very high fever, drowsiness, heart abnormalities, difficulty in concentrating, hallucinations, and agitation, as well as low body temperature, dilated pupils, convulsions, low blood pressure, and coma.

The drug must be eliminated from the body as quickly as possible. Call your doctor or poison control center for more information. The patient may have to be taken to a hospital emergency room. ALWAYS bring the medicine bottle with you.

Special Information

This drug can cause drowsiness, dizziness, or blurred vision.
Be careful while driving or operating any kind of equipment.
Do not use alcohol or any other depressant while taking
Cyclobenzaprine.

Generic Name

Cyproheptadine Hydrochloride

Brand Name

Cyprodine
Periactin

Type of Drug

Phenothiazine-type antihistamine.

Prescribed for

Relief of symptoms associated with allergies, drug allergies,
colds or upper respiratory infections, infection or itching of
the extremities, insect bites, and general itching.

General Information

Cyproheptadine Hydrochloride is an antihistamine. Any effect
it exerts is due to its ability to counteract the effects of
histamine, a chemical released by the body as part of allergic or sensitivity reactions. Histamine is also released as a
part of the body's reaction to the common cold or similar
respiratory infections. Cyproheptadine Hydrochloride is especially useful in treating symptoms of allergy, itching, and the
common cold. It has been reported to cause weight gain and
has even been tried as an appetite stimulant.

Cautions and Warnings

Do not take Cyproheptadine Hydrochloride if you are allergic
to it or to other phenothiazine-type drugs such as Chlorpromazine and Prochlorperazine. Signs of allergies to phenothiazines include sore throat, fever, unusual bleeding or
bruising, rash, blurred vision, and yellowing of the skin.

Although this drug is usually not a problem for people with heart, liver, and stomach problems, they would do well to avoid taking it.

Possible Side Effects

Most frequent: sedation, sleeplessness, dizziness, disturbed coordination. Less common: itching, rash, drug allergy, sensitivity to sunlight, excessive perspiration, chills, dryness of the mouth, nose, and throat. Other possible side effects: lowered blood pressure, headache, palpitations, rapid heartbeat.

Possible Adverse Drug Effects

Effects on the blood system, confusion, restlessness, excitation, nervousness, irritability, sleeplessness, euphoria, tingling in the hands and feet, blurred vision, double vision, ringing in the ears, convulsions, stomach upset, loss of appetite, vomiting, nausea, diarrhea, constipation, thickening of mucus and other bronchial secretions resulting in tightness in the chest, wheezing, stuffed nose. Cyproheptadine Hydrochloride may also produce adverse effects common to the phenothiazine class of drugs, such as tremors, a spastic, uncontrollable motion, and (rarely) a form of jaundice (yellowing of the skin and eyes).

Drug Interactions

Alcohol will increase the drowsiness or sleepiness that can be produced by Cyproheptadine Hydrochloride, so avoid drinking excessive amounts of alcoholic beverages. Taking Cyproheptadine Hydrochloride with another sedative, tranquilizer, barbiturate, or hypnotic drug can increase drowsiness and other symptoms of depression.

Cyproheptadine Hydrochloride can influence the effectiveness of any high blood pressure medicine you are taking.

If you have Parkinson's disease, you probably should not be taking this type of antihistamine; it is known to produce specific adverse drug effects in people with Parkinson's disease. An MAO inhibitor may interact with Cyproheptadine Hydrochloride to prolong the drying effect of the antihistamine, causing dry mouth and blurred vision.

Usual Dose

Adult: 4 to 20 milligrams daily.
Child (age 7 to 14): 4 milligrams 2 to 3 times per day.
Child (age 2 to 6): 2 to 3 milligrams per day.
The maximum daily dose for adults is 32 milligrams; for children age 7 to 14, 16 milligrams; for children age 2 to 6, 12 milligrams.
The liquid form of this medicine is very bitter. To improve the taste you can mix it with fruit juice, milk, or a carbonated beverage.

Overdosage

Symptoms are depression or stimulation (especially in children), dry mouth, fixed or dilated pupils, flushing of the skin, and stomach upset. Take the patient to a hospital emergency room immediately. ALWAYS bring the medicine container to the hospital. Do not induce vomiting. After having taken this drug the patient might breathe in the vomit, causing serious lung damage.

Special Information

Cyproheptadine Hydrochloride can produce sleepiness. Be careful if you are driving or operating hazardous machinery.

Brand Name

Darvocet-N

Ingredients

Acetaminophen
Propoxyphene Napsylate

Type of Drug

Analgesic.

Prescribed for

Relief of mild to moderate pain.

General Information

Propoxyphene Napsylate, the major ingredient in this product, is a chemical derivative of Methadone, a narcotic used for pain relief. It is estimated that Propoxyphene Napsylate is about half to two-thirds as strong a pain reliever as Codeine and about as effective as Aspirin.

Do not drink excessive amounts of alcohol when taking this medicine. Be extra careful when driving or operating machinery. Do not take this medicine if you are pregnant or think you may be pregnant.

Cautions and Warnings

Do not take this drug if you are allergic to either ingredient. It may produce physical or psychological drug dependence (addiction) after long periods of time. The major sign of dependence is anxiety when the drug is suddenly stopped. Darvocet-N abuse can lead to toxic effects on the kidneys from the Acetaminophen ingredient of this drug (see "Possible Adverse Drug Effects" below).

Possible Side Effects

Dizziness, sedation, nausea, vomiting. These effects usually disappear if you lie down and relax for a few moments.

Possible Adverse Drug Effects

Darvocet-N can produce constipation, abdominal pain, skin rash, light-headedness, weakness, headache, euphoria, and minor visual disturbances. Long-term use may lead to adverse effects caused by the Acetaminophen portion of Darvocet-N: anemias and changes in the composition of blood. Allergic reactions are rash, itching, and fever.

Drug Interactions

Interaction with alcohol, tranquilizers, sedatives, hypnotics, or antihistamines may produce tiredness, dizziness, light-headedness, and other signs of depression.

Usual Dose

1 to 2 tablets every 4 hours to relieve pain.

Take with a full glass of water or with food to reduce the possibility of stomach upset.

Overdosage

Symptoms are restlessness and difficulty in breathing, leading to stupor or coma, blue color of the skin, anemia, yellowing of the skin and/or whites of the eyes, rash, fever, stimulation, excitement, and delirium followed by depression, coma, and convulsions. The patient should be taken to a hospital emergency room immediately. ALWAYS bring the medicine bottle.

Brand Name

Darvon Compound-65

Ingredients

Aspirin
Caffeine
Phenacetin
Propoxyphene Hydrochloride

Other Brand Names

Note: The following products have the same combination of ingredients in the same or different concentrations.

Bexophene
Darvon Compound-65
Dolene Compound 65
Elder 65 Compound
Margesic Compound No. 65
Pargesic Compound 65
Progesic Compound-65
Propoxyphene Hydrochloride Compound
Proxagesic Compound-65
Repro Compound 65
Scrip-Dyne Compound
SK-65 Compound

Type of Drug

Analgesic combination.

Prescribed for

Relief of mild to moderate pain.

General Information

Propoxyphene Hydrochloride, the major ingredient in this product, is a chemical derivative of Methadone, a narcotic used for pain relief. It is estimated that Propoxyphene Hydrochloride is about half to two-thirds as strong a pain reliever as Codeine and about as effective as Aspirin.

Do not drink excessive amounts of alcohol when taking this medicine. Be extra careful when driving or operating machinery. Do not take this medicine if you are pregnant or think you may be pregnant.

Cautions and Warnings

Do not take Darvon Compound-65 if you know you are allergic or sensitive to it. Long-term use of this medicine may cause drug dependence or addiction. Use this drug with extreme caution if you suffer from asthma or other breathing problems. Darvon Compound-65 affects the central nervous system, producing sleepiness, tiredness, and/or inability to concentrate.

Possible Side Effects

Most frequent: light-headedness, dizziness, sleepiness, nausea, vomiting, loss of appetite, sweating. If these effects occur, consider calling your doctor and asking him about lowering the dose you are taking. Usually the side effects disappear if you simply lie down.

More serious side effects of Darvon Compound-65 are shallow breathing or difficulty in breathing.

Possible Adverse Drug Effects

Euphoria (feeling high), weakness, sleepiness, headache, agitation, uncoordinated muscle movement, minor hallucinations, disorientation and visual disturbances, dry mouth, loss of appetite, constipation, flushing of the face, rapid heartbeat, palpitations, faintness, urinary difficulties or hesitancy, reduced sex drive and/or potency, itching, skin rashes.

Drug Interactions

Interaction with alcohol, tranquilizers, barbiturates, or sleeping pills produces tiredness, sleepiness, or inability to concentrate, and seriously increases the depressive effect of Darvon Compound-65.

The Aspirin component of Darvon Compound-65 can affect anticoagulant (blood-thinning) therapy. Be sure to discuss this with your doctor so that the proper dosage adjustment can be made.

Usual Dose

1 capsule every 4 hours as needed for pain.

Overdosage

Symptoms are depression of respiration (breathing), extreme tiredness progressing to stupor and then coma, cold and clammy skin, slowing down of the heartbeat, convulsions, and cardiac arrest. The patient should be taken to a hospital emergency room immediately. ALWAYS bring the medicine bottle.

Special Information

Drowsiness may occur: be careful when driving or operating machinery.

Take with food or ½ glass of water to prevent stomach upset.

The Phenacetin ingredient of Darvon Compound-65 may be toxic to your kidneys; do not take this medication for longer than 10 days unless you are so directed by your doctor.

Brand Name

Demazin

Ingredients

Chlorpheniramine Maleate
Phenylephrine

Other Brand Name

Decohist

Type of Drug

Decongestant; antihistamine.

Prescribed for

Relief of sneezing, runny nose, and nasal congestion associated with the common cold, allergy, or other upper respiratory conditions.

General Information

Demazin is one of many products marketed to relieve the symptoms of the common cold. Most of these products contain ingredients to relieve a scratchy throat; and several of them may contain ingredients to suppress cough, or to help eliminate unwanted mucus. All these products are good only for the relief of symptoms and do not treat the underlying problem such as the cold virus or other infections.

Demazin may be bought over the counter, without a prescription.

Cautions and Warnings

Can cause excessive tiredness or drowsiness, restlessness, and nervousness with inability to sleep.

Possible Side Effects

Tremor, headache, palpitations, elevation of blood pressure, sweating, sleeplessness, loss of appetite, nausea, vomiting, dizziness, constipation.

Drug Interactions

Interaction with alcoholic beverages may produce excessive drowsiness and/or sleepiness, or inability to concentrate.

Do not self-medicate with additional over-the-counter drugs for the relief of cold symptoms: taking Demazin with such drugs may result in aggravation of high blood pressure, heart disease, diabetes, or thyroid disease.

Do not take Demazin if you are taking or suspect you may be taking a monoamine oxidase (MAO) inhibitor: severe elevation in blood pressure may result.

Usual Dose

Adult and child (over age 6): 2 teaspoonfuls every 4 hours.
Child (under age 6): 1 teaspoonful every 4 to 6 hours.

Generic Name

Demeclocycline

Brand Name

Declomycin

Type of Drug

Broad-spectrum antibiotic effective against gram-positive and gram-negative organisms.

Prescribed for

Bacterial infections such as gonorrhea, infections of the mouth, gums, and teeth, Rocky Mountain spotted fever and other fevers caused by ticks and lice from a variety of carriers, urinary tract infections, and respiratory system infections such as pneumonia and bronchitis.

These diseases are produced by gram-positive and gram-negative organisms such as diplococci, staphylococci, streptococci, gonococci, *E. coli,* and *Shigella*.

Demeclocycline has also been used successfully to treat some skin infections, but it is not considered the first-choice antibiotic for the treatment of general skin infections or wounds.

Demeclocycline has been used experimentally to treat the disease syndrome of inappropriate antidiuretic hormone (SIADH), where excess amounts of antidiuretic hormone are produced by the body.

General Information

Demeclocycline works by interfering with the normal growth cycle of the invading bacteria, preventing them from reproducing and thus allowing the body's normal defenses to fight off the infection. This process is referred to as bacteriostatic action. Demeclocycline has also been used along with other medicines to treat amoebic infections of the intestinal tract, known as amoebic dysentery. It is also prescribed for diseases caused by ticks, fleas, and lice.

Demeclocycline has been successfully used for the treatment of adolescent acne, in small doses over a long period of time. Adverse effects or toxicity in this type of therapy are almost unheard of.

Since the action of this antibiotic depends on its concentration within the invading bacteria, it is imperative that you completely follow your doctor's directions.

Cautions and Warnings

You should not use Demeclocycline if you are pregnant.

Demeclocycline when used in children has been shown to interfere with the development of the long bones and may retard growth.

Exceptions would be when Demeclocycline is the only effective antibiotic available and all risk factors have been made known to the patient.

Demeclocycline should not be given to people with known liver disease or kidney or urine excretion problems. You should avoid taking high doses of Demeclocycline or undergoing extended Demeclocycline therapy if you will be exposed to sunlight for a long period, because this antibiotic can interfere with your body's normal sun-screening mechanism, possibly causing a severe sunburn. If you have a known history of allergy to Demeclocycline, you should avoid taking this drug or other drugs within this category such as Aureomycin, Terramycin, Rondomycin, Vibramycin, Tetracycline, and Minocycline.

This drug is very likely to cause skin sensitivity, which has the appearance of a severe sunburn.

Possible Side Effects

As with other antibiotics, the common side effects of Demeclocycline are stomach upset, nausea, vomiting, diarrhea, and rash. Less common side effects include hairy tongue and itching and irritation of the anal and/or vaginal region. If these symptoms appear, consult your physician immediately. Periodic physical examinations and laboratory tests should be given to patients who are on long-term Demeclocycline.

Possible Adverse Drug Effects

Loss of appetite, peeling of the skin, sensitivity to the sun, fever, chills, anemia, possible brown spotting of the skin, decrease in kidney function, weakness, thirst, excessive urination, damage to the liver.

Drug Interactions

Demeclocycline (a bacteriostatic drug) may interfere with the action of bactericidal agents such as Penicillin. It is not advisable to take both during the same course of therapy.

The antibacterial effect of Demeclocycline is neutralized when taken with food, some dairy products (such as milk and cheese), and antacids.

Don't take multivitamin products containing minerals at the same time as Demeclocycline, or you may reduce the antibiotic's effectiveness. You may take these two medicines at least 2 hours apart.

People receiving anticoagulation therapy (blood-thinning agents) should consult their doctor, since Demeclocycline will interfere with this form of therapy. An adjustment in the anticoagulant dosage may be required.

Usual Dose

Adult: 600 milligrams per day.

Child (age 9 and over): 3 to 6 milligrams per pound per day.

Child (under age 8): should avoid Demeclocycline, as it has been shown to produce serious discoloration of the permanent teeth.

Take on an empty stomach 1 hour before or 2 hours after meals.

Storage

Demeclocycline can be stored at room temperature.

Special Information

Do *not* take after the expiration date on the label. The decomposition of Demeclocycline produces a highly toxic substance which can cause serious kidney damage.

Generic Name

Desipramine

Brand Names

Norpramin
Pertofrane

Type of Drug

Antidepressant.

Prescribed for

Depression with or without symptoms of anxiety.

General Information

Desipramine and other members of this group are effective in treating symptoms of depression. They can elevate your mood, increase physical activity and mental alertness, improve appetite and sleep patterns. These drugs are mild sedatives and therefore useful in treating mild forms of depression associated with anxiety. You should not expect instant results with this medicine: benefits are usually seen after 1 to 4 weeks. If symptoms are not affected after 6 to 8 weeks, contact your doctor. Occasionally this drug and other members of the group of drugs have been used in treating night-time bed-wetting in the young child, but they do not produce long-lasting relief, and therapy with one of them for nighttime bed-wetting is of questionable value.

Cautions and Warnings

Do not take Desipramine if you are allergic or sensitive to this or other members of this class of drug: Doxepin, Nortriptyline, Imipramine, Protriptyline, and Amitriptyline. The drugs should not be used if you are recovering from a heart attack. Desipramine may be taken with caution if you have a history of epilepsy or other convulsive disorders, difficulty in urination, glaucoma, heart disease, or thyroid disease. Desipramine can interfere with your ability to perform tasks which require concentration, such as driving or operating machinery. Desipramine will pass from mother to unborn child: consult your doctor before taking this medicine if you are pregnant.

Possible Side Effects

Changes in blood pressure (both high and low), abnormal heart rates, heart attack, confusion, especially in elderly patients, hallucinations, disorientation, delusions, anxiety, restlessness, excitement, numbness and tingling in the extremities, lack of coordination, muscle spasms or tremors, seizures and/or convulsions, dry mouth, blurred vision, constipation, inability to urinate, rash, itching, sensitivity to bright light or sunlight, retention of fluids, fever, allergy, changes in composition of blood, nausea, vomiting, loss of appetite, stomach upset, diarrhea, enlargement of the breasts in males and females, increased or decreased sex drive, increase or decrease of blood sugar.

Possible Adverse Drug Effects

Infrequent: agitation, inability to sleep, nightmares, feeling of panic, peculiar taste in the mouth, stomach cramps, black coloration of the tongue, yellowing eyes and/or skin, changes in liver function, increased or decreased weight, perspiration, flushing, frequent urination, drowsiness, dizziness, weakness, headache, loss of hair, nausea, not feeling well.

Drug Interactions

Interaction with monoamine oxidase (MAO) inhibitors can cause high fevers, convulsions, and occasionally death. Don't take MAO inhibitors until at least 2 weeks after Desipramine has been discontinued.

Desipramine interacts with Guanethidine, a drug used to treat high blood pressure: if your doctor prescribes Desipramine and you are taking medicine for high blood pressure, be sure to discuss this with him.

Desipramine increases the effects of barbiturates, tranquilizers, other depressive drugs, and alcohol. Don't drink alcohol if you take this medicine.

Taking Desipramine and thyroid medicine will enhance the effects of the thyroid medicine. The combination can cause abnormal heart rhythms.

Large doses of Vitamin C (Ascorbic Acid) can reduce the effect of Desipramine. Drugs such as Bicarbonate of Soda or Acetazolamide will increase the effect of Desipramine.

Usual Dose

Adult: 75 to 300 milligrams per day. The dose of this drug must be tailored to patient's need. Patients taking high doses of this drug should have regular heart examinations to check for side effects.

Adolescent or elderly: lower doses are recommended, usually 25 to 150 milligrams per day.

This drug should not be taken by children.

Overdosage

Symptoms are confusion, inability to concentrate, hallucinations, drowsiness, lowered body temperature, abnormal heart rate, heart failure, large pupils of the eyes, convulsions, severely lowered blood pressure, stupor, and coma (as well as agitation, stiffening of body muscles, vomiting, and high fever). The patient should be taken to a hospital emergency room immediately. ALWAYS bring the medicine bottle.

Generic Name

Dexamethasone

Brand Names

Decadron   Hexadrol
Dexone   SK-Dexamethasone
Dezone

Type of Drug

Adrenal cortical steroid.

Prescribed for

Reduction of inflammation. There is a wide range of disorders for which Dexamethasone is prescribed, from skin rash to cancer. The drug may be used as a treatment for adrenal gland disease, since one of the hormones produced by the adrenal gland is very similar to Dexamethasone. If patients are not producing sufficient adrenal hormones, Dexamethasone may be used as replacement therapy. It may also be prescribed for the treatment of bursitis, arthritis, severe skin reactions such as psoriasis or other rashes, severe allergic conditions, asthma, drug or serum sickness, severe, acute, or chronic allergic inflammation of the eye and surrounding areas such as conjunctivitis, respiratory diseases including pneumonitis, blood disorders, gastrointestinal diseases including ulcerative colitis, and inflammation of the nerves, heart, or other organs.

General Information

Dexamethasone is one of many adrenal cortical steroids used in medical practice today. The major differences between Dexamethasone and other adrenal cortical steroids are potency of medication and variation in some secondary effects. Choice of an adrenal cortical steroid to be used for a specific disease is usually a matter of doctor preference and past experience. Other adrenal cortical steroids include Cortisone, Hydrocortisone, Prednisolone, Triamcinolone, Methylprednisolone, Meprednisone, Paramethasone, Fluprednisolone, Prednisone, Betamethasone, and Fludrocortisone.

Dexamethasone may be used as eyedrops, eye ointment, topical cream, intranasal spray, or for oral inhalation as well as in an oral tablet.

Cautions and Warnings

Because of the effect of Dexamethasone on your adrenal gland, it is essential that the dose be tapered from a large dose down to a small dose over a period of time. Do not stop taking this medication suddenly and/or without the advice of your doctor. If you do, you may cause a failure of the adrenal gland with extremely serious consequences.

Dexamethasone has a strong anti-inflammatory effect, and may mask some signs of infections. If new infections appear during the use of Dexamethasone therapy, they may be difficult to diagnose and may grow more rapidly due to your decreased resistance. If you think you are getting an infection during the time that you are taking Dexamethasone, you should contact your doctor, who will prescribe appropriate therapy.

If you are taking Dexamethasone, you should not be vaccinated against any infectious diseases, because of inability of the body to produce the normal reaction to vaccination. Discuss this with your doctor before he administers any vaccination.

If you suspect that you are pregnant and are taking Dexamethasone, report it immediately to your doctor. If you are taking Dexamethasone and have just given birth, do not nurse; used prepared formulas instead.

Possible Side Effects

Stomach upset is one of the more common side effects of Dexamethasone, which may in some cases cause gastric or duodenal ulcers. If you notice a slight stomach upset when you take your dose of Dexamethasone, take this medication with food or a small amount of antacid. If stomach upset continues or bothers you, notify your doctor. Other side effects: retention of water, heart failure, potassium loss, muscle weakness, loss of muscle mass, loss of calcium which may result in bone fractures and a condition known as aseptic necrosis of the femoral and humoral heads (this means the ends of the large bones in the hip may degenerate from loss of calcium), slowing down of wound healing, black-and-blue marks on the skin, increased sweating, allergic skin rash, itching, convulsions, dizziness, headache.

Possible Adverse Drug Effects

May cause irregular menstrual cycles, slowing down of growth in children, particularly after the medication has been taken for long periods of time, depression of the adrenal and/or pituitary glands, development of diabetes, increased pressure of the fluid inside the eye, hypersensitivity or allergic reactions, blood clots, insomnia, weight gain, increased appetite, nausea, and feeling of ill health. Psychic derangements may appear which range from euphoria to mood swings, personality changes, and severe depression. Dexamethasone may also aggravate existing emotional instability.

Drug Interactions

Dexamethasone and other adrenal corticosteroids may interact with Insulin and oral antidiabetic drugs, causing an increased requirement of the antidiabetic drugs.

Interaction with Phenobarbital, Ephedrine, and Phenytoin may reduce the effect of Dexamethasone by increasing its removal from the body.

If a doctor prescribes Dexamethasone you should discuss any oral anticoagulant (blood-thinning) drugs you are taking: the dose of them may have to be changed.

Interaction with diuretics such as Hydrochlorothiazide may cause you to lose blood potassium. Be aware of signs of lowered potassium level such as weakness, muscle cramps, and tiredness, and report them to your physician. Eat high potassium foods such as bananas, citrus fruits, melons, and tomatoes.

Usual Dose

Initial dose: 0.75 to 9 milligrams per day. The dose of this medicine must be individualized to the patient's need, although it is always desirable to take the lowest effective dose of Dexamethasone. Stressful situations may cause a

need for a temporary increase in your Dexamethasone dose.
This drug must be tapered off slowly and not stopped abruptly. This drug may be taken every other day instead of every
day.

Overdosage

There is no specific treatment for overdosage of adrenal
cortical steroids. Symptoms are anxiety, depression and/or
stimulation, stomach bleeding, increased blood sugar, high
blood pressure, and retention of fluid. The patient should be
taken to a hospital emergency room immediately, where
stomach pumping, oxygen, intravenous fluids, and other
supportive treatments are available.

Generic Name

Dexchlorpheniramine Maleate

Brand Name

Polaramine

Type of Drug

Antihistamine.

Prescribed for

Seasonal allergy, stuffed and runny nose, itching of the eyes,
scratchy throat caused by allergy, and other allergic symptoms such as itching, rash, or hives.

General Information

Antihistamines generally, and Dexchlorpheniramine Maleate
specifically, act by blocking the release of the chemical substance histamine from the cell. Antihistamines work by drying
up the secretions of the nose, throat, and eyes.

Cautions and Warnings

Dexchlorpheniramine Maleate should not be used if you are
allergic to this drug. It should be avoided or used with
extreme care if you have narrow angle glaucoma (pressure
in the eye), stomach ulcer or other stomach problems,

enlarged prostate, or problems passing urine. It should not be used by people who have deep-breathing problems such as asthma.

Dexchlorpheniramine Maleate can cause dizziness, drowsiness, and lowering of blood pressure, particularly in the elderly patient. Young children can show signs of nervousness, increased tension, and anxiety.

Possible Side Effects

Occasional: itching, rash, sensitivity to light, excessive perspiration, chills, dryness of mouth, nose, and throat, lowering of blood pressure, headache, rapid heartbeat, sleeplessness, dizziness, disturbed coordination, confusion, restlessness, nervousness, irritability, euphoria (feeling high), tingling of the hands and feet, blurred vision, double vision, ringing in the ears, stomach upset, loss of appetite, nausea, vomiting, constipation, diarrhea, difficulty in urination, tightness of the chest, wheezing, nasal stuffiness.

Possible Adverse Drug Effects

Use with care if you have a history of asthma, glaucoma, thyroid disease, heart disease, high blood pressure, or diabetes.

Drug Interactions

Dexchlorpheniramine Maleate should not be taken with MAO inhibitors.

Interaction with tranquilizers, sedatives, and sleeping medication will increase the effects of these drugs: it is extremely important that you discuss this with your doctor so that doses of these drugs can be properly adjusted.

Be extremely cautious when drinking while taking Dexchlorpheniramine Maleate, which will enhance the intoxicating effect of alcohol. Alcohol also has a sedative effect.

Usual Dose

Adult: 2 milligrams 3 to 4 times per day.
Child (under age 12): 1 milligram 3 to 4 times per day.
Infant: 0.5 milligram 3 to 4 times per day.

Overdosage

Symptoms are depression or stimulation (especially in children), dry mouth, fixed or dilated pupils, flushing of the skin, and stomach upset. Take the patient to a hospital emergency room immediately, if you cannot make him vomit. ALWAYS bring the medicine bottle.

Special Information

Antihistamines produce a depressing effect: be extremely cautious when driving or operating heavy equipment.

The safety of Dexchlorpheniramine Maleate in pregnancy has not been established. A breast-feeding mother should avoid taking this medicine, since it is known to pass from the mother to the baby through the milk.

Generic Name

Dextroamphetamine (D-Amphetamine)

Brand Names

Dexampex
Dexedrine
Ferndex
Oxydess
Spancap

Type of Drug

Central nervous system stimulant.

Prescribed for

Short-term (a couple of weeks) aid to diet control, abnormal behavioral syndrome in children, narcolepsy (uncontrollable and unpredictable desire to sleep).

General Information

When taking this medicine as part of a weight control program it is usual to experience a decrease in drug effectiveness because your body is breaking down the drug faster. Do not increase the amount of drug you are taking: simply stop taking the medicine.

The use of D-Amphetamine (as well as other drugs) in the treatment of minimal brain dysfunction in children is extremely controversial and must be judged by a physician qualified to treat the disorder. Children whose problems are judged to have been produced by their surroundings or by primary psychiatric disorders may not be helped by D-Amphetamine.

Cautions and Warnings

D-Amphetamine is highly abusable and addictive. It must be used with extreme caution. People with hardening of the arteries (arteriosclerosis), heart disease, high blood pressure, thyroid disease, or glaucoma, or who are sensitive or allergic to any amphetamine, should not take this medication. D-Amphetamine should not be used by pregnant women (it may cause birth defects).

Possible Side Effects

Palpitations, restlessness, overstimulation, dizziness, sleeplessness, increased blood pressure, rapid heartbeat.

Possible Adverse Drug Effects

Euphoria, hallucinations, muscle spasms and tremors, headache, dryness of the mouth, unpleasant taste, diarrhea, constipation, stomach upset, itching, loss of sex drive, (rarely) psychotic drug reactions.

Drug Interactions

D-Amphetamine should not be given at the same time or within 14 days following the use of MAO inhibitors. This may cause severe lowering of the blood pressure.

D-Amphetamine may also decrease the effectiveness of Guanethidine.

Usual Dose

Narcolepsy: 5 to 60 milligrams per day, depending on individual need.

Abnormal behavior syndrome: 2.5 to 40 milligrams per day, depending on child's age and response to the drug.

Weight control: 5 to 30 milligrams per day in divided doses ½ to 1 hour before meals; or, as a long-acting dose, once in the morning.

Overdosage

Symptoms are tremors, muscle spasms, restlessness, exaggerated reflexes, rapid breathing, hallucinations, confusion, panic, and overaggressive behavior, followed by depression and exhaustion after the central nervous system stimulation wears off, as well as abnormal heart rhythms, changes in blood pressure, nausea, vomiting, diarrhea, convulsions, and coma. The patient should be taken to a hospital emergency room immediately. ALWAYS bring the medicine container.

Special Information

Do not take this medicine after 6 to 8 hours before you plan to go to sleep, or it will interfere with a sound and restful night's sleep.

Generic Name

Dextrothyoxine Sodium

Brand Name

Choloxin

Type of Drug

Antihyperlipidemic.

Prescribed for

Lowering blood cholesterol levels. Triglyceride levels may also be affected by Dextrothyroxine Sodium. May also be used to treat thyroid disease in patients who cannot take other thyroid drugs.

General Information

This drug is interesting in that it is a close cousin to Levothyroxine Sodium, a thyroid drug. It is thought to lower blood cholesterol by stimulating the liver to remove more cholesterol from the blood than usual. The lowering of blood cholesterol levels may have an effect on the development of heart disease, although no one knows for sure. This drug is only part of the therapy for high blood cholesterol levels. Diet and weight control are also very important. Remember, this medicine is not a substitute for dietary restrictions or other activities prescribed by your doctor.

Cautions and Warnings

Dextrothyroxine Sodium should not be taken by people with heart disease of any kind, severe high blood pressure, advanced liver or kidney disease, or a history of iodism.

Although no serious effects have been reported, this drug should not be used by women who are pregnant or breast-feeding.

This drug is not meant to help people lose weight. In large doses, it will not reduce appetite but can cause serious side effects.

This drug should be discontinued for 2 weeks before surgery. It could interact with the general anesthetic drugs to cause heart problems.

Possible Side Effects

The fewest side effects from Dextrothyroxine Sodium are experienced by people with normal thyroid function and no heart disease. The risk of side effects is increased if you have an underactive thyroid gland and is greatest if you have both thyroid and heart disease.

The most common side effects are heart palpitations and other effects related to heart function. Other side effects include sleeplessness, nervousness, weight loss, sweating, flushing, increased body temperature, hair loss, menstrual irregularity, and an unusual need to urinate. Dextrothyroxine Sodium can also cause upset stomach, nausea and vomiting, constipation, diarrhea, and loss of appetite.

Possible Adverse Drug Effects

Headache, change in sex drive (increase or decrease), hoarseness, dizziness, ringing or buzzing in the ears, swelling of the arms and legs, not feeling well, tiredness, visual disturbances, psychic changes, tingling in the hands or feet, muscle pain, rashes. Some rather bizarre subjective complaints have been linked to this drug.

Drug Interactions

May interact with digitalis drugs to yield adverse effects on the heart. Dextrothyroxine Sodium may increase the effects of the oral anticoagulant drugs. Some patients may need their anticoagulant dose reduced by 30 percent. Dextrothyroxine Sodium will increase the effect of other drugs being given for underactive thyroid.

The drug may increase blood sugar levels in diabetic patients. Diabetics may need an adjustment in their Insulin or oral antidiabetic drug therapy while taking Dextrothyroxine Sodium.

Usual Dose

Adult: up to 8 milligrams per day.

Child: up to 4 milligrams per day; approximately 0.05 milligrams per pound.

Overdosage

Symptoms are headache, irritability, nervousness, sweating, and rapid heartbeat, with unusual stomach rumbling and with or without cramps, chest pains, heart failure, and shock. The patient should be taken to a hospital emergency room immediately. ALWAYS bring the medicine bottle.

Special Information

Contact your doctor if you develop chest pain, heart palpitations, sweating, diarrhea, or a rash.

Generic Name

Diazepam

Brand Name

Valium

Type of Drug

Tranquilizer.

Prescribed for

Relief of symptoms of anxiety, tension, fatigue, or agitation.

General Information

Diazepam is a member of the chemical group of drugs known as benzodiazepines. These drugs are used as either antianxiety agents, anticonvulsants, or sedatives (sleeping pills). They exert their effects by relaxing the large skeletal muscles and by a direct effect on the brain. In doing so, they can relax you and make you either more tranquil or sleepier, depending on the drug and how much you use. Many doctors prefer Diazepam and the other members of this class to other drugs that can be used for the same effect. Their reason is that the benzodiazepines tend to be safer, have fewer side effects, and are usually as, if not more, effective.

These drugs are generally used in any situation where they can be a useful adjunct.

Benzodiazepine tranquilizing drugs can be abused if taken for long periods of time and it is possible to develop withdrawal symptoms if you discontinue the therapy abruptly. Withdrawal symptoms include tremor, muscle cramps, stomach cramps, vomiting, insomnia, agitation, sweating, and even convulsions.

Cautions and Warnings

Do not take Diazepam if you know you are sensitive or allergic to this drug or to other benzodiazepines such as Chlordiazepoxide, Oxazepam, Clorazepate, Lorazepam, Prazepam, Flurazepam, and Clonazepam.

Diazepam and other members of this drug group may aggravate narrow angle glaucoma, but if you have open angle glaucoma you may take the drugs. In any case, check this information with your doctor. Diazepam can cause tiredness, drowsiness, inability to concentrate, or similar symptoms. Be careful if you are driving, operating machinery, or performing other activities which require concentration. Avoid taking this drug during the first 3 months of pregnancy except under strict supervision of your doctor.

Possible Side Effects

Most common: mild drowsiness during the first few days of therapy, especially in the elderly or debilitated. If drowsiness persists, contact your doctor.

Possible Adverse Drug Effects

Major adverse reactions: confusion, depression, lethargy, disorientation, headache, inactivity, slurred speech, stupor, dizziness, tremor, constipation, dry mouth, nausea, inability to control urination, changes in sex drive, irregular menstrual cycle, changes in heart rhythm, lowered blood pressure, retention of fluids, blurred or double vision, itching, rash, hiccups, nervousness, inability to fall asleep, (occasional) liver dysfunction. If you experience any of these reactions stop taking the medicine and contact your doctor immediately.

Drug Interactions

Diazepam is a central nervous system depressant. Avoid alcohol, tranquilizers, narcotics, barbiturates, MAO inhibitors, antihistamines, and other medicines used to relieve depression. Smoking may reduce the effectiveness of Diazepam. The effects of Diazepam may be prolonged when taken together with Cimetidine.

Usual Dose

Adult: 2 to 40 milligrams per day as individualized for maximum benefit, depending on symptoms and response to treatment.

Elderly: if debilitated, will usually require less of the drug to control tension and anxiety.

Child: 1 to 2½ milligrams 3 to 4 times per day; possibly more if needed to control anxiety and tension. Diazepam should not be given to children under age 6 months.

Overdosage

Symptoms are confusion, sleep or sleepiness, lack of response to pain such as a pin stick, shallow breathing, lowered blood pressure, and coma. The patient should be taken to a hospital emergency room immediately. ALWAYS bring the medicine bottle.

Special Information

Do not drink alcohol or take other depressive drugs, such as tranquilizers, sleeping pills, narcotics, or barbiturates, when taking Diazepam.

Generic Name

Dicloxacillin Sodium

Brand Names

Dycill   Pathocil
Dynapen   Veracillin

Type of Drug

Broad-spectrum antibiotic.

Prescribed for

Gram-positive bacterial infections. Gram-positive bacteria
(pneumococci, streptococci, and staphylococci) are organisms which usually cause diseases such as pneumonia, infections of the tonsils and throat, venereal disease, meningitis
(infection of the spinal column), and septicemia (general
infection of the bloodstream). This drug is best used to treat
infections resistant to Penicillin, although it may be used as
initial treatment for some patients.

General Information

Dicloxacillin Sodium is manufactured in the laboratory by
fermentation and by general chemical reaction, and is classified as a semisynthetic antibiotic. Because the effectiveness
of the antibiotic is determined by the drug's ability to affect
the cell wall of the invading bacteria, it is very important that
the patient completely follow the doctor's prescribing directions. These directions include spacing of doses as well as
the number of days the patient should continue taking the
medicine. If they are not followed, the effect of the antibiotic
is severely reduced. To ensure the maximum effect, you
should take the medication on an empty stomach, either 1
hour before or 2 hours after meals. Another antibiotic closely
related to Dicloxycillin Sodium is Cloxacillin Sodium (Tegopen).
This drug is taken in the same doses and exerts the same
effects as Dicloxacillin Sodium.

Cautions and Warnings

If you have a known history of allergy to Penicillin you
should avoid taking Dicloxacillin Sodium, since the drugs
are chemically similar. The most common allergic reaction

to Dicloxacillin Sodium, as well as to the other penicillins, is a hivelike rash over the body with itching and redness. It is important to tell your doctor if you have ever taken this drug or penicillins before and if you have experienced any adverse reaction to the drug such as rash, itching, or difficulty in breathing.

Possible Side Effects

Common: stomach upset, nausea, vomiting, diarrhea, possible rash. Less common: hairy tongue, itching or irritation around the anus and or vagina, stomach pain with or without bleeding.

Drug Interactions

The effect of Dicloxacillin Sodium can be significantly reduced when taken with other antibiotics. Consult your doctor if you are taking both during the same course of therapy. Otherwise, Dicloxacillin Sodium is generally free of interactions with other medications.

Usual Dose

Adult (and child weighing 88 pounds or more): 125 to 250 milligrams every 6 hours. In severe infections, 500 milligrams may be needed.
Child (less than 88 pounds): 5½ to 11 milligrams per pound of body weight per day in divided doses.

Storage

Dicloxacillin Sodium can be stored at room temperature.

Special Information

Do not take Dicloxacillin Sodium after the expiration date on the label.
The safety of the drug in pregnancy has not been established.

Generic Name

Dicyclomine Hydrochloride

Brand Names

Bentomine
Bentyl
Dibent

Dilomine
Di-Spaz

Type of Drug

Gastrointestinal anticholinergic agent.

Prescribed for

Relief of stomach upset and spasms. This medication is sometimes prescribed to treat morning sickness during the early months of pregnancy.

General Information

Dicyclomine Hydrochloride works by reducing spasms in muscles of the stomach and other parts of the gastrointestinal tract. In doing so, it helps relieve some of the uncomfortable symptoms associated with peptic ulcer, irritable bowel and/or colon, spastic colon, and other gastrointestinal disorders. It only relieves symptoms. It does not cure the underlying disease.

Cautions and Warnings

Dicyclomine Hydrochloride should not be used if you know you are sensitive or allergic to it. Do not use this medicine if you have glaucoma, asthma, obstructive disease of the gastrointestinal tract, or other serious gastrointestinal disease. Because this drug reduces your ability to sweat, its use in hot climates may cause heat exhaustion. The safety of this drug for pregnant or nursing women has not been established.

Possible Side Effects

Difficulty in urination, blurred vision, rapid heartbeat, rash, sensitivity to light, headache, flushing of the skin, nervousness, dizziness, weakness, drowsiness, nausea, vomiting, fever, nasal congestion, heartburn, constipation, loss of sense of taste.

Possible Adverse Drug Effects

Elderly patients taking this drug may develop mental confusion or excitement.

Drug Interactions

Interaction with antihistamines, phenothiazines, long-term use of corticosteroids, tranquilizers, antidepressants, and some narcotic painkillers may cause blurred vision, dry mouth, or drowsiness. Antacids should not be taken together with Dicyclomine Hydrochloride, or they will reduce the absorption of the Dicyclomine Hydrochloride.

Do not use with MAO inhibitor drugs, which will tend to prevent excretion of Dicyclomine Hydrochloride from the body and thus increase its effect.

Usual Dose

10 to 30 milligrams 3 to 4 times per day.

Special Information

Dry mouth from Dicyclomine Hydrochloride can be relieved by chewing gum or sucking hard candy; constipation can be treated by using a stool-softening laxative.

Generic Name

Diethylpropion Hydrochloride

Brand Names

Depletite   Tepanil
Tenuate   Tepanil Ten-Tab
Tenuate Dospan

Type of Drug

Nonamphetamine appetite depressant.

Prescribed for

Suppression of appetite and treatment of obesity.

General Information

Although Diethylpropion Hydrochloride is not an amphetamine, it can produce the same adverse effects as the amphetamine appetite suppressants.

Cautions and Warnings

Do not use Diethylpropion Hydrochloride if you have heart disease, high blood pressure, thyroid disease, or glaucoma, or if you are sensitive or allergic to this or similar drugs.

Furthermore, do not use this medication if you are emotionally agitated or have a history of drug abuse.

Possible Side Effects

Palpitations, high blood pressure, overstimulation, nervousness, restlessness, drowsiness, sedation, weakness, dizziness, inability to sleep, tremor, headache, dry mouth, nausea, vomiting, diarrhea and other intestinal disturbances, rash, itching, changes in sex drive, hair loss, muscle pain, difficulty in passing urine, sweating, chills, blurred vision, fever.

Usual Dose

25 milligrams 3 times per day 1 hour before meals; an additional tablet may be given in midevening, if needed to suppress the desire for midnight snacks. Sustained-release tablets or capsules of 75 milligrams (Tenuate Dospan, Tepanil Ten-Tab, Weh-Less Timecelles); 1 per day usually in midmorning.

Overdosage

Symptoms are restlessness, tremor, shallow breathing, confusion, hallucinations, and fever, followed by fatigue and depression, with additional symptoms such as high or possibly low blood pressure, cold and clammy skin, nausea, vomiting, diarrhea, and stomach cramps. The patient should be taken to a hospital emergency room immediately. ALWAYS bring the medicine bottle.

Special Information

Use for only a few weeks as an adjunct to diet, under strict supervision of your doctor.

Medicine alone will not take off weight. You must limit and modify your food intake, preferably under medical supervision.

Generic Name

Diethylstilbestrol

Brand Names

DES
Stilbestrol

Type of Drug

Estrogen.

Prescribed for

Hormone replacement; diseases which require increases in estrogen levels in the blood for effective treatment of symptoms associated with menopause.

General Information

Because of the potential development of secondary disease after a long period of taking Diethylstilbestrol, the decision to take this medication chronically should be made cautiously by you and your doctor.

Cautions and Warnings

Estrogens have been reported to increase the risk of certain types of cancer in postmenopausal women taking this type of drug for prolonged periods of time: this risk tends to depend upon the duration of treatment and on the dose of the estrogen being taken. When long-term estrogen therapy is indicated for the treatment of menopausal symptoms, the lowest effective dose should be used. If you have to take Diethylstilbestrol for extended periods of time, you should see your doctor at least twice a year so that he can assess your current condition and your need to continue the drug therapy. If you are taking an estrogenic product and experience vaginal bleeding of a recurrent, abnormal, or persistent nature, contact your doctor immediately. If you are pregnant you should not use this or any other estrogenic substance, since these drugs, if used during the earlier stages of pregnancy, may seriously damage the offspring. If you have active thrombophlebitis or any other disorder associated with the formation of blood clots, you probably should not take this drug. If you feel that you have a disorder associated with blood clots and you have been taking Diethylstilbestrol or a similar product, you should contact your doctor immediately so that he can evaluate your situation and decide about stopping the drug therapy.

Prolonged continuous administration of estrogenic substances to certain animal species has increased the frequency of cancer in these animals, and there is evidence that these drugs may increase the risk of various cancers in humans. This drug should be taken with caution by women with a strong family history of breast cancer or those who have breast nodules, fibrocystic disease of the breast, or abnormal mammogram. Furthermore, long-term use of Diethylstilbestrol may expose a woman to a two to threefold increase in chance of developing gallbladder disease. It is possible that women taking Diethylstilbestrol for extended periods of time may experience some of the same development of long-term adverse effects as women who have taken oral contraceptives for extended periods of time. These long-term problems may include thromboembolic disease or the development of various disorders associated with the development of blood clots, liver cancer or other liver tumors, high blood pressure, glucose intolerance or a development of a symptom similar to diabetes or the aggravation of diabetes in patients who had this disease before they started the estrogen, and high blood levels of calcium in certain classes of patients.

Possible Side Effects

Breakthrough bleeding, spotting, changes in menstrual flow, dysmenorrhea, premenstrual-type syndrome, resumption of menorrhea, vaginal infection with candida, cystitislike syndrome, enlargement or tenderness of the breasts, nausea, vomiting, abdominal cramps, feeling of bloatedness, jaundice or yellowing of the skin or whites of the eyes, skin rash, loss of scalp hair, development of new hairy areas. Lesions of the eye have been associated with estrogen therapy. If you wear contact lenses and are taking estrogens, it is possible that you will become intolerant to the lenses. You may also experience headache—possibly migraine—dizziness, depression, weight changes, retention of water, and changes in sex drive.

Usual Dose

0.2 to 3 milligrams per day, depending upon the disease being treated and patient's response. Some diseases or patients may require up to 15 milligrams per day.

Overdosage

Overdose may cause nausea and withdrawal bleeding in

adult females. Serious adverse effects have not been reported after accidental overdosage in children.

Generic Name

Digitoxin

Brand Names

Crystodigin
De-Tone
Purodigin

Type of Drug

Cardiac glycoside.

Prescribed for

Congestive heart failure and other heart abnormalities.

General Information

This medication is generally used for long periods of time.

Cautions and Warnings

Do not use this drug if you know you are allergic or sensitive to Digitalis. Long-term use of Digitoxin can cause the body to lose potassium, especially since Digitoxin is generally used in combination with a diuretic drug. For this reason, be sure to eat a well-balanced diet and emphasize foods which are high in potassium such as bananas, citrus fruits, melons, and tomatoes.

Possible Side Effects

Most common: loss of appetite, nausea, vomiting, diarrhea, blurred or disturbed vision. If you experience any of these problems, discuss them with your doctor immediately.

Possible Adverse Drug Effects

Enlargement of the breasts has been reported after long-term use of Digitoxin, but this is uncommon. Allergy or sensitivity to Digitoxin is also uncommon.

Drug Interactions

Diuretics (drugs which increase the production of urine) including Furosemide, Chlorothiazide, and Hydrochlorothiazide can reduce the potassium in your blood and interact with Digitoxin.

If you are a long-term Digitoxin user, avoid over-the-counter drugs used to relieve coughs, colds, or allergies if they contain stimulants which may aggravate your heart condition. If you feel you must have medication to relieve the symptoms of colds, ask your doctor or pharmacist which medicines do not contain stimulants.

Usual Dose

Adult: The first dose—known as the digitalizing dose—is 2 milligrams over about 3 days, or 0.4 milligram per day for 4 days. Maintenance dose ranges from 0.05 to 0.03 milligram daily.

Elderly: Lower doses, as the elderly are more sensitive to adverse effects.

Infant or child: The first dose depends on age but can be from 0.01 milligram per pound to 0.02 milligram per pound. Maintenance dose is one-tenth the first dose.

Overdosage

Symptoms are loss of appetite, nausea, vomiting, diarrhea, headache, weakness, feeling of not caring, blurred vision, yellow or green spots before the eyes, yellowing of the skin and eyes, or changes in heartbeat. Contact your doctor immediately if any of these symptoms appear. Early signs of overdose in children are changes in heart rhythm. Vomiting, diarrhea, and eye trouble are frequently seen in older people.

Generic Name

Digoxin

Brand Names

Lanoxin
SK-Digoxin

Type of Drug

Cardiac glycoside.

Prescribed for

Congestive heart failure, and other heart abnormalities.

General Information

This medication is generally used for long periods of time.

Cautions and Warnings

Do not use this drug if you know you are allergic or sensitive to Digitalis. Long-term use of Digoxin can cause the body to lose potassium, especially since Digoxin is generally used in combination with a diuretic drug. For this reason, be sure to eat a well-balanced diet and emphasize foods which are high in potassium, such as bananas, citrus fruits, melons, and tomatoes.

Possible Side Effects

Most common: loss of appetite, nausea, vomiting, diarrhea, blurred or disturbed vision. If you experience any of these problems, discuss them with your doctor immediately.

Possible Adverse Drug Effects

Enlargement of the breasts has been reported after long-term use of Digoxin, but this is uncommon. Allergy or sensitivity to Digoxin is also uncommon.

Drug Interactions

Diuretics (drugs which increase the production of urine), including Furosemide, Chlorothiazide, and Hydrochlorothiazide, can reduce the potassium in your blood and interact with Digoxin.

If you are a long-term Digoxin user avoid over-the-counter drugs used to relieve cough, colds, or allergies if they contain stimulants which may aggravate your heart condition. If you feel you must have medication to relieve the symptoms of colds, contact your doctor or pharmacist for information about medicine which does not contain stimulating ingredients.

Usual Dose

Adult: the first dose—known as the digitalizing dose—is 1 to 1.5 milligrams. Maintenance dose ranges from 0.125 to 0.5 milligram.

Elderly: lower dose, as the elderly are more sensitive to adverse effects.

Infant or child: substantially lower dose.

Overdosage

If symptoms of loss of appetite, nausea, vomiting, diarrhea, headache, weakness, feeling of not caring, blurred vision, yellow or green spots before the eyes, yellowing of the skin and eyes, or changes in heartbeat appear, contact your doctor immediately. Early signs of overdose in children are changes in heart rhythm; vomiting, diarrhea, and eye trouble are frequently seen in older people.

Special Information

Do not stop taking this medicine unless your doctor tells you to. Avoid nonprescription medicine containing stimulants. Your pharmacist can tell you which nonprescription medicine is safe for you. Call your doctor if you develop loss of appetite, stomach pains, nausea or vomiting, diarrhea, unusual tiredness or weakness, visual disturbances, or mental depression. There are considerable variations among Digoxin tablets made by different manufacturers. Do not change brands of Digoxin without telling your doctor.

Brand Name

Dimetane Expectorant-DC

Ingredients

Brompheniramine Maleate
Codeine Phosphate
Guaifenesin
Phenylephrine Hydrochloride
Phenylpropanolamine Hydrochloride

Type of Drug

Decongestant; expectorant.

Prescribed for

Relief of cough, nasal congestion, runny nose, and other symptoms associated with the common cold, viruses, or other upper respiratory diseases. The drug may also be used to treat allergies, asthma, ear infections, or sinus infections.

General Information

Dimetane Expectorant-DC is one of almost 100 products marketed to relieve the symptoms of the common cold and other upper respiratory infections. These products contain medicine to relieve congestion, act as an antihistamine, relieve or suppress cough, and help you to cough up mucus. They may contain medicine for each purpose, or may contain a combination of medicines. Some combinations leave out the antihistamine, the decongestant, or the expectorant. You must realize while taking Dimetane Expectorant-DC or similar products that these drugs are good only for the relief of symptoms and will not treat the underlying problem, such as a cold virus or other infections.

Cautions and Warnings

Can cause excessive tiredness or drowsiness.
   This product should not be used for newborn infants or taken by pregnant or nursing mothers. People with glaucoma or difficulty in urinating should avoid this drug and other drugs containing antihistamines.

Possible Side Effects

Dry mouth, blurred vision, difficulty passing urine, headache, palpitations, (possibly) constipation, nervousness, dizziness, restlessness or even inability to sleep.

Drug Interactions

Taking Dimetane Expectorant-DC with an MAO inhibitor can produce a severe elevation in blood pressure. Consult your doctor first.
   Dimetane Expectorant-DC contains Codeine. Drinking alcoholic beverages while taking this drug may produce excessive drowsiness and/or sleepiness, or inability to concentrate.

Usual Dose

1 to 2 teaspoons 4 times per day.

Special Information

Take with a full glass of water to reduce stomach upset and
help remove excessive mucus from the throat.

Brand Name

Dimetapp Extentabs

Ingredients

Brompheniramine
Phenylephrine
Phenylpropanolamine

Other Brand Names

Bromophen	Midatap
Eldatapp	Normatane
Histatapp	Puretapp
Leder-BP Sequels	Tagatap

Type of Drug

Long-acting combination antihistamine-decongestant.

Prescribed for

Relief of cough, nasal congestion, runny nose, and other
symptoms associated with the common cold, viruses, or other
upper respiratory diseases.

General Information

Dimetapp Extentabs is one of many products marketed to
relieve the symptoms of the common cold. These products
contain medicine to relieve nasal congestion or to dry up
runny noses or relieve a scratchy throat; and several of
them may contain ingredients to suppress cough, or to help
eliminate unwanted mucus. All these products are good only
for the relief of symptoms and will not treat the underlying
problem, such as a cold virus or other infections.

Cautions and Warnings

Can cause excessive tiredness or drowsiness.

This product should not be used for newborn infants or taken by pregnant or nursing mothers. People with glaucoma or difficulty in urinating should avoid this drug and other drugs containing antihistamines.

Possible Side Effects

Mild drowsiness has been seen in patients taking Dimetapp.

Possible Adverse Drug Effects

Infrequent: restlessness, tension, nervousness, tremor, weakness, inability to sleep, headache, palpitations, elevation of blood pressure, sweating, sleeplessness, loss of appetite, nausea, vomiting, dizziness, constipation.

Drug Interactions

Interaction with alcoholic beverages may produce excessive drowsiness and/or sleepiness, or inability to concentrate. Also avoid sedatives, tranquilizers, antihistamines, and sleeping pills.

Do not self-medicate with additional over-the-counter drugs for the relief of cold symptoms; taking Dimetapp Extentabs with such drugs may result in aggravation of high blood pressure, heart disease, diabetes, or thyroid disease.

Do not take Dimetapp Extentabs if you are taking or suspect you may be taking a monoamine oxidase (MAO) inhibitor: severe elevation in blood pressure may result.

Usual Dose

1 tablet morning and night.

Special Information

Since drowsiness may occur during use of Dimetapp Extentabs, be cautious while performing mechanical tasks requiring alertness.

Generic Name

Diphenhydramine Hydrochloride

Brand Names

Benachlor	Diphenadril
Bendylate	Fenylhist
Benadryl	Nordryl
Diahist	SK-Diphenhydramine
Diphen	Valdrene

Type of Drug

Antihistamine.

Prescribed for

Seasonal allergy, stuffed and runny nose, itching of the eyes, scratchy throat caused by allergy, and other allergic symptoms such as itching, rash, or hives. In addition, Diphenhydramine Hydrochloride has been used for motion sickness and, with other drugs, for Parkinson's disease.

General Information

Antihistamines generally, and Diphenhydramine Hydrochloride specifically, act by blocking the release of the chemical substance histamine from the cell. Antihistamines work by drying up the secretions of the nose, throat, and eyes.

Cautions and Warnings

Diphenhydramine Hydrochloride should not be used if you are allergic to this drug. It should be avoided or used with extreme care if you have glaucoma (pressure in the eye), stomach ulcer or other stomach problems, enlarged prostate, or problems passing urine. It should not be used by people who have deep-breathing problems such as asthma.

Diphenhydramine Hydrochloride can cause dizziness, drowsiness, and lowering of blood pressure, particularly in the elderly patient. Young children can show signs of nervousness, increased tension, and anxiety.

Possible Side Effects

Occasional: itching, rash, sensitivity to light, perspiration, chills, dryness of the mouth, nose, and throat, lowering of blood pressure, headache, rapid heartbeat, sleeplessness, dizziness, disturbed coordination, confusion, restlessness, nervousness, irritability, euphoria (feeling high), tingling of the hands and feet, blurred vision, double vision, ringing in the ears, stomach upset, loss of appetite, nausea, vomiting, constipation, diarrhea, difficulty in urination, tightness of the chest, wheezing, nasal stuffiness.

Possible Adverse Drug Effects

Use with care if you have a history of asthma, glaucoma, thyroid disease, heart disease, high blood pressure, or diabetes.

Drug Interactions

Diphenhydramine Hydrochloride should not be taken with MAO inhibitors.

Interaction with tranquilizers, sedatives, and sleeping medication will increase the effects of these drugs; it is extremely important that you discuss this with your doctor so that doses of these drugs can be properly adjusted.

Be extremely cautious when drinking while taking Diphenhydramine Hydrochloride, which will enhance the intoxicating effect of the alcohol. Alcohol also has a sedative effect.

Usual Dose

Adult: 25 to 50 milligrams 3 to 4 times per day.

Child (over 20 pounds): 12½ to 25 milligrams 3 to 4 times per day.

Overdosage

Symptoms are depression or stimulation (especially in children), dry mouth, fixed or dilated pupils, flushing of the skin, and stomach upset. Take the patient to a hospital emergency room immediately, if you cannot make him vomit. ALWAYS bring the medicine bottle.

Special Information

Antihistamines produce a depressant effect: be extremely cautious when driving or operating heavy equipment.

The safety of Diphenhydramine Hydrochloride in pregnancy

has not been established. A breast-feeding mother should avoid taking this medication, since it is known to pass from the mother to the baby through the milk.

Generic Name

Dipyridamole

Brand Name

Persantine

Type of Drug

Antianginal agent.

Prescribed for

Prevention of attacks of angina pectoris; generally used for chronic treatment of angina, not for the immediate pain of an attack.

General Information

Dipyridamole is one of many drugs used in the treatment of angina and is also being studied as a possible addition to the treatment of stroke. In such studies, the drug is examined for its possible ability to affect platelets, a component of blood involved in clotting. When used for angina, Dipyridamole increases the flow of blood to the heart muscle in order to provide the heart with sufficient oxygen.

Possible Side Effects

Headache, dizziness, nausea, flushing, weakness, mild stomach upset, possible skin rash.

Possible Adverse Drug Effects

Dipyridamole has, on rare occasions, been reported to aggravate angina pectoris.

Drug Interactions

May interact with anticoagulant (blood-thinning drugs); patients taking anticoagulants and Dipyridamole should be checked periodically by their physician. Aspirin has an effect

similar to Dipyridamole on the platelets and may increase
the chances of bleeding due to loss of platelet effectiveness
when taken with Dipyridamole.

Usual Dose

50 milligrams 3 times per day 1 hour before meals with a full
glass of water.

Special Information

Dipyridamole may take 2 or 3 months to exert a therapeutic
effect.

Brand Name

Diupres

Ingredients

Chlorothiazide
Reserpine

Type of Drug

Antihypertensive.

Prescribed for

High blood pressure.

General Information

Diupres is a good example of a drug taking advantage of a
drug interaction. Each of the drug ingredients works by different mechanisms to lower your blood pressure. The Chlorothiazide relaxes the muscles in your veins and arteries and
also helps reduce the volume of blood flowing through those
blood vessels. Reserpine works on the nervous system to
reduce the efficiency of nerve transmissions which are contributing to the increased pressure. These drugs complement
each other so that their combined effect is better than the
effect of either one alone.

It is essential that you take your medicine exactly as prescribed for maximum benefit.

An ingredient in this drug may cause excessive loss of potassium, which may lead to a condition called hypokalemia. Warning signs are dryness of mouth, excessive thirst, weakness, drowsiness, restlessness, muscle pains or cramps, muscular fatigue, lack of urination, abnormal heart rhythms, and upset stomach. If warning signs occur, call your doctor. You may need potassium from some outside source. This may be done by either taking a potassium supplement or by eating foods such as bananas, citrus fruits, melons, and tomatoes, which have high concentrations of potassium.

This drug should be stopped at the first sign of despondency, early morning insomnia, loss of appetite, or sexual impotence. Drug-induced depression may persist for several months after the drug has been discontinued; it has been known to be severe enough to result in suicide attempts. This drug should be used with care by women of childbearing age.

Cautions and Warnings

Do not take this drug if you have a history of mental depression, active peptic ulcer, or ulcerative colitis, or if you are sensitive or allergic to either of its ingredients, to similar drugs of the Chlorothiazide group, or to sulfa drugs. If you have a history of allergy or bronchial asthma, you may also have a sensitivity or allergy to the Chlorothiazide ingredient. Although the Chlorothiazide ingredient has been used to treat specific conditions in pregnancy, unsupervised use by pregnant women should be avoided; the drug will cross the placenta and pass into the unborn child, possibly causing problems. The Chlorothiazide ingredient will also pass into the breast milk of nursing mothers.

Possible Side Effects

Loss of appetite, stomach irritation, nausea, vomiting, cramps, diarrhea, constipation, dizziness, headache, tingling in the arms and legs, restlessness, chest pains, abnormal heart rhythms, drowsiness, depression, nervousness, anxiety, nightmares, glaucoma, blood disorders, itching, fever, difficulty in breathing, muscle spasms, gout, weakness, high blood sugar, sugar in urine, blurred vision, stuffed nose, dryness of the mouth, rash. Occasional: impotence or decreased sex drive.

Drug Interactions

Interaction with Digitalis or Quinidine may cause abnormal heart rhythms.

Interaction with drugs containing lithium may lead to toxic effects of lithium.

Avoid over-the-counter cough, cold, or allergy remedies containing stimulant drugs which may raise your blood pressure.

Usual Dose

Must be individualized to patient's response.

Brand Name

Donnagel-PG

Ingredients

Alcohol   Kaolin
Atropine Sulfate   Pectin
Hyoscine Hydrobromide   Powdered Opium
Hyoscyamine Sulfate

Other Brand Names

Amogel-PG
Kaodonna-PG
Kaomead-PG
Kapectolin-PG

Type of Drug

Antidiarrheal.

Prescribed for

Relief of diarrhea.

General Information

Donnagel-PG works by reducing the mobility of the intestine, reducing secretions from the stomach and other parts of the gastrointestinal tract, and absorbing excessive fluids and other unusual materials which may be present in the stomach. This is one of many products available for the symptomatic treatment of diarrhea. Although it is effective in reducing diarrhea, it does not treat the underlying causes of the problem.

Cautions and Warnings

Do not take Donnagel-PG if you are allergic to any of its ingredients or if you have glaucoma or serious kidney or liver disease.

Possible Side Effects

Blurred vision, dry mouth, and difficulty in urination will occur only in a small number of people, usually when the recommended dosage is exceeded.

Drug Interactions

Donnagel-PG should not be taken at the same time as any other drug. The Kaolin and Pectin in this product will prevent other medications from being absorbed into the bloodstream. This is especially true of antibiotics.

Donnagel-PG occasionally interacts with large quantities of alcoholic beverages to cause excessive sleepiness, drowsiness, and inability to concentrate.

The Atropine Sulfate and Hyoscyamine Sulfate in Donnagel-PG can interact with antihistamines and drugs with side effects similar to those of antihistamines, exaggerating such effects as dry mouth, difficulty urinating, constipation, and blurred vision. If this becomes a problem, consult your doctor.

Usual Dose

Adult: 2 tablespoons taken immediately after each episode of diarrhea; then 2 tablespoons every 3 hours as needed.

Child (30 pounds and over): 1 to 2 teaspoons every 3 hours as needed.

Child (10 to 30 pounds): 1 teaspoon every 3 hours as needed.

Child (up to 10 pounds): ½ teaspoon every 3 hours as needed.

Brand Name

Donnatal

Ingredients

Atropine Sulfate
Hyoscine Hydrobromide
Hyoscyamine
Phenobarbital

Other Brand Names

Hyosophen   Setamine
Malatal   Spalix
Neoquess   Spaslin
Pylora #1   Spasmolin
Relaxadon   Spasmophen
Sedacord   Vanatal
Sedralex

Products with slightly different concentrations of the same ingredients are:

Barbidonna   Hybephen
Donnatal No 2   Kinesed
Donphen Tablets   Palbar

Type of Drug

Anticholinergic combination.

Prescribed for

Symptomatic relief of stomach spasm and other forms of cramps. Donnatal may also be prescribed for the treatment of motion sickness.

General Information

Donnatal is a mild antispasmodic sedative drug. It is only used to relieve symptoms, not to treat the cause of the symptoms. In addition to the brand names listed above, there are 40 to 50 other drug products which are anticholinergic combinations with the same properties. All are used to relieve cramps, and all are about equally effective. Some have

additional ingredients to reduce or absorb excess gas in the
stomach, to coat the stomach, or to control diarrhea.

Cautions and Warnings

Donnatal should not be used by people with glaucoma, rapid
heartbeat, severe intestinal disease such as ulcerating colitis,
serious kidney or liver disease, or a history of allergy to any
of the ingredients of this drug. Donnatal and other drugs of
this class can reduce the patient's ability to sweat. Therefore
if you take this type of medication, avoid extended heavy
exercise and the excessive high temperature of summer.

Possible Side Effects

Most common: blurred vision, dry mouth, difficulty in urination, flushing, dry skin.

Possible Adverse Drug Effects

Infrequent: rapid or unusual heartbeat, increased sensitivity
to strong light, loss of taste sensation, headache, difficulty in
passing urine, nervousness, tiredness, weakness, dizziness,
inability to sleep, nausea, vomiting, fever, stuffy nose, heartburn, loss of sex drive, decreased sweating, constipation,
bloated feeling, allergic reactions such as fever and rash.

Drug Interactions

Although Donnatal contains only a small amount of Phenobarbital, it is wise to avoid excessive amounts of alcohol or
other drugs which are sedative in action. Be careful when
driving or operating equipment. Other Phenobarbital interactions are probably not significant, but are possible with anticoagulants, adrenal corticosteroids, tranquilizers, narcotics,
sleeping pills, Digitalis or other cardiac glycosides, and
antihistamines.
    Some phenothiazine drugs, tranquilizers, antidepressants,
and narcotics may increase the side effects of the Atropine
Sulfate contained in Donnatal, causing dry mouth, difficulty
in urination, and constipation.

Usual Dose

  Adult: 1 to 2 tablets, capsules, or teaspoons 3 to 4 times
per day.
  Child: Half the adult dose, if necessary.

Overdosage

Symptoms are dry mouth, difficulty in swallowing, thirst, blurred vision, sensitivity to strong light, flushed, hot dry skin, rash, fever, abnormal heart rate, high blood pressure, difficulty in urination, restlessness, confusion, delirium, and difficulty in breathing. The patient should be taken to a hospital emergency room immediately. ALWAYS bring the medicine bottle.

Special Information

Dry mouth from Donnatal can be relieved by chewing gum or sucking hard candy; constipation can be treated with a stool-softening laxative.

Safety for pregnant or nursing women has not been established.

Generic Name

Doxepin Hydrochloride

Brand Names

Adapin
Sinequan

Type of Drug

Antidepressant.

Prescribed for

Primary depression or depression secondary to disorders such as alcoholism, other major organic diseases such as cancer, or other illnesses which may have a strong psychological impact on a patient.

General Information

Doxepin Hydrochloride and other members of this group are effective in treating symptoms of depression. They can elevate your mood, increase physical activity and mental alertness, and improve appetite and sleep patterns. The drugs are mild sedatives and therefore useful in treating mild forms of depression associated with anxiety. You should not expect instant results with this medicine: benefits are usually seen after 1 to 4 weeks of therapy. If symptoms are not changed after 6 to 8 weeks, contact your doctor.

Cautions and Warnings

Unlike other tricyclic antidepressants, Doxepin Hydrochloride should not be given to children under age 12 and cannot be used to treat nighttime bed-wetting. Do not take Doxepin Hydrochloride if you are allergic or sensitive to this or other members of this class of drug: Imipramine, Nortriptyline, Amitriptyline, Desipramine, and Protriptyline. The drugs should not be used if you are recovering from a heart attack. Doxepin Hydrochloride may be taken with caution if you have a history of epilepsy or other convulsive disorders, difficulty in urination, glaucoma, heart disease, or thyroid disease. Doxepin Hydrochloride can interfere with your ability to perform tasks which require concentration, such as driving or operating machinery. Do not stop taking this medicine without first discussing it with your doctor, since stopping may cause you to become nauseated, weak, and headachy. Doxepin Hydrochloride will pass from mother to unborn child: consult your doctor before taking this medicine if you are pregnant.

Possible Side Effects

Changes in blood pressure (both high and low), abnormal heart rate, heart attack, confusion, especially in elderly patients, hallucinations, disorientation, delusions, anxiety, restlessness, excitement, numbness and tingling in the extremities, lack of coordination, muscle spasm or tremors, seizures and/or convulsions, dry mouth, blurred vision, constipation, inability to urinate, rash, itching, sensitivity to bright light or sunlight, changes in composition of blood, nausea, vomiting, loss of appetite, stomach upset, diarrhea, enlargement of the breasts in males and females, increased or decreased sex drive, and increased or decreased blood sugar.

Possible Adverse Drug Effects

Infrequent: agitation, inability to sleep, nightmares, feeling of panic, peculiar taste in the mouth, stomach cramps, black coloration of the tongue, yellowing eyes and/or skin, changes in liver function, increased or decreased weight, excessive perspiration, flushing, frequent urination, drowsiness, dizziness, weakness, headache, loss of hair, nausea, not feeling well.

Drug Interactions

Interaction with MAO inhibitors can cause high fevers, convulsions, and (occasionally) death. Don't take MAO inhibitors until at least 2 weeks after Doxepin Hydrochloride has been discontinued.

Doxepin Hydrochloride interacts with Guanethidine and Clonidine, drugs used to treat high blood pressure: if your doctor prescribes Doxepin Hydrochloride and you are taking medicine for high blood pressure, be sure to discuss this with him.

Doxepin Hydrochloride increases the effects of barbiturates, tranquilizers, other depressive drugs, and alcohol. Don't drink alcoholic beverages if you take Doxepin Hydrochloride.

Taking Doxepin Hydrochloride and thyroid medicine will enhance the effects of the thyroid medicine. The combination can cause abnormal heart rhythms. The combination of Doxepin Hydrochloride and Reserpine may cause overstimulation.

Large doses of Vitamin C (Ascorbic Acid), oral contraceptives, or smoking can reduce the effect of Doxepin Hydrochloride. Drugs such as Bicarbonate of Soda, Acetazolamide, Quinidine, or Procainamide will increase the effect of Doxepin Hydrochloride. Ritalin and phenothiazine drugs such as Thorazine and Compazine block the metabolism of Doxepin Hydrochloride, causing it to stay in the body longer. This can cause possible overdose.

The combination of Doxepin Hydrochloride with large doses of the sleeping pill Ethchlorvynol has caused patients to experience passing delirium.

Usual Dose

Initial dose is a moderate 10 to 25 milligrams 3 times per day; the low dose reduces drowsiness during the first few days. The doctor may then increase or decrease the dose according to individual response, giving 50 to 300 milligrams per day. This drug should not be given to children under age 12.

Overdosage

Symptoms are confusion, inability to concentrate, hallucinations, drowsiness, lowered body temperature, abnormal heart rate, heart failure, large pupils of the eyes, convulsions, severely lowered blood pressure, stupor, and coma (as well as agitation, stiffening of body muscles, vomiting, and high fever). The patient should be taken to a hospital emergency room immediately. ALWAYS bring the medicine bottle.

Storage

Liquid Doxepin Hydrochloride should not be diluted until just before use. Dilute in about 4 ounces of water or juice just before you take it.

Generic Name

Doxycycline

Brand Names

Doxy-C   Vibramycin
Doxychel   Vibra Tabs

Type of Drug

Broad-spectrum antibiotic effective against gram-positive and gram-negative organisms.

Prescribed for

Bacterial infections such as gonorrhea, infections of the mouth, gums, and teeth, Rocky Mountain spotted fever and other fevers caused by ticks and lice from a variety of carriers, urinary tract infections, and respiratory system infections such as pneumonia and bronchitis.

These diseases may be produced by gram-positive or gram-negative organisms such as diplococci, staphylococci, streptococci, gonococci, E. coli, and Shigella.

Doxycycline has also been used successfully to treat some skin infections, but is not considered the first-choice antibiotic for the treatment of general skin infections or wounds. It may be used to prevent "traveler diarrhea."

General Information

Doxycycline works by interfering with the normal growth cycle of the invading bacteria, preventing them from reproducing and thus allowing the body's normal defenses to fight off the infection. This process is referred to as bacteriostatic action. Doxycycline has also been used along with other medicines to treat amoebic infections of the intestinal tract, known as amoebic dysentery. It is also prescribed for diseases caused by ticks, fleas, and lice.

Doxycycline has been successfully used for the treatment of adolescent acne, in small doses over a long period of time. Adverse effects or toxicity in this type of therapy are almost unheard of.

Since the action of this antibiotic depends on its concentration within the invading bacteria, it is imperative that you completely follow the doctor's directions.

Cautions and Warnings

You should not use Doxycycline if you are pregnant. In general, children up to age 8 should also avoid Doxycycline as it has been shown to produce serious discoloration of the permanent teeth. Doxycycline when used in children has been shown to interfere with the development of long bones and may retard growth.

Exceptions would be when Doxycycline is the only effective antibiotic available and all risk factors have been made known to the patient.

Doxycycline should not be given to people with known liver disease. You should avoid taking high doses of Doxycycline therapy if you will be exposed to sunlight for a long period because this antibiotic may interfere with your body's normal sun-screening mechanism, possibly causing severe sunburn. If you have a known history of allergy to Doxycycline you should avoid taking this drug or other drugs within this category such as Aureomycin, Terramycin, Rondomycin, Vibramycin, Demeclocycline, Tetracycline, and Minocycline.

Possible Side Effects

As with other antibiotics, the common side effects of Doxycycline are stomach upset, nausea, vomiting, diarrhea, and rash. Less common side effects include hairy tongue and itching and irritation of the anal and/or vaginal region. If these symptoms appear, consult your physician immediately. Periodic physical examinations and laboratory tests should be given to patients who are on long-term Doxycycline.

Possible Adverse Drug Effects

Loss of appetite, peeling of the skin, sensitivity to the sun, fever, chills, anemia, possible brown spotting of the skin, decrease in kidney function, damage to the liver.

Drug Interactions

Doxycycline (a bacteriostatic drug) may interfere with the action of bactericidal agents such as Penicillin. It is not advisable to take both.

Don't take multivitamin products containing minerals at the same time as Doxycycline, or you will reduce the antibiotic's effectiveness. Space the taking of these two medicines at least 2 hours apart.

People receiving anticoagulation therapy (blood-thinning agents) should consult their doctor, since Doxycycline will interfere with this form of therapy. An adjustment in the anticoagulant dosage may be required.

Anticonvulsant drugs such as Carbamazepine, Phenytoin, and barbiturates may increase the elimination of Doxycycline from the body, requiring higher or more frequent doses of the antibiotic.

Usual Dose

Adult: first day, 200 milligrams given as 100 milligrams every 12 hours. Maintenance, 100 milligrams per day in 1 to 2 doses. The maintenance dose may be doubled in severe infections.

Child (101 pounds and over): the usual adult dose may be given.

Child (under 101 pounds): first day, 2 milligrams per pound of body weight divided in 2 doses. Maintenance, 1 milligram per pound as a single daily dose. (Double the maintenance dose for severe infections.)

An increased incidence of side effects is observed if the dose is over 200 milligrams per day.

Storage

Doxycycline can be stored at room temperature.

Special Information

Do *not* take after the expiration date on the label. The decomposition of Doxycycline produces a highly toxic substance which can cause serious kidney damage. You may take Doxycycline with food or milk to reduce stomach upset.

Brand Name

Drixoral

Other Brand Names

Disophrol
Histarall
Spenhist S.A.

Ingredients

Dexbrompheniramine Maleate
Pseudoephedrine Sulfate

Type of Drug

Long-acting combination antihistamine-decongestant.

Prescribed for

Relief of sneezing, runny nose, and nasal congestion associated with the common cold, allergy, or other upper respiratory condition.

General Information

Drixoral is one of many products marketed to relieve the symptoms of the common cold. Most of these products contain ingredients to relieve nasal congestion or to dry up runny noses or relieve a scratchy throat; and several of them may contain ingredients to suppress cough, or to help eliminate unwanted mucus. All these products are good only for the relief of symptoms and do not treat the underlying problem, such as a cold virus or other infections.

Cautions and Warnings

If you are pregnant you should not take this drug.

Possible Side Effects

Mild drowsiness has been seen in patients taking Drixoral.

Possible Adverse Drug Effects

Infrequent: restlessness, tension, nervousness, tremor, weakness, inability to sleep, headache, palpitations, elevation of blood pressure, sweating, sleeplessness, loss of appetite, nausea, vomiting, dizziness, constipation.

Drug Interactions

Interaction with alcoholic beverages may cause excessive drowsiness and/or sleepiness, or inability to concentrate. Also avoid sedatives, tranquilizers, antihistamines, sleeping pills, thyroid medicine, or antihypertensive drugs such as Reserpine or Guanethidine.

Do not self-medicate with over-the-counter drugs for the relief of cold symptoms: taking Drixoral with such drugs may aggravate high blood pressure, heart disease, diabetes, or thyroid disease.

Do not take Drixoral if you are taking or suspect you may be taking a monoamine oxidase (MAO) inhibitor; severe elevation in blood pressure may result.

Usual Dose

Adult and child (age 12 and over): 1 tablet morning and night.

Child (under age 12): not recommended.

Special Information

Since drowsiness may occur during use of Drixoral, be cautious while performing mechanical tasks requiring alertness.

If this drug upsets your stomach it should be taken with food.

Brand Name

Dyazide

Ingredients

Hydrochlorothiazide
Triamterene

Type of Drug

Diuretic.

Prescribed for

High blood pressure or any condition where it is desirable to eliminate excess fluid from the body.

General Information

Dyazide is a combination of two diuretics and is a convenient, effective approach for the treatment of diseases where the elimination of excess fluids is required. One of the ingredients in Dyazide has the ability to hold potassium in the body while producing a diuretic effect. This balances off the other ingredient, Hydrochlorothiazide, which normally causes a loss of potassium from outside sources.

Cautions and Warnings

Do not use Dyazide if you have nonfunctioning kidneys, if you may be allergic to this drug or any sulfa drug, or if you have a history of allergy or bronchial asthma. Dyazide may be used to treat specific conditions in pregnant women, but the decision to use this medication by pregnant women should be weighed carefully because the drug may cross the placental barrier into the blood of the unborn child. Dyazide may appear in the breast milk of nursing mothers. Do not take any potassium supplements together with Dyazide unless specifically directed to do so by your doctor.

Possible Side Effects

Drowsiness, lethargy, headache, gastrointestinal upset, cramping and diarrhea, rash, mental confusion, fever, feeling of ill health, enlargement of the breasts, inability to achieve or maintain erection in males, irregular menstrual cycles, or deepening of the voice in females.

Possible Adverse Drug Effects

Loss of appetite, headache, tingling in the toes and fingers, restlessness, anemias or other effects on components of the blood, unusual sensitivity to sunlight, dizziness when rising quickly from a sitting position. Dyazide can also produce muscle spasms, gout, weakness, and blurred vision.

Drug Interactions

Dyazide will increase (potentiate) the action of other blood-pressure-lowering drugs. This is beneficial, and the drug is frequently used to help lower blood pressure in patients with hypertension.

The possibility of developing imbalances in body fluids (electrolytes) is increased if you take other medications such as Digitalis and adrenal corticosteroids while you are taking Dyazide.

If you are taking an oral antidiabetic drug and begin taking Dyazide, the antidiabetic dose may have to be altered.

Lithium Carbonate should not be taken with Dyazide because the combination may increase the risk of lithium toxicity.

Avoid over-the-counter cough, cold, or allergy remedies containing stimulant drugs which can aggravate your condition.

Usual Dose

1 capsule twice per day.

Special Information

Take Dyazide exactly as prescribed.

Brand Name

Equagesic

Ingredients

Aspirin
Ethoheptazine
Meprobamate

Other Brand Names

Hepto
Mepro Compound
Meprogesic

Type of Drug

Analgesic combination.

Prescribed for

Pain relief in patients who suffer muscle spasms, sprains, strains, or bad backs.

General Information

Equagesic is a combination product containing a tranquilizer, a muscle relaxant, and Aspirin; it is used for the relief of pain associated with muscle spasms. The tranquilizer (Meprobamate) in this combination opens it to many drug interactions, especially with other tranquilizers or depressant drugs, which can result in habituation and possible drug dependence. Equagesic may be effective in providing temporary relief from pain and muscle spasm. If you are taking Equagesic, you must follow any other instructions your doctor gives you to help treat the basic problem.

Cautions and Warnings

Do not take Equagesic if you are allergic to any of the ingredients contained in it. If you are pregnant or are nursing, talk to your physician before you take Equagesic, because this combination may cause adverse effects in the unborn infant or child.

Possible Side Effects

Most frequent: nausea, vomiting, stomach upset, dizziness, drowsiness. Less frequent: allergy, itching, rash, fever, fluid in the arms and/or legs, occasional fainting spells, spasms of bronchial muscles leading to difficulty in breathing.

Possible Adverse Drug Effects

People taking Equagesic have occasionally experienced effects on components of the blood system. Equagesic has also caused blurred vision.

Drug Interactions

Two of the ingredients in Equagesic may cause sleepiness, drowsiness, or, in high doses, difficulty in breathing. Avoid interaction with other drugs that produce the same effect, for example, barbiturates, narcotics, tranquilizers, sleeping pills, and some antihistamines. Do not drink alcoholic beverages with Equagesic, because the depressive effect of the alcohol will be increased.

If you are taking an anticoagulant (blood-thinning medication) and have been given a new prescription for Equagesic, be sure that your doctor is aware that there is Aspirin in Equagesic. Aspirin affects the ability of your blood to clot and can necessitate a change in the dose of your anticoagulant.

Usual Dose

1 or 2 tablets 3 to 4 times per day as needed for the relief of pain associated with skeletal muscle spasms.

Overdosage

Equagesic overdoses are serious. Symptoms are drowsiness, feeling of light-headedness, desire to go to sleep, nausea, and vomiting. The patient should be taken to a hospital emergency room immediately. ALWAYS bring the medicine bottle.

Special Information

If you experience stomach upset with Equagesic, take with food or water.

Generic Name

Ergot Alkaloids Dihydrogenated

Brand Names

Circanol	Hydergine Oral Tabs
Deapril-ST	Spengine
Dihydroergotoxine Methane- sulfonate	Tri-Ergone
	Trigot
Gerigine	

Type of Drug

Psychotherapeutic.

Prescribed for

Alzheimer's disease; depression, confusion, forgetfulness, antisocial behavior, and dizziness in the elderly.

General Information

Ergot Alkaloids Dihydrogenated has improved the supply of blood to the brain in test animals and reduces heart rate and muscle tone in blood vessels. Some studies have shown the drug to be very effective in relieving mild symptoms of mental impairment, while others have found it to be only moderately effective. It has been most beneficial in patients whose symptoms are due to the effects of high blood pressure in the brain.

Cautions and Warnings

Do not use this drug if you are allergic or sensitive to Ergot or any of its derivatives.

Possible Side Effects

Ergot Alkaloids Dihydrogenated does not produce serious side effects. Since the tablet is taken under the tongue, you may experience some irritation, nausea, or stomach upset.

Usual Dose

1 tablet under the tongue 3 times per day.

Special Information

The results of this drug are gradual. Frequently they are not seen for 3 to 4 weeks.

Dissolve the tablets under the tongue: they are not effective if swallowed whole.

Generic Name

Erythromycin

Brand Names

Bristamycin
Delta-E
E.E.S.
E-Mycin
Eramycin
Erypar
Erythrocin
Erythromycin Ethyl-succinate
Ethril

Ilosone
Ilotycin
Pediamycin
Pfizer-E
Robimycin
RP-Mycin
SK-Erythromycin
Wyamycin

Type of Drug

Bacteriostatic antibiotic, effective against gram-positive organisms such as streptococcus, staphylococcus, and gonococcus.

Prescribed for

Infections of the upper and lower respiratory tract; infections of the mouth, gums, and teeth; infections of the nose, ears, and sinuses. May be used for mild to moderate skin infections, but is not considered the antibiotic of choice. Can also be effective against amoebas of the intestinal tract, which cause amoebic dysentery and legionnaire's disease.

Erythromycin is a relatively safe antibiotic. It is used instead of Penicillin for mild to moderate infections in people who are allergic to the penicillin class of antibiotics.

Note: Erythromycin is not the antibiotic of choice for severe infections.

General Information

Erythromycin works by interfering with the normal growth cycle of the invading bacteria, preventing them from reproducing and thus allowing the body's normal defenses to fight off the infection. This process is referred to as bacteriostatic action.

Erythromycin is absorbed from the gastrointestinal tract, but it is deactivated by the acid content of the stomach. Because of this, the tablet form of this drug is formulated in such a way as to bypass the stomach and dissolve in the intestine.

Erythromycin is used primarily for infections of the mouth, nose, ears, sinuses, throat, and lungs. It can also be used to treat venereal disease and pelvic inflammatory disease in people who have allergies and/or sensitivity to the penicillin class of antibiotics.

Because the action of this antibiotic depends on its concentration within the invading bacteria, it is imperative that you follow the doctor's directions regarding the spacing of the doses as well as the number of days you should continue taking the medication. The effect of the antibiotic is severely reduced if these instructions are not followed.

Cautions and Warnings

Erythromycin is excreted primarily through the liver. People with liver disease or damage should exercise caution. Those on long-term therapy with Erythromycin are advised to have periodic blood tests.

Erythromycin is available in a variety of formulations. One formula, Erythromycin Estolate, has occasionally produced fatigue, nausea, vomiting, abdominal cramps, and fever. If you are susceptible to stomach problems, Erythromycin may cause mild to moderate stomach upset. Discontinuing the drug will reverse this condition.

Possible Side Effects

Most common: nausea, vomiting, stomach cramps, diarrhea. Less common: hairy tongue, itching, irritation of the anal and/or vaginal region. If any of these symptoms appear, consult your physician immediately.

Possible Adverse Drug Effects

Erythromycin should not be given to people with known sensitivity to this antibiotic. It may cause a yellowing of the skin and eyes. If this occurs, discontinue the drug and notify your doctor immediately.

Drug Interactions

Erythromycin is relatively free of interactions with other medicines. However, there seems to be a neutralizing effect between it and Lincomycin and Clindamycin. Erythromycin interferes with the elimination of Theophylline from the body. This may cause toxic effects of Theophylline overdose.

Usual Dose

Adult: 250 to 500 milligrams every 6 hours.

Children: 50 to 200 milligrams per pound of body weight per day in divided doses, depending upon age, weight, and severity of infection.

Take 1 hour before or 2 hours after meals.

Doses of E.E.S., Pediamycin, and Wyamycin are 60 percent higher, due to different chemical composition of the Erythromycin formulation.

Special Information

The safety of Erythromycin in pregnancy has not been established.

Generic Name

Ethchlorvynol

Brand Name

Placidyl

Type of Drug

Sedative-hypnotic.

Prescribed for

Inability to sleep.

General Information

Sleep is produced within 30 minutes and lasts 4 to 8 hours.

Cautions and Warnings

Patients who are allergic to this drug and patients with rash or porphyria should not take Ethchlorvynol. Continued use may cause physical and psychological dependence.

Possible Side Effects

Skin rash, dizziness.

Possible Adverse Drug Effects

There have been reports of nausea, morning hangover, excitation, and blurring of the vision.

Drug Interactions

The combination of Ethchlorvynol and Amitriptyline can make you delirious. Avoid combining them.

   Do not take this drug with alcohol, antihistamines, or other depressants.

Usual Dose

   Adult: 500 milligrams by mouth at bedtime; for severe insomnia, 750 or even 1000 milligrams. Patients may be instructed, if they awaken during the night, to take an additional 100 to 200 milligrams to help them get back to sleep. Only the smallest effective dose of Ethchlorvynol should be used, since the drug can be abused and can be addictive.

Overdosage

Large amounts of Ethchlorvynol can be fatal, and the drug is frequently used in suicide attempts. Symptoms are coma, lowered body temperature followed by fever, absence of normal reflexes and pain responses after pinches and needle or pin sticks, and shallow breathing. The patient should be taken to a hospital emergency room immediately. ALWAYS bring the medicine bottle.

People who have taken Ethchlorvynol for a long time may show signs of chronic overdosage: loss of memory, inability to concentrate, shakes, tremors, loss of reflexes, slurring of speech, and general sense of depression. Abrupt discontinuation of Ethchlorvynol often causes withdrawal reactions of nervousness, anxiety, seizures, cramping, chills, numbness of the extremities, and general behavior changes. Chronic overdosage is best treated by withdrawing of the drug over a period of days or weeks.

Storage

Ethchlorvynol capsules must be protected from heat and moisture. They should not be refrigerated. The best place to keep them is at room temperature; for example, in a night or bed table.

Special Information

If you feel giddy or get an upset stomach from this drug, take it after eating.

Generic Name

Fenoprofen Calcium

Brand Name

Nalfon

Type of Drug

Nonsteroid anti-inflammatory.

Prescribed for

Relief of pain and inflammation of joints and muscles; arthritis, mild to moderate pain of menstrual cramps, dental surgery and extractions, and athletic injuries such as sprains and strains.

General Information

Fenoprofen Calcium is one of several new drugs used to treat various types of pain and belongs to the chemical group known as propionic acid derivatives. These drugs reduce inflammation and share side effects, the most common of which are upset stomach and possible formation of ulcers. The drugs are roughly comparable to Aspirin in controlling the symptoms of arthritis and other pain, and are used by some people who cannot tolerate Aspirin.

Cautions and Warnings

Do not take Fenoprofen Calcium if you are allergic or sensitive to this drug, Aspirin, or other nonsteriod anti-inflammatory drugs. Fenoprofen Calcium may cause stomach ulcers. This drug should not be used by patients with severe kidney disease. The safety of this drug for pregnant women has not been established and it is not recommended for them.

Possible Side Effects

Stomach upset, blurred vision, darkening of stool, changes in color vision, rash, weight gain, retention of fluids.

Possible Adverse Drug Effects

Most frequent: stomach upset, dizziness, headache, drowsiness, ringing in the ears. Others: heartburn, nausea, vomiting, bloating, gas in the stomach, stomach pain, diarrhea, constipation, dark stool, nervousness, insomnia, depression, confusion, tremor, loss of appetite, fatigue, itching, rash, double vision, abnormal heart rhythm, anemia or other changes in the composition of the blood, changes in liver function, loss of hair, tingling in the hands and feet, fever, breast enlargement, lowered blood sugar, effects on the kidneys. If symptoms appear, stop taking the medicine and see your doctor immediately.

Drug Interactions

Fenoprofen Calcium increases the action of Phenytoin, sulfa drugs, drugs used to control diabetes, and drugs used to thin the blood. If you are taking any of these medicines, be sure to discuss it with your doctor, who will probably change the dose of the other drug.

An adjustment in the dose of Fenoprofen Calcium may be needed if you take Phenobarbital.

Usual Dose

Adult: 300 to 600 milligrams 4 times per day, to start. Doses may be increased if needed, up to 3200 milligrams per day. If upset stomach occurs, take each dose with food, milk, or antacid.

Child: not recommended.

Generic Name

Ferrous Sulfate

Brand Names

Courac	Ferralyn
Feosol	Fero-Gradumet
Feosol Spansules	Mol-Iron
Fer-In-Sol	Sterasol
Ferospace	

Type of Drug

Iron-containing product.

Prescribed for

Iron deficiency of the blood.

General Information

Ferrous Sulfate is used to treat anemias due to iron deficiency. Other anemias will not be affected by this drug. Ferrous Sulfate works by being incorporated into red blood cells where it can help carry oxygen throughout the body. Iron is absorbed only in a small section of the gastrointestinal tract called the duodenum. Sustained-release preparations of iron should only be used to help minimize the stomach discomfort that Ferrous Sulfate can cause, since any drug which passes the duodenum (in the upper part of the small intestine) cannot be absorbed.

Other drugs may also provide a source of iron to treat

iron deficiency anemia. The iron in these products may be combined with other vitamins or with special extracts as in the product Trinsicon, where iron is combined with vitamin B-12, Folic Acid and Intrinsic Factor.

Cautions and Warnings

Do not take Ferrous Sulfate if you have a history of stomach upset, peptic ulcer, or ulcerative colitis.

Possible Side Effects

Stomach upset and irritation, nausea, diarrhea, constipation.

Drug Interactions

Ferrous Sulfate will interfere with absorption of oral Tetracycline. Separate the doses by at least 2 hours.

Antacids will interfere with the absorption of iron; again, separate doses by 2 hours.

In either case, avoid taking iron supplements (unless absolutely necessary) until your other medical condition clears up.

Usual Dose

1 to 3 tablets per day.

Overdosage

Symptoms appear after 30 minutes to several hours: lethargy (tiredness), vomiting, diarrhea, stomach upset, change in pulse to weak and rapid, and lowered blood pressure—or, after massive doses, shock, black and tarry stools due to massive bleeding in the stomach or intestine, and pneumonia. Quickly induce vomiting and feed the patient eggs and milk until he can be taken to a hospital for stomach pumping. Be sure to call a doctor right away. The patient must be taken to the hospital as soon as possible, since stomach pumping should not be performed after the first hour of iron ingestion because there is a danger of perforation of the stomach wall. In the hospital emergency room measures to treat shock, loss of water, loss of blood, and respiratory failure may be necessary. ALWAYS bring the medicine bottle.

Special Information

Iron salts impart a black color to stools and are slightly constipating. If stools become black and tarry in consistency, however, there may be some bleeding in the stomach or intestine. Discuss it with your doctor.

Iron salts and iron-containing products are best absorbed on an empty stomach; but if they upset your stomach, take with meals or immediately after meals.

Brand Name

Fiorinal

Ingredients

Aspirin
Butalbital
Caffeine
Phenacetin

Other Brand Names

Forbutol	I-PAC
Idenal	Lanorinal
Isobutal	Marnal
Isollyl	Ten-Shun

Type of Drug

Nonnarcotic analgesic combination.

Prescribed for

Relief of headache pain or other types of pain.

General Information

Fiorinal is one of many combination products containing barbiturates and analgesics. These products often also contain tranquilizers or narcotics, and Acetaminophen may be substituted for Aspirin.

Cautions and Warnings

Fiorinal can cause drug dependence or addiction. Use this drug with caution if you have asthma or problems in breathing. It can affect your ability to drive a car or operate machinery. Do not drink alcoholic beverages while taking Fiorinal. The Aspirin component in this drug can interfere with the normal coagulation of blood. This is especially important if you are taking blood-thinning medication.

Possible Side Effects

Major: light-headedness, dizziness, sedation, nausea, vomiting, sweating, stomach upset, loss of appetite, (possible) mild stimulation.

Possible Adverse Side Effects

Weakness, headache, sleeplessness, agitation, tremor, uncoordinated muscle movements, mild hallucinations, disorientation, visual disturbances, feeling high, dry mouth, loss of appetite, constipation, flushing of the face, changes in heart rate, palpitations, faintness, difficulty in urination, skin rashes, itching, confusion, rapid breathing, diarrhea.

Drug Interactions

Interaction with alcohol, tranquilizers, barbiturates, sleeping pills, or other drugs that produce depression can cause tiredness, drowsiness, and inability to concentrate.

Interaction with Prednisone, steroids, Phenylbutazone, or alcohol can irritate your stomach.

The dose of anticoagulant (blood-thinning) drugs will have to be changed by your physician if you begin taking Fiorinal, which contains Aspirin.

Usual Dose

1 to 2 tablets or capsules every 4 hours or as needed. Maximum of 6 doses per day.

Take with a full glass of water or with food to reduce the possibility of stomach upset.

Overdosage

Symptoms are difficulty in breathing, nervousness progressing to stupor or coma, pinpointed pupils of the eyes, cold clammy skin and lowered heart rate and/or blood pressure, nausea, vomiting, dizziness, ringing in the ears, flushing, sweating, and thirst. The patient should be taken to a hospital emergency room immediately. ALWAYS bring the medicine bottle.

Special Information

Drowsiness may occur. The Phenacetin ingredient of Fiorinal may be dangerous to your kidneys, so do not take for an extended period unless so directed by your doctor.

Brand Name

Fiorinal with Codeine

Ingredients

Aspirin
Butalbital
Caffeine
Codeine
Codeine Phosphate
Phenacetin

Type of Drug

Narcotic analgesic combination.

Prescribed for

Relief of headache pain or other types of pain.

General Information

Fiorinal with Codeine is one of many combination products containing barbiturates and analgesics. These products often also contain tranquilizers or narcotics, and Acetaminophen may be substituted for Aspirin.

Cautions and Warnings

Fiorinal with Codeine can cause drug dependence or addiction. Use this drug with caution if you have asthma or problems in breathing. It can affect your ability to drive a car or operate machinery.

Possible Side Effects

Major: light-headedness, dizziness, sedation, nausea, vomiting, sweating, stomach upset, loss of appetite, (possible) mild stimulation.

Possible Adverse Drug Effects

Weakness, headache, sleeplessness, agitation, tremor, unco-ordinated muscle movements, mild hallucinations, disorientation, visual disturbances, feeling high, dry mouth, loss of appetite, constipation, flushing of the face, changes in heart rate, palpitations, faintness, difficulty in urination, rashes, itching, confusion, rapid breathing, diarrhea.

Drug Interactions

Interaction with alcohol, tranquilizers, barbiturates, sleeping pills, or other drugs that produce depression can cause tiredness, drowsiness, and inability to concentrate.

Interaction with Prednisone, steroids, Phenylbutazone, or alcohol can irritate your stomach.

The dose of anticoagulant (blood-thinning) drugs will have to be changed by your physician if you begin taking Fiorinal with Codeine, which contains Aspirin.

Usual Dose

1 to 2 tablets or capsules every 4 hours or as needed. Maximum of 6 doses per day.

Take with a full glass of water or with food to reduce the possibility of stomach upset.

Overdosage

Symptoms are difficulty in breathing, nervousness progressing to stupor or coma, pinpointed pupils of the eyes, cold clammy skin and lowered heart rate and/or blood pressure, nausea, vomiting, dizziness, ringing in the ears, flushing, sweating, and thirst. The patient should be taken to a hospital emergency room immediately. ALWAYS bring the medicine bottle.

Special Information

Drowsiness may occur. The Phenacetin ingredient of Fiorinal with Codeine may be dangerous to your kidneys, so do not take for an extended period unless so directed by your doctor.

Generic Name

Fluocinolone Acetonide

Brand Names

Fluonid	Synalar-HP
Flurosyn	Synemol
Synalar	

Type of Drug

Topical corticosteroid.

Prescribed for

Relief of skin inflammation of local skin area, itching, or other skin problems.

General Information

Fluocinolone Acetonide is one of many adrenal cortical steroids used in medical practice today. The major differences between Fluocinolone Acetonide and other adrenal cortical steroids are potency of medication and variation in some secondary effects. In most cases the choice of adrenal cortical steroids to be used in a specific disease is a matter of doctor preference and past experience. Other adrenal cortical steroids include Cortisone, Hydrocortisone, Prednisone, Prednisolone, Triamcinolone, Methylprednisolone, Meprednisone, Paramethasone, Fluprednisolone, Dexamethasone, Betamethasone, and Fludrocortisone.

Cautions and Warnings

Fluocinolone Acetonide should not be used if you have viral diseases of the skin (herpes), fungal infections of the skin (athlete's foot), or tuberculosis of the skin, nor should it be used in the ear if the eardrum is perforated. People with a history of allergies to any of the components of the ointment, cream, or gel should not use this drug.

Possible Side Effects

Itching, irritation, dryness, and redness of the skin.

Special Information

Clean the skin before applying Fluocinolone Acetonide to prevent secondary infection. Apply in a very thin film (effectiveness is based on contact area and not on the thickness of the layer applied).

Generic Name

Fluocinonide Ointment/Cream/Gel

Brand Names

Lidex
Lidex-E
Topsyn

Type of Drug

Topical corticosteroid.

Prescribed for

Relief of skin inflammation of local skin area, itching, or
other skin problems.

General Information

Fluocinonide is used to relieve the symptom of any itching,
rash, or inflammation of the skin. It does not treat the underlying cause of the skin problem, only the symptom. It exerts
this effect by interfering with natural body mechanisms that
produce the rash, itching, etc., in the first place. If you use
this drug without finding the cause of the problem, the
condition may return after you stop using the drug. Fluocinonide should not be used without your doctor's consent
because it could cover an important reaction, one that may
be valuable to him in treating you.

Cautions and Warnings

Fluocinonide should not be used if you have viral diseases
of the skin (herpes), fungal infections of the skin (athlete's
foot), or tuberculosis of the skin, nor should it be used in the
ear if the eardrum is perforated. People with a history of
allergies to any of the components of the ointment, cream,
or gel should not use this drug.

Possible Side Effects

Itching, irritation, dryness and redness of the skin.

Special Information

Clean the skin before applying Fluocinonide to prevent secondary infection. Apply a very thin film (effectiveness is based on contact area and not on the thickness of the layer applied).

Generic Name

Fluoxymesterone

Brand Names

Halotestin
Ora-Testryl

Type of Drug

Androgenic (male) hormone.

Prescribed for

Diseases in which male hormone replacement or augmentation is needed; male menopause.

General Information

This is a member of the androgenic or male hormone group, which includes Testosterone, Methyl Testosterone, Calusterone, and Dromostanolone Propionate. (The last two are used primarily to treat breast cancer in women.) Females taking any androgenic drug should be careful to watch for deepening of the voice, oily skin, acne, hairiness, increased libido, and menstrual irregularities, effects related to the so-called virilizing effects of these hormones. Virilization is a sign that the drug is starting to produce changes in secondary sex characteristics. The drugs should be avoided if possible by young boys who have not gone through puberty.

Cautions and Warnings

Men with unusually high blood levels of calcium, known or suspected cancer of the prostate, or prostate destruction or disease, cancer of the breast, or with liver, heart, or kidney disease should not use this medication. Women who are pregnant should not use Fluoxymesterone since it may affect the unborn child.

Possible Side Effects

In males: Inhibition of testicle function, impotence, chronic erection of the penis, enlargement of the breast.

In females: unusual hairiness, baldness in a pattern similar to that seen in men, deepening of the voice, enlargement of the clitoris. These changes are usually irreversible once they have occurred. Females also experience increases in blood calcium and menstrual irregularities.

In both sexes: changes in libido, flushing of the skin, acne, habituation, excitation, chills, sleeplessness, water retention, nausea, vomiting, diarrhea. Symptoms resembling stomach ulcer may develop. Fluoxymesterone may affect levels of blood cholesterol.

Drug Interactions

Fluoxymesterone may increase the effect of oral anticoagulants; dosage of the anticoagulant may have to be decreased. It may have an effect on the glucose tolerance test, a blood test used to screen for diabetes mellitus.

Usual Dose

2 to 30 milligrams per day, depending upon the disease being treated and patient's response.

Special Information

Fluoxymesterone and other androgens are potent drugs. They must be taken only under the close supervision of your doctor and never used casually. The dosage and clinical effects of the drug vary widely and require constant monitoring.

Generic Name

Fluphenazine Hydrochloride

Brand Names

Permitil
Prolixin

Type of Drug

Phenothiazine antipsychotic.

Prescribed for

Psychotic disorders, moderate to severe depression with anxiety, control of agitation or aggressiveness of disturbed children, alcohol withdrawal symptoms, intractable pain, and senility.

General Information

Fluphenazine Hydrochloride and other members of the phenothiazine group act on a portion of the brain called the hypothalamus. The drugs affect parts of the hypothalamus that control metabolism, body temperature, alertness, muscle tone, hormone balance, and vomiting, and may be used to treat problems related to any of these functions.

Cautions and Warnings

Fluphenazine Hydrochloride should not be taken if you are allergic to one of the drugs in the broad classification of phenothiazine drugs. Do not take it if you have blood, liver, kidney, or heart disease, very low blood pressure, or Parkinson's disease. This medication is a tranquilizer and can have a depressive effect, especially during the first few days of therapy. Care should be taken when performing activities requiring a high degree of concentration, such as driving. If you are taking this medication and become pregnant, contact your doctor immediately.

Possible Side Effects

Most common: drowsiness, especially during the first or second week of therapy. If the drowsiness becomes troublesome, contact your doctor.

Possible Adverse Drug Effects

Can cause jaundice (yellowing of the whites of the eyes or skin), usually in 2 to 4 weeks. The jaundice usually goes away when the drug is discontinued, but there have been cases when it did not. If you notice this effect or if you develop symptoms such as fever and generally not feeling well, contact your doctor immediately. Less frequent: changes in components of the blood including anemias, raised or lowered blood pressure, abnormal heart rate, heart attack, feeling faint or dizzy.

Phenothiazines can produce "extrapyramidal effects," such as spasms of the neck muscles, severe stiffness of the back muscles, rolling back of the eyes, convulsions, difficulty in swallowing, and symptoms associated with Parkinson's disease. These effects look very serious, but disappear after the drug has been withdrawn; however, symptoms of the face, tongue, and jaw may persist for as long as several years, especially in the elderly with a history of brain damage. If you experience extrapyramidal effects, contact your doctor immediately.

Fluphenazine Hydrochloride may cause an unusual increase in psychotic symptoms or may cause paranoid reactions, tiredness, lethargy, restlessness, hyperactivity, confusion at night, bizarre dreams, inability to sleep, depression, and euphoria. Other reactions are itching, swelling, unusual sensitivity to bright lights, red skin, and rash. There have been cases of breast enlargement, false positive pregnancy tests, changes in menstrual flow in females, and impotence and changes in sex drive in males. Fluphenazine Hydrochloride may also cause dry mouth, stuffy nose, headache, nausea, vomiting, loss of appetite, change in body temperature, loss of facial color, excessive salivation, excessive perspiration, constipation, diarrhea, changes in urine and stool habits, worsening of glaucoma, blurred vision, weakening of eyelid muscles, and spasms in bronchial and other muscles, as well as increased appetite, fatigue, excessive thirst, and changes in the coloration of skin, particularly in exposed areas.

Drug Interactions

Fluphenazine Hydrochloride should be taken with caution in combination with barbiturates, sleeping pills, narcotics, or any other medication which may produce a depressive effect. Avoid alcohol.

Usual Dose

0.5 to 10 milligrams per day in divided doses. (The lowest effective dose should be used.) Few people will require more than 3 milligrams per day, although some have required 20 milligrams or more per day.

Elderly: Geriatric patients usually require lower doses of this drug than younger adults because they metabolize it more slowly.

Overdosage

Symptoms are depression, extreme weakness, tiredness, desire to go to sleep, coma, lowered blood pressure, uncontrolled muscle spasms, agitation, restlessness, convulsions, fever, dry mouth, and abnormal heart rhythms. The patient should be taken to a hospital emergency room immediately. ALWAYS bring the medicine bottle.

Generic Name

Flurandrenolide

Brand Names

Cordran Ointment/Lotion/Tape
Cordran SP Cream

Type of Drug

Corticosteroid.

Prescribed for

Relief of inflammation in a local skin area, itching, or other skin problems.

General Information

Flurandrenolide is used to relieve the symptom of any itching, rash, or inflammation of the skin. It does not treat the underlying cause of the skin problem, only the symptom. It exerts this effect by interfering with natural body mechanisms that produced the rash, itching, etc., in the first place. If you use this drug without finding the cause of the problem, the condition may return after you stop using the drug. Flurandrenolide should not be used without your doctor's consent because it could cover an important reaction, one that may be valuable to him in treating you.

Cautions and Warnings

Flurandrenolide should not be used if you have viral diseases of the skin (herpes), fungal infections of the skin (athlete's foot), or tuberculosis of the skin, nor should it be used in the ear if the eardrum has been perforated. Don't use this medicine if you are allergic to any of the components of the ointment, cream, lotion, or tape.

Possible Side Effects

Burning sensations, itching, irritation, dryness of the skin, secondary infection.

Special Information

Clean the skin before applying Flurandrenolide in a very thin film (effectiveness is based on contact area and not on the thickness of the layer applied).

Generic Name

Flurazepam

Brand Name

Dalmane

Type of Drug

Sedative-sleeping medicine.

Prescribed for

Insomnia or sleeplessness, frequent nighttime awakening, or waking up too early in the morning.

General Information

Flurazepam is a member of the chemical group of drugs known as benzodiazepines. These drugs are used as either antianxiety agents, anticonvulsants, or sedatives (sleeping pills). They exert their effects by relaxing the large skeletal muscles and by a direct effect on the brain. In doing so, they can relax you and make you either more tranquil or sleepier, depending on the drug and how much you use. Many doctors prefer Flurazepam and the other members of this class to other drugs that can be used for the same effect. Their reason is that the benzodiazepines tend to be safer, have fewer side effects, and are usually as, if not more, effective.

These drugs are generally used in any situation where they can be a useful adjunct.

Benzodiazepine tranquilizing drugs can be abused if taken for long periods of time, and it is possible to develop withdrawal symptoms if you discontinue the therapy abruptly. Withdrawal symptoms include convulsions, tremor, muscle cramps, stomach cramps, insomnia, agitation, diarrhea, vomiting, sweating, and even convulsions.

Cautions and Warnings

Do not take Flurazepam if you know you are sensitive or allergic to this drug or to other benzodiazepines such as Chlordiazepoxide, Oxazepam, Clorazepate, Diazepam, Lorazepam, Prazepam, and Clonazepam.

Flurazepam and other members of this drug group may aggravate narrow angle glaucoma, but if you have open angle glaucoma you may take the drugs. In any case, check this information with your doctor. Flurazepam can cause tiredness, drowsiness, inability to concentrate, or similar symptoms. Be careful if you are driving, operating machinery, or performing other activities which require concentration. Avoid taking this drug during the first 3 months of pregnancy except under strict supervision of your doctor.

Possible Side Effects

Most common: mild drowsiness during the first few days of therapy, especially in the elderly or debilitated. If drowsiness persists, contact your doctor.

Possible Adverse Drug Effects

Major adverse reactions: confusion, depression, lethargy, disorientation, headache, lack of activity, slurred speech, stupor, dizziness, tremor, constipation, dry mouth, nausea, inability to control urination, changes in sex drive, irregular menstrual cycle, changes in heart rhythm, lowered blood pressure, retention of fluids, blurred or double vision, itching, rash, hiccups, nervousness, inability to fall asleep, (occasional) liver dysfunction. If you experience any of these reactions stop taking the medicine and contact your doctor immediately.

Drug Interactions

Flurazepam is a central nervous system depressant. Avoid

alcohol, tranquilizers, narcotics, sleeping pills, barbiturates, MAO inhibitors, antihistamines, and other medicines used to relieve depression.

Usual Dose

15 to 30 milligrams at bedtime. Must be individualized for maximum benefit.

Overdosage

Symptoms are confusion, sleep or sleepiness, lack of response to pain such as a pin stick, shallow breathing, lowered blood pressure, and coma. The patient should be taken to a hospital emergency room immediately. ALWAYS bring the medicine bottle.

Generic Name

Furosemide

Brand Name

Lasix

Type of Drug

Diuretic.

Prescribed for

Congestive heart failure, cirrhosis of the liver, kidney dysfunction, high blood pressure, and other conditions where it may be desirable to rid the body of excess fluid.

General Information

Furosemide causes the production of urine by affecting the kidneys. It may also cause lowered blood pressure. Furosemide is particularly useful as a very strong drug with great diuretic potential, when a drug with less diuretic potential would fail to produce the desired therapeutic effect.

Cautions and Warnings

Furosemide if given in excessive quantities will cause depletion of water and electrolytes. It should not be taken without constant medical supervision and unless the dose has been adjusted to your particular needs. You should not take this drug if your production of urine has been decreased abnormally by some type of kidney disease, or if you feel you may be allergic to it or if you have experienced an allergic reaction to it in the past. Although Furosemide has been used to treat specific conditions in pregnancy, it should generally not be used to treat a pregnant woman because of its potential effects on the unborn child. If your doctor feels that your case warrants the use of Furosemide, the decision to use this drug must be made by you and your doctor based on the potential benefits derived from this drug as opposed to the potential problems that may be associated with its use. If you must take this drug during the period that you are nursing a newborn baby, you should stop nursing and feed the baby prepared formulas. Excessive use of Furosemide will result in dehydration or reduction in blood volume, and may cause circulatory collapse and other related problems, particularly in the elderly. In addition, because of the potent effect that this drug has on the electrolytes in the blood—potassium, sodium, carbon dioxide, and others—frequent laboratory evaluations of these electrolytes should be performed during the few months of therapy, and periodically afterward.

Possible Side Effects

If you are taking Furosemide you should be aware that changes may develop in potassium and other electrolyte concentrations in your body. In the case of lower potassium produced by Furosemide (hypokalemia), you may observe these warning signs: dryness of the mouth, thirst, weakness, lethargy, drowsiness, restlessness, muscle pains or cramps, muscular tiredness, low blood pressure, decreased frequency of urination and decreased amount of urine produced, abnormal heart rate, and stomach upset including nausea and vomiting. To treat this, potassium supplements are given in the form of tablets, liquids, or powders or by increased consumption of potassium-rich foods such as bananas, citrus fruits, melons, and tomatoes.

Furosemide may alter the metabolism of sugar in your body. If you have diabetes mellitus, you may develop high blood sugar or sugar in the urine while you are taking the drug. To treat this problem, the dose of drugs that you are taking to treat your diabetes will have to be altered.

In addition, people taking Furosemide have experienced one or more of the following side effects: abdominal discomfort, nausea, vomiting, diarrhea, rash, dizziness, lightheadedness, weakness, headache, blurred vision, fatigue, jaundice or yellowing of the skin or whites of the eyes, acute attacks of gout, ringing in the ears, reversible periodic impairment in hearing. There have also been some reported cases of irreversible hearing loss.

Possible Adverse Drug Effects

Dermatitis, unusual skin reactions, tingling in the extremities, postural hypotension (or dizziness on rising quickly from a sitting or lying position), anemia of various types. Rare: a sweet taste in the mouth, burning feeling in the stomach and/or mouth, thirst, increased perspiration, frequent urination.

Drug Interactions

Furosemide will increase (potentiate) the action of other blood-pressure-lowering drugs. This is beneficial, and is frequently used to help lower blood pressure in patients with hypertension.

The possibility of developing electrolyte imbalances in body fluids is increased if you take other medications such as Digitalis and adrenal corticosteroids while you are taking Furosemide.

If you are taking Furosemide because of congestive heart failure and are also taking Digitalis, loss of potassium may significantly affect the toxicity of Digitalis. For this reason, foods which are high in potassium, including bananas, citrus fruits, melons, and tomatoes, should be given high priority in your daily diet.

If you are taking an oral antidiabetic drug and begin taking Furosemide, the antidiabetic dose may have to be altered.

If you are taking Lithium Carbonate, you should probably not take a diuretic, which by reducing the elimination of lithium from the blood adds a high risk of lithium toxicity.

Interaction with aminoglycoside antibiotics may cause periodic hearing losses; make sure your doctor knows you are taking Furosemide before he gives you an injection of an aminoglycoside.

If you are taking high doses of Aspirin to treat arthritis or similar diseases, and you begin to take Furosemide, you may have to lower the dose of Aspirin because of the effect Furosemide has on passage of Aspirin through the kidneys.

If you are taking Furosemide for the treatment of high blood pressure or congestive heart failure, avoid over-the-counter drug products for the treatment of coughs, colds, and allergies which may contain stimulant drugs. Check with your pharmacist, who can give you accurate information about any over-the-counter drug and its potential interactions with Furosemide.

Usual Dose

Adult: 20 to 80 milligrams per day, depending on disease and patient's response. Doses of 600 milligrams per day or even more have been prescribed.

Infant or child: 4 to 5 milligrams per pound of body weight daily in a single dose. If therapy is not successful, the dose may be increased by steps of 2 to 5 milligrams, but not to more than 14 to 15 milligrams per day.

Maintenance doses are adjusted to the minimum effective level.

Special Information

If the amount of urine you produce each day is dropping or if you suffer from significant loss of appetite, muscle weakness, tiredness, or nausea while taking this drug, contact your doctor immediately.

Generic Name

Gamma Benzene Hexachloride (Lindane)

Brand Names

GBH
Kwell

Type of Drug

Parasiticide.

Prescribed for

Topical treatment of head lice, crab lice, and scabies.

General Information

Gamma Benzene Hexachloride is considered to be the most effective agent against lice and scabies by many authorities. It should only be used when prescribed by a physician because it cannot prevent infestation, it can only treat it. Also, this medication is extremely irritating, particularly when applied to the eyelids and genital areas. If allowed to remain in contact with the skin for too long, Gamma Benzene Hexachloride will be absorbed directly into the bloodstream, causing signs of drug overdose.

Possible Side Effect

Skin rash.

Usual Dose

For head lice: pour 1 ounce of shampoo on the affected area; rub vigorously; be sure to wet all hairy areas. Wet hair with warm water and work into a full lather for at least 4 minutes. Rinse hair thoroughly and rub with a dry towel. Comb with a fine-tooth comb to remove any remaining nit shells. A second application is usually not needed, but may be made after 24 hours if necessary. The drug should not be used more than twice in 1 week. The shampoo may also be used for crab lice.

For crab lice: after a bath or shower, apply a thin layer of lotion to hairy areas and over the skin of adjacent areas. Leave on for 12 to 24 hours, then wash thoroughly and put on freshly laundered or dry-cleaned clothing. Repeat after 4 days if necessary.

For scabies: after a bath or shower, apply a thin layer of the lotion over the entire skin surface. Leave on for 24 hours, then wash thoroughly. If necessary, a second and third weekly application may be made.

Overdosage

Anyone who ingests this drug accidentally should be taken to a hospital emergency room immediately. When taken internally, Gamma Benzene Hexachloride is a stimulant; the patient may require Phenobarbital or a similar depressant to neutralize the effect.

If contact with your eyes occurs during shampoo or other use, flush the eyes and surrounding area with water. If irritation or sensitization occurs, discontinue use and call a doctor.

Brand Name

Gaviscon

Ingredients

Alginic Acid
Aluminum Hydroxide Dried Gel
Magnesium Trisilicate
Sodium Bicarbonate

Type of Drug

Antacid.

Prescribed for

Heartburn, acid indigestion, or sour stomach.

General Information

Gaviscon is one of many commercial antacid products on the market. Antacids are used by many people for the relief of temporary symptoms associated with indigestion caused by drugs, food, or disease. For more information on Antacids see page 42.

Cautions and Warnings

Do not use this antacid if you are on a sodium-restricted diet.

Possible Side Effects

Occasional constipation or diarrhea if taken in large quantities.

Drug Interactions

Do not take this drug if you are taking a Tetracycline derivative, antibiotic, Digoxin, Phenytoin, Quinidine, Warfarin, or oral iron supplement. The antacid may interfere with the effective absorption of these drugs.

Usual Dose

Chew 2 to 4 tablets 4 times per day, as needed. Do not take more than 16 tablets per day.

Overdosage

Take the patient to an emergency facility. Bring the medication.

Storage

Store the medication at room temperature in a dry place.

Special Information

Do not swallow these tablets whole—they must be chewed.

Generic Name

Glutethimide

Brand Names

Doriden
Dormtabs

Type of Drug

Sedative-hypnotic.

Prescribed for

Inability to sleep.

General Information

Sleep is produced within 30 minutes and lasts 4 to 8 hours.

Cautions and Warnings

Glutethimide should not be used if you are sensitive or allergic to it. It can be addictive.

Possible Side Effect

Skin rash.

Possible Adverse Drug Effects

There have been reports of nausea, morning hangover, rash, excitation, and blurred vision.

Drug Interactions

Do not take this drug with alcohol and/or other depressants such as sedatives, hypnotics, and antihistamines which may produce drowsiness or sleepiness.

Doses of anticoagulant (blood-thinning) drugs such as Warfarin may require adjustment because of increased effects. Dosage adjustment will also be required when you stop taking Glutethimide.

Usual Dose

1 tablet at bedtime; if necessary, repeat after 4 hours.

Overdosage

Large amounts of Glutethimide can be fatal, and the drug is frequently used in suicide attempts. Symptoms are coma, lowered body temperature followed by fever, absence of normal reflexes and pain responses after pinches and needle or pin sticks, and shallow breathing. The patient should be taken to a hospital emergency room immediately.

People who have taken Glutethimide for a long time may show signs of chronic overdosage: loss of memory, inability to concentrate, shakes, tremors, loss of reflexes, slurring of speech, and general sense of depression. Abrupt discontinuation of Glutethimide often causes withdrawal reactions of nervousness, anxiety, seizures, cramping, chills, numbness of the extremities, and general behavior changes. Chronic overdosage is best treated by withdrawing the drug over a period of days or weeks.

Generic Name

Guanethidine Sulfate

Brand Name

Ismelin

Type of Drug

Antihypertensive.

Prescribed for

High blood pressure.

General Information

Guanethidine Sulfate affects the section of the nervous system which controls pressure in the major blood vessels. Its blood-pressure-lowering effect is enhanced when taken along with other medicines, such as diuretics.

Cautions and Warnings

Patients who may be allergic to this drug, who are taking an MAO inhibitor, or who also have a tumor called a pheochromocytoma should not take Guanethidine Sulfate.

Possible Side Effects

Dizziness, weakness, especially on rising quickly from a sitting or prone position, slowed heartbeat, increased bowel movements, possibly severe diarrhea, male impotence (difficult ejaculation), retention of fluid in the body.

Possible Adverse Drug Effects

Difficulty in breathing, fatigue, nausea, vomiting, increased frequency of nighttime urination, difficulty in controlling urinary function, itching, rash, loss of scalp hair, dry mouth, involuntary lowering of eyelids, blurred vision, muscle aches and spasms, mental depression, chest pains (angina pectoris), tingling in the chest, stuffed nose, weight gain, asthma in some patients. This drug may affect kidney function.

Drug Interactions

Guanethidine Sulfate may interact with digitalis drugs to slow heart rates excessively. When taken with other blood-pressure-lowering drugs it can lower pressure excessively. Otherwise, this is a useful interaction that is sometimes used in treating hypertension (high blood pressure).

Drugs with stimulant properties (antidepressants, decongestants), oral contraceptives, and some antipsychotic drugs (phenothiazines, etc.) may reduce the effectiveness of Guanethidine Sulfate. The drug should not be taken together with MAO inhibitors, which should be stopped at least 1 week before taking Guanethidine Sulfate.

Avoid over-the-counter cough, cold, or allergy medicines which may contain stimulants. Check with your doctor or pharmacist before combining these medicines.

Usual Dose

10 milligrams per day to start. Dose is adjusted according to patient's need. Average daily requirement is 25 to 50 milligrams.

Overdosage

Symptoms are basically exaggerated or prolonged side effects, including dizziness, weakness, slowed heartbeat, and possible diarrhea. Call your doctor immediately if the symptoms appear or if you think you have these symptoms.

Special Information

Do not stop taking this medication unless specifically directed to. Call your doctor if you develop frequent diarrhea or are often dizzy or faint. Alcoholic beverages, heat, and strenuous exercise may increase the chances of dizziness or faintness developing.

Generic Name

Halazepam

Trade Name

Paxipam

Type of Drug

Tranquilizer.

Prescribed for

Relief of symptoms of anxiety, tension, fatigue, and agitation.

General Information

Halazepam is a member of the chemical group of drugs

known as benzodiazepines. These drugs are used either as antianxiety agents, anticonvulsants, or sedatives (sleeping pills). They exert their effects by relaxing the large skeletal muscles and by a direct effect on the brain. In doing so, they can relax you and make you either more tranquil or sleepier, depending upon which drug you use and how much you take. Many doctors prefer the benzodiazepines to other drugs that can be used for the same effects. Their reason is that these drugs tend to be safer, have fewer side effects, and are usually as, if not more, effective. The benzodiazepines are generally prescribed in any situation where they can be a useful adjunct.

The benzodiazepines, including Halazepam, can be abused if taken for long periods of time and it is possible to experience withdrawal symptoms if you stop taking the drug abruptly. Withdrawal symptoms include tremor, muscle cramps, stomach cramps, vomiting, insomnia, and convulsions.

Cautions and Warnings

Do not take Halazepam if you know you are sensitive or allergic to this drug or other benzodiazepines such as Diazepam, Oxazepam, Chlorazepate, Lorazepam, Prazepam, Flurazepam, and Clonazepam. Halazepam and other members of this group can aggravate narrow angle glaucoma, but if you have open angle glaucoma you may take the drug. In any case, check with your doctor. Halazepam can cause tiredness, drowsiness, inability to concentrate, or similar symptoms. Be careful if you are driving, operating machinery, or performing other activities which require concentration. Avoid taking this drug during the first 3 months of pregnancy except under strict supervision of your doctor.

Possible Side Effects

Most common: mild drowsiness during the first few days of therapy, especially in the elderly or debilitated. If drowsiness persists, contact your doctor.

Possible Adverse Drug Effects

Major adverse reactions: confusion, depression, lethargy, disorientation, headache, inactivity, slurred speech, stupor, dizziness, tremor, constipation, dry mouth, nausea, inability to control urination, changes in sex drive, irregular menstrual cycle, changes in heart rhythm, lowered blood pressure, fluid retention, blurred or double vision, itching, rash, hiccups, nervousness, inability to fall asleep, and occasional liver dysfunction. If you experience any of these symptoms, stop taking the medicine and contact your doctor immediately.

Drug Interactions

Halazepam is a central nervous system depressant. Avoid alcohol, other tranquilizers, narcotics, barbiturates, MAO inhibitors, antihistamines, and medicine used to relieve depression. Taking Halazepam with these drugs may result in excessive depression, tiredness, sleepiness, difficulty breathing, or similar symptoms. Smoking may reduce the effectiveness of Halazepam by increasing the rate at which it is broken down in the body. The effects of Halazepam may be prolonged when taken together with Cimetidine.

Usual Dose

60 to 160 milligrams per day. The dose must be tailored to the individual needs of the patient. Elderly or debilitated patients will require less of the drug to control anxiety and tension. This drug should not be used in children.

Overdosage

Symptoms are: confusion, sleepiness, lack of response to pain such as a pin stick, shallow breathing, lowered blood pressure, and coma. The patient should be taken to a hospital emergency room. ALWAYS bring the medicine bottle.

Special Information

Do not drink alcoholic beverages or take other depressive drugs, such as tranquilizers, sleeping pills, narcotics, or barbiturates when taking Halazepam. Tell your doctor if you become pregnant or are nursing an infant. Take care while driving or operating machinery.

Generic Name

Haloperidol

Brand Name

Haldol

Type of Drug

Butyrophenone antipsychotic.

Prescribed for

Psychotic disorders and to help control an unusual disorder: Gilles de la Tourette's syndrome; short-term treatment of hyperactive children.

General Information

Haloperidol is one of many nonphenothiazine agents used in the treatment of psychosis. The drugs in this group are usually about equally effective when given in therapeutically equivalent doses. The major differences are in type and severity of side effects. Some patients may respond well to one and not at all to another: this variability is not easily explained and is thought to result from inborn biochemical differences.

Cautions and Warnings

Haloperidol should not be used by patients who are allergic to it. Patients with blood, liver, kidney, or heart disease, very low blood pressure, or Parkinson's disease should avoid this drug.

Possible Side Effects

Most common: drowsiness, especially during the first or second week of therapy. If the drowsiness becomes trouble-some, contact your doctor.

Possible Adverse Drug Effects

Halperidol can cause jaundice (yellowing of the whites of the eyes or skin), usually in 2 to 4 weeks. The jaundice usually goes away when the drug is discontinued, but there have been cases when it did not. If you notice this effect or if you develop fever and generally do not feel well, contact your doctor immediately. Less frequent: changes in components of the blood including anemias, raised or lowered blood pressure, abnormal heartbeat, heart attack, feeling faint or dizzy.

Butyrophenone drugs can produce extrapyramidal effects such as spasms of the neck muscles, severe stiffness of the back muscles, rolling back of the eyes, convulsions, difficulty in swallowing, and symptoms associated with Parkinson's disease. These effects look very serious but disappear after the drug has been withdrawn; however, symptoms of the face, tongue, and jaw may persist for several years, especially in the elderly with a long history of brain disease. If you experience these extrapyramidal effects contact your doctor immediately.

Haloperidol may cause an unusual increase in psychotic symptoms or may cause paranoid reactions, tiredness, lethargy, restlessness, hyperactivity, confusion at night, bizarre dreams, inability to sleep, depression, or euphoria. Other reactions are itching, swelling, unusual sensitivity to bright lights, red skin, and rash. There have been cases of breast enlargement, false positive pregnancy tests, changes in menstrual flow in females, impotence and changes in sex drive in males.

Haloperidol may also cause dry mouth, stuffy nose, headache, nausea, vomiting, loss of appetite, change in body temperature, loss of facial color, excessive salivation, excessive perspiration, constipation, diarrhea, changes in urine and stool habits, worsening of glaucoma, blurred vision, weakening of eyelid muscles, and spasms in bronchial and other muscles, as well as increased appetite, fatigue, excessive thirst, and changes in the coloration of skin, particularly in exposed areas.

Drug Interactions

Haloperidol should be taken with caution in combination with barbiturates, sleeping pills, narcotics, or any other medication which produces a depressive effect. Avoid alcohol.

Haloperidol may increase the need for anticonvulsant medicine in patients who must take both drugs. It may interfere with oral anticoagulant drugs. Any dosage adjustment necessary can easily be made by your doctor.

Usual Dose

Adult: ½ to 2 milligrams 2 to 3 times per day. Dose may be increased according to patient's need up to 100 milligrams per day.

Child: not recommended.

Overdosage

Symptoms are depression, extreme weakness, tiredness, desire to go to sleep, coma, lowered blood pressure, uncontrolled muscle spasms, agitation, restlessness, convulsions, fever, dry mouth, and abnormal heart rhythms. The patient should be taken to a hospital emergency room immediately. ALWAYS bring the medicine bottle.

Special Information

Haloperidol has been associated with birth defects but this has not definitely been established. Pregnant women should only use this drug when absolutely necessary.

Generic Name

Hydralazine Hydrochloride

Brand Names

Apresoline
Dralzine

Type of Drug

Antihypertensive.

Prescribed for

Essential hypertension (high blood pressure).

General Information

Although the mechanism of action is not completely understood, it is felt that Hydralazine Hydrochloride lowers blood pressure by enlarging the blood vessels throughout the body.

Cautions and Warnings

Long-term administration of large doses of Hydralazine Hydrochloride may produce an arthritislike syndrome in some people, although symptoms of this problem usually disappear when the drug is discontinued. Fever, chest pain, not feeling well, or other unexplained symptoms should be reported to your doctor.

Possible Side Effects

Common: headache, loss of appetite, nausea, vomiting, diarrhea, rapid heartbeat, chest pain.

Possible Adverse Drug Effects

Most frequent: stuffy nose, flushing, tearing in the eyes, itching and redness of the eyes, numbness and tingling of the hands and feet, dizziness, tremors, muscle cramps, depression, disorientation, anxiety. Less frequent: itching, rash, fever, chills, (occasional) hepatitis, constipation, difficulty in urination, adverse effects on the normal composition of the blood.

Drug Interactions

Hydralazine Hydrochloride should be used with caution by patients who are taking MAO inhibitors.

Usual Dose

Tailored to your needs, like other antihypertensive drugs. Most people begin with 40 milligrams per day for the first few days, then increase to 100 milligrams per day for the rest of the first week. Dose increases until the maximum effect is seen.

Overdosage

If symptoms of extreme lowering of blood pressure, rapid heartbeat, headache, generalized skin flushing, chest pains, and poor heart rhythms appear, contact your doctor immediately.

Special Information

Take this medicine exactly as prescribed.

Do not self-medicate with over-the-counter cough, cold, or

allergy remedies whose stimulant ingredients will increase blood pressure.

This drug should not be used if you are pregnant unless it is very strictly monitored by your doctor.

Generic Name

Hydrochlorothiazide

Brand Names

Chlorzide	Hydro-Z
Diaqua	Hyperetic
Diu-Scrip	Jen-Diril
Esidrix	Lexor
Hydro-Schlor	Oretic
HydroDIURIL	SK Hydrochlorothiazide
Hydromal	Zide

Type of Drug

Diuretic.

Prescribed for

Congestive heart failure, cirrhosis of the liver, kidney malfunction, high blood pressure, and other conditions where it is necessary to rid the body of excess fluid.

General Information

This drug is a member of the class known as thiazide diuretics. Thiazides act on the kidneys to stimulate the production of large amounts of urine. They also cause you to lose bicarbonate, chloride, and potassium ions from the body. They are used as part of the treatment of any disease where it is desirable to eliminate large quantities of body water. These diseases include heart failure, some kidney diseases, and liver disease.

Cautions and Warnings

Do not take Hydrochlorothiazide if you are allergic or sensitive to this drug, similar drugs of this group, or sulfa drugs.

If you have a history of allergy or bronchial asthma, you may also have a sensitivity or allergy to Hydrochlorothiazide. Although this drug has been used to treat specific conditions in pregnancy, unsupervised use by pregnant patients should be avoided. Hydrochlorothiazide will cross the placenta and pass into the unborn child, possibly causing problems. The drug will pass into the breast milk of nursing mothers.

Possible Side Effects

Hydrochlorothiazide will cause a lowering of potassium in the body. Signs of low potassium are dryness of the mouth, thirst, weakness, lethargy, drowsiness, restlessness, muscle pains or cramps, muscular tiredness, low blood pressure, decreased frequency of urination and decreased amount of urine produced, abnormal heart rate, stomach upset including nausea and vomiting.

To treat this, potassium supplements are given in the form of tablets, liquids, or powders, or by increased consumption of foods such as bananas, citrus fruits, melons, and tomatoes.

Possible Adverse Drug Effects

Loss of appetite, stomach upset, nausea, vomiting, cramping, diarrhea, constipation, dizziness, headache, tingling of the toes and fingers, restlessness, changes in blood composition, sensitivity to sunlight, rash, itching, fever, difficulty in breathing, allergic reactions, dizziness when rising quickly from a sitting or lying position, muscle spasms, weakness, blurred vision.

Drug Interactions

Hydrochlorothiazide will increase (potentiate) the action of other blood-pressure-lowering drugs. This is beneficial, and is frequently used to help lower blood pressure in patients with hypertension.

The possibility of developing imbalances in body fluids (electrolytes) is increased if you take medications such as Digitalis and adrenal corticosteroids while you take Hydrochlorothiazide.

If you are taking an oral antidiabetic drug and begin taking Hydrochlorothiazide, the antidiabetic dose may have to be altered.

Lithium Carbonate should not be taken with Hydrochlorothiazide because the combination may increase the risk of lithium toxicity.

If you are taking Hydrochlorothiazide for the treatment of high blood pressure or congestive heart failure, avoid over-the-counter medicines for the treatment of coughs, colds, and allergies: such medicines may contain stimulants. If you are unsure about them, ask your pharmacist.

Usual Dose

Adult: 25 to 200 milligrams per day, depending on condition treated. Maintenance dose, 25 to 100 milligrams per day; some patients may require up to 200 milligrams per day. It is recommended that you take this drug early in the morning, thus avoiding the possibility of your sleep being disturbed by the need to urinate.

Child: 1 milligram per pound of body weight per day in 2 doses.

Infant (under age 6 months): 1½ milligrams per pound per day in 2 doses.

The dose, individualized to your response, must be altered until maximum therapeutic response at minimum effective dose is reached.

Overdosage

Symptoms are large amount of urination, fatigue, and coma. The patient should be taken to a hospital emergency room immediately. ALWAYS bring the medicine bottle.

Brand Name

Hydropres

Ingredients

Hydrochlorothiazide
Reserpine

Type of Drug

Antihypertensive.

Prescribed for

High blood pressure.

General Information

Hydropres is a good example of a drug taking advantage of a drug interaction. Each of the drug ingredients works by different mechanisms to lower your blood pressure. The Hydrochlorothiazide relaxes the muscles in your veins and arteries and also helps reduce the volume of blood flowing through those blood vessels. Reserpine works on the nervous system to reduce the efficiency of nerve transmissions which are contributing to the increased pressure. These drugs complement each other so that their combined effect is better than the effect of either one alone.

It is essential that you take your medicine exactly as prescribed for maximum benefit.

An ingredient in this drug may cause excessive loss of potassium, which may lead to a condition called hypokalemia. Warning signs are dryness of mouth, excessive thirst, weakness, drowsiness, restlessness, muscle pains or cramps, muscular fatigue, lack of urination, abnormal heart rhythms, and upset stomach. If warning signs occur, call your doctor. You may need potassium from some outside source. This may be done by either taking a potassium supplement or by eating foods such as bananas, citrus fruits, melons, and tomatoes, which have high concentrations of potassium.

This drug should be stopped at the first sign of despondency, early morning insomnia, loss of appetite, or sexual impotence. Drug-induced depression may persist for several months after the drug has been discontinued; it has been known to be severe enough to result in suicide attempts. This drug should be used with care by women of childbearing age.

Cautions and Warnings

Do not take this drug if you have a history of mental depression, active peptic ulcer, or ulcerative colitis, or if you are sensitive or allergic to either of its ingredients, to similar drugs of the Hydrochlorothiazide group, or to sulfa drugs. If you have a history of allergy or bronchial asthma, you may also have a sensitivity or allergy to the Hydrochlorothiazide ingredient. Although the Hydrochlorothiazide ingredient has been used to treat specific conditions in pregnancy, unsupervised use by pregnant women should be avoided; the drug will cross the placenta and pass into the unborn child, possibly causing problems. The Hydrochlorothiazide ingredient will also pass into the breast milk of nursing mothers.

Possible Side Effects

Loss of appetite, stomach irritation, nausea, vomiting, cramps, diarrhea, constipation, dizziness, headache, tingling in the arms and legs, restlessness, chest pains, abnormal heart rhythms, drowsiness, depression, nervousness, anxiety, nightmares, glaucoma, blood disorders, rash, itching, fever, difficulty in breathing, muscle spasms, gout, weakness, high blood sugar, sugar in urine, blurred vision, stuffed nose, dryness of the mouth. Occasional: impotence or decreased sex drive.

Drug Interactions

Interaction with Digitalis or Quinidine may cause abnormal heart rhythms.

Interaction with drugs containing lithium may lead to toxic effects of lithium.

Avoid over-the-counter cough, cold, or allergy remedies containing stimulant drugs which may raise your blood pressure.

Usual Dose

Must be individualized to patient's response.

Generic Name

Hydroxyzine Hydrochloride

Brand Names

Atarax
Vistaril

Type of Drug

Antihistamine with antinausea and antianxiety properties.

Prescribed for

Nausea and vomiting; the management of emotional stress such as anxiety, tension, agitation or itching caused by allergies.

General Information

Hydroxyzine Hydrochloride may be of value in relieving temporary anxiety such as stress of dental or other minor surgical procedures, acute emotional problems, and the management of anxiety associated with stomach and digestive disorders, skin problems, and behavior difficulties in children. This drug has also been used in the treatment of alcoholism.

Cautions and Warnings

Hydroxyzine Hydrochloride should not be used if you know you are sensitive or allergic to this drug, or during early pregnancy.

Possible Side Effects

The primary side effect of Hydroxyzine Hydrochloride is drowsiness, but this disappears in a few days or when the dose is reduced. At higher doses, you may experience dry mouth and occasional tremors or convulsions.

Drug Interactions

Hydroxyzine Hydrochloride has a depressive effect on the nervous system, producing drowsiness and sleepiness. It should not be used with alcohol, sedatives, tranquilizers, antihistamines, or other depressants.

Usual Dose

Adult: 25 to 100 milligrams 3 to 4 times per day.
Child (age 6 and over): 5 to 25 milligrams 3 to 4 times per day.
Child (under age 6): 5 to 10 milligrams 3 to 4 times per day.

Special Information

Be aware of the depressive effect of Hydroxyzine Hydrochloride: be careful when driving or operating heavy or dangerous machinery.

Generic Name

Ibuprofen

Brand Name

Motrin

Type of Drug

Nonsteroid anti-inflammatory.

Prescribed for

Relief of pain and inflammation of joints and muscles; arthritis, mild to moderate pain of menstrual cramps, dental surgery and extractions, and athletic injuries such as sprains and strains.

General Information

Ibuprofen is one of several new drugs used to treat various types of pain and belongs to the chemical group known as propionic acid derivatives. These drugs reduce inflammation and share side effects, the most common of which are upset stomach and possible formation of ulcers. The drugs are roughly comparable to Aspirin in controlling the symptoms of arthritis and other pain and are used by some people who cannot tolerate Aspirin.

Cautions and Warnings

Do not take Ibuprofen if you are allergic or sensitive to this drug, Aspirin, or other nonsteroid anti-inflammatory drugs. Ibuprofen may cause stomach ulcers. This drug should not be used by patients with severe kidney disease. The safety of this drug for pregnant women has not been established and it is not recommended for them.

Possible Side Effects

Stomach upset, blurred vision, darkening of stool, changes in color vision, rash, weight gain, retention of fluids.

Possible Adverse Drug Effects

Most frequent: stomach upset, dizziness, headache, drowsiness, ringing in the ears. Others: heartburn, nausea, vomiting, bloating, gas in the stomach, stomach pain, diarrhea, constipation, dark stool, nervousness, insomnia, depression, confusion, tremor, loss of appetite, fatigue, itching, rash, double vision, abnormal heart rhythm, anemia or other changes in the composition of the blood, changes in liver function, loss of hair, tingling in the hands and feet, fever, breast enlargement, lowered blood sugar, effects on the kidneys. If symptoms appear, stop taking the medicine and see your doctor immediately.

Drug Interactions

Ibuprofen increases the action of Phenytoin, sulfa drugs, drugs used to control diabetes, and drugs used to thin the blood. If you are taking any of these medicines, be sure to discuss it with your doctor, who will probably change the dose of the other drug.

An adjustment in the dose of Ibuprofen may be needed if you take Phenobarbital.

Usual Dose

900 to 1600 or even 2400 milligrams per day. Take with meals to reduce stomach upset.

Generic Name

Imipramine

Brand Names

Antipress
Imavate
Janimine
Presamine

SK-Pramine
Tofranil
Tofranil-PM (long-acting
   dosage form)

Type of Drug

Antidepressant.

Prescribed for

Depression with or without symptoms of anxiety.

General Information

Imipramine and other members of this group are effective in treating symptoms of depression. They can elevate your mood, increase physical activity and mental alertness, improve appetite and sleep patterns. These drugs are mild sedatives and therefore useful in treating mild forms of depression associated with anxiety. You should not expect instant results with this medicine: benefits are usually seen after 1 to 4 weeks. If symptoms are not affected after 6 to 8 weeks, contact your doctor. Occasionally this drug and other members of the group of drugs have been used in treating night-time bed-wetting in the young child, but they do not produce long-lasting relief, and therapy with one of them for night-time bed-wetting is of questionable value.

Cautions and Warnings

Do not take Imipramine if you are allergic or sensitive to this or other members of this class of drug: Doxepin, Nortriptyline, Amitriptyline, Desipramine, and Protriptyline. The drugs should not be used if you are recovering from a heart attack. Imipramine may be taken with caution if you have a history of epilepsy or other convulsive disorders, difficulty in urination, glaucoma, heart disease, or thyroid disease. Imipramine can interfere with your ability to perform tasks which require concentration, such as driving or operating machinery. Do not stop taking this medicine without first discussing it with your doctor, since stopping may cause you to become nauseated, weak, and headachy. Imipramine will pass from mother to unborn child: consult your doctor before taking this medicine if you are pregnant.

Possible Side Effects

Changes in blood pressure (both high and low), abnormal heart rates, heart attack, confusion, especially in elderly patients, hallucinations, disorientation, delusions, anxiety, restlessness, excitement, numbness and tingling in the extremities, lack of coordination, muscle spasms or tremors, seizures and/or convulsions, dry mouth, blurred vision, constipation, inability to urinate, rash, itching, sensitivity to bright light or sunlight, retention of fluids, fever, allergy, changes in composition of blood, nausea, vomiting, loss of appetite, stomach upset, diarrhea, enlargement of the breasts in males and females, increased or decreased sex drive, increased or decreased blood sugar.

Possible Adverse Drug Effects

Infrequent: agitation, inability to sleep, nightmares, feeling of panic, peculiar taste in the mouth, stomach cramps, black coloration of the tongue, yellowing eyes and/or skin, changes in liver function, increased or decreased weight, perspiration, flushing, frequent urination, drowsiness, dizziness, weakness, headache, loss of hair, nausea, not feeling well.

Drug Interactions

Interaction with Monoamine oxidase (MAO) inhibitors can cause high fevers, convulsions, and occasionally death. Don't take MAO inhibitors until at least 2 weeks after Imipramine has been discontinued.

Imipramine interacts with Guanethidine and Clonidine, drugs used to treat high blood pressure: if your doctor prescribes Imipramine and you are taking medicine for high blood pressure, be sure to discuss this with him.

Imipramine increases the effects of barbiturates, tranquilizers, other depressive drugs, and alcohol. Don't drink alcoholic beverages if you take this medicine.

Taking Imipramine and thyroid medicine will enhance the effects of the thyroid medicine. The combination can cause abnormal heart rhythms. The combination of Imipramine and Reserpine may cause overstimulation.

Large doses of Vitamin C (Acsorbic Acid), oral contraceptives, or smoking can reduce the effect of Imipramine. Drugs such as Bicarbonate of Soda, Acetazolamide, Quinidine, or Procainamide will increase the effect of Imipramine. Ritalin and phenothiazine drugs such as Thorazine and Compazine block the metabolism of Imipramine, causing it to stay in the body longer. This can cause possible overdose.

The combination of Imipramine with large doses of the sleeping pill Ethchlorvynol has caused patients to experience passing delirium.

Usual Dose

Adult: initial dose, about 75 milligrams per day in divided doses; then increased or decreased as judged necessary by your doctor. The individualized dose may be less than 75 or up to 200 milligrams. Long-term patients being treated for depression may be given extended-acting medicine daily at bedtime or several times per day.

Adolescent or elderly: initial dose, 30 or 40 milligrams per day. These patients require less of the drug because of increased sensitivity. Maintenance dose is usually less than 100 milligrams per day.

Child: dose for nighttime bed-wetting is 25 milligrams per day (age 6 and over), an hour before bedtime. If relief of bed-wetting does not occur within 1 week, the dose is increased to a daily 50 to 75 milligrams, depending on age; often in midafternoon and at bedtime. (A dose greater than 75 milligrams will increase side effects without increasing effectiveness.) The medication should be gradually tapered off; this may reduce the probability that the bed-wetting will return.

Overdosage

Symptoms are confusion, inability to concentrate, hallucinations, drowsiness, lowered body temperature, abnormal heart rate, heart failure, large pupils of the eyes, convulsions, severely lowered blood pressure, stupor, and coma (as well as agitation, stiffening of body muscles, vomiting, and high fever). The patient should be taken to a hospital emergency room immediately. ALWAYS bring the medicine bottle.

Brand Name

Inderide

Ingredients

Hydrochlorothiazide
Propranolol

Type of Drug

Antihypertensive.

Prescribed for

High blood pressure.

General Information

Inderide is a combination of two proven antihypertensive drugs. One of these works by affecting body ions (sodium and potassium); the other works by affecting the nerves which control the dilating of your blood vessels. The more dilated (open) these vessels are, the lower the blood pressure. This combination is good so long as both ingredients are present in the right amounts. If you need more or less of one ingredient than the other, you must take the ingredients as separate pills. Often, doctors are able to lower your blood pressure most effectively by manipulating the doses of one drug or the other.

Cautions and Warnings

Do not take this drug if you are allergic to either of the active ingredients or to sulfa drugs. If you have a history of heart failure, asthma, or upper respiratory disease, Inderide may aggravate the situation.

Possible Side Effects

May decrease the heart rate, aggravate heart failure or some other heart diseases, cause a tingling in the hands or feet, light-headedness, depression, sleeplessness, weakness, tiredness, feeling of not caring, hallucinations, visual disturbances, disorientation, loss of short-term memory, nausea, vomiting, upset stomach, cramps, diarrhea, constipation, allergic reactions including: sore throat, rash, and fever. Inderide can also cause adverse effects on the blood.

Inderide can cause a lowering of body potassium (hypokalemia). The signs of this include dryness of the mouth, weakness, thirst, lethargy, drowsiness, restlessness, muscle pains or cramps, muscle tiredness, low blood pressure, decreased frequency of urination. To treat this, potassium supplements are given as tablets, liquids, or powders. You may increase your natural consumption of potassium by eating more bananas, citrus fruits, melons, or tomatoes.

Possible Adverse Drug Effects

Loss of appetite, dizziness, headache, increased sensitivity to the sun, dizziness when rising quickly from a sitting or lying position, muscle spasms and loss of hearing (it comes back after the drug has been stopped).

Drug Interactions

Inderide may interact with Reserpine and similar drugs to cause very low blood pressure, slowed heart rate, and dizziness.

Inderide may cause a need for the alteration of your daily dose of oral antidiabetic drug.

Inderide should not be taken with lithium drugs since there is an increased possibility of lithium toxicity. This drug may interact with digitalis drugs to cause abnormal heart rhythms. This effect results from potassium loss and may be prevented by taking extra potassium.

Usual Dose

4 tablets of either strength per day. The dose of this drug must be tailored to your needs for maximum benefit.

Overdosage

In case of overdosage contact your doctor or poison control center immediately. The patient may have to be taken to a hospital emergency room for treatment. ALWAYS bring the medicine bottle with you.

Special Information

Do not stop taking this medicine unless your doctor tells you to.

If you develop rash, severe muscle pains, or difficulty in breathing, call your doctor.

Avoid any over-the-counter drugs containing stimulants. If you are unsure which ones to avoid, ask your pharmacist.

Generic Name

Indomethacin

Brand Name

Indocin

Type of Drug

Nonsteroid anti-inflammatory.

Prescribed for

Arthritis and other forms of inflammation of joints and muscles.

General Information

Indomethacin is one of the newer nonsteroid anti-inflammatory drugs available over the last 10 years or so; it has pain-relieving, fever-lowering, and inflammation-reducing effects, but we do not know exactly how these effects are produced. It also can produce serious side effects at high doses. For this reason, the drug should be taken with caution.

Cautions and Warnings

Use Indomethacin with extra caution if you have a history of ulcers, bleeding diseases, or allergic reaction to Aspirin. Indomethacin should be avoided by pregnant women, nursing mothers, children under age 14, and patients with nasal polyps. This drug is not a simple pain reliever; it should be used only under the strict supervision of your doctor.

Possible Side Effects

Indomethacin may produce severe stomach upset or other reactions. It has caused ulcers in all portions of the gastrointestinal tract, including the esophagus, stomach, small intestine, and large intestine. For this reason any unusual stomach upset, nausea, vomiting, loss of appetite, gas, gaseous feeling, or feeling of being bloated must be reported immediately to your doctor. Indomethacin may cause blurred vision: this is an important side effect and must be reported to your doctor immediately. If you develop a persistent headache while taking Indomethacin, report this to your doctor immediately and stop taking the drug.

Indomethacin may aggravate preexisting psychiatric disturbances, epilepsy, or Parkinson's disease. It may cause reduction in metal alertness and coordination which can affect you particularly while driving, operating a machine or appliance, or engaging in any activity requiring alertness and concentration.

Possible Adverse Drug Effects

On rare occasions Indomethacin can cause effects on the liver, and anemia or other effects on components of the blood. People who are allergic to the drug can develop reactions including a rapid fall in blood pressure, difficulty in breathing, itching, and rashes. It has also caused ringing in the ears, retention of fluids in the body, elevation of blood pressure, passing of blood in the urine, loss of hair, (occasional) vaginal bleeding, and increased blood sugar.

Drug Interactions

Avoid alcohol, which will aggravate any problem with drowsiness or lack of alertness.

Probenecid (Benemid) increases the amount of Indomethacin in your blood by reducing its elimination from the body. This interaction will reduce the amount of Indomethacin required.

If you are taking an anticoagulant (blood-thinning) drug and start taking Indomethacin, you probably will experience no serious interaction, but your doctor should know that you are taking both drugs so he can monitor the anticoagulant during the first week or two of Indomethacin therapy, in case dosage adjustment may be required.

Since Indomethacin causes stomach upset in many patients and can be a source of ulcers, it should be taken with food or antacids. Adrenal corticosteroids, Aspirin, or other drugs may aggravate this problem. Space Indomethacin and such drugs at least 2 to 3 hours apart to minimize irritating effects on the stomach.

Usual Dosage

50 to 150 milligrams per day, individualized to patient's needs.

Special Information

If you are allergic to Aspirin, you may be allergic to Indomethacin.

Generic Name

Insulin

Brand Names

Insulin for Injection

Actrapid	Pork Regular Iletin II
Beef Regular Iletin	Regular Iletin
Beef Regular Iletin II	Velosulin

Insulin Zinc Suspension

Beef Lente Insulin	Lente Iletin II
Lentard	Monotard
Lente Iletin	

Insulin Zinc Suspension, Extended

Ultralente Iletin	Ultratard
Ultralente Insulin	

Insulin Zinc Suspension, Prompt

Semilente Insulin   Semitard

Isophane Insulin Suspension and Insulin Injection

Mixtard

Isophane Insulin Suspension (NPH)

Beef NPH Iletin   NPH Iletin
Beef NPH Iletin II   Pork NPH Iletin II
Insulatard NPH   Protaphane
Isophane Insulin

Protamine Zinc Insulin Suspension

Beef Protamine, Zinc and Iletin
Pork Protamine, Zinc and Iletin
Protamine, Zinc and Iletin
Protamine Zinc Insulin

Type of Drug

Antidiabetic.

Prescribed For

Diabetes mellitus that cannot be controlled by dietary restriction. Insulin may also be used in a hospital to treat hyperkalemia (high blood potassium levels).

General Information

Insulin is a complex hormone normally produced by the pancreas. Diabetes develops when we do not make enough insulin or when the insulin we do make is not effective in our bodies. At the present, the Insulin we use as a drug we get from animals. Insulin derived from pork is closer in chemical structure to our own insulin than that derived from beef. It causes fewer reactions.

Insulin used for injection is the unmodified material derived from the animal source. It starts to work quickly, and lasts only 6 to 8 hours. People using only Insulin injection must take several injections per day. Pharmaceutical scientists have been able to add on to the Insulin molecule so as to help extend the time over which the drug can exert its effect. Insulin Zinc Suspension, like Insulin for injection, is considered rapid-acting. It starts to work in 30 to 60 minutes and lasts 12 to 16 hours.

Intermediate-acting Insulin starts working 1 to 1½ hours after injection and continues to work for 24 hours. Isophane Insulin Suspension and Insulin Zinc Suspension are intermediate-acting forms of Insulin. Long-acting Insulin begins working 4 to 8 hours after injection and its effect lasts for 36 hours or more. Protamine Zinc Insulin Suspension and Insulin Zinc Suspension, Extended, are long-acting types of Insulin.

Other factors have a definite influence on patients' response to Insulin: diet, amount of regular exercise, and other medicines being used.

Because Insulin is derived from a natural source, there are a number of normal contaminants in the products. In recent years, processes have been developed to remove many of these contaminants. The first process resulted in single-peak Insulin, with only one high point of drug effect, making the action of the drug more predictable and therefore safer. Today, all Insulin sold in the United States is single-peak. The second refinement resulted in purified Insulin. Several purified Insulin products are available. The advantage of purified Insulin over single-peak is that it produces fewer reactions at the injection site.

Cautions and Warnings

Patients taking Insulin *must* also follow the diet that has been prescribed. Be sure to take exactly the dose prescribed. Too much Insulin will cause lowering of the blood sugar and too little will not control the diabetes. Avoid alcoholic beverages.

Possible Side Effects

Allergic reactions.

Drug Interactions

Insulin may affect blood potassium levels and can therefore affect digitalis drugs. Patients on Insulin who begin taking oral contraceptive pills, adrenal corticosteroids (by mouth), Epinephrine, or thyroid hormones may have an increased need for Insulin. Thiazide diuretic drugs can raise blood sugar levels and cause a need for more Insulin. The blood-sugar-lowering effects of Insulin can be increased by MAO inhibitor drugs, Phenylbutazone, Sulfinpyrazone, Tetracycline, alcoholic beverages, and anabolic steroid drugs (Oxymetholone, Oxandrolone, Methandrostenolone, Ethylestrenol, Stanozolol, Nandrolone). Patients taking these drugs may require a decrease in their Insulin dosage.

Usual Dose

The dose and kind of Insulin must be individualized to the patient's need. Insulin is generally injected ½ hour before meals; the longer-acting forms are taken ½ hour before breakfast. Since Insulin can only be given by injection, patients must learn to give themselves their Insulin subcutaneously (under the skin) or have a family member or friend give them their injection. Hospitalized patients may receive Insulin injection directly into a vein.

Special Information

You may develop low blood sugar if you take too much Insulin, work or exercise more strenuously than usual, skip a meal, take Insulin too long before a meal, or vomit before a meal. Signs of low blood sugar may be fatigue, headache, drowsiness, nausea, tremulous feeling, sweating, or nervousness. If you develop any of these signs while taking Insulin, your blood sugar may be too low. The usual treatment for low blood sugar is eating a candy bar or lump of sugar, which diabetics should carry with them at all times. If the signs of low blood sugar do not clear up within 30 minutes, call your doctor. You may need further treatment.

If your Insulin is in suspension form, you must evenly distribute the suspended particles throughout the liquid before taking the dose out. Do this by rotating the vial and turning it over several times. Do not shake the vial too strenuously.

Insulin products are generally stable at room temperatures for about 2 years. They must be kept away from direct sunlight. Most manufacturers, however, still recommend that Insulin be stored in a refrigerator or a cool place whenever possible. Insulin should not be put in a freezer or exposed to very high temperatures; this can affect its stability. Partly used vials of Insulin should be thrown away after several weeks if not used.

Some Insulin products can be mixed. Do it only if so directed by your doctor. Insulin for injection may be mixed with Isophane Insulin Suspension and Protamine Zinc Insulin in any proportion. Insulin Zinc Suspension, Insulin Zinc Suspension (Prompt), and Insulin Zinc Suspension (Extended) may also be mixed in any proportions. Insulin for injection and Insulin Zinc Suspension must be mixed immediately before using.

Generic Name

Isosorbide Dinitrate

Brand Names

Iso-Bid	Isotrate
Isogard	Isotrate Timecelles
Isordil	Sorate
Isordil Sublingual	Sorbide T.D.
Isordil Tembids	Sorbitrate
Isordil Titradose	Sorbitrate SA

Type of Drug

Antianginal agent.

Prescribed for

Relief of heart or chest pain associated with angina pectoris; also, control or prevention of recurrence of chest or heart pain.

General Information

Isosorbide Dinitrate belongs to the class of drugs known as nitrates, which are used to treat pain associated with heart problems. The exact nature of their action is not fully understood. However, they are believed to relax muscles of veins and arteries.

Cautions and Warnings

If you know that you are allergic or sensitive to this drug or other drugs for heart pain such as Nitroglycerin, do not use Isosorbide Dinitrate. Anyone who has a head injury or has recently had a head injury should use this drug with caution.

Possible Side Effects

Flushing of the skin and headache are common, but should disappear after your body has had an opportunity to get used to the drug. You may experience dizziness and weakness in the process.

There is a possibility of blurred vision and dry mouth; if this happens stop taking the drug and call your physician.

Possible Adverse Drug Effects

Nausea, vomiting, weakness, sweating, rash with itching, redness, possible peeling. If these signs appear, discontinue the medication and consult your physician.

Drug Interactions

If you take Isosorbide Dinitrate, do not self-medicate with over-the-counter cough and cold remedies, since many of them contain ingredients which may aggravate heart disease.

Interaction with large amounts of whiskey, wine, or beer can cause rapid lowering of blood pressure resulting in weakness, dizziness, and fainting.

Usual Dose

Average daily dose, 40 milligrams. The drug may be given in doses from 5 milligrams 2 to 3 times per day to 40 milligrams 4 times per day.

Special Information

Take Isosorbide Dinitrate on an empty stomach unless you get a headache which cannot be controlled by the usual means, when the medication can be taken with meals. If you take this drug sublingually (under the tongue) be sure the tablet is fully dissolved before swallowing the drug.

Generic Name

Isoxsuprine Hydrochloride

Brand Names

Vasodilan
Vasoprine

Type of Drug

Vasodilator.

Prescribed for

Relief of symptoms arising from chronic organic brain syndrome; specifically, loss of memory and other intellectual functions. Also used to prevent the progress of this disease and at times to help reverse the disease process.

General Information

Isoxsuprine Hydrochloride works by helping to increase the amount of blood supplied to the brain, by acting on the nerves that control muscles in the major blood vessels, which relaxes the muscles and allows more blood to flow to the brain. Many studies have questioned the effectiveness of this drug. However, it continues to be widely used and prescribed.

Possible Side Effects

Isoxsuprine Hydrochloride can cause low blood pressure. In this condition blood tends to stay in the arms and legs and less is available to the brain, resulting in light-headedness or dizziness. To avoid this, if you are taking Isoxsuprine Hydrochloride or any other vasodilator do not stand for long periods and be careful not to get out of bed or stand up too quickly.

Possible Adverse Drug Effects

Rapid heartbeat, nausea, vomiting, dizziness, stomach distress, severe rash. If you develop a rash, stop taking the drug and consult your doctor immediately.

Drug Interactions

Alcoholic beverages increase the effect of Isoxsuprine Hydro-chloride and can cause dizziness or faintness.

Usual Dose

10 to 20 milligrams 3 to 4 times per day.

Generic Name

Levodopa (L-Dopa)

Brand Names

Bendopa
Dopar
Lavodopa

Type of Drug

Anti-Parkinsonian.

Prescribed for

Parkinson's disease.

General Information

Parkinson's disease can develop as a result of brain inflammation or damage to the central nervous system caused by carbon monoxide poisoning or manganese poisoning. It usually develops in the elderly because of hardening of the arteries. In many cases, the cause of Parkinson's disease is not known. Levodopa works by entering into the brain where it is converted to dopamine, a chemical found in the central nervous system. The new dopamine replaces what is deficient in people with Parkinson's disease. Another drug used to treat Parkinson's Disease is Amantadine (Symmetrel). Although it has been shown to increase the amount of dopamine in the brain, no one knows how it works.

Cautions and Warnings

Patients with severe heart or lung disease, asthma, or kidney, liver, or hormone diseases should be cautious about using this drug. Do not take it if you have a history of stomach

ulcer. People with a history of psychosis must be treated
with extreme care; this drug can cause depression with
suicidal tendencies. Pregnant women should take this drug
only if it is absolutely necessary. Women taking this drug
must not breast-feed their infants.

Possible Side Effects

Muscle spasms, inability to control arms, legs, or facial muscles, loss of appetite, nausea, vomiting (with or without
stomach pain), dry mouth, difficulty eating, dribbling saliva
from the corners of the mouth (due to poor muscle control),
tiredness, hand tremors, headache, dizziness, numbness,
weakness and a faint feeling, confusion, sleeplessness, grinding of the teeth, nightmares, euphoria, hallucinations, delusions, agitation and anxiousness, feeling of general ill health.

Possible Adverse Drug Effects

Heart irregularities or palpitations, dizziness when standing
or arising in the morning, mental changes (depression, with
or without suicidal tendencies; paranoia; loss of some intellectual function), difficulty urinating, muscle twitching, burning of the tongue, bitter taste, diarrhea, constipation, unusual
breathing patterns, double or blurred vision, hot flashes,
weight gain or loss, darkening of the urine or sweat.

Rare adverse effects include stomach bleeding, development of an ulcer, high blood pressure, convulsions, adverse
effects on the blood, difficulty controlling the eye muscles,
feeling of being stimulated, hiccups, loss of hair, hoarseness, decreasing size of male genitalia, and retention of fluids.

Drug Interactions

The effect of Levodopa is increased when it is used together
with an anticholinergic drug (such as Trihexyphenidyl). If
one of these drugs is stopped, the change must be gradual
to allow for adjustments in the other one. Levodopa can
interact with drugs for high blood pressure to cause further
lowering of pressure. Dosage adjustments in the high blood
pressure medication may be needed. Methyldopa (a drug for
high blood pressure) may increase the effects of Levodopa.

The effects of Levodopa may be antagonized by Reserpine, benzodiazepine drugs, phenothiazine-type tranquilizing
drugs, Phenytoin, Papaverine, and Vitamin B_6.

Patients taking MAO inhibitor drugs should stop taking them 2 weeks before starting to take Levodopa.

Levodopa may increase the effects of stimulants such as amphetamines, Ephedrine, Epinephrine, Isoproterenol, and the tricycline antidepressant drugs.

Levodopa will affect the blood sugar of diabetic patients. Adjustments in dosages of antidiabetic medicine may be needed.

Usual Dose

0.5 to 8 grams per day. Dosage must be individualized to patient's need.

Overdosage

People taking an overdose of Levodopa must be treated in a hospital emergency room. ALWAYS bring the prescription bottle with you.

Special Information

This drug can cause upset stomach; each dose should be taken with food. Do not take any vitamin preparation which contains Vitamin B_6; be careful while driving or operating any machinery.

Call your doctor *immediately* if any of the following occur: abnormal urine test for sugar (diabetics), uncontrollable movement of the face, eyelids, mouth, tongue, neck, arms, hands, or legs, mood changes, palpitations or irregular heartbeats, difficulty urinating, severe nausea or vomiting.

Generic Name

Levothyroxine Sodium

Brand Names

Levoid	Noroxine
Levothroid	Synthroid
L-T-S	Thyrolar

Type of Drug

Thyroid replacement.

Prescribed for

Replacement of thyroid hormone or low output of hormone from the thyroid gland.

General Information

Levothyroxine Sodium is one of several thyroid replacement products available. The major difference between these products is in effectiveness in treating certain phases of thyroid disease.

Cautions and Warnings

If you have hyperthyroid disease or high output of thyroid hormone you should not use Levothyroxine Sodium. Symptoms of hyperthyroid disease include headache, nervousness, sweating, rapid heartbeat, chest pains, and other signs of central nervous system stimulation. If you have heart disease or high blood pressure, thyroid therapy should not be used unless it is clearly indicated and supervised by your physician. If you develop chest pains or other signs of heart disease while you are taking thyroid medication, contact your doctor immediately.

Possible Side Effects

Most common: palpitations of the heart, rapid heartbeat, abnormal heart rhythms, weight loss, chest pains, shaking of the hands, headache, diarrhea, nervousness, menstrual irregularity, inability to sleep, sweating, inability to stand heat. These symptoms may be controlled by adjusting the dose of the medication. If you are suffering from one or more side effects, you must contact your doctor immediately so that the proper dose adjustment can be made.

Drug Interactions

Interaction of Levothyroxine Sodium with Cholestyramine (Questran) can be avoided by spacing the two doses at least 4 hours apart.

Avoid over-the-counter products containing stimulant drugs, such as many drugs used to treat coughs, colds, or allergies, which will affect your heart and may cause symptoms of overdosage.

Thyroid replacement therapy may increase the effect of

anticoagulant (blood-thinning) drugs such as Warfarin or Bishydroxycoumarin. Be sure you report this to your physician as it will be necessary to reduce the dose of your anticoagulant drug by approximately one-third at the beginning of thyroid therapy (to avoid hemorrhage). Further adjustments may be made later after your doctor reviews your blood tests.

Diabetics may have to increase their dose of Insulin or oral antidiabetic drugs. Changes in dose must be made by a doctor.

Usual Dose

Initial dose, as little as 25 micrograms per day; then increased in steps of 25 micrograms once every 3 to 4 weeks, depending upon response, with final dose of 100 to 200 micrograms per day, or even 300 to 400 micrograms if needed to achieve normal function.

Overdosage

Symptoms are headache, irritability, nervousness, sweating, rapid heartbeat with unusual stomach rumbling and with or without cramps, chest pains, heart failure, and shock. The patient should be taken to a hospital emergency room immediately. ALWAYS bring the medicine bottle.

Brand Name

Librax

Ingredients

Chlordiazepoxide
Clidinium Bromide

Type of Drug

Anticholinergic combination.

Prescribed for

Anxiety and spasms associated with gastrointestinal disease. Librax may be specifically prescribed as an adjunct in the treatment of organic or functional gastrointestinal disorders and in the management of peptic ulcers, gastritis, irritable bowel syndrome, spastic colon, and mild ulcerative colitis.

General Information

Librax is one of many combinations of this class containing an anticholinergic or antispasmodic drug and a tranquilizer such as Chlordiazepoxide. All the drugs in this class will provide symptomatic relief only, and will not treat an underlying disease: it is important that you realize while taking this medication that you should actively pursue the treatment of the underlying cause of this problem if one is present and can be found.

Cautions and Warnings

Librax should not be used if you know you are sensitive or allergic to either of its ingredients, Chlordiazepoxide (Librium) and Clidinium Bromide (Quarzan), or to any benzodiazepine drug, which is related to Chlordiazepoxide. Do not use this medicine if you have glaucoma, or if you have a history of prostatic hypertrophy and bladder-neck obstruction.

Some people may develop dependence on Librax because of its tranquilizer components.

Possible Side Effects

Most common: mild drowsiness (usually experienced during the first few days of therapy), dry mouth, difficulty in urination, constipation. These side effects may be accentuated in the elderly or debilitated person. If they persist, discuss these problems with your doctor, since it is possible that you may be taking too much of the drug for your system—or the side effects may be so bothersome as to suggest the possibility of using a different medication.

Possible Adverse Drug Effects

Infrequent: confusion, depression, lethargy, disorientation, headache, lack of activity, slurring of speech, stupor, dizziness, tremor, constipation, nausea, difficulty in urination, changes in sex drive, menstrual irregularity, changes in heart rhythm, stuffed nose, fever, heartburn, suppression of lactation in females, bloated feeling, drug allergy or allergic reaction to the drug including itching, rash, and less common manifestations. Most people taking Librax experience few truly bothersome effects and although the effects listed may be a problem, in most patients they do not constitute a severe difficulty.

Drug Interactions

The central nervous system depressant (tranquilizer) or the atropinelike drug (anticholinergic) in Librax may interact with alcoholic beverages or depressant drugs such as other tranquilizers, narcotics, barbiturates, or even antihistamines, causing excessive tiredness or sleepiness.

Both Librax ingredients may be potentiated (increased in effect) by MAO inhibitors: you may wish to discuss with your doctor the possibility of avoiding the combination.

The anticholinergic ingredient in Librax may be inhibited by certain drugs used to treat high blood pressure, including Guanethidine (Ismelin) and Reserpine. Discuss this with your doctor.

Usual Dose

1 to 2 capsules 3 to 4 times per day, usually before meals and at bedtime. Amount and scheduling of medication may vary according to disease and patient's response.

Overdosage

Symptoms are dry mouth, difficulty in swallowing, thirst, blurred vision, inability to tolerate bright lights, flushed, hot dry skin, rash, high temperatures, palpitations and other unusual heart rhythms, feeling that you must urinate but difficulty in doing so, restlessness or depression, confusion, delirium, possible coma and/or lack of reflexes, and lowered respiration (breathing) and blood pressure. The patient should be taken to a hospital emergency room immediately. ALWAYS bring the medicine bottle.

Brand Name

Limbitrol

Ingredients

Amitriptyline
Chlordiazepoxide

Type of Drug

Antianxiety-antidepressant combination.

Presribed for

Moderate to severe anxiety and depression.

General Information

This combination contains two drugs often used by themselves. Some reports have stated that this combination takes effect sooner than other treatments. Symptoms that may respond to this treatment are sleeplessness, feelings of guilt or worthlessness, agitation, anxiety, suicidal thoughts, and appetite loss.

Cautions and Warnings

Do not take this drug if you are allergic to either of the ingredients or related drugs. It should be used with caution if you have a history of heart disease, epilepsy or other convulsive disorder, difficulty urinating, glaucoma, or thyroid disease.

This combination can cause drowsiness or dizziness. While taking this drug, drive and operate equipment with extreme caution. Avoid alcoholic beverages.

Possible Side Effects

Mild drowsiness, changes in blood pressure, abnormal heart rates, heart attacks, confusion (especially in elderly patients), hallucinations, disorientation, delusions, anxiety, restlessness, excitement, numbness and tingling in the extremities, blurred vision, constipation, difficult urination, lack of coordination, muscle spasms, seizures or convulsions, dry mouth, blurred vision, rash, itching, sensitivity to the sun or bright light, retention of fluids, fever, drug allergy, changes in blood composition, nausea, vomiting, loss of appetite, stomach upset, diarrhea, enlargement of the breasts, changes in sex drive, changes in blood sugar.

Possible Adverse Drug Effects

Confusion, depression, lethargy, disorientation, headache, inactivity, slurred speech, stupor, dizziness, changes in menstrual cycle, blurred or double vision, inability to fall asleep, nightmares, feeling of panic, peculiar taste in the mouth, stomach cramps, black coloration of the tongue, yellowing of the eyes or skin, changes in liver function, changes in weight, sweating, flushing, loss of hair, feeling of ill health.

Drug Interactions

Avoid MAO inhibitors while taking this combination. The addition of MAO inhibitors can cause fever and convulsions. Do not take this drug together with Guanethidine. If you are taking high blood pressure medicine with this combination, consult with your doctor. Do not take this combination with alcohol, sleeping pills, or other depressive drugs.

Large doses of Vitamin C can reduce the effect of Amitriptyline, one ingredient of Limbitrol.

Usual Dose

1 tablet 3 to 4 times per day.

Overdosage

May cause confusion, drowsiness, difficulty concentrating, abnormal heart rate, convulsions, and coma. Bring the patient to a hospital emergency room and ALWAYS bring the medicine bottle.

Generic Name

Lithium

Brand Names

Cibalith-S Syrup
Eskalith
Lithane
Lithium Carbonate

Lithium Citrate Syrup
Lithobid
Pfi-Lith

Type of Drug

Antipsychotic, antimanic.

Prescribed for

Treatment of the manic phase of manic-depressive illness.

General Information

Lithium is the only medicine which is effective as an antimanic drug. It reduces the level of manic episodes and may produce normal activity within the first 3 weeks of treatment. Typical manic symptoms include rapid speech, elation, hyperactive movements, need for little sleep, grandiose ideas, poor judgment, aggressiveness, and hostility.

Cautions and Warnings

This drug should not be given to patients with heart or kidney disease, dehydration, low blood sodium, or to patients who take diuretic drugs. If such patients require Lithium they must be very closely monitored by their doctors.

Lithium may affect routine mental or physical activity. Take care while driving or operating machinery. Lithium has been associated with adverse effects on the unborn fetus. It should be used by pregnant women only if absolutely necessary. Its safety has not been established for children under age 12.

Possible Side Effects

Side effects of Lithium are directly associated with the amount of this drug in the blood. At usual doses, the patient may develop a fine hand tremor, thirst, and excessive urination. Mild nausea and discomfort may be present during the first few days of treatment. At higher levels, diarrhea, vomiting, drowsiness, muscle weakness and poor coordination, giddiness, ringing in the ears, and blurred vision, may occur.

Possible Adverse Drug Effects

The following body systems can be affected by Lithium, producing symptoms which tend to become worse with more of this drug in the body: muscles, nerves, central nervous system (blackouts, seizures, dizziness, incontinence, slurred speech, coma), heart and blood vessels, stomach and intestines, kidney and urinary tract, skin, thyroid gland. Lithium can also cause changes in tests used to monitor heart-brain function and can cause dry mouth and blurred vision.

Drug Interactions

When combined with Haloperidol, Lithium may cause an unusual set of symptoms including weakness, tiredness, fever and confusion. In a few patients these symptoms have been followed by permanent brain damage.

Lithium may reduce the effect of Chlorpromazine.

The drug is counteracted by Sodium Bicarbonate, Acetazolamide, Urea, Mannitol, and Aminophylline, which increase the rate at which Lithium is released from the body.

Long-term use of thiazide diuretic drugs may decrease the clearance of Lithium from the body. Salt (sodium chloride) is directly related to this drug in the body. You will retain more of the drug than normal if the salt level in your body is low, and will hold less if you have a high salt level. It is essential to maintain a normal diet, including salt and fluid intake, while taking Lithium, since it can cause a natural reduction in body salt levels.

Usual Dose

Must be individualized to each patient's need. Most patients will respond to 600 milligrams 3 times per day at first, then will require 300 milligrams 3 to 4 times per day.

Overdosage

Toxic levels of Lithium are only slightly above the levels required for treatment. If any of the following symptoms occur, stop taking the medicine and call your doctor immediately: diarrhea, vomiting, tremors, drowsiness, or poor coordination.

Special Information

Lithium may cause drowsiness. If you are taking this drug be cautious while driving or operating any machinery.

Brand Name

Lomotil

Ingredients

Atropine Sulfate
Diphenoxylate

Other Brand Names

Colonaid	Lomoxate
Diaction	Lonox
Enoxa	Lo-Trol
Lofene	Low-Quel
Loflo	Nor-Mil
Lomanate	SK-Diphenoxylate

Type of Drug

Antidiarrheal.

Prescribed for

Symptomatic treatment of diarrhea.

General Information

Lomotil and other antidiarrheal agents should only be used for short periods: they will relieve the diarrhea, but not its underlying causes. Sometimes these drugs should not be used even though there is diarrhea present: people with some kinds of bowel, stomach, or other disease may be harmed by taking antidiarrheal drugs. Obviously, the decision to use Lomotil must be made by your doctor. Do not use Lomotil without his advice.

Cautions and Warnings

Do not take Lomotil if you are allergic to this medication or any other medication containing Atropine, or if you are jaundiced (yellowing of the whites of the eyes and/or skin) or are suffering from diarrhea caused by antibiotics such as Clindamycin or Lincomycin. Do not use Lomotil if you are pregnant, because the ingredients in this medication will cross into the blood system of the unborn child. If you are nursing a newborn baby, Lomotil will appear in the breast milk and can affect the newborn infant.

Possible Side Effects

Most common: dryness of the skin inside the nose or mouth, flushing or redness of the face, fever, unusual heart rates, inability to urinate.

Possible Adverse Drug Effects

People taking Lomotil for extended periods may experience abdominal discomforts, swelling of the gums, interference with normal breathing, feeling of numbness in the extremities, drowsiness, restlessness, rashes, nausea, sedation, vomiting, headache, dizziness, depression, feeling unwell, lethargy, loss of appetite, euphoria, itching, and coma.

Drug Interactions

Lomotil, a depressant on the central nervous system, may cause tiredness or inability to concentrate, and may thus increase the effect of sleeping pills, tranquilizers, and alcohol. Avoid drinking large amounts of alcoholic beverages while taking Lomotil.

Usual Dose

Adult: 4 tablets per day until diarrhea has stopped; then reduce to the lowest level that will control diarrhea (usually 2 tablets per day or less).

For children age 2 to 12 the liquid form, supplied with a dropper calibrated to deliver medication as desired in milliliters, is used.

Child (age 8 to 12, or about 60 to 80 pounds): 4 milliliters 5 times per day.

Child (age 5 to 8, or about 45 to 60 pounds): 4 milliliters 4 times per day.

Child (age 2 to 5, or about 26 to 45 pounds): 4 milliliters 3 times per day.

Child (under age 2): not recommended.

Overdosage

Lomotil overdose is generally accidental: patients, feeling that the prescribed amount has not cured their diarrhea, will take more medication on their own. Symptoms of overdosage (particularly effects on breathing) may not be evident until 12 to 30 hours after the medication has been taken. Symptoms are dryness of skin, mouth, and/or nose, flushing, fever and abnormal heart rates with possible lethargy, coma, or depression of breathing. The patient should be taken to a hospital emergency room immediately. ALWAYS bring the medicine bottle.

Special Information

Lomotil may cause drowsiness and difficulty concentrating: be careful while driving or operating any appliance or equipment.

Generic Name

Loperamide

Brand Name

Imodium

Type of Drug

Antidiarrheal.

Prescribed for

Symptomatic treatment of diarrhea.

General Information

Loperamide and other antidiarrheal agents should only be used for short periods: they will relieve the diarrhea, but not its underlying causes. Sometimes these drugs should not be used even though there is diarrhea present: people with some kinds of bowel, stomach, or other disease may be harmed by taking antidiarrheal drugs. Obviously, the decision to use the drug must be made by your doctor; do not use it without his advice.

Cautions and Warnings

Do not use Loperamide if you are allergic or sensitive to it or if you suffer from diarrhea associated with colitis. Also, do

not use when intestinal toxins from bacteria such as *E. coli,*
Salmonella, or *Shigella* are present or with certain drugs
such as Clindamycin. Pregnant women and nursing mothers
should avoid taking this drug. Loperamide is not known to
be addictive.

Possible Side Effects

The incidence of side effects from Loperamide is low. Stomach and abdominal pain, bloating or other discomfort, constipation, dryness of the mouth, dizziness, tiredness, nausea
and vomiting, and rash are possible.

Drug Interactions

Loperamide, a depressant on the central nervous system,
may cause tiredness and inability to concentrate, and may
thus increase the effect of sleeping pills, tranquilizers, and
alcohol. Avoid drinking large amounts of alcoholic beverages while taking Loperamide.

Usual Dose

Adult or child (age 12 and over): 2 capsules to start, followed by 1 capsule after each loose stool, up to 8 capsules
per day maximum. Improvement should be seen in 2 days.
People with long-term (chronic) diarrhea usually need 2 to 4
capsules per day. This drug usually is effective within 10
days or not at all.

Child (under age 12): not recommended.

Overdosage

Symptoms are constipation, irritation of the stomach and
tiredness. Large doses cause vomiting. The patient should
be taken to the emergency room immediately. ALWAYS bring
the medicine bottle.

Special Information

Loperamide may cause drowsiness and difficulty concentrating: be careful while driving or operating any appliance or
equipment.

Generic Name

Lorazepam

Brand Name
Ativan

Type of Drug
Tranquilizer.

Prescribed for
Relief of symptoms of anxiety, tension, fatigue, or agitation.

General Information
Lorazepam is a member of the chemical group of drugs known as benzodiazepines. These drugs are used as either antianxiety agents, anticonvulsants, or sedatives (sleeping pills). They exert their effects by relaxing the large skeletal muscles and by a direct effect on the brain. In doing so, they can relax you and make you either more tranquil or sleepier, depending on the drug and how much you use. Many doctors prefer Lorazepam and the other members of this class to other drugs that can be used for the same effect. Their reason is that the benzodiazepines tend to be safer, have fewer side effects, and are usually as, if not more, effective.

These drugs are generally used in any situation where they can be a useful adjunct.

Benzodiazepine tranquilizing drugs can be abused if taken for long periods of time and it is possible to develop withdrawal symptoms if you discontinue the therapy abruptly. Withdrawal symptoms include convulsions, tremor, muscle cramps, stomach cramps, vomiting, and sweating.

Cautions and Warnings
Do not take Lorazepam if you know you are sensitive or allergic to this drug or to other benzodiazepines such as Chlordiazepoxide, Oxazepam, Clorazepate, Diazepam, Prazepam, Flurazepam, and Clonazepam.

Lorazepam and other members of this drug group may aggravate narrow angle glaucoma, but if you have open angle glaucoma you may take the drugs. In any case, check this information with your doctor. Lorazepam can cause tiredness, drowsiness, inability to concentrate, or similar symptoms. Be careful if you are driving, operating machinery, or performing other activities which require concentration. Avoid taking this drug during the first 3 months of pregnancy except under strict supervision of your doctor.

Possible Side Effects

Most common: mild drowsiness during the first few days of therapy, especially in the elderly or debilitated. If drowsiness persists, contact your doctor.

Possible Adverse Drug Effects

Major: confusion, depression, lethargy, disorientation, headache, lack of activity, slurred speech, stupor, dizziness, tremor, constipation, dry mouth, nausea, inability to control urination, changes in sex drive, irregular menstrual cycle, changes in heart rhythm, lowered blood pressure, retention of fluids, blurred or double vision, itching, rash, hiccups, nervousness, inability to fall asleep, (occasional) liver dysfunction. If you experience any of these reactions stop taking the medicine and contact your doctor immediately.

Drug Interactions

Lorazepam is a central nervous system depressant. Avoid alcohol, tranquilizers, narcotics, sleeping pills, barbiturates, MAO inhibitors, antihistamines, and other medicines used to relieve depression.

Usual Dose

Adult: 2 to 10 milligrams per day as individualized for maximum benefit, depending on symptoms and response to treatment, which may call for a dose outside the range given. Most people require 2 to 6 milligrams per day. 2 to 4 milligrams may be taken at bedtime for sleep.

Elderly: usually require less of the drug to control anxiety and tension.

Child: should not use.

Overdosage

Symptoms are confusion, sleep or sleepiness, lack of response to pain such as a pin stick, shallow breathing, lowered blood pressure, and coma. The patient should be taken to a hospital emergency room immediately. ALWAYS bring the medicine bottle.

Generic Name

Maprotiline

Brand Name

Ludiomil

Type of Drug

Antidepressant.

Prescribed for

Depression with or without symptoms of anxiety.

General Information

Maprotiline and other members of this group are effective in treating symptoms of depression. They can elevate your mood, increase physical activity and mental alertness, improve appetite and sleep patterns. These drugs are mild sedatives and therefore useful in treating mild forms of depression associated with anxiety. You should not expect instant results with this medicine: benefits are usually seen after 1 to 4 weeks. If symptoms are not affected after 6 to 8 weeks, contact your doctor. Occasionally other members of this group of drugs have been used in treating nighttime bed-wetting in the young child, but they do not produce long-lasting relief, and therapy with one of them for nighttime bed-wetting is of questionable value.

Cautions and Warnings

Do not take Maprotiline if you are allergic or sensitive to this or other members of this class of drug: Doxepin, Nortriptyline, Imipramine, Desipramine, Protriptyline, and Amitriptyline. The drugs should not be used if you are recovering from a heart attack. Maprotiline may be taken with caution if you have a history of epilepsy or other convulsive disorders, difficulty in urination, glaucoma, heart disease, or thyroid disease. Maprotiline can interfere with your ability to perform tasks which require concentration, such as driving or operating machinery. Maprotiline will pass from mother to unborn child: consult your doctor before taking this medicine if you are pregnant.

Possible Side Effects

Changes in blood pressure (both high and low), abnormal heart rates, heart attack, confusion, especially in elderly patients, hallucinations, disorientation, delusions, anxiety, restlessness, excitement, numbness and tingling in the extremities, lack of coordination, muscle spasms or tremors, seizures and/or convulsions, dry mouth, blurred vision, constipation, inability to urinate, rash, itching, sensitivity to bright light or sunlight, retention of fluids, fever, allergy, changes in composition of blood, nausea, vomitig, loss of appetite, stomach upset, diarrhea, enlargement of the breasts in males and females, increased or decreased sex drive, increased or decreased blood sugar.

Possible Adverse Drug Effects

Infrequent: agitation, inability to sleep, nightmares, feeling of panic, development of a peculiar taste in the mouth, stomach cramps, black coloration of the tongue, yellowing eyes and/or skin, changes in liver function, increased or decreased weight, increased perspiration, flushing, frequent urination, drowsiness, dizziness, weakness, headache, loss of hair, nausea, not feeling well.

Drug Interactions

Interaction with monoamine oxidase (MAO) inhibitors can cause high fevers, convulsions, and occasionally death. Don't take MAO inhibitors until at least 2 weeks after Maprotiline has been discontinued.

Maprotiline interacts with Guanethidine, a drug used to treat high blood pressure: if your doctor prescribes Maprotiline and you are taking medicine for high blood pressure, be sure to discuss this with him.

Maprotiline increases the effects of barbiturates, tranquilizers, other depressive drugs, and alcohol. Don't drink alcoholic beverages if you take this medicine.

Taking Maprotiline and thyroid medicine will enhance the effects of the thyroid medicine. The combination can cause abnormal heart rhythms.

Large doses of Vitamin C (Ascorbic Acid) can reduce the effect of Maprotiline. Drugs such as Bicarbonate of Soda or Acetazolamide will increase the effect of Maprotiline.

Usual Dose

Adult: 75 to 225 milligrams per day. Hospitalized patients may need up to 300 milligrams per day. The dose of this drug must be tailored to patient's need.

Elderly: lower doses are recommended for people over 60 years of age, usually 50 to 75 milligrams per day.

Overdosage

Symptoms are confusion, inability to concentrate, hallucinations, drowsiness, lowered body temperature, abnormal heart rate, heart failure, large pupils of the eyes, convulsions, severely lowered blood pressure, stupor, and coma (as well as agitation, stiffening of body muscles, vomiting, and high fever). The patient should be taken to a hospital emergency room immediately. ALWAYS bring the medicine bottle.

Brand Name

Marax

Ingredients

Ephedrine Sulfate
Hydroxyzine Hydrochloride
Theophylline

Other Brand Names

Asminorel	Theophedrizine
E.T.H. Compound	Theophozine
Hydrophed	Theozine
T.E.H. Compound	

Type of Drug

Antiasthmatic combination product.

Prescribed for

Relief of asthma symptoms or other upper respiratory disorders.

General Information

Marax is one of several antiasthmatic combination products prescribed for the relief of asthmatic symptoms and other breathing problems. These products contain drugs which help relax the bronchial muscles, drugs which increase the diameter of the breathing passages, and a mild tranquilizer to help relax the patient. Other products in this class may contain similar ingredients along with other medicine to help eliminate mucus from the breathing passages.

Cautions and Warnings

Take the drug with food to help prevent stomach upset.

This drug should not be taken if you have severe kidney or liver disease.

Possible Side Effects

Large doses of Marax can produce excitation, shakiness, sleeplessness, nervousness, rapid heartbeat, chest pains, irregular heartbeat, dizziness, dryness of the nose and throat, headache, and sweating. Occasionally people have been known to develop hesitation or difficulty in urination. Marax may also cause stomach upset, diarrhea, and possible bleeding, so you are advised to take this drug with food.

Possible Adverse Drug Effects

Excessive urination, heart stimulation, drowsiness, muscle weakness, muscle twitching, unsteady walk. These effects can usually be controlled by having your doctor adjust the dose.

Drug Interactions

Marax may cause sleeplessness and/or drowsiness. Do not take this drug with alcoholic beverages.

Taking Marax or similar medicines with an MAO inhibitor can produce severe interaction. Consult your doctor first.

Marax or similar products taken together with Lithium Carbonate will increase the excretion of lithium; they have neutralized the effect of Propranolol. Erythromycin and similar antibiotics cause the body to hold Theophylline, leading to possible side effects.

Usual Dose

Adult: 1 tablet 2 to 4 times per day.

Child (over age 5): ½ tablet 2 to 4 times per day. Syrup, 1 teaspoon 3 to 4 times per day.

Child (age 2 to 5): Syrup, ½ teaspoon 3 to 4 times per day.

Take doses at least 4 hours apart. The dose is adjusted to severity of disease and patient's ability to tolerate side effects.

Generic Name

Meclizine

Brand Names

Antivert
Bonine
Dizmiss
Motion Cure
Wehvert

Type of Drug

Antiemetic, antivertigo agent.

Prescribed for

Relief of nausea, vomiting, and dizziness associated with motion sickness or disease affecting the middle ear.

General Information

Meclizine is an antihistamine used to treat or prevent nausea, vomiting, and motion sickness. It takes a little longer to start working than most other drugs of this type but its effects last much longer (1 to 2 days). The specific method by which Meclizine acts on the brain to prevent dizziness and the nausea associated with it is not fully understood. In general, Meclizine does a better job of preventing motion sickness than of treating the symptoms once they are present.

Use with caution in children as a treatment for vomiting or

nausea. This drug may obscure symptoms important in reaching the diagnosis of underlying disease. Meclizine is one of several drugs prescribed for the relief of nausea, vomiting, or dizziness that do not cure any underlying problems.

Cautions and Warnings

Do not take this medication if you think you are allergic to it. Women who are pregnant or who feel they may become pregnant while they are taking this medication should not take Meclizine. Meclizine has been associated with birth defects in children.

Possible Side Effects

Most common: drowsiness, dry mouth, blurred vision.

Possible Adverse Drug Effects

Infrequent: difficulty in urination, constipation. Adverse effects are usually not cause for great concern. If they become serious, discuss them with your doctor.

Drug Interactions

Meclizine may cause sleepiness, tiredness, or inability to concentrate. Avoid tranquilizers, sleeping pills, alcoholic beverages, barbiturates, narcotics, and antihistamines, which can add to these effects.

Usual Dose

25 to 50 milligrams 1 hour before travel; repeat every 24 hours for duration of journey. For control of dizziness (diseases affecting middle ear, etc.), 25 to 100 milligrams per day in divided doses. This drug should not be given to children.

Special Information

Meclizine may cause tiredness, sleepiness, and inability to concentrate. Be extremely careful while driving or operating any machinery, appliances, or delicate equipment.

Generic Name

Medroxyprogesterone Acetate

Brand Names

Amen
Curretab
Provera

Type of Drug

Progestogen.

Prescribed for

Irregular menstrual bleeding.

General Information

Because of the potential development of secondary disease
after a long period of taking Medroxyprogesterone Acetate,
the decision to take this medication chronically should be
made cautiously by you and your doctor. Your continued
need for chronic therapy with Medoxyprogesterone Acetate
should be evaluated at least every 6 months to be sure that
this therapy is absolutely necessary.

Cautions and Warnings

Do not take this drug if you have a history of blood clots or
similar disorders, a history of convulsions, liver disease,
known or suspected breast cancer, undiagnosed vaginal bleeding or miscarriage. You should not be taking the drug if you
are pregnant, since Medroxyprogesterone Acetate has been
known to produce masculinization in the female unborn child.

Possible Side Effects

Breakthrough bleeding, spotting, changes in or loss of menstrual flow, retention of water, increase or decrease in weight,
jaundice, rash (with or without itching), mental depression.

Possible Adverse Drug Effects

A significant association has been demonstrated between
the use of progestogen drugs and the following serious
adverse effect: development of blood clots in the veins,

lungs, or brain. Other possible adverse effects: changes in libido or sex drive, changes in appetite and mood, headache, nervousness, dizziness, tiredness, backache, loss of scalp hair, growth of hair in unusual quantities or places, itching, symptoms similar to urinary infections, unusual rashes.

Usual Dose

5 to 10 milligrams per day for 5 to 10 days beginning on what is assumed to be the 16th to 21st day of the menstrual cycle.

Special Information

At the first sign of sudden, partial, or complete loss of vision, leg cramps, water retention, unusual vaginal bleeding, migraine headache, or depression, or if you think you have become pregnant, stop the drug immediately and call your doctor.

Generic Name

Megestrol Acetate

Brand Name

Megace

Type of Drug

Progestational hormone.

Prescribed for

Cancer of the breast or endometrium.

General Information

Megestrol Acetate has been used quite successfully in the treatment of the cancers cited above. It exerts its effect by acting as a hormonal counterbalance in areas rich in estrogen (breast and endometrium). Other progestational hormones such as Norethindrone (Norlutin, Norlutate) may be used to treat cancer of the endometrium or uterus or to correct hormone imbalance.

Cautions and Warnings

This drug should only be used for its two specifically approved indications. The use of this drug should be accompanied by close, continued contact with your doctor.

Possible Side Effects

Back or stomach pain, headache, nausea, vomiting. If any of these symptoms appear, contact your doctor immediately.

Possible Adverse Drug Effects

Should be used with caution if you have a history of blood clots in the veins.

Usual Dose

40 to 320 milligrams per day.

Generic Name

Meperidine

Brand Names

Demerol
Meperidine Hydrochloride

Type of Drug

Narcotic analgesic.

Prescribed for

Moderate to severe pain.

General Information

Meperidine is a narcotic drug with potent pain-relieving effect. It is also used before surgery to reduce patient anxiety and help bring the patient into the early stages of anesthesia. Meperidine is probably the narcotic analgesic most commonly used in American hospitals. Its effects compare favorably with those of Morphine Sulfate, the standard against which other narcotics are judged.

Meperidine is a narcotic drug with some pain-relieving and cough-suppressing activity. As an analgesic it is useful for mild to moderate pain. 25 to 50 milligrams of Meperidine are approximately equal in pain-relieving effect to 2 Aspirin tablets (650 milligrams). Meperidine may be less active than Aspirin for types of pain associated with inflammation, since Aspirin reduces inflammation and Meperidine does not. Meperidine suppresses the cough reflex but does not cure the underlying cause of the cough. In fact, sometimes it may not be desirable to overly suppress cough, because cough suppression reduces your ability to naturally eliminate excess mucus produced during a cold or allergy attack.

Cautions and Warnings

The side effects of narcotic drugs are exaggerated when the patient has a head injury, brain tumor, or other head problem. Narcotics can also hide the symptoms of head injury. They should be used with extreme caution in patients with head injuries.

Possible Side Effects

Most frequent: light-headedness, dizziness, sleepiness, nausea, vomiting, loss of appetite, sweating. If these occur, consider calling your doctor and asking him about lowering your present dose of Meperidine. Usually the side effects disappear if you simply lie down.

More serious side effects of Meperidine are shallow breathing or difficulty in breathing.

Possible Adverse Drug Effects

Euphoria (feeling high), weakness, sleepiness, headache, agitation, uncoordinated muscle movement, minor hallucinations, disorientation and visual disturbances, dry mouth, loss of appetite, constipation, flushing of the face, rapid heartbeat, palpitations, faintness, urinary difficulties or hesitancy, reduced sex drive and/or potency, itching, skin rashes, anemia, lowered blood sugar, and a yellowing of the skin and/or whites of the eyes. Narcotic analgesics may aggravate convulsions in those who have had convulsions in the past.

Drug Interactions

Because of its depressant effect and potential effect on breathing, Meperidine should be taken with extreme care in combination with alcohol, sleeping medicine, tranquilizers, or other depressant drugs.

Usual Dose

Adult: 50 to 150 milligrams every 3 to 4 hours as needed.
Child: 0.5 to 0.8 milligram per pound every 3 to 4 hours as needed, up to the adult dose.

Overdosage

Symptoms are depression of respiration (breathing), extreme tiredness progressing to stupor and then coma, pinpointed pupils of the eyes, no response to stimulation such as a pin stick, cold and clammy skin, slowing down of the heartbeat, lowering of blood pressure, convulsions, and cardiac arrest. The patient should be taken to a hospital emergency room immediately. ALWAYS bring the medicine bottle.

Special Information

If you are taking Meperidine, be extremely careful while driving or operating machinery. Avoid alcoholic beverages. Call your doctor if this drug makes you very nauseated or constipated or if you have trouble breathing. This drug may be taken with food to reduce stomach upset.

Generic Name

Meprobamate

Brand Names

Bamate	Miltown
Coprobate	Neuramate
Equanil	Protran
Evenol	Sedabamate
F.M.	SK-Bamate
Meprospan	Tranmep

Type of Drug

Tranquilizer.

Prescribed for

Relief of anxiety and tension, and to promote sleep in anxious or tense patients.

General Information

Meprobamate and the other drugs in its chemical group are used as either antianxiety agents, anticonvulsants, or sedatives (sleeping pills). This drug exerts effects by relaxing the large skeletal muscles and by a direct effect on the brain. In doing so, it can relax you and make you either more tranquil or sleepier, depending on the drug and how much you use.

Meprobamate is generally used in any situation where it can be a useful adjunct.

Meprobamate can be abused if taken for long periods of time and it is possible to develop withdrawal symptoms if you discontinue the therapy abruptly. Withdrawal symptoms include convulsions, tremor, muscle or stomach cramps, vomiting, and sweating.

Cautions and Warnings

You should not take Meprobamate if you are allergic to it or if you feel that you may be allergic to a related drug such as Carisoprodol, Mebutamate, Tybamate, or Carbromal. Severe physical and psychological dependence has been experienced by people taking Meprobamate for long periods of time. The drug can produce chronic intoxication after prolonged use or if used in greater than recommended doses, leading to adverse effects such as slurred speech, dizziness, and general sleepiness or depression. If this is true of a friend of yours who is taking this drug, you should discuss this matter with him/her and urge the friend to see a doctor. Or if it is true of you, see your doctor. Sudden withdrawal of Meprobamate after prolonged and excessive use may result in drug withdrawal symptoms including severe anxiety, loss of appetite, sleeplessness, vomiting, tremors, muscle twitching, severe sleepiness, confusion, hallucinations, and possibly convulsions. Such withdrawal symptoms usually begin 12 to 48 hours after Meprobamate has been stopped and may last 1 to 4 days. When someone has taken this medication in excessive quantities for weeks, months, or longer, the medication must be gradually reduced over a period of 1 or 2 weeks in order to avoid these withdrawal symptoms. If you are taking Meprobamate you should be aware that this drug may cause inability to perform usual tasks which require coordination, such as driving or operating machinery, and you must be extremely careful when performing such tasks.

Use with extreme caution if you are in the first 3 months of pregnancy or if you suspect that you may be pregnant; minor tranquilizers have been associated with a small incidence of birth defects. If you are pregnant and are taking this medication, you should discuss it with your doctor.

Possible Side Effects

Most common: drowsiness, sleepiness, dizziness, slurred speech, headache, weakness, tingling in the arms and legs, euphoria, and possibly excitement or paradoxical reactions such as overstimulation.

Possible Adverse Drug Effects

Infrequent: nausea, vomiting, diarrhea, abnormal heart rhythms, low blood pressure, itching, rash, effects on various components of the blood. Quite rarely there has been severe hypersensitivity or allergic reactions producing high fever, chills, closing of the throat (bronchospasm), loss of urinary function, and other severe symptoms.

Drug Interactions

Interactions with other drugs that produce depression of the central nervous system can cause sleepiness, tiredness, and tranquilization. Interaction with other tranquilizers, alcoholic beverages in excessive quantities, narcotics, barbiturates and other sleeping pills, or antihistamines can cause excessive depression, sleepiness, and fatigue.

Usual Dose

Adult (when used as a tranquilizer): 1200 to 1600 milligrams per day in divided doses; maximum permissible, 2400 milligrams per day.

Child (age 6 to 12): 100 to 200 milligrams 2 to 3 times per day.

Should not be given to children under age 6.

Overdosage

In attempted suicide or accidental overdose, symptoms are extreme drowsiness, lethargy, stupor, and coma, with possible shock and respiratory collapse (breathing stops).

The overdosed patient must be taken to a hospital emergency room immediately. ALWAYS bring the medicine bottle. Some people have died after taking 30 tablets, others have survived after taking 100.

The overdose is much worse if there is interaction with a large quantity of alcohol or another depressant: a much smaller dose of Meprobamate can produce fatal results.

After a large overdose, the patient will go to sleep very quickly and blood pressure, pulse, and breathing levels will be greatly reduced. After the patient is taken to the hospital his stomach should be pumped and respiratory assistance and other supportive therapy given.

Special Information

Elderly or debilitated (physically below par) people are especially sensitive to Meprobamate and should take it with care. The same dose taken in the past may produce excessive depression and be uncomfortable or dangerous.

Generic Name

Mesoridazine

Brand Names

Serentil

Type of Drug

Phenothiazine antipsychotic.

Prescribed for

Psychotic disorders, moderate to severe depression with anxiety, control of agitation or aggressiveness of disturbed children, alcohol withdrawal symptoms, intractable pain, and senility.

General Information

Mesoridazine and other members of the phenothiazine group act on a portion of the brain called the hypothalamus. They affect parts of the hypothalamus that control metabolism, body temperature, alertness, muscle tone, hormone balance, and vomiting, and may be used to treat problems related to any of these functions.

Cautions and Warnings

Mesoridazine should not be taken if you are allergic to one of the drugs in the broad classification known as phenothiazine drugs. Do not take Mesoridazine if you have any blood, liver, kidney, or heart disease, very low blood pressure, or Parkinson's disease. This medication is a tranquilizer and can have a depressive effect, especially during the first few days of therapy. Care should be taken when performing activities requiring a high degree of concentration, such as driving. If you are taking this medication and become pregnant contact your doctor immediately.

This drug should be used with caution and under strict supervision of your doctor if you have glaucoma, epilepsy, ulcers, or difficulty passing urine.

Avoid insecticides and extreme exposure to heat.

Possible Side Effects

Most common: drowsiness, especially during the first or second week of therapy. If the drowsiness becomes troublesome, contact your doctor.

Possible Adverse Drug Effects

Mesoridazine can cause jaundice (yellowing of the whites of the eyes or skin), usually in 2 to 4 weeks. The jaundice usually goes away when the drug is discontinued, but there have been cases when it did not. If you notice this effect or if you develop symptoms such as fever and generally not feeling well, contact your doctor immediately. Less frequent: changes in components of the blood including anemias, raised or lowered blood pressure, abnormal heart rates, heart attack, feeling faint or dizzy.

Phenothiazines can produce "extrapyramidal effects," such as spasm of the neck muscles, rolling back of the eyes, convulsions, difficulty in swallowing, and symptoms associated with Parkinson's disease. These effects look very serious but go away after the drug has been withdrawn; however, symptoms of the face, tongue, and jaw may persist for as long as several years, especially in the elderly with a history of brain damage. If you experience extrapyramidal effects, contact your doctor immediately.

Mesoridazine may cause an unusual increase in psychotic symptoms or may cause paranoid reactions, tiredness, lethargy, restlessness, hyperactivity, confusion at night, bizarre dreams, inability to sleep, depression, and euphoria. Other reactions are itching, swelling, unusual sensitivity to bright lights, red skin (particularly in exposed areas) and rash. There have been cases of breast enlargement, false positive pregnancy tests, changes in menstrual flow in females, and impotence and changes in sex drive in males, stuffy nose, headache, nausea, vomiting, loss of appetite, change in body temperature, loss of facial color, excessive salivation and perspiration, constipation, diarrhea, changes in urine and stool habits, worsening of glaucoma, blurred vision, weakening of eyelid muscles and spasms in bronchial and other muscles, increased appetite, and excessive thirst.

Drug Interactions

Mesoridazine should be taken with caution in combination with barbiturates, sleeping pills, narcotics, other tranquilizers, or any other medication which may produce a depressive effect. Avoid alcohol.

Usual Dose

30 to 400 milligrams per day, depending on the condition being treated.

Overdosage

Symptoms are depression, extreme weakness, tiredness, desire to go to sleep, coma, lowered blood pressure, uncontrolled muscle spasms, agitation, restlessness, convulsions, fever, dry mouth, and abnormal heart rhythms. The patient should be taken to a hospital emergency room immediately. ALWAYS bring the medicine bottle.

Special Information

This drug may turn the color of your urine to pink or reddish brown.

Generic Name

Metaproterenol

Brand Names

Alupent
Metaprel

Type of Drug

Bronchodilator.

Prescribed for

Asthma and spasm of the bronchial muscles.

General Information

This is one of the newer drugs used in the treatment of
asthma and similar conditions. It can be taken both as a
tablet and by inhalation. This drug may be used together
with other drugs to produce the desired relief from asthmatic symptoms. It begins working 15 to 30 minutes after a
dose and its effects may last for up to 4 hours.

Cautions and Warnings

This drug should be used with caution by patients who have
angina, heart disease, high blood pressure, a history of stroke
or seizures, diabetes, thyroid disease, prostate disease, or
glaucoma. This drug should be used by women who are
pregnant or breast-feeding only when absolutely necessary.
The potential hazard to the unborn child or nursing infant is
not known at this time.

Older patients, over age 60, are more likely to experience
the adverse effects of this drug.

Possible Side Effects

Restlessness, anxiety, fear, tension, sleeplessness, tremors,
convulsions, weakness, dizziness, headache, flushing, pallor,
sweating, nausea; also vomiting, loss of appetite, muscle
cramps, urinary difficulties.

Possible Adverse Drug Effects

Metaproterenol can cause some side effects on the heart

and cardiovascular system, such as high blood pressure, abnormal heart rhythms, and angina. It is less likely to cause these effects than some of the older drugs.

Drug Interactions

The effect of this drug may be increased by antidepressant drugs, some antihistamines, and Levothyroxine. This drug may antagonize the effects of Reserpine or Guanethidine.

Usual Dose

Oral doses are as follows:

Adult and Child (over 60 pounds, or over age 9): 60 to 80 milligrams per day.

Child (under 60 pounds, or age 6 to 9): 30 to 40 milligrams per day.

Inhalation doses are as follows:

Adult and Child (over age 12): 2 or 5 puffs every 3 to 4 hours.

Do not use more than 12 puffs per day. The inhalation form of the drug is not recommended for children under age 12.

Overdosage

Symptoms of Metaproterenol overdose are palpitation, abnormal heart rhythms, rapid or slow heartbeat, chest pain, high blood pressure, fever, chills, cold sweat, blanching of the skin, nausea, vomiting, sleeplessness, delirium, tremor, pinpoint pupils, convulsions, coma, and collapse. If you or someone you know has taken an overdose of this drug call your doctor or bring the patient to a hospital emergency room. ALWAYS remember to bring the prescription bottle or inhaler with you.

Special Information

Do not take more than the amount prescribed for you. If the tablets cause an upset stomach, take each dose with food.

Generic Name

Methaqualone Hydrochloride

Brand Names

Mequin
Parest
Quáálude

Type of Drug

Sedative-hypnotic.

Prescribed for

Inability to sleep

General Information

Methaqualone Hydrochloride begins to produce drowsiness
within 10 to 20 minutes and sleep lasts for several hours.
This drug has been implicated in suicides and accidental
deaths. Particular attention should be paid to the drug interactions of Methaqualone Hydrochloride. Aged, highly agitated, or very ill people may be especially sensitive to this drug
and require smaller doses to produce sleep.

Cautions and Warnings

Do not take Methaqualone Hydrochloride if you are allergic
or sensitive to it. It can be addictive.

Possible Side Effects

Headache, hallucinations, hangover, fatigue, nausea, dizziness, rash.

Possible Adverse Drug Effects

Infrequent: tingling in the extremities, restlessness and anxiety, anemias, dry mouth, loss of appetite, vomiting, diarrhea, stomach upset, sweating, itching.

Drug Interactions

Avoid interaction with alcohol, other sleeping medicine, tranquilizers, or other depressants, which can lead to profound
depression of respiration (breathing) and, eventually, death.

Usual Dose

Adult: up to 400 milligrams.
Child: do not use.

Overdosage

Large amounts of Methaqualone Hydrochloride can be fatal, and the drug is frequently used in suicide attempts. Symptoms are coma, lowered body temperature followed by fever, absence of normal reflexes and pain responses after pinches or needle or pin sticks, and shallow breathing. The patient should be taken to a hospital emergency room immediately. ALWAYS bring the medicine bottle.

People who have taken Methaqualone Hydrochloride for a long time may show signs of chronic overdosage: loss of memory, inability to concentrate, shakes, tremors, loss of reflexes, slurred speech, and general sense of depression. Abrupt discontinuation of Methaqualone Hydrochloride often causes withdrawal reactions of nervousness, anxiety, seizures, cramping, chills, numbness of the extremities, and general behavior changes. Chronic overdosage is best treated by withdrawing the drug over a period of days or weeks.

Special Information

Do not attempt to drive or operate any equipment, appliances, or machinery while under the influence of Methaqualone Hydrochloride.

Generic Name

Methenamine Hippurate

Brand Names

Hippurate
Urex

Other Brand Names

Mandelamine (Methenamine Mandelate)

Type of Drug

Urinary anti-infective.

Prescribed for

Chronic urinary tract infections.

General Information

This drug and other methenamine salts work by turning into formaldehyde and ammonia when the urine is acidic. These drugs do not break down in the blood. They must be taken with large doses (4 to 12 grams per day) of Ascorbic Acid (Vitamin C) or Ammonium Chloride tablets. The formaldehyde kills any bacteria in the urinary tract.

Cautions and Warnings

Patients with kidney disease, dehydration, or severe liver disease should not use this drug. Pregnant women should only take this drug if absolutely necessary. Studies suggest it may be safe during the last three months of pregnancy, but are not conclusive.

Possible Side Effects

Large doses for long periods of time may cause bladder irritation, painful and frequent urination, and protein or blood in the urine. This drug may cause elevation in liver enzymes.

Possible Adverse Drug Effects

Upset stomach, rash.

Drug Interactions

Do not take with sulfa drugs, since the sulfas can form a precipitate in the urine when mixed with Methenamine Hippurate, which may lead to a kidney stone.

Sodium Bicarbonate and Acetazolamide will decrease the effect of Methenamine Hippurate by making the drug less acidic.

Usual Dose

Adult: 1 gram twice per day.
Child (age 6 to 12): ½ to 1 gram twice per day.

Special Information

Take Methenamine Hippurate with food to minimize upset stomach. Avoid foods (e.g., milk) or drugs (e.g., bicarbonate of soda) that are low in acid content or alkaline. Take each dose every 12 hours with plenty of water. Call your doctor if you develop pain when urinating or severe upset stomach.

Generic Name

Methocarbamol

Brand Names

Delaxin
Forbaxin
Marbaxin
Metho
Robamol

Robaxin
SK-Methocarbamol
Spenaxin
Tumol

Type of Drug

Skeletal muscle relaxant.

Prescribed for

Partial treatment for the relief of pain and other discomforts associated with acute conditions such as sprains, strains, or bad backs.

General Information

Methocarbamol is one of several drugs available for the relief of pain caused by spasms of large skeletal muscles. These drugs give symptomatic relief only. They should not be the only form of therapy used. If you are taking Methocarbamol, follow any other instructions given by your doctor about rest, physical therapy, or other measures to help relieve your problem.

Cautions and Warnings

The effect of Methocarbamol on the pregnant female has not been studied. It may have an effect on the unborn child: if you are pregnant, you should not use this medicine unless it is absolutely necessary and this problem has been considered by your physician.

Possible Side Effects

Most common: light-headedness, dizziness, drowsiness, nausea, drug allergy (itching and rash), conjunctivitis with nasal congestion, blurred vision, headache, fever.

Drug Interactions

Other drugs which, like Methocarbamol, may cause drowsiness, sleepiness, or lack of ability to concentrate must be taken with extreme caution: sleeping pills, tranquilizers, barbiturates, narcotics, and alcoholic beverages.

Usual Dose

Adult: initial dose, 1500 milligrams 4 times per day for 48 to 72 hours; then 1500 milligrams 3 times per day, 1000 milligrams 4 times per day, or 750 milligrams every 4 hours.

Overdosage

Symptoms are central nervous system depression, desire to sleep, weakness, lassitude, and difficulty in breathing. The patient should be taken to a hospital immediately. ALWAYS bring the medicine bottle.

Special Information

Methocarbamol may cause drowsiness, sleepiness, and inability to concentrate: this can affect you if you drive or operate any sort of appliance, equipment, or machinery.

Generic Name

Methyclothiazide

Brand Names

Aquatensen
Enduron

Type of Drug

Diuretic.

Prescribed for

Congestive heart failure, cirrhosis of the liver, kidney malfunction, high blood pressure, and other conditions where it is necessary to rid the body of excess fluid.

General Information

This drug is a member of the class known as thiazide diuretics. Thiazides act on the kidneys to stimulate the production of large amounts of urine. They also cause you to lose bicarbonate, chloride, and potassium ions from the body. They are used as part of the treatment of any disease where it is desirable to eliminate large quantities of body water. These diseases include heart failure, some kidney diseases, and liver disease.

Cautions and Warnings

Do not take Methyclothiazide if you are allergic or sensitive to this drug, similar drugs of this group, or sulfa drugs. If you have a history of allergy or bronchial asthmas, you may also have a sensitivity or allergy to Methyclothiazide. Although this drug has been used to treat specific conditions in pregnancy, unsupervised use by pregnant patients should be avoided. Methyclothiazide will cross the placenta and pass into the unborn child, possibly causing problems. The drug will pass into the breast milk of nursing mothers.

Possible Side Effects

Methyclothiazide will cause a lowering of potassium in the body. Signs of low potassium levels are dryness of the mouth, thirst, weakness, lethargy, drowsiness, restlessness, muscle pains or cramps, muscular tiredness, low blood pressure, decreased frequency of urination and decreased amount of urine produced, abnormal heart rate, and stomach upset including nausea and vomiting.

To treat this, potassium supplements are given in the form of tablets, liquids, or powders, or by increased consumption of foods such as bananas, citrus fruits, melons, and tomatoes.

Possible Adverse Drug Effects

Loss of appetite, stomach upset, nausea, vomiting, cramping, diarrhea, constipation, dizziness, headache, tingling of the toes and fingers, restlessness, changes in blood composition, sensitivity to sunlight, rash, itching, fever, difficulty in breathing, allergic reactions, dizziness when rising quickly from a sitting or lying position, muscle spasms, weakness, blurred vision.

Drug Interactions

Methyclothiazide will increase (potentiate) the action of other blood-pressure-lowering drugs. This is beneficial, and is frequently used to help lower blood pressure in patients with hypertension.

The possibility of developing imbalances in body fluids (electrolytes) is increased if you take medications such as Digitalis and adrenal corticosteroids while you take Methyclothiazide.

If you are taking an oral antidiabetic drug and begin taking Methyclothiazide, the antidiabetic drug dose may have to be altered.

Lithium Carbonate should not be taken with Methyclothiazide because the combination may increase the risk of lithium toxicity.

If you are taking this drug for the treatment of high blood pressure or congestive heart failure, avoid over-the-counter medicines for the treatment of coughs, colds, and allergies: such medicines may contain stimulants. If you are unsure about them, ask your pharmacist.

Usual Dose

Adult: 2½ to 10 milligrams per day. Thiazide diuretic doses must be adjusted toward maximum effect with minimum medication. Eventual dose is often 5 milligrams or less.

Overdosage

Symptoms are unusually frequent and excessive urination, fatigue, and coma. The patient should be taken to a hospital emergency room. ALWAYS bring the medicine bottle.

Generic Name

Methyldopa

Brand Name

Aldomet

Type of Drug

Antihypertensive.

Prescribed for

High blood pressure.

General Information

Methyldopa is usually prescribed with one or more of the other high blood pressure medications or a diuretic.

Cautions and Warnings

You should not take Methyldopa if you have hepatitis or active cirrhosis or if you have ever developed a sign or symptom of reaction to Methyldopa. No unusual effects have been noted in patients using the drug while they are pregnant, but the possibility of damage to the unborn child should be kept in mind.

Possible Side Effects

Most people have little trouble with Methyldopa, but it can cause transient sedation during the first few weeks of therapy or when the dose is increased. Transient headache or weakness are other possible early symptoms.

Possible Adverse Drug Effects

Dizziness, light-headedness, tingling in the extremities, unusual muscle spasms, decreased mental acuity, and psychic disturbances including nightmares, mild psychosis, or depression; also changes in heart rate, increase of pain associated with angina pectoris, retention of water, resulting weight gain, and orthostatic hypotension (dizziness when rising suddenly from a sitting or lying position), as well as nausea, vomiting, constipation, diarrhea, mild dryness of the mouth, and sore and/or black tongue. The drug may cause liver disorders: you may develop jaundice (yellowing of the skin and/or whites of the eyes), with or without fever, in the first 2 to 3 months of therapy. If you are taking Methyldopa for the first time, be sure your doctor checks your liver function, especially during the first 6 to 12 weeks of therapy. If you develop fever or jaundice, stop taking the drug and contact your physician immediately: if the reactions are due to Methyldopa, your temperature and/or liver abnormalities will reverse toward normal as soon as the drug is discontinued. Still other adverse effects are stuffed nose, breast enlargement, lactation (in females), impotence or decreased sex drive, mild symptoms of arthritis, and skin reactions.

Drug Interactions

Methyldopa will increase the effect of other blood pressure-lowering drugs. This is a desirable interaction which benefits patients with high blood pressure.

Avoid over-the-counter cough, cold, and allergy preparations containing stimulant drugs that can aggravate your high blood pressure. Information on over-the-counter drugs that are safe for you can be obtained from your pharmacist.

Methyldopa may increase the blood sugar, lowering effect of Tolbutamine or other oral antidiabetic drugs. If given together, with phenoxybenzamine, inability to control one's bladder (urinary incontinence) may result. The combination of Methyldopa and Lithium may cause symptoms of Lithium overdose, even though blood levels of Lithium do not change. Methyldopa when given together with Haloperidol may produce irritability, aggressiveness, assaultive behavior or other psychiatric symptoms.

Usual Dose

Adult: Starting dose, 250-milligram tablet 2 to 3 times per day for first 2 days. Dosage may be increased or decreased until blood pressure control is achieved. Maintenance dose, 500 milligrams to 3000 milligrams per day in 2 to 4 divided doses, per patient's needs.

Child: 5 milligrams per pound of body weight per day in 2 to 4 divided doses per patient's needs. Maximum dose, 30 milligrams per pound of body weight per day, up to 3 grams per day.

Special Information

Take this drug exactly as prescribed by your doctor so you can maintain maximum control over your high blood pressure.

A mild sedative effect is to be expected from Methyldopa and will resolve within several days.

Do not stop taking this medicine unless you are told to by your doctor. Avoid nonprescription cough and cold medicines or diet pills which contain stimulants. Your pharmacist can give you more information on those nonprescription drugs to be avoided. Call your doctor if you develop fever, prolonged general tiredness, or unusual dizziness.

Generic Name

Methylphenidate

Brand Name

Ritalin

Type of Drug

Central Nervous System stimulant.

Prescribed for

Minimal brain dysfunction in children; psychological, educational, or social disorders; narcolepsy and mild depression.

General Information

Chronic or abusive use of Methylphenidate can cause the development of drug dependence or addiction; also the drug can cause severe psychotic episodes. The primary use for Methylphenidate is the treatment of minimal brain dysfunction in children. Common signs of this disease are short attention span, easy distractibility, emotional instability, impulsiveness, and moderate to severe hyperactivity. Children who suffer from this disorder will find it difficult to learn. There are many who feel that Methylphenidate is a temporary solution because it does not permanently change patterns of behavior. When Methylphenidate is used, it must be used with other special measures.

Cautions and Warnings

Do not take Methylphenidate if you are extremely tense or agitated, have glaucoma, are allergic to this drug, have high blood pressure, or have a history of epilepsy or other seizures.

Possible Side Effects

Most common in adults: nervousness and inability to sleep, which are generally controlled by reducing or eliminating the afternoon or evening dose. Most common in children: loss of appetite, stomach pains, weight loss (especially during prolonged periods of therapy), difficulty sleeping, and abnormal heart rhythms.

Possible Adverse Drug Effects

Infrequent in adults: skin rash, itching, fever, symptoms similar to arthritis, loss of appetite, nausea, dizziness, abnormal heart rhythms, headache, drowsiness, changes in blood pressure or pulse, chest pains, stomach pains, psychotic reactions, effects on components of the blood, loss of some scalp hair.

Drug Interactions

Methylphenidate will decrease the effectiveness of Guanethidine, a drug used to treat high blood pressure.

Interaction with MAO inhibitors may vastly increase the effect of Methylphenidate and cause problems.

Interaction with anticoagulants (blood-thinning drugs), some drugs used to treat epilepsy or other kinds of convulsions, Phenylbutazone and Oxyphenbutazone, and antidepressant drugs will slow the rate at which these drugs are broken down by the body, making more of them available in the bloodstream. Thus it may be necessary to lower the dose of them.

Usual Dose

Adult: 10 or 20 to 30 or even 60 milligrams per day in divided doses 2 to 3 times per day, preferably 30 to 45 minutes before meals.

Child (over age 6): Initial dose, 5 milligrams before breakfast and lunch; then increase in steps of 5 to 10 milligrams each week as required, but not to exceed 60 milligrams per day.

Doses should be tailored to individual needs; the doses listed here are only guidelines.

Overdosage

Symptoms are stimulation of the nervous system such as vomiting, agitation, tremors (uncontrollable twitching of the muscles), convulsions followed by coma, euphoria, confusion, hallucinations, delirium, sweating, flushing (face, hands, and extremities will be red), headache, high fever, abnormal heart rate, high blood pressure, and dryness of the mouth and nose. The patient should be taken to a hospital emergency room. ALWAYS bring the medicine bottle.

Special Information

Methylphenidate can cause temporary drowsiness: be careful while driving or operating an automobile, machine, or appliance. If you take Methylphenidate regularly, avoid alcoholic beverages; they will add to the drowsiness problem.

Generic Name

Methylprednisolone

Brand Name

Medrol

Type of Drug

Adrenal cortical steroid.

Prescribed for

Reduction of inflammation. The variety of disorders for which Methylprednisolone is prescribed is almost endless, from skin rash to cancer. The drug may be used as a treatment for adrenal gland disease, since one of the hormones produced by the adrenal gland is very similar to Methylprednisolone. If patients are not producing sufficient adrenal hormones, Methylprednisolone may be used as replacement therapy. It may also be prescribed for the treatment of bursitis, arthritis, severe skin reactions such as psoriasis or other rashes, severe allergic conditions, asthma, drug or serum sickness, severe acute or chronic allergic inflammation of the eye and surrounding areas such as conjunctivitis, respiratory diseases including pneumonitis, blood disorders, gastrointestinal diseases including ulcerative colitis, and inflammation of the nerves, heart, or other organs.

General Information

Methylprednisolone is one of many adrenal cortical steroids used in medical practice today. The major differences between Methylprednisolone and other adrenal cortical steroids are potency of medication and variation in some secondary effects. In most cases the choice of adrenal cortical steroids to be used in a specific disease is a matter of doctor preference and past experience. Other adrenal cortical steroids include Cortisone, Hydrocortisone, Prednisone, Prednisolone, Triamcinolone, Meprednisone, Paramethasone, Fluprednisolone, Dexamethasone, Betamethasone, and Fludrocortisone.

Cautions and Warnings

Because of the effect of Methylprednisolone on your adrenal gland, it is essential that the dose be tapered from a large dose down to a small dose over a period of time. Do not stop taking this medication suddenly and/or without the advice of your doctor. If you do, you may cause a failure of the adrenal gland with extremely serious consequences. Methylprednisolone has a strong anti-inflammatory effect, and may mask some signs of infections. If new infections appear during the use of Methylprednisolone therapy, they may be difficult to discover and may grow more rapidly due to your decreased resistance. If you think you are getting any kind of infection during the time that you are taking Methylprednisolone, you should contact your doctor, who will prescribe appropriate therapy. If you are taking Methylprednisolone you should not be vaccinated against infectious disease, because of inability of the body to produce the normal reaction to the vaccination. Discuss this with your doctor before he administers any vaccination. If you suspect that you have become pregnant and are taking Methylprednisolone, report it immediately to your doctor. If you are taking Methylprednisolone and have just given birth, do not nurse; use prepared formulas instead.

Possible Side Effects

Stomach upset is one of the more common side effects of Methylprednisolone, which may in some cases cause gastric or duodenal ulcers. If you notice a slight stomach upset when you take your dose of Methylprednisolone, take this medication with food or with a small amount of antacid. If stomach upset continues, notify your doctor. Other side effects: retention of water, heart failure, potassium loss, muscle weakness, loss of muscle mass, loss of calcium from bones which may result in bone fractures and a condition known as aseptic necrosis of the femoral and humoral heads (this means the ends of the large bones in the hip may degenerate from loss of calcium), slowing down of wound healing, black-and-blue marks on the skin, increased sweating, allergic skin rash, itching, convulsions, dizziness, headache.

Possible Adverse Drug Effects

May cause irregular menstrual cycles, slowing down of growth in children, particularly after the medication has been taken for long periods of time, depression of the adrenal and/or pituitary glands, development of diabetes, increased pressure of the fluid inside the eye, hypersensitivity or allergic reactions, blood clots, insomnia, weight gain, increased appetite, nausea, and feeling of ill health. Psychic derangements may appear which range from euphoria to mood swings, personality changes, and severe depression. Methylprednisolone may also aggravate existing emotional instability.

Drug Interactions

Methylprednisolone and other adrenal corticosteroids may interact with Insulin or oral antidiabetic drugs, causing an increased requirement of the antidiabetic drugs.

Interaction with Phenobarbital, Ephedrine, and Phenytoin may reduce the effect of Methylprednisolone by increasing its removal from the body.

If a doctor prescribes Methylprednisolone you should discuss any oral anticoagulant (blood-thinning) drugs you are taking; their dose may have to be changed.

Interaction with diuretics such as Hydrochlorothiazide may cause you to lose blood potassium. Be aware of signs of lowered potassium level such as weakness, muscle cramps, and tiredness, and report them to your physician. It is recommended that you eat high-potassium foods such as bananas, citrus fruits, melons, and tomatoes.

Usual Dose

Initial dose, 4 to 48 milligrams; maintenance dose, as determined by your doctor based on your response.

Overdosage

There is no specific treatment for overdosage of adrenal cortical steroids. Symptoms are anxiety, depression and/or stimulation, stomach bleeding, increased blood sugar, high blood pressure, and retention of fluid. The patient should be taken to a hospital emergency room immediately, where stomach pumping, oxygen, intravenous fluids, and other supportive treatment are available.

Generic Name

Methyltestosterone

Brand Names

Android
Metandren
Oreton
Testred
Virilon

Type of Drug

Androgenic (male) hormone.

Prescribed for

Diseases in which male hormone replacement or augmentation is needed; male menopause.

General Information

This is a member of the androgenic or male hormone group, which includes Testosterone, Calusterone, and Dromostanolone Propionate. (The last two are used primarily to treat breast cancer in women.) Females taking any androgenic drug should watch for deepening of the voice, oily skin, acne, hairiness, increased libido, and menstrual irregularities, which may be related to the so-called virilizing effects of these hormones. Virilization is a sign that the drug is starting to produce changes in secondary sex characteristics. The drugs should be avoided if possible by boys who have not gone through puberty.

Cautions and Warnings

Men who have an unusually high blood level of calcium, known or suspected cancer of the prostate, or prostate destruction or disease, cancer of the breast, liver, heart, or kidney disease should not use this medication. Women who are pregnant should not use Methyltestosterone, since it may affect the unborn child.

Possible Side Effects

In males: inhibition of testicle function, impotence, chronic erection of the penis, enlargement of the breast.

In females: unusual hairiness, baldness in a pattern similar to that seen in men, deepening of the voice, enlargement of the clitoris. These changes are usually irreversible once they have occurred. Females also experience menstrual irregularities and increases in blood calcium.

Possible Adverse Drug Effects

In both sexes: changes in libido, flushing of the skin, acne, mild dependence on the drug, excitation, chills, sleeplessness, water retention, nausea, vomiting, diarrhea. Symptoms resembling stomach ulcer may develop. Methyltestosterone may affect level of blood cholesterol.

Drug Interactions

Methyltestosterone may increase the effect of oral anticoagulants; dosage of the anticoagulant may have to be decreased. The drug may have an effect on the glucose tolerance test, a blood test used to screen people for diabetes mellitus.

Usual Dose

10 to 300 milligrams per day, depending upon the disease being treated and patient's response.

Special Information

Methyltestosterone and other androgens are potent drugs. They must be taken only under the close supervision of your doctor and never used casually. The dosage and clinical effects of the drug vary widely and require constant monitoring.

Generic Name

Methyprylon

Brand Name

Noludar

Type of Drug

Sedative-hypnotic.

Prescribed for

Inability to sleep.

General Information

This drug works in about 45 minutes. Its effect lasts for 5 to 8 hours. It should not be used continuously for long periods of time.

Cautions and Warnings

Methyprylon should not be used if you are sensitive or allergic to it. It can be addictive.

Possible Side Effects

Skin rash.

Possible Adverse Drug Effects

People who have taken Methyprylon for a long time may show signs of chronic overdosage: loss of memory, inability to concentrate, shakes, tremors, loss of reflexes, slurred speech, and general sense of depression. Abrupt discontinuation of Methyprylon often causes withdrawal reactions of nervousness, anxiety, seizures, cramping, chills, numbness of the extremities, and general behavior changes. Chronic overdosage is best treated by withdrawing the drug over a period of days or weeks.

There have been reports of nausea, morning hangover, rash, excitation, and blurred vision.

Drug Interactions

Do not take this drug with alcohol and/or other depressants such as sedatives, hypnotics, and antihistamines which may produce drowsiness or sleepiness.

Doses of anticoagulant (blood-thinning) drugs such as Warfarin may require adjustment because of increased effects. Dosage adjustment will also be required when you stop taking Methyprylon.

Usual Dose

200 to 400 milligrams at bedtime.

Overdosage

Large amounts of Methyprylon can be fatal, and the drug is

frequently used in suicide attempts. Symptoms are coma, lowered body temperature followed by fever, absence of normal reflexes and pain responses after pinches and needle or pin sticks, and shallow breathing. The patient should be taken to a hospital emergency room immediately.

Generic Name

Metoclopramide

Brand Name

Reglan

Type of Drug

Gastrointestinal stimulant.

Prescribed for

Symptoms of diabetic gastroparesis (stomach paralysis), including nausea, vomiting, fullness after meals, and loss of appetite. Also used to facilitate certain X-ray diagnostic procedures. Used experimentally for the relief of nausea and vomiting caused by anticancer drugs.

General Information

This drug stimulates movement of the upper gastrointestinal tract but does not stimulate excess stomach acids or other secretions. Recently, it has been investigated in the U.S. as an antinauseant for patients receiving anticancer drugs. It has been used extensively for this purpose in Europe and South America. Although it is not known exactly how the drug works, its results may be caused by the direct effect of Metoclopramide on special receptors in the brain. Its value as an antiemetic is about the same as that of other currently available drugs.

Cautions and Warnings

This drug should not be used where stimulation of the gastrointestinal tract could be dangerous (bleeding ulcers, etc.) and should not be used if you are allergic to the drug. This drug can cause "extrapyramidal" side effects similar to those caused by phenothiazine drugs. Do not take the two classes of drugs together. Extrapyramidal effects occur in only about 0.2 percent of the people taking the drug and usually include restlessness and involuntary movements of arms and legs, face, tongue, lips, or other parts of the body. This drug should be used by pregnant women or nursing mothers only when absolutely necessary.

Possible Side Effects

Restlessness, drowsiness, tiredness.

Possible Adverse Drug Effects

Sleeplessness, headache, dizziness, nausea, upset stomach.

Drug Interactions

The effects of Metoclopramide on the stomach are antagonized by narcotics and anticholinergic drugs. Metoclopramide may interact with alcohol, sedatives, or other depressant drugs to produce excessive sleepiness or tiredness. Because of its effects on the gastrointestinal tract, this drug may affect the passage of drugs through the stomach or intestines into the bloodstream.

Usual Dose

Adult: 1 to 2 tablets before meals and at bedtime. Single doses of 1 to 2 tablets are used before X-ray diagnostic procedures.

Child (age 6 to 14): One-quarter to half the adult dose.

Child (under age 6): 0.05 milligram per pound of body weight per dose.

Overdosage

Symptoms are drowsiness, disorientation, restlessness, or uncontrollable muscle movements. Symptoms usually disappear within 24 hours after the drug has been stopped. Anticholinergic drugs will antagonize these symptoms.

Special Information

Take exactly as directed. When taking this drug for nausea, be sure to take the medicine 1 hour before meals and at bedtime.

Generic Name

Metoprolol

Brand Name

Lopressor

Type of Drug

Beta-adrenergic blocking agent.

Prescribed for

High blood pressure.

General Information

This drug is very much like Propranolol but it has a more specific effect on the heart and a less specific effect on receptors in the blood vessels and respiratory tract. This means that the drug causes less difficulty in breathing and has a more specific effect on heart functions.

Cautions and Warnings

Metoprolol should be used with care if you have a history of asthma, upper respiratory disease, or seasonal allergy, which may be made worse by the effects of this drug.

Possible Side Effects

Metoprolol may decrease the heart rate; may aggravate a condition of congestive heart failure; and may produce lowered blood pressure, tingling in the extremities, light-headedness, mental depression including inability to sleep, weakness, and tiredness. It may also produce a mental depression which is reversible when the drug is withdrawn, visual disturbances, hallucinations, disorientation, and short-term memory loss. Patients taking Metoprolol may experience nausea, vomiting, stomach upset, abdominal cramps and diarrhea, or constipation. If you are allergic to this drug, you may show typical reactions associated wth drug allergies, including sore throat, fever, difficulty in breathing, and various effects on the blood system. Metoprolol may induce bronchospasms (spasms of muscles in the bronchi), which will make any existing asthmatic condition or any severe upper respiratory disease worse.

Possible Adverse Drug Effects

Occasionally, patients taking Metoprolol may experience emotional instability, or a feeling of detachment or personality change, or the drug may produce unusual effects on the blood system.

Drug Interactions

This drug will interact with any psychotropic drug, including the MAO inhibitors, which stimulates one of the adrenergic segments of the nervous system. Since this information is not generally known, you should discuss the potential problem of using Metoprolol with your doctor if you are taking any psychotropic or psychiatric drug.

Metoprolol may cause increased effectiveness of Insulin or oral antidiabetic drugs. If you are diabetic, discuss the situation with your doctor; a reduction in dose of antidiabetic medication will probably be made.

Metoprolol may reduce the effectiveness of Digitalis on your heart. Any dose of Digitalis medication will have to be altered. If you are taking Digitalis for a purpose other than congestive heart failure, the effectiveness of the Digitalis may be increased by Metoprolol, and the dose of Digitalis may have to be reduced.

Metoprolol may interact with certain other drugs to produce lowering of blood pressure. This interaction often has positive results in the treatment of patients with high blood pressure.

Do not self-medicate with over-the-counter cold, cough, or allergy remedies which may contain stimulant drugs that will aggravate certain types of heart disease and high blood pressure, or other ingredients that may antagonize the effects of Metoprolol. Double-check with your doctor or pharmacist before taking any over-the-counter medication.

Usual Dose

100 to 450 milligrams per day. The dosage of this drug must be tailored to patient's need.

Overdosage

Symptoms are slowed heart rate, heart failure, lowered blood pressure, and spasms of the bronchial muscles which make it difficult to breathe. The patient should be taken to a hospital emergency room where proper therapy can be given. ALWAYS bring the medicine bottle with you.

Special Information

This drug may make you tired, so take care when driving or

when operating machinery. Call your doctor if you become dizzy or develop diarrhea. Do not stop taking this medicine abruptly unless you are told to do so by your doctor, or serious heart pain (angina) may develop.

Generic Name

Metronidazole

Brand Name

Flagyl

Type of Drug

Amoebicide.

Prescribed for

Acute amoebic dysentery; vaginal infections (trichomonas); and diseases caused by some parasites.

General Information

Metronidazole may be prescribed for asymptomatic disease when the doctor feels that the use of this drug is indicated; specifically, asymptomatic females may be treated with this drug when vaginal examination shows evidence of trichomonas. Because trichomonas infection of the vaginal area is a veneral disease, asymptomatic sexual partners of treated patients should be treated simultaneously if the organism has been found to be present in the woman's genital tract, in order to prevent reinfection of the partner. The decision to treat an asymptomatic male partner who does not have the organism present is an individual one and must be made by the doctor.

Cautions and Warnings

If you have a history of blood disease or if you know that you are sensitive or allergic to Metronidazole you should not use this drug. It should not be used during the first 3 months of pregnancy.

Metronidazole has been shown to be carcinogenic (cancer-inducing) in mice and possibly in rats. This drug should not be used unnecessarily and should only be used in specific conditions for which it is normally prescribed.

Possible Side Effects

Most common: symptoms in the gastrointestinal tract, including nausea (sometimes accompanied by headache), loss of appetite, occasional vomiting, diarrhea, stomach upset, abdominal cramping, and constipation. A sharp, unpleasant metallic taste is also associated with the use of this drug. Dizziness and, rarely, incoordination have been reported. Numbness or tingling in the extremities and occasional joint pains have been associated with Metronidazole therapy as have confusion, irritability, depression, inability to sleep, and weakness. Itching and a sense of pelvic pressure have been reported.

Possible Adverse Drug Effects

Rarely: fever, increased urination, incontinence, decrease of libido.

Drug Interactions

Avoid alcoholic beverages: interaction with metronidazole may cause abdominal cramps, nausea, vomiting, headaches, and flushing. Modification of the taste of alcoholic beverages has also been reported.

People taking oral anticoagulant (blood-thinning) drugs such as Warfarin will have to have their dose of Warfarin changed, because Metronidazole increases the effect of anticoagulants.

Usual Dose

Adult: for the treatment of amoebic dysentery, 3 tablets 3 times per day for 5 to 10 days.

Child: Amoebic dysentery, 16 to 23 milligrams per pound of body weight daily divided in 3 equal doses, for 10 days.

For trichomonal infections, 1 tablet 3 times per day for 7 days.

Special Information

Follow your doctor's dosage instructions faithfully and don't stop until the full course of therapy has been taken.

The occasional darkening of urine of patients taking Metronidazole is of uncertain clinical significance and is probably not important.

Generic Name

Miconazole Nitrate

Brand Names

Monistat
Monistat-Derm

Type of Drug

Antifungal.

Prescribed for

Treatment of fungus infections in the vagina, on the skin, and in the blood.

General Information

Miconazole Nitrate is used as a vaginal cream or topical cream, or by intravenous injection. When given as an injection to hospitalized patients, it is effective against serious fungal infections. When used for vaginal infections, it is effective against several nonfungus types of organisms, as well as fungus-type infections of the vaginal tract. On the skin, it is used for common fungus infections such as athlete's foot or jock itch.

Cautions and Warnings

Do not use Miconazole Nitrate if you know you are allergic to it. Pregnant women should avoid using the vaginal cream during the first 3 months of pregnancy. They should use it during the next 6 months only if it is absolutely necessary.

Possible Side Effects

After intravenous injection: vein irritation, itching, rash, nausea, vomiting, fever, drowsiness, diarrhea, loss of appetite, flushing. After vaginal administration: itching, burning or irritation, pelvic cramps, hives, rash, headache. After application to the skin: irritation, burning.

Usual Dose

Intravenous: 200 to 3600 milligrams per day.

Vaginal: One applicatorful into the vagina at bedtime for 7 days.

Topical: Apply to affected areas of skin twice a day for up to 1 month.

Special Information

When using the vaginal cream, insert the whole applicatorful of cream high into the vagina and be sure to complete the full course of treatment prescribed for you. Call your doctor if you develop burning or itching.

Generic Name

Minocycline

Brand Name

Minocin

Type of Drug

Broad-spectrum antibiotic effective against gram-positive and gram-negative organisms.

Prescribed for

Bacterial infections such as gonorrhea, infections of the mouth, gums, teeth, Rocky Mountain spotted fever and other fevers caused by ticks and lice from a variety of carriers, urinary tract infections, and respiratory system infections such as pneumonia and bronchitis.

These diseases are produced by gram-positive and gram-negative organisms such as diplococci, staphylococci, streptococci, gonococci, E. coli, and Shigella.

Minocycline has also been successfully used to treat some skin infections, but it is not considered the first-choice antibiotic for the treatment of general skin infections or wounds.

General Information

Minocycline works by interfering with the normal growth cycle of the invading bacteria, preventing them from reproducing and thus allowing the body's normal defenses to fight off the infection. This process is referred to as bacteriostatic action. Minocycline has also been used along with other medicines to treat amoebic infections of the intestinal tract, known as amoebic dysentery. It is also prescribed for diseases caused by ticks, fleas, and lice.

Minocycline has been successfully used for the treatment of adolescent acne, in small doses over a long period of time. Adverse effects or toxicity in this type of therapy are almost unheard of.

Since the action of this antibiotic depends on its concentration within the invading bacteria, it is imperative that you completely follow your doctor's directions.

Cautions and Warnings

You should not use Minocycline if you are pregnant. Minocycline when used in children has been shown to interfere with the development of the long bones and may retard growth.

Exceptions would be when Minocycline is the only effective antibiotic available and all risk factors have been made known to the patient.

Minocycline should not be given to people with known liver disease or kidney or urine excretion problems. You should avoid taking high doses of Minocycline or undergoing extended Minocycline therapy if you will be exposed to sunlight for a long period because this antibiotic can interfere with your body's normal sun-screening mechanism, possibly causing a severe sunburn. If you have a known history of allergy to Minocycline you should avoid taking this drug or other drugs within this category such as Aureomycin, Terramycin, Rondomycin, Vibramycin, Demeclocycline, and Tetracycline.

Possible Side Effects

As with other antibiotics, the common side effects of Minocycline are stomach upset, nausea, vomiting, diarrhea, and skin rash. Less common side effects include hairy tongue and itching and irritation of the anal and/or vaginal region. If these symptoms appear, consult your physician immediately. Periodic physical examinations and laboratory tests should be given to patients who are on long-term Minocycline.

Possible Adverse Drug Effects

Loss of appetite, peeling of the skin, sensitivity to the sun, fever, chills, anemia, possible brown spotting of the skin, decrease in kidney function, damage to the liver.

Drug Interactions

Minocycline (a bacteriostatic drug) may interfere with the action of bactericidal agents such as Penicillin. It is not advisable to take both during the same course of therapy.

The antibacterial effect of Minocycline is neutralized when taken with food, some dairy products (such as milk and cheese), and antacids.

Don't take multivitamin products containing minerals at the same time as Minocycline, or you may reduce the antibiotic's effectiveness. You may take these two medicines at least 2 hours apart.

People receiving anticoagulation therapy (blood-thinning agents) should consult their doctor, since Minocycline will interfere with this form of therapy. An adjustment in the anticoagulant dosage may be required.

Usual Dose

Adult: first dose, 200 milligrams, followed by 100 milligrams every 12 hours. Or 100 to 200 milligrams may be given to start, followed by 50 milligrams 4 times per day.

Child (age 9 and over): approximately 2 milligrams per pound of body weight initially, followed by 1 milligram per pound every 12 hours.

Child (up to age 8): not recommended, as the drug has been shown to produce serious discoloration of the permanent teeth.

Storage

Minocycline can be stored at room temperature.

Special Information

Do *not* take after the expiration date on the label. The decom-

MULTICOLORED

Achromycin 250 mg **p. 477**	**Achromycin** 500 mg **p. 477**	**Adapin** 25 mg **p. 179**	**Amoxil** 250mg **p. 38**
Antivert 12.5 mg **p. 270**	**Antivert** 25 mg **p. 270**	**Azolid** **p. 390**	**Benadryl** 25 mg **p. 170**
Benadryl 50 mg **p. 170**	**Butazolidin** **p. 390**	**Carbritral** **p. 371**	**Cleocin** 150 mg **p. 109**
Combid **p. 120**	**Compazine** 10 mg **p. 414**	**Compazine** 15 mg **p. 414**	**Dalmane** 15 mg **p. 210**
Dalmane 30 mg **p. 210**	**Darvon Compound** **p. 418**	**Darvon Compound-65** **p. 135**	**Dexedrine** 10 mg **p. 149**

A

MULTICOLORED

Dexedrine 15 mg p. 149	Dilantin 100 mg p. 393	Donnatal p. 177	Dyazide p. 186
Dycill 500 mg p. 156	Dynapen 250 mg p. 156	Dynapen 500 mg p. 156	Equagesic p. 188
Eskalith p. 257	Fastin 30 mg p. 389	Feosol p. 197	Fiorinal #1 p. 199
Fiorinal #2 p. 199	Fiorinal #3 p. 199	Histaspan 8 mg p. 98	Histaspan 12 mg p. 98
Ilosone 250 mg p. 191	Indocin 25 mg p. 240	Indocin 50 mg p. 240	Isordil 40 mg p. 246

B

Keflex 250 mg **p. 85**	**Larotid** 250 mg **p. 38**	**Librium** 5 mg **p. 92**	**Librium** 10 mg **p. 92**
Librium 25 mg **p. 92**	**Loxitane** 10 mg **p. 573**	**Macrodantin** 50 mg **p. 331**	**Meclizine HCL** 12.5 mg **p. 270**
Meprospan 200 mg **p. 276**	**Meprospan** 400 mg **p. 276**	**Minipress** 2 mg **p. 404**	**Minipress** 5 mg **p. 404**
Minocin 100 mg **p. 308**	**Naldecon** **p. 322**	**Nalfon** 200 mg **p. 195**	**Nalfon** 300 mg **p. 195**
Natabec Rx **p. 326**	**Navane** 1 mg **p. 486**	**Navane** 2 mg **p. 486**	**Navane** 5 mg **p. 486**

MULTICOLORED

Navane 10 mg p. 486	**Navane** 20 mg p. 486	**Nembutal Sodium** 50 mg p. 371	**Nicobid** 250 mg p. 327
Nitro-Bid Plateau 2.5 mg p. 333	**Nitro-Bid Plateau** 6.5 mg p. 333	**Nitrospan** 2.5 mg p. 333	**Noludar** 300 mg p. 299
Norgesic p. 335	**Norgesic Forte** p. 335	**Novafed A** p. 426	**Omnipen** 250 mg p. 40
Omnipen 500 mg p. 40	**Ornade** p. 348	**Pamelor** 25 mg p. 337	**Panmycin** 250 mg p. 270
Pavabid 150 mg p. 360	**Pathocil** 250 mg p. 156	**Phenaphen** w/Codeine #2 p. 13	**Phenaphen** w/Codeine #3 p. 13

D

MULTICOLORED

Phenaphen w/Codeine #4 13	**Polycillin** 250 mg p. 40	**Polycillin** 500 mg p. 40	**Polymox** 250 mg p. 38
Ponstel 250 mg p. 577	**Proloid** 32 mg (½ grain) p. 489	**Proloid** 65 mg (1 grain) p. 489	**Proloid** 100 mg (1½ grain) p. 489
Proloid 200 mg (3 grain) p. 489	**Pronestyl** 375 mg p. 412	**Pronestyl** 500 mg p. 412	**Propoxyphene Compound-65** p. 135
Restoril 15 mg p. 469	**Restoril** 30 mg p. 469	**Rimactane** 300 mg p. 435	**Serax** 10 mg p. 352
Serax 15 mg p. 352	**Serax** 30 mg p. 352	**Sinequan** 25 mg p. 179	**Sinequan** 100 mg p. 179

E

SK-Diphen-hydramine 50 mg **p. 170**	SK-Lygen 10 mg **p. 92**	Slo-Phyllin 125 mg **p. 48**	Slo-Phyllin 250 mg **p. 48**
Sudafed S.A. 120 mg **p. 426**	Sumycin 500 mg **p. 477**	Synalgos **p. 465**	Synalgos-DC **p. 465**
Tegopen 250 mg **p. 156**	Tegopen 500 mg **p. 156**	Teldrin 8 mg **p. 49**	Teldrin 12 mg **p. 49**
Terrastatin **p. 317**	Tetracycline 250 mg **p. 477**	Tetracycline 500 mg **p. 477**	Tetrex 500 mg **p. 477**
Theophyl-SR 125 mg **p. 480**	Theophyl-SR 250 mg **p. 480**	Thorazine 30 mg **p. 100**	Thorazine 75 mg **p. 100**

F

MULTICOLORED

Thorazine 150 mg **p. 100**	Thorazine 300 mg **p. 100**	Thyrolar #1 **p. 251**	Thyrolar #2 **p. 251**
Thyrolar #3 **p. 251**	Tigan 100 mg **p. 511**	Tofranil-PM 100 mg **p. 235**	Tranxene 7.5 mg **p. 114**
Tuinal 50 mg **p. 520**	Tuinal 100 mg **p. 520**	Tuinal 200 mg **p. 520**	Tuss Ornade **p. 524**
Vibramycin 50 mg **p. 182**	Virilon 10 mg **p. 298**	Vistaril 50 mg **p. 232**	Wymox 250 mg **p. 38**
Wymox 500 mg **p. 38**			

WHITE/GRAY

Actifed p. 18	Aldactazide p. 21	Aldactone 25 mg p. 452	Aldoril 25 mg p. 24
Aldoril 50 mg p. 24		Aminodur 300 mg p. 480	Aminophylline 100 mg p. 480
Aminophylline 200 mg p. 480	Antabuse 500 mg p. 581	Artane 2 mg p. 510	Artane 5 mg p. 510
Ativan ½ mg p. 264	Ativan 1 mg p. 264	Ativan 2 mg p. 264	Bactrim DS p. 442
Bayer Aspirin 325 mg p. 53	Bendectin p. 66	Bentyl w/Phenobarbital p. 67	Brethine 2.5 mg p. 471

H

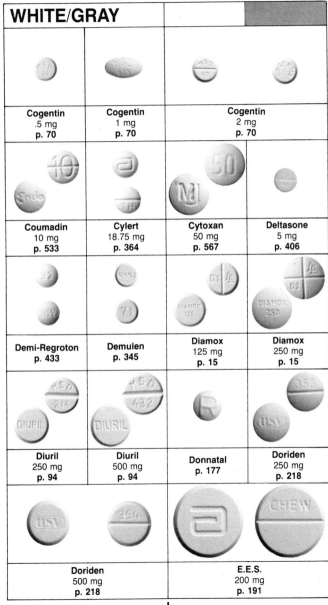

WHITE/GRAY			

| **Cogentin** .5 mg p. 70 | **Cogentin** 1 mg p. 70 | **Cogentin** 2 mg p. 70 | |

| **Coumadin** 10 mg p. 533 | **Cylert** 18.75 mg p. 364 | **Cytoxan** 50 mg p. 567 | **Deltasone** 5 mg p. 406 |

| **Demi-Regroton** p. 433 | **Demulen** p. 345 | **Diamox** 125 mg p. 15 | **Diamox** 250 mg p. 15 |

| **Diuril** 250 mg p. 94 | **Diuril** 500 mg p. 94 | **Donnatal** p. 177 | **Doriden** 250 mg p. 218 |

| **Doriden** 500 mg p. 218 | | **E.E.S.** 200 mg p. 191 | |

I

WHITE/GRAY

Duricef 1 gram p. 560	**Elixophyllin** 200 mg p. 480	**Empirin Analgesic** p. 53	**Empirin w/Codeine 2** p. 48
Empirin w/Codeine 3 p. 48	**Empirin w/Codeine 4** p. 48	**E-Mycin** 333 mg p. 191	**Entozyme**
Equanil 200 mg p. 276	**Equanil** 400 mg p. 276	**Eskalith** p. 257	**Feosol** 200 mg p. 197
Fiorinal p. 199	**Flagyl** 250 mg p. 305	**Gantrisin** 500 mg p. 461	**Haldol** .5 mg p. 224
Hydergine Sublingual .5 mg p. 190	**Hydergine** 1 mg p. 190	**Hydergine Sublingual** 1 mg p. 190	**Idenal** p. 199

J

WHITE/GRAY

Inderide 40/25 p. 238	Inderide 80/25 p. 238	Isoclor p. 98	Isordil Sublingual 5 mg p. 246
Isordil 10 mg p. 246	Lanoxin .25 mg p. 164	Lasix 20 mg p. 212	Lasix 40 mg p. 212
Lasix 80 mg p. 212	Leukeran 2 mg p. 567	Limbitrol 10-25 p. 256	Lomotil p. 260
Loniten 10 mg p. 311	Lo/Ovral p. 345	Marax p. 268	Medrol 4 mg p. 295
Medrol 16 mg p. 295	Mellaril 50 mg p. 484	Meprobamate 400 mg p. 276	Meticorten 1 mg p. 406

K

WHITE/GRAY

Meticorten 5 mg **p. 406**	**Miltown** 400 mg **p. 276**	**Minipress** 1 mg **p. 404**	**Motrin** 300 mg **p. 233**
Mysoline 250 mg **p. 409**	**Noludar** 200 mg **p. 299**	**Norlutin** 5 mg **p. 273**	**Norinyl 1 + 50** **p. 345**
Optimine 1 mg **p. 60**	**Oretic** 50 mg **p. 228**	**Oreton Methyl** 10 mg **p. 298**	**Ortho-Novum** 1/80-21 **p. 345**
	Orinase 500 mg **p. 498**	**Ovral** **p. 345**	**Ovral 28** **p. 345**
Ovulen 21 **p. 345**	**Penicillin VK** 500 mg **p. 368**	**Pentids** 400 mg **p. 366**	**Pen-Vee-K** 250 mg **p. 368**

L

WHITE/GRAY

Pen-Vee-K 500 mg **p. 368**	**Periactin** **p. 131**	**Phenobarbital** 16 mg **p. 387**	**Phenobarbital** 65 mg **p. 387**
Prednisone 5 mg **p. 406**	**Principen** 500 mg **p. 40**	**Pro-Banthine** 7.5 mg **p. 417**	**Provera** 10 mg **p. 272**
Quäälude 300 mg **p. 284**	**Quinidine Sulfate** 200 mg **p. 431**	**Quinine Sulfate** 5 grain **p. 557**	**Reglan** 10 mg **p. 301**
Renese 1 mg **p. 561**	**Ritalin** 10 mg **p. 293**	**Robaxin-750** 750 mg **p. 287**	**SK-Amitriptyline** 10 mg **p. 31**
SK-Diphenoxylate **p. 260**	**SK-Methocarbam-ol** 500 mg **p. 287**	**SK-Methocarbam-ol** 750 mg **p. 287**	**SK-Probenecid** 500 mg

M

WHITE/GRAY

SK-Reserpine 0.25 mg **p. 562**	**SK-Soxazole** 500 mg **p. 461**	**Slo-Phyllin** 100 mg **p. 48**	**Slo-Phyllin** 200 mg **p. 48**
Soma (Carisoprodol) **p. 81**	**Sustaire** 100 mg **p. 480**	**Sustaire** 300 mg **p. 480**	**Synthroid** .05 mg **p. 251**
Tagamet 200 mg **p. 107**	**Tagamet** 300 mg **p. 107**	**Tapazole** 5 mg **p. 491**	**Tapazole** 10 mg **p. 491**
Tavist	**Tegretol** **p. 578**	**Tenuate** 25 mg **p. 159**	**Tenuate Dospan** 75 mg **p. 159**
Theolair 125 mg **p. 480**	**Theolair** 250 mg **p. 480**	**Theophyl** 100 mg **p. 480**	**Thiosulfil Forte** **p. 455**

N

WHITE/GRAY

Armour Thyroid 16 mg p. 491	Armour Thyroid 32 mg p. 491	Armour Thyroid 65 mg p. 491	Armour Thyroid 195 mg p. 491
Armour Thyroid 325 mg p. 491	Tolectin 200 mg p. 500		Tolinase 100 mg p. 495
Tolinase 250 mg p. 495	Tranxene 3.75 mg p. 114	Tranxene 15 mg p. 114	Trimpex 100 mg p. 516
Tylenol 325 mg p. 11	Tylenol w/Codeine #2 p. 13	Tylenol w/Codeine #3 p. 13	Tylenol w/Codeine #4 p. 13
Urex p. 285	Valium 2 mg p. 153	Vasodilan 10 mg p. 248	Vasodilan 20 mg p. 248

WHITE/GRAY

V-Cillin K 250 mg p. 368	V-Cillin K 500 mg p. 368	Zyloprim 100 mg p. 26	

RED/PINK

Azo Gantrisin p. 62	Butisol Sodium 100 mg p. 77	Choledyl 100 mg p. 354	Coumadin Sodium 5 mg p. 533
Darvocet-N 50 mg p. 133	Darvocet-N 100 mg p. 133	Darvon 32 mg p. 418	Darvon 65 mg p. 418
Didrex 50 mg p. 73	Dimetane 8 mg p. 75	Disophrol pp. 75, 185	Diupres 250 mg p. 173

P

RED/PINK

Diupres 500 mg p. 173	**Dolene** 65 mg p. 418	**E.E.S.** 400 mg p. 191
Elavil 100 mg p. 31	**Enduron** 5 mg p. 288	**Erythrocin** 250 mg p. 191

Erythrocin 500 mg p. 191	**Erythromycin Base** 500 mg p. 191	**Esidrix** 25 mg p. 228
Etrafon 2-25 p. 504	**Etrafon 4-25** p. 504	**Haldol** 2 mg p. 224	**Ilotycin** 250 mg p. 191
Isordil 5 mg p. 246	**Lopressor** 50 mg p. 302	**Medrol** 2 mg p. 295

Q

RED/PINK

Natalins Rx p. 325	**Norlutate** 5 mg p. 273	**Peri-Colace** p. 377	**Persantine** 50 mg p. 172
Persantine 75 mg p. 172	**Placidyl** 500 mg p. 194	**Polaramine** 2 mg p. 147	**Polaramine** 4 mg p. 147
Polaramine 6 mg p. 147	**Preludin** 75 mg p. 380	**Propoxyphene HCL 65 mg** p. 418	**Prostaphlin** 250 mg p. 350
Prostaphlin 500 mg p. 350	**Purodigin** 0.1 mg p. 163	**Regroton** p. 433	**Rela** 350 mg p. 81
Seconal 50 mg p. 440	**Seconal** 100 mg p. 440	**Septra** p. 442	**Septra DS** p. 442

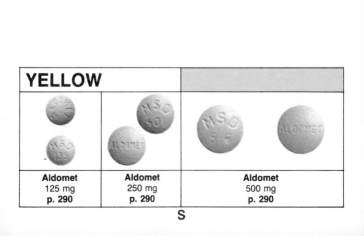

RED/PINK			
Ser-Ap-Es p. 444	**Sinequan** 10 mg p. 179	**Sinequan** 50 mg p. 179	**Singlet** p. 449
Sinubid p. 451	**Sumycin** 250 mg p. 477	**Symmetrel** 100 mg p. 249	**Synthroid** .2 mg p. 251
Tolectin 400 mg p. 500	**Wyamycin S** 250 mg p. 191	**Wyamycin S** 500 mg p. 191	**Zaroxolyn** 2.5 mg p. 561

YELLOW		
Aldomet 125 mg p. 290	**Aldomet** 250 mg p. 290	**Aldomet** 500 mg p. 290

S

YELLOW

Apresoline 10 mg **p. 226**	**Atarax** 50 mg **p. 232**	**Azolid** 100 mg **p. 390**	**Benemid**
Chlor-Trimeton 4 mg **p. 98**	**Chlor-Trimeton** 8 mg **p. 98**	**Choloxin** 2 mg **p. 151**	**Clinoril** 150 mg **p. 463**
Clinoril 200 mg **p. 463**	**Compazine** 5 mg **p. 414**	**Compazine** 10 mg **p. 414**	**Coumadin** 7.5 mg **p. 533**
Dilantin 50 mg **p. 393**	**Elavil** 25 mg **p. 31**	**Endep** 75 mg **p. 31**	**Esidrix** 50 mg **p. 228**
Etrafon 2-10 **p. 504**	**Flexeril** 10 mg **p. 129**	**Folic Acid** 1 mg	**Furadantin** 50 mg **p. 331**

T

YELLOW

Geocillin p. 560	**Haldol** 1 mg p. 224	**Imuran** 50 mg p. 569	**Inderal** 80 mg p. 420
Ionamin 30 mg p. 389	**Ismelin** 10 mg p. 219	**Isordil** 40 mg p. 246	**K-Tab** 750 mg p. 400
Kaon-Cl 500 mg p. 400	**Lanoxin** 125 mg p. 164	**Macrodantin** 100 mg p. 331	**Naprosyn** 250 mg p. 324
NegGram 250 mg pp. 331–32	**NegGram** 1 gram pp. 331–32	**Nembutal** 30 mg p. 371	**Nembutal** 100 mg p. 371
Norlestrin 1/50 p. 345	**Ortho-Novum** 1/50☐21 mg p. 345	**Oxytetracycline** 250 mg p. 478	**Pathibamate** 200 mg p. 411

U

YELLOW

Pathibamate 400 mg **p. 411**	**Percodan** **p. 375**	**Plegine** 35 mg **p. 380**	**Premarin** 1.25 mg **p. 124**
Pro-Banthine **w/Phenobarbital** **p. 411**	**Prolixin** 2.5 mg **p. 207**	**Pronestyl** 250 mg **p. 412**	**Quibron** **p. 427**
Ritalin 5 mg **p. 293**	**Ritalin** 20 mg **p. 293**	**Sansert** **p. 578**	**SK-Amitriptyline** 50 mg **p. 31**
SK-Erythromycin 500 mg **p. 191**	**Sorbitrate** 10 mg **p. 246**	**Synthroid** .1 mg **p. 251**	**Terramycin** 250 mg **p. 478**
Triavil 4-25 **p. 504**	**Valium** 5 mg **p. 153**	**Vivactil** 10 mg **p. 423**	**Yutopar** 10 mg **p. 437**

V

BLUE/PURPLE

Anaprox 275 mg **p. 324**	**Apresoline** 25 mg **p. 226**	**Apresoline** 50 mg **p. 226**	**Bentyl** 10 mg **p. 157**
Bentyl 20 mg **p. 157**	**Butisol Sodium** 15 mg **p. 77**	**Corgard** 40 mg **p. 320**	**Corgard** 80 mg **p. 320**
Corgard 120 mg **p. 320**	**Coumadin** 2 mg **p. 533**	**Cyclospasmol** 200 mg **p. 127**	**Diabinese** 100 mg **p. 103**
Diabinese 250 mg **p. 103**	**Dianabol** 5 mg **p. 561**	**Dimetapp** **p. 168**	**Disalcid** 500 mg **p. 577**
Diulo 5 mg **p. 561**	**Doxycycline** Hyclate 100 mg **p. 182**	**Elavil** 10 mg **p. 31**	**Elavil** 150 mg **p. 31**

W

BLUE/PURPLE

Hygroton 50 mg p. 105	**Inderal** 20 mg p. 420	**Isordil** 30 mg p. 246	**Limbitrol 5-12.5** p. 256
Lopressor 100 mg p. 302	**Oreton Methyl Bucal** 10 mg p. 298	**PBZ-SR** 100 mg p. 517	**Percodan** p. 375
Premarin 2.5 mg p. 124	**SK-Pramine** 25 mg p. 235	**SK-Pramine** 50 mg p. 235	**Sodium Amytal** 200 mg p. 34
Sorbitrate 20 mg p. 246	**Stelazine** 1 mg p. 507	**Stelazine** 2 mg p. 507	**Stelazine** 5 mg p. 507
Stelazine 10 mg p. 507	**Synthroid** .15 mg p. 251	**Tigan** 250 mg p. 511	**Tranxene** 3.75 mg p. 114

X

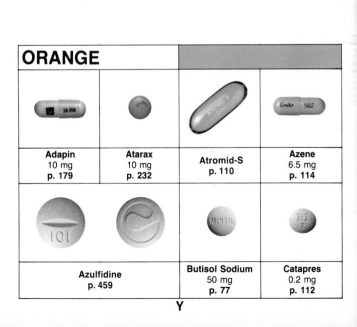

BLUE/PURPLE

Triavil 2-10 p. 504	**Valium** 10 mg p. 153	**Vibramycin** 100 mg p. 182	**Xanax** 1 mg p. 28
Zaroxolyn 5 mg p. 561			

ORANGE

Adapin 10 mg p. 179	**Atarax** 10 mg p. 232	**Atromid-S** p. 110	**Azene** 6.5 mg p. 114
Azulfidine p. 459		**Butisol Sodium** 50 mg p. 77	**Catapres** 0.2 mg p. 112

ORANGE

Chlor-Trimeton 12 mg **p. 98**	**Clonopin** 0.5 mg **p. 573**	**Coumadin** 2.5 mg **p. 533**	
Cyclospasmol 100 mg **p. 127**	**Cylert** 37.5 mg **p. 364**	**Deltasone** 20 mg **p. 406**	**Depakene** 250 mg **p. 527**
Dexedrine 5 mg **p. 149**	**Diamox Sequel** 500 mg **p. 15**	**Dimetane** 4 mg **p. 75**	**Elavil** 75 mg **p. 31**
Empracet **w/Codeine #3** **p. 13**	**E-Mycin** 250 mg **p. 191**	**Endep** 10 mg **p. 31**	**Endep** 25 mg **p. 31**
Endep 50 mg **p. 31**	**Endep** 150 mg **p. 31**	**Enovid E** **p. 345**	**Etrafon 4-10** **p. 504**

ORANGE

Hydrochloro-thiazide 25 mg **p. 228**	Hydrochloro-thiazide 50 mg **p. 228**	HydroDIURIL 25 mg **p. 228**	HydroDIURIL 50 mg **p. 228**
HydroDIURIL 100 mg **p. 228**	Hygroton 25 mg **p. 105**	Inderal 10 mg **p. 420**	Klotrix 10 mg **p. 400**
Minocin 50 mg **p. 308**	Moban 5 mg **p. 573**	Moduretic 5/50 **p. 313**	Motrin 400 mg **p. 233**
Motrin 600 mg **p. 233**	Nalfon 600 mg **p. 195**	Noctec 250 mg **p. 90**	Noctec 500 mg **p. 90**
Oreton Methyl 25 mg **p. 298**	Persantine 25 mg **p. 172**	Pro-Banthine 15 mg **p. 417**	Procardia 10 mg **p. 329**

AA

ORANGE

Provera 2.5 mg **p. 272**	**Slow-K** 600 mg **p. 400**	**Sodium Amytal** 50 mg **p. 34**	**Synthroid** .025 mg **p. 251**
Talwin 50 mg **p. 369**	**Thorazine** 25 mg **p. 100**	**Thorazine** 50 mg **p. 100**	**Thorazine** 100 mg **p. 100**
Triavil 2-25 **p. 504**	**Triavil 4-50** **p. 504**		**Trilisate** 500 mg **p. 53**
Uticillin VK 250 mg **p. 368**	**Vibra Tabs** 100 mg **p. 182**	**Xanax** 0.5 mg **p. 28**	**Zyloprim** 300 mg **p. 26**

GREEN

Atarax 25 mg **p. 232**	**Bactrim** **p. 442**	**Butisol Sodium** 30 mg **p. 77**	**Centrax** 5 mg **p. 402**
Drixoral **p. 185**	**Edecrin** 50 mg **p. 561**	**Fiorinal** **p. 199**	**Gantanol** **p. 457**
Haldol 5 mg **p. 224**	**Haldol** 10 mg **p. 224**	**Halotestin** **p. 205**	**Hydropres** 25 mg **p. 230**
Hydropres 50 mg **p. 230**	**Imodium** **p. 262**	**Inderal** 40 mg **p. 420**	**Isordil** 20 mg **p. 246**
Keflex 500 mg **p. 85**	**Librax** **p. 253**	**Megace** 20 mg **p. 273**	**Mellaril** 10 mg **p. 484**

GREEN

Mellaril 100 mg **p. 484**	**Novahistine LP** **p. 342**		**Moban** 25 mg **p. 573**
Parafon Forte **p. 361**	**PBZ** 50 mg **p. 517**	**Premarin** .3 mg **p. 124**	**Procan SR** 250 mg **p. 412**
Prochlorperazine 5 mg **p. 414**	**Prochlorperazine** 10 mg **p. 414**	**Salutensin** **p. 438**	**SK-Amitriptyline** 25 mg. **p. 31**
SK-Chloral Hydrate **p. 90**	**SK-Diphen- hydramine** 25 mg **p. 170**	**Sorbitrate** 5 mg **p. 246**	**Synthroid** .3 mg **p. 251**
Veracillin 250 mg **p. 156**	**Vistaril** 25 mg **p. 232**	**Wygesic** **p. 418**	

BROWN

Aldoril 15 mg **p. 24**	**Aldoril** 30 mg **p. 24**	**Catapres** 0.1 mg **p. 112**	**Elavil** 50 mg **p. 31**
Maolate 400 mg **p. 96**	**Mandelamine** **p. 285**	**Mellaril** 25 mg **p. 484**	**Mol-Iron** **p. 197**
Nystatin **p. 344**	**Oxacillin** 250 mg **p. 350**	**Parnate** 10 mg **p. 574**	**Premarin** .625 mg **p. 124**
Pyridium 100 mg **p. 378**	**Pyridium** 200 mg **p. 378**	**Pyridium Plus** **p. 378**	**Serentil** 10 mg **p. 279**
Serentil 50 mg **p. 279**	**Sulfasalazine** 500 mg **p. 459**	**Tandearil** 100 mg **p. 357**	**Thorazine** 10 mg **p. 100**

BROWN

Tofranil 10 mg p. 235	**Tofranil** 25 mg p. 235	**Tofranil** 50 mg p. 235	**Tofranil-PM** 75 mg p. 235
Tranxene-SD 22.5 mg p. 114	**Triavil 4-10** p. 504	**Tussionex** p. 522	

FF

DRUG INTERACTIONS

A drug interaction occurs when the effect of a drug is altered by another drug, a food, a chemical, or the environment.

Who May Suffer a Drug Interaction:

1. *People taking several medications.* The more drugs you take, the greater the likelihood of an interaction. Commonly used over-the-counter products such as laxatives, antacids, and cough and cold remedies have the potential for interacting.

2. *People taking combinations of drugs known to have interacted in the past.* This may seem an obvious point; however, drug interactions are not completely predictable. A friend may have taken a suspect combination with no ill effects, but that doesn't necessarily mean you will be able to tolerate the same combination.

3. *People with certain diseases.* Patients with diabetes, thyroid disease, liver disease, alcoholism, or kidney disease may break down drugs differently resulting in a changed or increased susceptibility to drug interactions.

4. *Elderly people.* As people get older their ability to handle drugs changes. They are more likely to experience interactions.

Other Factors

Your susceptibility to drug interactions is also affected by:

1. *Diet and environmental factors,* such as air pollution, smoking, and the presence of chemicals in the environment.

2. *General susceptibility.* Some people are genetically more susceptible to interactions. There is no way to take this factor into account yet, though we know it exists.

3. *How the drug is given.* Some interactions occur only when the drug is taken by mouth, others are affected by the order in which drugs are taken or when they are taken.

4. *How much of the drug is taken.* The more of the drug you take and the longer you take it, the greater the likelihood of interactions.

5. *Sex.* There is little information to substantiate sex differences, but it appears that women are more susceptible than men to interactions.

What to Do

If you experience what you think may be a drug interaction, notify your doctor immediately. Generally, he will do one of the following:

1. Discontinue one of the offending drugs or alter your diet to avoid interaction.

2. Alter the dose of an interactant to compensate for the interaction.

3. Treat the interaction effect with another medication.

4. Evaluate the interaction, decide it is not significant, and ignore it.

5. Evaluate what you think is an interaction and determine that it is not, in fact, an interaction but a usual side effect of one of the drugs.

The drug interaction table lists the more important potential interactions. This table is *not* meant to be a complete listing of all interactions and does not contain every possible problem. It is merely a reference source for the more common problems.

ALCOHOL

May Interact With:	To Produce:
Acetaminophen	Increased risk of liver damage.
Anticoagulants (blood-thinning drugs)	May affect blood coagulation in people who are chronic, heavy drinkers.
Anitdiabetic drugs (including Insulin)	Severe lowering of blood sugar. Can also cause stomach cramps, nausea, vomiting.
Antihistamines, sleeping pills, sedatives, tranquilizers, narcotics, Propoxyphene (large amounts)	Excessive sedation, sleepiness, lack of coordination, difficulty in concentrating. Has been associated with serious accidents and severe breathing difficulty leading to coma and death. People with heart disease are particularly prone to this interaction. Avoid drinking or operating machinery.
Aspirin	May increase amount of blood lost due to stomach bleeding normally caused by Aspirin. People with gastrointestinal disease and those taking large doses of Aspirin are most affected
Caffeine	May mask true degree of uncoordination
Disulfiram (Antabuse)	Life-threatening reactions
Isoniazid (tuberculosis drug)	Intoxication after taking unusually small amounts of alcohol. Avoid driving. Small amount may make Isoniazid less effective.
Lithium drugs, antidepressants, Phenylbutazone, Oxyphenbutazone; rare with Griseofulvin, Atropine (in many OTC drugs)	Lack of coordination, difficulty in concentrating, sedation. Avoid driving.
Metronidazole	May cause stomach cramps, nausea, vomiting, general aversion to alcohol.
Phenytoin	May decrease the effectiveness of Phenytoin. Usually seen only in chronic, heavy drinkers.

ANTIBIOTICS

	May Interact With:	To Produce:
Chloramphenicol	Antidiabetics	Low blood sugar
Chloramphenicol	Anticoagulants	Bleeding
Chloramphenicol	Phenytoin	Increased toxic effects from Phenytoin
Erythromycin	Theophylline	Nausea, vomiting, palpitations
Griseofulvin	Anticoagulants	Less anticoagulant effect. More anticoagulant may be needed
Isoniazid	Alcohol	Intoxication may make Isoniazid less effective and more toxic
Isoniazid	Antacids containing aluminum	Decreased Isoniazid effectiveness
Isoniazid	Disulfiram (Antabuse)	Psychotic reaction

ANTIBIOTICS (Continued)

May Interact With:	To Produce:	
Isoniazid	Phenytoin	Increased Phenytoin side effects
Lindomycin	Kaolin, Pectin	Decreased antibiotic effect
Miconazole	Anticoagulants	Bleeding
Nalidixic Acid	Anticoagulants	Bleeding
Rifampin	Adrenal corticosteroids	Less steroid effect
Rifampin	Anticoagulants	Less anticoagulant effect
Rifampin	Antidiabetics	Raised blood sugar
Rifampin	Methadone	Narcotic withdrawal symptoms
Rifampin	Oral contraceptives	Less contraceptive effect
Sulfa drugs	Anticoagulants	Bleeding
Sulfa drugs	Antidiabetics	Low blood sugar
Tetracycline drugs	Antacids, Zinc-containing drugs	Decreased antibiotic effect
Tetracycline drugs	Barbiturates Carbamazepine (Tegretol), Iron-containing drugs	Decreased antibiotic effect (especially Doxycycline)
Tetracycline drugs	Oral contraceptives	Less contraceptive effect

ANTICOAGULANTS (Warfarin, etc.)

May Interact With:	To Produce:
Alcohol (chronic abuse)	Need for more anticoagulant
Allopurinol	Bleeding
Antidiabetics	Low blood sugar
Aspirin, Chloral Hydrate, Chloramphenicol, Clofibrate (Atromid-S), Cimetidine (Tagamet), Disulfiram (Antabuse), D-Thyroxine (Choloxin), Hormones (Male), Quinidine or Quinine, Sulfa drugs, Sulfinpyrazone (Anturante), Thyroid Hormone, Vitamin E	Bleeding
Indomethacin, Metronidazole, Nalidixic Acid, Oxyphenbutazone, Phenylbutazone	Bleeding (possible)

ANTICOAGULANTS (Warfarin, etc.) (Continued)

May Interact With:	To Produce:
Barbiturates Cholestyramine (Questran), Glutethimide, Griseofulvin, Oral contraceptives, Rifampin (Rifadin, Rimactane)	Need for more anticoagulant
Phenytoin	Increased Phenytoin side effects

ANTIHYPERTENSIVES

	May Interact With:	To Produce:
Clonidine	Antidepressants, Stimulants*, Propranolol, Tolazoline (Priscoline)	Increased blood pressure
Clonidine	Levodopa	Decreased Levodopa effect
Clonidine	Oral Antidiabetics	Decreased awareness of low blood sugar
Guanethidine	Antidepressants, Phenothiazines (Thioridazine, Chlorpromazine, Prochlorperazine, etc.)	Increased blood pressure
Guanethidine	Antidiabetics	Low blood sugar
Methyldopa	Haloperidol	Increase in Haloperidol side effects
Methyldopa	Lithium drugs	Increase in side effects of lithium drugs
Propranolol (Inderal)	Barbiturates	Increased blood pressure
Propranolol (Inderal)	Cimetidine (Tagamet)	Slow pulse, fainting
Propranolol	Oral Antidiabetics	Decreased awareness of low blood sugar
All blood-pressure-lowering drugs	Stimulants*	Increased blood pressure
	*Often found in nose drops and sprays, and in over-the-counter cold and allergy remedies.	

DIURETICS

	May Interact With:	To Produce:
Furosemide	Phenytoin	Increased diuresis
Furosemide	Propranolol	Increased Propranolol effects
Spironolactone	Aspirin	Loss of body sodium

DIURETICS (Continued)

Spironolactone	**May Interact With:** Potassium drugs	**To Produce:** Unusually high blood levels of potassium
Thiazide diuretics, Furosemide	Adrenal corticosteroids (Prednisone, Hydrocortisone, etc.)	Low blood level of potassium
Thiazide diuretics, Furosemide	Digitalis drugs (including Digoxin)	Increased Digitalis side effects (due to potassium loss)
Thiazide diuretics, Furosemide	Indomethacin	Decreased Furosemide effect
Thiazide diuretics, Furosemide	Lithium drugs	Increase in Lithium side effects
Triamterene	Potassium drugs	Unusually high blood levels of potassium

ORAL ANTIDIABETICS (Tolbutamide, etc.)

May Interact With:	**To Produce:**
Alcoholic Beverages	Minor stomach cramps and nausea; low blood sugar (acute intoxication); high blood sugar (chronic alcohol abuse)
Anticoagulants Aspirin, Chloramphenicol, Clofibrate, Guanethidine, MAO Inhibitors, Methyldopa, Oxyphenbutazone, Phenylbutazone, Propranolol, Sulfa drugs	Low blood sugar
Clonidine	Masks warning symptoms of low blood sugar
Contraceptives, Oral	High blood sugar
Rifampin (Rifadin, Rimactane)	High blood sugar (possible)

PSYCHOTROPIC DRUGS

Antidepressants	**May Interact With:** Barbiturates	**To Produce:** Less antidepressant effect
Antidepressants	Clonidine, Guanethidine	Increased blood pressure
Antidepressants	MAO inhibitors	Fever, convulsions (possible)
Antidepressants	Stimulants*	High blood pressure
Diazepam, Oxazepam, Flurazepam, Chlordiazepoxide	Alcoholic beverages	Sleepiness; sedation; loss of coordination and difficulty in concentrating. Don't use this combination and drive
Haloperidol	Lithium drugs, Methyldopa	Increased Haloperidol side effects

PSYCHOTROPIC DRUGS (Continued)

	May Interact With:	To Produce:
Imipramine	Phenytoin	Increased Phenytoin toxication
Lithium drugs	Haloperidol	Increased Haloperidol side effects
Lithium drugs	Thiazide diuretics, Furosemide, Ethacrynic Acid, Methyldopa, Indomethacin	Increased side effects of lithium drugs
MAO inhibitors (Furoxone, Marplan, Eutonyl, Nardil, Matulane, Parnate)	Antidepressants	Fever, convulsions
	Antidiabetics	Low blood sugar
	Levodopa	Rapid rise in blood pressure
	Meperidine	Changes in blood pressure
MAO inhibitors	Stimulants*, Certain foods	Rapid rise in blood pressure
Phenothiazines (Chlorpromazine, Thioridazine, etc.)	Guanethidine	Increased blood pressure
Phenothiazines	Levodopa	Decrease in Levodopa effect
	*Often found in nose drops and sprays, and in over-the-counter cold and allergy remedies.	

OTHER DRUGS

	May Interact With:	To Produce:
Adrenal corticosteroids (Prednisone, Hydrocortisone, etc.)	Barbiturates	Decreased steroid effect
Adrenal corticosteroids	Phenytoin, Rifampin (Rifadin, Rimactane)	Decreased steroid effect
Adrenal corticosteroids	Thiazide diuretics, Furosemide, Ethyacrynic Acid	Increased potassium loss
Allopurinol	Anticoagulants	Bleeding
Allopurinol	Cytoxan	Increased Cytoxan effects
Allopurinol	6-MP (Purinethol)	Increased 6-MP side effects
Allopurinol	Imuran	Increased Imuran side effects
Antacids	Digitalis drugs (including Digoxin)	Increased Digitalis effects
Antacids	Indomethacin	Decreased Indomethacin effects
Antacids	Isoniazid	Decreased Isoniazid effect (with antacids containing aluminum only)

OTHER DRUGS (Continued)

	May Interact With:	To Produce:
Antacids	Tetracycline antibiotics	Decreased antibiotic effect
Aspirin	Alcohol	Increase in stomach bleeding normally associated with Aspirin
Aspirin	Anticoagulants	Bleeding
Aspirin	Antidiabetics	Low blood sugar
Aspirin	Dipyridamole (Persantine)	Bleeding
Aspirin	Methotrexate	Increase in Methotrexate side effects, methotrexate toxicity
Aspirin	Probenecid (Benemid)	Decrease in Probenecid effect
Barbiturates	Adrenal corticosteroids (e.g., Prednisone)	Decreased steroid effect
Barbiturates	Alcohol (chronic abuse)	Decreased barbiturate effectiveness
Barbiturates	Alcohol (acute intoxication), tranquilizers, sleeping pills	Increased sedation; sleepiness; loss of concentration and coordination. This interaction has led to accidental and other deaths and should be avoided
Barbiturates	Anticoagulants	Decreased anticoagulant effect
Barbiturates	Antidepressants	Decreased antidepressant effect
Barbiturates	Quinidine	Decreased Quinidine effect
Barbiturates	Tetracycline drugs	Decreased antibiotic effect
Chloral Hydrate	Alcohol	Oversedation; loss of concentration and coordination. This interaction has led to accidental and other deaths
Chloral Hydrate	Anticoagulants	Bleeding
Cholestyramine	Anticoagulants	Decreased anticoagulant effect
Cholestyramine	Digitalis drugs (e.g., Digoxin)	Decreased Digitalis effect
Cholestyramine	Thyroid Hormone	Decreased Thyroid Hormone effect
Cimetidine	Anticoagulant	Bleeding
Cimetidine	Narcotics	Increased effect of Cimetidine
Cimetidine	Phenytoin	Increased Phenytoin effect
Cimetidine	Propranolol	Increased Propranolol effect
Cimetidine	Theophylline	Increased Theophylline effect
Cimetidine	Valium, Librium	Increased drowsiness
Digitalis drugs (Digoxin, Digitoxin, etc.)	Amphotericin-B	Increased Digitalis side effects

OTHER DRUGS (Continued)

	May Interact With:	To Produce:
Digitalis drugs	Antacids, Cholestyramine (Questran), Kaolin, Pectin (Kaopectate)	Decreased Digitalis effectiveness
Digitalis drugs	Quinidine, Quinine	Increased Digitalis side effects
Digitalis drugs	Stimulants*	Possible abnormal heart rhythms
Digitalis drugs	Thiazide diuretics, Ethacrynic Acid, Furosemide	Increased Digitalis side effects
Levodopa	MAO inhibitors	Rapid rise in blood pressure
Levodopa	Papaverine, Phenothiazine drugs, Phenytoin, Pyridoxine	Decreased Levodopa effect
Oral contraceptives	Anticoagulants	Less Anticoagulant effect
Oral contraceptives	Rifampin (Rifadin, Rimactane)	Decreased contraceptive effect (could lead to pregnancy)
Phenytoin	Adrenal corticosteroids	Decreased steroid effect
Phenytoin	Alcohol (acute intoxication)	Increased Phenytoin side effects
Phenytoin	Alcohol (chronic abuse)	Decreased Phenytoin effect
Phenytoin	Anticoagulants, Chloramphenicol	Increased Phenytoin effect
Phenytoin	Furosemide	Decreased Furosemide effect
Phenytoin	Haldol	Decreased Haldol effect
Phenytoin	Isoniazid	Increased Phenytoin side effects
Phenytoin	Levodopa	Decreased Levodopa effect
Phenytoin	Quinidine	Decreased Quinidine effect
Phenytoin	Phenylbutazone	Increased Phenytoin toxicity
Quinidine	Barbiturates, Phenytoin	Decreased Quinidine effect
Stimulants*	Antidepressants	Increased blood pressure
Stimulants*	Digitalis drugs	May cause unusual heart rhythms
Stimulants*	Drugs for high blood pressure	Increased blood pressure
Stimulants*	MAO inhibitors	Rapid increase in blood pressure
Thyroid Hormone	Anticoagulants	Bleeding
Thyroid Hormone	Cholestyramine (Questran)	Decreased Thyroid Hormone effect
	*Often found in nose drops and sprays, and in over-the-counter cold and allergy remedies.	

position of Minocycline produces a highly toxic substance which can cause serious kidney damage.

Generic Name

Minoxidil

Brand Name

Loniten

Type of Drug

Antihypertensive.

Prescribed for

Severe high blood pressure not controllable with other drugs.

General Information

This drug can cause severe adverse effects on the heart. It is usually given together with a beta-blocking antihypertensive drug (Propranolol, Metoprolol, Nadolol, etc.) to prevent rapid heartbeat and a diuretic to prevent fluid accumulation. Some patients may have to be hospitalized when treatment with this drug is started, to avoid too rapid a drop in blood pressure.

Minoxidil works by dilating peripheral blood vessels and allowing more blood to flow through arms and legs. This increased blood flow reduces the resistance levels in central vessels (heart, lungs, kidneys, etc.) and therefore reduces blood pressure. Its effect on blood pressure can be seen $\frac{1}{2}$ hour after a dose is taken and lasts up to 3 days. Patients usually take the medicine once or twice a day. Maximum drug effect occurs as early as 3 days after the drug is started, if the dose is large enough (40 milligrams per day).

Cautions and Warnings

This drug should not be used by people with pheochromocytoma, a rare tumor in which extra body stimulants (catecholamines) are made. Minoxidil may cause the accumulation of water and sodium in the body, leading to heart failure. It also increases heart rate. To protect you from these side effects, Minoxidil must be given with other drugs, a diuretic and a beta-adrenergic blocker. This drug should be avoided by pregnant women or nursing mothers unless taking it is absolutely necessary. The effect of this drug on the unborn baby is not known. It has not been carefully studied in patients who have suffered a heart attack within the past month.

Possible Side Effects

Water and sodium retention can develop, leading to heart failure. Also, some patients taking this drug may develop fluid in the sacs surrounding the heart. This is treated with diuretic drugs.

Eighty percent of people taking this drug experience thickening, elongation, and darkening of body hair within 3 to 6 weeks after starting Minoxidil. This is usually first noticed on the temples, between the eyebrows, between the eyebrows and hairline, or on the upper cheek. Later on it will extend to the back, arms, legs, and scalp. This effect stops when the drug is stopped and symptoms will disappear in 1 to 6 months. Electrocardiogram changes occur in 60 percent of patients but are usually not associated with any symptoms. Some other laboratory tests (blood, liver, kidney) may be affected by Minoxidil.

Possible Adverse Drug Effects

Minoxidil may interact with Guanethidine to produce dizziness when rising from a sitting or lying position.

Usual Dose

Adult and child (age 12 and over): 5 milligrams to start; may be increased to 40 milligrams per day. Do not take more than 100 milligrams per day. The daily dose of Minoxidil must be tailored to each patient's needs.

Child (under age 12): 0.1 milligram per pound per day to start; may be increased to 0.5 milligram per pound per day. Do not use more than 50 milligrams per day. The daily dose of Minoxidil must be tailored to each patient's needs.

Minoxidil is usually given together with a diuretic (Hydrochlorothiazide, 100 milligrams per day; Chlorthalidone, 50 to 100 milligrams per day; or Furosemide, 80 milligrams per day) and a beta-adrenergic blocker (Propranolol, 80 to 160 milligrams per day; or the equivalent dose of another drug). People who cannot take a beta-adrenergic blocker may take Methyldopa, 500 to 1500 milligrams per day, instead. 0.2 to 0.4 milligram per day of Clonidine may also be used.

Overdosage

Symptoms may be those associated with too low blood pressure. Contact your doctor or poison control center if an overdose of Minoxidil occurs.

Special Information

Since Minoxidil is usually given with two other medications, a beta-adrenergic blocker and a diuretic, do not discontinue any of these drugs unless told to do so by your doctor. Take all medication exactly as prescribed.

This drug may be taken at any time. It is not affected by food or liquid intake. The effect of this drug on body hair (see "Possible Side Effects") is a nuisance but not dangerous. Do not stop taking Minoxidil because of it.

Call your doctor if you experience an increase in your pulse of 20 or more beats per minute, weight gain of more than 5 pounds, unusual swelling of your arms and/or legs, face, or stomach, chest pain, difficulty in breathing, dizziness, or fainting spells.

Do not take over-the-counter drugs containing stimulants. If you are unsure which drugs to avoid, ask your pharmacist.

Brand Name

Moduretic

Ingredients

Amiloride
Hydrochlorothiazide

Type of Drug

Diuretic.

Prescribed for

High blood pressure or any condition where it is desirable to eliminate excess fluid from the body.

General Information

Moduretic is a combination of two diuretics and is a convenient, effective approach for the treatment of diseases where the elimination of excess fluids is required. One of the ingredients in Moduretic, Amiloride, holds potassium in the body while producing a diuretic effect. This balances the Hydrochlorothiazide, which often causes a loss of potassium.

Combination drugs such as Moduretic should only be used when you need the exact amount of ingredients contained in the product and when your doctor feels you would benefit from taking one dose per day.

Cautions and Warnings

This drug should not be used by people with diabetes or kidney disease or those who are allergic to either of these ingredients or to sulfa drugs. This drug may cause abnormally high blood potassium levels. Since too much potassium in your blood can be fatal, your doctor should test blood potassium levels periodically. This drug should only be used by pregnant women or nursing mothers if absolutely necessary.

Possible Side Effects

Headache, weakness, tiredness, dizziness, difficulty in breathing, abnormal heart rhythms, nausea, loss of appetite, diarrhea, stomach and abdominal pains, decrease in blood potassium, rash, itching, leg pains.

Possible Adverse Drug Effects

Feeling sick, chest and back pain, heart palpitations, dizziness when rising from a sitting or lying position, angina pain, constipation, stomach bleeding, stomach upset, appetite changes, feeling of being bloated, hiccups, thirst, vomiting, stomach gas, gout, dehydration, flushing, muscle cramps or spasms, joint pain, tingling in the arms or legs, feeling of numbness, stupor, sleeplessness, nervousness, depression, sleepiness, confusion, visual disturbances, bad taste in the mouth, stuffed nose, sexual impotence, urinary difficulties, dry mouth, adverse effects on the blood system, fever, shock, allergic reactions, jaundice, liver damage, sugar in the blood or urine, unusual sensitivity to the sun, restlessness.

Drug Interactions

Moduretic will add to (potentiate) the action of other blood-pressure-lowering drugs. Since this is beneficial, it is frequently used to help lower blood pressure in patients with hypertension.

The possibility of developing imbalances in body fluids (electrolytes) is increased if you take other medications such as Digitalis and adrenal corticosteroids while you are taking Moduretic.

If you are taking an oral antidiabetic drug and begin taking Moduretic, the antidiabetic dose may have to be altered.

Lithium Carbonate should not be taken with Moduretic because the combination may increase the risk of lithium toxicity.

Avoid over-the-counter cough, cold, or allergy remedies containing stimulant drugs which can aggravate your condition.

Moduretic may interfere with the oral blood-thinning drugs such as Warfarin by making the blood more concentrated (thicker).

Usual Dose

1 to 2 tablets per day.

Overdosage

Signs are tingling in the arms or legs, weakness, fatigue, slow heartbeat, a sickly feeling, dryness of the mouth, lethargy, restlessness, muscle pains or cramps, low blood pressure, rapid heartbeat, urinary difficulty, nausea, or vomiting. A patient who has taken a Moduretic overdose should be taken to a hospital emergency room. ALWAYS bring the medicine bottle.

Special Information

This drug can affect your concentration. Do not drive or operate machinery while taking it.

Brand Name

Mycolog Cream/Ointment

Ingredients

Gramicidin
Neomycin
Nystatin
Triamcinolone Acetonide

Type of Drug

Topical adrenal corticosteroid combination.

Prescribed for

Relief of infected rash or inflammation.

General Information

Mycolog Cream/Ointment is used to relieve the symptoms of itching, rash, or inflammation of the skin. It does not treat the underlying cause of the skin problem, but only the symptoms. It exerts this effect by interfering with natural body mechanisms that produced the rash, itching, etc., in the first place. If you use this drug without finding the cause of the problem, you may find that the problem returns after you stop using it. Mycolog Cream/Ointment should not be used without your doctor's consent because it could cover an important reaction, one that may be of value to him in treating you.

Cautions and Warnings

Do not use Mycolog Cream/Ointment if you are allergic to any of its ingredients. This drug should not be used in the eyes, or the external ear if the eardrum is perforated, unless you are specifically directed to do so by your doctor. Severe local infections require antibiotic therapy. If you have some Mycolog Cream/Ointment left over from an old prescription, do not use it without first contacting your doctor. If this medication fails to help you or a new infection develops on your skin while you are using it, contact your doctor so that appropriate treatment can be given.

Possible Side Effects

Most frequent: burning sensation, itching, irritation of the skin, dryness, secondary infection after prolonged use of this medication.

Usual Dose

Apply to affected areas several times daily.

Special Information

Clean the skin before applying Mycolog Cream/Ointment, to prevent secondary infection. Apply in a very thin film (effectiveness is based on contact area and not on thickness of the layer applied).

Brand Name

Mysteclin-F

Other Brand Name

Tetrastatin

Ingredients

Amphotericin-B
Tetracycline

Type of Drug

Broad-spectrum antibiotic antifungal combination.

Prescribed for

Bacterial infections such as gonorrhea, infections of the mouth, gums and teeth, Rocky Mountain spotted fever and other fevers caused by ticks and lice from a variety of carriers, urinary tract infections, and respiratory system infections such as pneumonia and bronchitis.

These diseases may be produced by gram-positive or gram-negative organisms such as diplococci, staphylococci, streptococci, gonococci, E. coli, and Shigella.

Mysteclin-F has also been successfully used to treat some skin infections, but is not considered the first-choice antibiotic for the treatment of general skin infections or wounds.

General Information

Mysteclin-F works by interfering with the normal growth cycle of the invading bacteria, preventing them from reproducing and thus allowing the body's normal growth defenses to fight off the infection. This process is referred to as bacteriostatic action. Mysteclin-F has also been used along with other medicines to treat amoebic infections of the intestinal tract, known as amoebic dysentery. It is also prescribed for diseases caused by ticks, fleas, and lice. This combination should be used only by people who are susceptible to developing candida (fungus) when taking tetracycline.

Since the action of this antibiotic depends on its concentration within the invading bacteria, it is imperative that you, the patient, completely follow the doctor's directions.

Cautions and Warnings

You should not use Mysteclin-F if you are pregnant. Mysteclin-F, when used in children, has been shown to interfere with the development of the long bones and may retard growth.

Exceptions would be when Mysteclin-F is the only effective antibiotic available and all risk factors have been made known to the patient.

Mysteclin-F should not be given to people with known liver disease or to people with kidney or urine excretion problems. You should avoid taking high doses of Mysteclin-F or undergoing extended Mysteclin-F therapy if you will be exposed to sunlight for a long period because this antibiotic can interfere with your body's normal sun-screening mechanism, possibly causing severe sunburn. If you have a known history of allergy to Mysteclin-F you should avoid taking this drug or other drugs within this category such as Aureomycin, Terramycin, Rondomycin, Vibramycin, Tetracycline, Demeclocycline, and Minocycline.

Possible Side Effects

Amphotericin-B, when given by mouth, is not absorbed into the blood system. For this reason there are few side effects associated with Amphotericin-B in this combination.

As with other antibiotics, the common side effects of Mysteclin-F are stomach upset, nausea, vomiting, diarrhea, and rash. Less common side effects include hairy tongue and itching and irritation of the anal and/or vaginal region. If these symptoms appear, consult your physician immediately. Periodic physical examinations and laboratory tests should be given to patients who are on long-term Mysteclin-F.

Possible Adverse Drug Effects

Loss of appetite, peeling of the skin, sensitivity to the sun, fever, chills, anemia, possible brown spotting of the skin, decrease in kidney function, damage to the liver.

Drug Interactions

Mysteclin-F (a bacteriostatic drug) may interfere with the action of bactericidal agents such as Penicillin. It is not advisable to take both.

The antibacterial effect of Mysteclin-F is neutralized when taken with food, some dairy products (such as milk and cheese), and antacids.

Don't take multivitamin products containing minerals at the same time as Mysteclin-F, or you will reduce the antibiotic's effectiveness. Space the taking of these two medicines at least 2 hours apart.

People receiving anticoagulation therapy (blood-thinning agents) should consult their doctor, since Mysteclin-F will interfere with this form of therapy. An adjustment in the anticoagulant dosage may be required.

Usual Dose

Adult: 250 to 500 milligrams 4 times per day.

Child (age 9 and over): 10 to 20 milligrams per pound of body weight per day in divided doses taken 1 hour before or 2 hours after meals.

Child (up to age 8): should avoid Mysteclin-F, as it has been shown to produce serious discoloration of the permanent teeth.

Special Information

Do not take outdated Mysteclin-F under any circumstances. Its decomposition produces a highly toxic substance which can cause serious kidney damage.

The only difference between Mysteclin-F and Tetracycline is that Mysteclin-F contains a small amount of Amphotericin-B to prevent the growth of fungal organisms in the intestine. Since the Amphotericin-B in Mysteclin-F is often ineffective in reducing the incidence of fungal infections, you may be better off taking plain Tetracycline. Discuss it with your doctor.

Generic Name

Nadolol

Brand Name

Corgard

Type of Drug

Beta-adrenergic blocking agent.

Prescribed for

High blood pressure; angina pectoris (a specific type of chest pain).

General Information

This drug is quite similar to Propranolol, another beta blocking agent. It has not been studied in as many kinds of problems as Propranolol, but it is very useful because it can be taken once a day. When used for high blood pressure, it is usually given with a diuretic such as Hydrochlorothiazide.

Cautions and Warnings

Nadolol should be used with care if you have a history of asthma or other upper respiratory disease or of heart failure. You should stop taking the drug several days before major surgery, if possible. Do not do this without telling your doctor. Nadolol can hide some symptoms of diabetes or thyroid disease. Pregnant women should use this drug only if it is absolutely necessary. No adverse effects on the unborn child have been reported.

Possible Side Effects

Nadolol may decrease the heart rate; may aggravate a condition of congestive heart failure; and may produce lowered blood pressure, tingling in the extremities, light-headedness, mental depression including inability to sleep, weakness, and tiredness. It may also produce a mental depression which is reversible when the drug is withdrawn, visual disturbances, hallucinations, disorientation, and short-term memory loss. Patients taking Nadolol may experience nausea, vomiting, stomach upset, abdominal cramps and diarrhea,

or constipation. If you are allergic to this drug, you may
show typical reactions associated with drug allergies, including sore throat, fever, difficulty in breathing, and various
effects on the blood system. Nadolol may induce bronchospasms (spasms of muscles in the bronchi), which will make
any existing asthmatic condition or any severe upper respiratory disease worse.

Possible Adverse Drug Effects

Occasionally, patients taking Nadolol may experience emotional instability, or a feeling of detachment or personality
change, or the drug may produce unusual effects on the
blood system.

Drug Interactions

This drug will interact with any psychotropic drug, including
the MAO inhibitors, which stimulates one of the adrenergic
segments of the nervous system. Since this information is
not generally known, you should discuss the potential problem of using Nadolol with your doctor if you are taking any
psychotropic or psychiatric drug.

Nadolol may cause increased effectiveness of Insulin or
oral antidiabetic drugs. If you are diabetic, discuss the situation with your doctor; a reduction in dose of antidiabetic
medication will probably be made.

Nadolol may reduce the effectiveness of Digitalis on your
heart. Any dose of Digitalis medication will have to be altered.
If you are taking Digitalis for a purpose other than congestive heart failure, the effectiveness of the Digitalis may be
increased by Nadolol, and the dose of Digitalis may have to
be reduced.

Nadolol may interact with certain other drugs to lower
blood pressure. This interaction often has positive results in
the treatment of patients with high blood pressure.

Do not self-medicate with over-the-counter cold, cough, or
allergy remedies which may contain stimulant drugs that
will aggravate certain types of heart disease and high blood
pressure, or other ingredients that may antagonize the effects
of Nadolol. Double-check with your doctor or pharmacist
before taking any over-the-counter medication.

Usual Dose

40 to 640 milligrams per day. Patients with bad kidneys may take their medication dosage as infrequently as once every 60 hours.

Overdosage

Symptoms are slowed heart rate, heart failure, lowered blood pressure, and spasms of the bronchial muscles which make it difficult to breathe. The patient should be taken to a hospital emergency room where proper therapy can be given. ALWAYS bring the medicine bottle with you.

Special Information

Nadolol may be taken at any time, without regard to meals. Since this drug is taken only once a day, be sure to take it at the same time every day. Do not stop taking the drug abruptly unless your doctor tells you to, or serious heart pain and other effects can occur. Call your doctor if you have trouble breathing when you exert yourself or are lying down, have a nighttime cough, or develop swollen ankles, arms, or legs.

Brand Name

Naldecon Tablets

Ingredients

Chlorpheniramine Maleate
Phenylephrine Hydrochloride
Phenylpropanolamine Hydrochloride
Phenytoloxamine Citrate

Type of Drug

Long-acting combination antihistamine-decongestant.

Prescribed for

Relief of sneezing, runny nose, and nasal congestion associated with the common cold, allergy, or other upper respiratory condition.

General Information

Naldecon Tablets are one of many products marketed to

relieve the symptoms of the common cold. Most of these products contain ingredients to relieve nasal congestion or to dry up runny noses or relieve a scratchy throat; and several of them may contain ingredients to suppress cough, or to help eliminate unwanted mucus. All these products are good only for the relief of symptoms and do not treat the underlying problem such as a cold virus or other infections.

Cautions and Warnings

Naldecon Tablets should not be given to pregnant women.

Possible Side Effects

Mild drowsiness.

Possible Adverse Drug Effects

Infrequent: restlessness, tension, nervousness, tremor, weakness, inability to sleep, headache, palpitations, elevation of blood pressure, sweating, sleeplessness, loss of appetite, nausea, vomiting, dizziness, constipation.

Drug Interactions

Interaction with alcoholic beverages, sedatives, tranquilizers, antihistamines, sleeping pills, thyroid medicine, and antihypertensive drugs such as Reserpine or Guanethidine may produce excessive drowsiness and/or sleepiness, or inability to concentrate.

Do not self-medicate with over-the-counter drugs for the relief of cold symptoms; taking Naldecon Tablets with such drugs may aggravate high blood pressure, heart disease, diabetes, or thyroid disese.

Do not take Naldecon Tablets if you are taking or suspect you may be taking a monoamine oxidase inhibitor: severe elevation in blood pressure may result.

Usual Dose

Adult and child (age 12 and over): 1 tablet 3 times per day.
Child (under age 12): not recommended.

Special Information

Since drowsiness may occur during use of Naldecon Tablets, be cautious while performing mechanical tasks requiring alertness.

If this drug upsets your stomach it should be taken with food.

Generic Name

Naproxen

Brand Name

Anaprox
Naprosyn

Type of Drug

Nonsteroid anti-inflammatory.

Prescribed for

Relief of pain and inflammation of joints and muscles; arthritis, mild to moderate pain of menstrual cramps, dental surgery and extractions, and athletic injuries such as sprains and strains.

General Information

Naproxen is one of several new drugs used to treat various types of pain and belongs to the chemical group known as propionic acid derivatives. These drugs reduce inflammation and share side effects, the most common of which are upset stomach and possible formation of ulcers. The drugs are roughly comparable to Aspirin in controlling the symptoms of arthritis and other pain and are used by some people who cannot tolerate Aspirin.

Cautions and Warnings

Do not take Naproxen if you are allergic or sensitive to this drug, Aspirin, or other nonsteroid anti-inflammatory drugs. Naproxen may cause stomach ulcers. This drug should not be used by patients with severe kidney disease. The safety of this drug for pregnant women has not been established and it is not recommended for them.

Possible Side Effects

Stomach upset, blurred vision, darkening of stool, changes in color vision, rash, weight gain, retention of fluids.

Possible Adverse Drug Effects

Most frequent: stomach upset, dizziness, headache, drowsiness, ringing in the ears. Others: heartburn, nausea, vomiting, bloating, gas in the stomach, stomach pain, diarrhea, constipation, dark stool, nervousness, insomnia, depression, confusion, tremor, loss of appetite, fatigue, itching, rash, double vision, abnormal heart rhythm, anemia or other changes in the composition of the blood, changes in liver function, loss of hair, tingling in the hands and feet, fever, breast enlargement, lowered blood sugar, effects on the kidneys. If symptoms appear, stop taking the medicine and see your doctor immediately.

Drug Interactions

Naproxen increases the action of Phenytoin, sulfa drugs, drugs used to control diabetes, and drugs used to thin the blood. If you are taking any of these medicines, be sure to discuss it with your doctor, who will probably change the dose of the other drug.

An adjustment in the dose of Naproxen may be needed if you take Phenobarbital.

Usual Dose

Adult: 250 milligrams morning and night, to start. Dose may be adjusted up to 750 milligrams per day, if needed.
Child: not recommended.

Brand Name

Natalins

Ingredients

Calcium	Vitamin B_3
Folic Acid	Vitamin B_6
Iodine	Vitamin B_{12}
Magnesium	Vitamin C
Vitamin A	Vitamin D
Vitamin B_1	Vitamin E
Vitamin B_2	

Type of Drug

Vitamin (with minerals).

Prescribed for

Prenatal vitamin supplement.

General Information

Natalins is one of many prenatal vitamin formulas which can be bought without a prescription. It does not contain Vitamin B_5, Biotin, Copper, or Zinc. The rationale for using prenatal vitamins is to see that the expectant mother receives sufficient vitamins and minerals to keep her healthy and support the growth of the baby she is carrying. Some people state that what vitamin pills provide can be obtained by eating the right foods. They are right; however, practical experience has told us that not all pregnant women eat everything they should. Therefore, most obstetricians prescribe a prenatal vitamin supplement for pregnant patients. There are many different combinations of these same vitamins with actions similar to Natalins, including Natabec RX, Materna, Stuart Pre-Natal and Mission Pre-Natal.

Cautions and Warnings

Do not take Natalins if you are allergic or sensitive to any of its ingredients.

Possible Side Effects

Indigestion, gastrointestinal intolerance.

Possible Adverse Drug Effects

Serious adverse effects are rare.

Usual Dose

1 tablet per day.

Brand Name

Neosporin Ophthalmic Solution

Ingredients

Gramicidin
Neomycin Sulfate
Polymyxin-B Sulfate

Type of Drug

Topical antibiotic for use in the eye.

Prescribed for

Superficial infections of the eye.

General Information

Neosporin Ophthalmic Solution is a combination of antibiotics which are effective against the most common eye infections. It is most useful when the infecting organism is one known to be sensitive to one of the three antibiotics contained in Neosporin Ophthalmic Solution. It is also useful when the infecting organism is not known, because of the drug's broad range of coverage.

Prolonged use of any antibiotic product in the eye should be avoided because of the possibility of developing sensitivity to the antibiotic. Frequent or prolonged use of antibiotics in the eye may result in the growth of other organisms such as fungi. If the infection does not clear up within a few days, contact your doctor.

Cautions and Warnings

Neosporin Ophthalmic Solution should not be used if you know you are sensitive to or have an allergy to this product or to any of the ingredients in it.

Possible Side Effects

Occasional local irritation after application to the eye.

Usual Dose

1 to 2 drops in the affected eye or eyes 2 to 4 times per day; more frequently if the infection is severe.

Generic Name

Nicotinic Acid (Niacin)

Brand Names

Diacin	Nicotinex
Niac	Nicotym
Nicobid	SK-Niacin
Nicocap	Span-Niacin
Nico 400 Plateau Caps	Tega-Span
Nicolar	Wampocap
nico-Span	

Type of Drug

Vitamin.

Prescribed for

Treatment of Nicotinic Acid deficiency (pellagra). Also, prescribed to help lower high blood levels of lipids or fats, and to help dilate or enlarge certain blood vessels.

General Information

Nicotinic Acid or Niacin, also known as Vitamin B_3, is essential to normal body function through the part it plays in enzyme activity. It is effective in lowering blood levels of fats and can help enlarge or dilate certain blood vessels, but we do not know exactly how it does these things. Normally, individual requirements of Nicotinic Acid are easily supplied in a well-rounded diet.

Cautions and Warnings

Do not take this drug if you are sensitive or allergic to it or to any related drugs or if you have liver disease, stomach ulcer, severely low blood pressure, or hemorrhage (bleeding). When used in normal doses Nicotinic Acid can be taken by pregnant women, but if it is used in high doses (to help lower blood levels of fats) there may be some problems. Therefore, if you are pregnant or nursing consult with your doctor.

Possible Side Effects

Most common: flushing (redness and a warm sensation in the face and hands).

Possible Adverse Drug Effects

Decreased sugar tolerance in diabetics, activation of stomach ulcers, jaundice (yellowing of the whites of the eyes and skin), stomach upset, oily skin, dry skin, possible aggravation of skin conditions such as acne, itching, high blood levels of uric acid, low blood pressure, temporary headache, tingling feeling, skin rash, abnormal heartbeats, dizziness.

Drug Interactions

Nicotinic Acid, which can enlarge blood vessels, can intensify the effect of antihypertensive (blood-pressure-lowering) drugs, causing postural hypotension (getting dizzy when you rise quickly from a sitting or lying position).

If you are diabetic, large doses of Nicotinic Acid can throw your blood sugar slightly out of control and your doctor may have to adjust either your diet or your drug therapy.

Usual Dose

Supplementary vitamin product: 25 milligrams per day.

Treatment of high blood levels of lipids or fats: initial dose, 500 milligrams to 3 grams per day with or after meals. (Take with cold water to assist in swallowing.) If 3 grams does not prove effective the dose may be increased slowly to a maximum of 6 grams per day.

The dose should be built up slowly so you can watch carefully for common side effects: flushing or redness of the face and extremities, itching, and stomach upset.

Generic Name

Nifedipine

Brand Name

Procardia

Type of Drug

Calcium channel blocker.

Prescribed for

Angina pectoris, Prinzmetal's angina.

General Information

Nifedipine is the first member of a new drug group to be marketed in the United States. It works by blocking the passage of calcium into heart and smoothe muscle. Since calcium is an essential factor in muscle contraction, any drug that affects calcium in this way will interfere with the contraction of these muscles. When this happens the amount of oxygen used by the muscles is also reduced. Therefore, Nifedipine is used in the treatment of angina, a type of heart pain related to poor oxygen supply to the heart muscles.

Also, Nifedipine dilates the vessels that supply blood to the heart muscles and prevents spasm of these arteries. Nifedipine only affects the movement of calcium into muscle cells. It does not have any effect on calcium in the blood.

Cautions and Warnings

Nifedipine may cause lowered blood pressure in some patients. Patients taking a beta-blocking drug who begin taking Nifedipine may develop heart failure or increased angina pain. Do not take this drug if you have had an allergic reaction to it. Pregnant women or nursing mothers should only use this drug if absolutely necessary.

Possible Side Effects

Dizziness, light-headedness, flushing, a feeling of warmth, headache, weakness, nausea, heartburn, muscle cramps, tremors, swelling of the arms or legs, nervousness, mood changes, heart palpitations, difficulty breathing, coughs, wheezing, stuffed nose, sore throat.

Possible Adverse Drug Effects

Less frequently: shortness of breath, diarrhea, cramps, stomach gas, muscle cramps, stiffness and inflammation of the joints, shakiness, jitteriness, blurred vision, difficulty sleeping, difficulty maintaining balance, itching, rash, fever, sweating, chills, sexual difficulties. In addition, some patients taking Nifedipine have experienced heart attack, heart failure, fluid in the lungs, and abnormal heart rhythms. The occurence of these serious effects have not been directly related to taking Nifedipine. Future research may tell us whether Nifedipine actually causes these problems or if the occurrence is merely coincidental. Nifedipine can cause increases in certain blood enzyme tests.

Drug Interactions

Nifedipine may interact with the beta-blocking drugs to cause heart failure, very low blood pressure, or an increased incidence of angina pain. However, in many cases these drugs have been taken together with no problem. Nifedipine may cause a lowering of blood pressure in patients already taking medicine to control their high blood pressure through interaction with the other antihypertensive drugs.

Usual Dose

30 to 120 milligrams per day. No patient should take more than 180 milligrams per day. If you have been taking Nifedipine, do not stop taking the drug abruptly. The dosage should be gradually reduced over a period of time.

Overdosage

Overdose of Nifedipine can cause low blood pressure. If you think you have taken an overdose of Nifedipine, call your doctor or go to a hospital emergency room. ALWAYS bring the medicine bottle.

Special Information

Take this drug 1 hour before or 2 hours after meals. Call your doctor if you develop swelling in the arms or legs, difficulty breathing, increased heart pains, dizziness or light-headedness, or lowered blood pressure.

Generic Name

Nitrofurantoin

Brand Names

Furadantin	Macrodantin
Furalan	Nitrex
Furan	Nitrodan
Furatoin	Urotoin

Type of Drug

Urinary anti-infective.

Prescribed for

Urinary tract infections by organisms susceptible to Nitrofurantoin. These organisms cause pyelonephritis, pyelitis, and cystitis.

General Information

Nitrofurantoin, like several other drugs (including Naladixic

Acid [NegGram]), is of value in treating urinary tract infections because it appears in large amounts in the urine. It should not be used to treat infections in other parts of the body.

Cautions and Warnings

Do not take Nitrofurantoin if you have kidney disease, if you are allergic to this agent, or if you are pregnant and near term. Infants under age 3 months should not be given this medication.

Possible Side Effects

Loss of appetite, nausea, vomiting, stomach pain, and diarrhea. Some people develop hepatitislike symptoms.

Side effects are less prominent when Macrodantin (large crystal form of Nitrofurantoin) is used rather than Furadantin (regular crystal size).

Possible Adverse Drug Effects

Fever, chills, cough, chest pain, difficulty in breathing, development of fluid in the lungs; if these occur in the first week of therapy they can generally be resolved by stopping the medication. If they develop after a longer time they can be more serious because they develop more slowly and are more difficult to associate with the drug. If you develop chest pains or difficulty in breathing while taking Nitrofurantoin, report the effects to your physician immediately. Other adverse effects: rashes, itching, asthmatic attacks in patients with history of asthma, drug fever, symptoms similar to arthritis, jaundice (yellowing of the whites of the eyes and/or skin), effects on components of the blood, headache, dizziness, drowsiness, temporary loss of hair. The oral liquid form of Nitrofurantoin can stain your teeth if you don't swallow the medicine rapidly.

This drug is known to cause changes in the blood. Therefore, it should be used only under strict supervision by your doctor.

Usual Dose

Adult: 50 to 100 milligrams 4 times per day.

Child (over age 3 months): 2 to 3 milligrams per pound of body weight in 4 divided doses.

Child (under age 3 months): not recommended.

Nitrofurantoin may be used in lower doses over a long period by people with chronic urinary infections.

Nitrofurantoin may be given with food or milk to help decrease stomach upset, loss of appetite, nausea, or other gastrointestinal symptoms. Continue to take this medicine at least 3 days after you stop experiencing symptoms of urinary tract infection.

Special Information

Nitrofurantoin may give your urine a brownish color: this is not dangerous.

Generic Name

Nitroglycerin

Brand Names

Ang-O-Span
Klavikordal
Niong
Nitro-Bid
Nitro-Bid Plateau Caps
Nitrocap T.D.
Nitrodisc Patches
Nitro-Dur Patches
Nitrol
Nitrolin
Nitronet
Nitrong
Nitrospan
Nitrostat
Nitro-T.D.
Transderm Nitro Patches
Trates Granucaps

Type of Drug

Antianginal agent.

Prescribed for

Prevention and treatment of chest pains associated with angina pectoris.

General Information

Nitroglycerin is available in several dosage forms, including sublingual tablets (which are taken under the tongue and are allowed to dissolve), capsules (which are swallowed), patches (which deliver Nitroglycerin through the skin over a 24-hour period), and ointment (which is usually spread over the chest wall, although it can be spread on any area of the body). Frequently patients may take one or more dosage forms of

Nitroglycerin to prevent and/or treat the attack of chest pain associated with angina.

Cautions and Warnings

You should not take Nitroglycerin if you are known to be allergic to it. Also, because Nitroglycerin will increase the pressure of fluid inside your head, it should be taken with great caution if head trauma or bleeding in the head is present.

Possible Side Effects

The most frequent side effect of Nitroglycerin is flushing of the skin. Headache is common and may be severe or persistent. Once in a while, episodes of dizziness and weakness have been associated with the use of Nitroglycerin. There is a possibility that you will experience blurred vision. If this occurs, stop taking the drug and call your physician.

Possible Adverse Drug Effects

Occasionally an individual exhibits a marked sensitivity to the blood-pressure-lowering effect of Nitroglycerin, causing severe responses of nausea, vomiting, weakness, restlessness, loss of facial color or pallor, perspiration, and collapse even with the usual therapeutic dose. Drug rash occasionally occurs.

Drug Interactions

If you are taking Nitroglycerin continuously, avoid excessive alcohol intake, which may cause lowering of blood pressure and resulting faintness and dizziness.

Avoid over-the-counter drugs containing stimulants, which may aggravate your heart disease. Such drugs are used to treat coughs, colds, and allergies, and as appetite suppressants.

Usual Dose

Only as much as is necessary to control chest pains. Since the sublingual dosage form (tablet taken under the tongue) acts within 10 to 15 seconds of being taken, the drug is only taken when necessary.

Long-acting (sustained-release) capsules or tablets are generally used to prevent chest pains associated with angina, with the dose being 1 capsule or tablet every 8 to 12 hours.

1 to 2 inches of Nitroglycerin ointment are squeezed from the tube onto a prepared piece of paper with markings on it. (Some patients may require as much as 4 to 5 inches.) The ointment is spread on the skin every 3 to 4 hours as needed for control of chest pains. The drug is absorbed through the skin. Application sites should be rotated to prevent skin inflammation and rash. Patches are placed on the chest once a day and left on for 24 hours.

Special Information

The sublingual form (tablets which are dissolved under the tongue) should be acquired from your pharmacist only in the original, unopened bottle, and the tablets must not be transferred to a secondary bottle or container; otherwise the tablets may lose potency. Close the bottle tightly after each use or the drug may evaporate from the tablets.

The sublingual form should produce a burning sensation under the tongue, which indicates that the drug is potent and will produce the desired effect. If there is no such sensation you must have the tablets replaced immediately.

Orthostatic hypotension, where more blood stays in the extremities and less becomes available to the brain, resulting in light-headedness or faintness if you rise suddenly from the prone position, can be a problem if you take Nitroglycerin over a long period of time. Avoid prolonged standing and be careful to stand up slowly.

Brand Name

Norgesic

Ingredients

Aspirin
Caffeine
Orphenadrine Citrate
Phenacetin

Type of Drug

Muscle relaxant combination.

Prescribed for

Muscle spasms.

General Information

The primary ingredient in Norgesic is Orphenadrine Citrate, a derivative of the antihistamine Diphenhydramine Hydrochloride (Benadryl). It is a moderately effective muscle relaxant which works by exerting a general sedative effect. The Aspirin and Phenacetin in Norgesic are there only for pain relief. Norgesic cannot solve the problems of pain due to muscle spasm: it can only temporarily relieve the pain. You must follow any additional advice given regarding exercise, diet, or immobilization to help solve the underlying problem.

Cautions and Warnings

Norgesic should not be used if you have a history of glaucoma, stomach ulcer, intestinal obstruction, difficulty in passing urine, or known sensitivity or allergy to this drug or any of its ingredients. It should not be used by pregnant women or children.

Be aware of the potential depressive effects of Norgesic: drowsiness, sleepiness, and inability to concentrate. These may affect your ability to drive or to operate machinery or equipment.

Possible Side Effects

Dryness of the mouth is usually the first side effect to appear. As the daily dose increases, other possible side effects include rapid heartbeat, palpitations, difficulty in urination, blurred vision, enlarged pupils, weakness, nausea, vomiting, headache, dizziness, constipation, drowsiness, rash, itching, running or stuffy nose, hallucinations, agitation, tremor, and stomach upset. Elderly patients taking this drug may occasionally experience some degree of mental confusion. Large doses or prolonged therapy may result in Aspirin intoxication with symptoms of ringing in the ears, headache, dizziness, fever, confusion, sweating, thirst, drowsiness, dimness of vision, rapid breathing, increased pulse rate, or diarrhea.

Drug Interactions

One of the ingredients in Norgesic is Aspirin, which may

significantly affect the effectiveness of oral anticoagulant (blood-thinning) drugs, may increase the effect of Probenecid, and may increase the blood-sugar-lowering effects of oral antidiabetic drugs such as Chlorpropamide and Tolbutamide.

Interaction with Propoxyphene may cause confusion, anxiety, tremors, or shaking.

Long-term users should avoid excessive alcohol intake, which may aggravate stomach upset and bleeding.

Usual Dose

1 to 2 tablets 3 to 4 times per day.

Special Information

Take with food or at least ½ glass of water to prevent stomach upset.

Generic Name

Nortriptyline

Brand Names

Aventyl
Pamelor

Type of Drug

Antidepressant.

Prescribed for

Depression with or without symptoms of anxiety.

General Information

Nortriptyline and other members of this group are effective in treating symptoms of depression. They can elevate your mood, increase physical activity and mental alertness, improve appetite and sleep patterns. These drugs are mild sedatives and therefore useful in treating mild forms of depression associated with anxiety. You should not expect instant results with this medicine: benefits are usually seen after 1 to 4 weeks. If symptoms are not affected after 6 to 8 weeks, contact your doctor. Occasionally this drug and other members of the group of drugs have been used in treating nighttime bed-wetting in the young child, but they do not produce long-lasting relief and therapy with one of them for nighttime bed-wetting is of questionable value.

Cautions and Warnings

Do not take Nortriptyline if you are allergic or sensitive to this or other members of this class of drug: Doxepin, Protriptyline, Imipramine, Desipramine, and Amitriptyline. The drugs should not be used if you are recovering from a heart attack. Nortriptyline may be taken with caution if you have a history of epilepsy or other convulsive disorders, difficulty in urination, glaucoma, heart disease, or thyroid disease. Nortriptyline can interfere with your ability to perform tasks which require concentration, such as driving or operating machinery. Nortriptyline will pass from mother to unborn child: consult your doctor before taking this medicine if you are pregnant.

Possible Side Effects

Changes in blood pressure (both high and low), abnormal heart rates, heart attack, confusion (especially in elderly patients), hallucinations, disorientation, delusions, anxiety, restlessness, excitement, numbness and tingling in the extremities, lack of coordination, muscle spasms or tremors, seizures and/or convulsions, dry mouth, blurred vision, constipation, inability to urinate, rash, itching, sensitivity to bright light or sunlight, retention of fluids, fever, allergy, changes in composition of blood, nausea, vomiting, loss of appetite, stomach upset, diarrhea, enlargement of the breasts in males and females, increased or decreased sex drive, increased or decreased blood sugar.

Possible Adverse Drug Effects

Infrequent: agitation, inability to sleep, nightmares, feeling of panic, development of a peculiar taste in the mouth, stomach cramps, black coloration of the tongue, yellowing eyes and/or skin, changes in liver function, increased or decreased weight, perspiration, flushing, frequent urination, drowsiness, dizziness, weakness, headache, loss of hair, nausea, not feeling well.

Drug Interactions

Interaction with monoamine oxidase (MAO) inhibitors can cause high fevers, convulsions, and occasionally death. Don't take MAO inhibitors until at least 2 weeks after Nortriptyline has been discontinued.

Nortriptyline interacts with Guanethidine, a drug used to treat high blood pressure: if your doctor prescribes Nortriptyline and you are taking medicine for high blood pressure, be sure to discuss this with him.

Nortriptyline increases the effects of barbiturates, tranquilizers, other depressive drugs, and alcohol. Don't drink alcoholic beverages if you take this medicine.

Taking Nortriptyline and thyroid medicine will enhance the effects of the thyroid medicine. The combination can cause abnormal heart rhythms.

Large doses of Vitamin C (Ascorbic Acid) can reduce the effect of Nortriptyline. Drugs such as Bicarbonate of Soda or Acetazolamide will increase the effect of Nortriptyline.

Usual Dose

Adult: 30 to 100 milligrams per day. The dose of this drug must be tailored to patient's need.

Elderly: lower doses are recommended, usually 30 to 50 milligrams per day.

Child: this drug should not be taken by children.

Overdosage

Symptoms are confusion, inability to concentrate, hallucinations, drowsiness, lowered body temperature, abnormal heart rate, heart failure, large pupils of the eyes, convulsions, severely lowered blood pressure, stupor, and coma (as well as agitation, stiffening of body muscles, vomiting, and high fever). The patient should be taken to a hospital emergency room immediately. ALWAYS bring the medicine bottle.

Generic Name

Noscapine

Brand Name

Tusscapine

Type of Drug

Nonnarcotic cough suppressant.

Prescribed for

Coughs due to colds or other respiratory infections.

Cautions and Warnings

Do not use this drug if you are allergic to Noscapine (which is rare). Do not use this drug for a serious cough or a cough with severe mucus congestion.

General Information

This drug is chemically related to Papaverine but has cough suppressant potency similar to that of Codeine, a narcotic drug. Noscapine does not have all the side effects associated with Codeine because it is not a narcotic.

Possible Side Effects

Nausea, drowsiness.

Drug Interactions

This drug can cause drowsiness when taken in high doses. Do not drink alcoholic beverages or take other drugs which can also cause drowsiness.

Usual Dose

Syrup doses are as follows.
  Adult: 1 to 2 teaspoons 3 to 4 times per day.
  Child (age 2 to 6): ½ to 1 teaspoon 3 to 4 times per day.
  Chewable tablet doses are as follows.
  Adult: 1 to 2 every 4 to 6 hours. Do not take more than 8 per day.
  Child (age 6 to 12): 1 tablet 3 to 4 times per day. Do not take more than 4 per day.

Overdosage

Primary sign of overdosage is drowsiness. In case of overdose, call your doctor or local poison control center.

Special Information

Take care while driving or operating equipment if you are taking Noscapine.

Brand Name

Novahistine Elixir

Ingredients

Chlorpheniramine
Phenylpropanolamine Hydrochloride

Other Brand Names

Alamine Liquid	Phenhist Elixir
Dehist Elixir	Rohistine Elixir
Midahist Elixir	Spen-Histine Elixir
Novamor Elixir	

Type of Drug

Decongestant combination.

Prescribed for

Relief of cough, nasal congestion, runny nose, and other symptoms associated with the common cold, viruses, or other upper respiratory diseases. The drug may also be used to treat allergies, asthma, ear infections, or sinus infections.

General Information

Novahistine Elixir is one of almost 100 products marketed to relieve the symptoms of the common cold and other upper respiratory infections. These products may contain medicine to relieve congestion, act as an antihistamine, relieve or suppress cough, and help you to cough up mucus. They may contain medicine for each purpose, or may contain a combination of medicines. Some combinations leave out the antihistamine, the decongestant, or the expectorant. You must realize while taking Novahistine Elixir or similar products that these drugs are good only for the relief of symptoms and will not treat the underlying problem, such as a cold virus or other infections.

Cautions and Warnings

Can cause excessive tiredness or drowsiness.

This product should not be used for newborn infants or taken by pregnant or nursing mothers. People with glaucoma or difficulty in urinating should avoid this drug and other drugs containing antihistamines.

Possible Side Effects

Dry mouth, blurred vision, difficulty passing urine, headache, palpitations, (possibly) constipation, nervousness, dizziness, restlessness or even inability to sleep.

Drug Interactions

Taking Novahistine Elixir with MAO inhibitors can produce severe interaction. Consult your doctor first.

Novahistine Elixir contains Chlorpheniramine. Drinking alcoholic beverages while taking this drug may produce excessive drowsiness and/or sleepiness, or inability to concentrate.

Usual Dose

1 to 2 teaspoons 4 times per day.

Special Information

Take with a full glass of water to reduce stomach upset and help remove excessive mucus from the throat.

Brand Name

Novahistine LP

Ingredients

Chlorpheniramine
Phenylephrine

Type of Drug

Long-acting combination antihistamine-decongestant.

Prescribed for

Relief of sneezing, runny nose, and nasal congestion associated with the common cold, allergy, or other upper respiratory condition.

General Information

Novahistine LP is one of many products marketed to relieve

the symptoms of the common cold. Most of these products contain ingredients to relieve nasal congestion or dry up runny noses or relieve a scratchy throat; several of them may contain ingredients to suppress cough or to help eliminate unwanted mucus. All these products are good only for the relief of symptoms and do not treat the underlying problem such as the cold virus or other infections.

Cautions and Warnings

If you are pregnant you should not take this drug.

Possible Side Effect

Mild drowsiness.

Possible Adverse Drug Effects

Infrequent: restlessness, tension, nervousness, tremor, weakness, insomnia, headache, palpitations, elevation of blood pressure, sweating, loss of appetite, nausea, vomiting, dizziness, constipation.

Drug Interactions

Interaction with alcoholic beverages may cause excessive drowsiness and/or sleepiness, or inability to concentrate. Do not take this drug with alcohol, sedatives, tranquilizers, antihistamines, sleeping pills, thyroid medicine, or antihypertensive drugs such as Reserpine or Guanethidine. Do not self-medicate with over-the-counter drugs for the relief of cold symptoms: taking Novahistine LP with such drugs may aggravate high blood pressure, heart disease, diabetes, or thyroid disease.

Do not take Novahistine LP if you are taking or suspect you may be taking a monoamine oxidase (MAO) inhibitor; severe elevation in blood pressure may result.

Usual Dose

Adult and child (age 12 and over): 1 to 2 tablets every 12 hours.

Child (under age 12): not recommended.

Special Information

Since drowsiness may occur during use of Novahistine LP,

be cautious while performing mechanical tasks requiring alertness.

If this drug upsets your stomach it should be taken with food.

Generic Name
Nystatin Vaginal Tablets

Brand Names
Korostatin
Mycostatin
Nilstat
O-V Statin

Type of Drug
Vaginal anti-infective.

Prescribed for
Fungal infection of the vagina.

General Information
Generally you will have relief of symptoms in 1 to 3 days. Nystatin Vaginal Tablets effectively control troublesome and unpleasant symptoms such as itching, inflammation, and discharge. In most cases, 2 weeks of therapy is sufficient for treatment, but prolonged treatment may be necessary. It is important that you continue using this medicine during menstruation. This drug has been used to prevent thrush or candida infection in the newborn infant by treating the mother for 3 to 6 weeks before her due date. At times the vaginal tablet has been used to treat candida infections of the mouth: the vaginal tablet is used as a lozenge and is allowed to be dissolved in the mouth and then swallowed.

Cautions and Warnings
Do not take this drug if you know you may be sensitive or allergic to Nystatin Vaginal Tablets.

Possible Side Effects
Nystatin Vaginal Tablets is virtually nontoxic, and is gener-

ally well tolerated. The only side effect reported has been intravaginal irritation: if this occurs, discontinue the drug and contact your doctor.

Usual Dose

1 to 2 tablets inserted high in the vagina daily.

Special Information

Do not stop taking the medication just because you begin to feel better. All the medication prescribed must be taken for at least 2 days after the relief of symptoms.

Generic Name

Oral Contraceptives (Combination)

Brand Names

Brevicon
Demulen
Enovid
Enovid-E
Loestrin
Lo/Ovral
Modicon

Norinyl
Norlestrin
Ortho-Novum
Ovcon
Ovral
Ovulen

Note: Brand names may appear with a number (e.g., Loestrin 28) that represents the number of tablets in each package, or with "FE," which indicates that iron pills are included.

Type of Drug

Oral contraceptive.

Prescribed for

Prevention of pregnancy.

General Information

These oral contraceptives (the Pill) are a combination of two natural female hormones, Estrogen and Progestin. These hormones control the menstrual cycle and prepare the woman's body to accept a fertilized egg: once the fertilized egg is implanted, no more eggs can be produced. The Pill works by preventing the production of eggs. Other products (Micronor, Nor Q-l, Ovrette) contain Progestin only.

Any woman taking the Pill should be fully aware of all the problems associated with this type of contraception and should discuss them fully with her doctor. Side effects may be avoided by changing from one product to another with differing quantities of estrogen and/or progestin. There are combinations with low, intermediate, or high concentrations of one hormone or another.

Cautions and Warnings

You should not use oral contraceptives if you have a history of blood clots of the veins or arteries, have a disease affecting blood coagulation, have known or suspected breast cancer, have undiagnosed or abnormal bleeding, or suspect you are pregnant.

Women with hepatitis or any other liver dysfunction should avoid taking the Pill. Smoking increases the risk of serious side effects on the heart.

Possible Side Effects

Nausea, abdominal cramps, bloating, vaginal bleeding, change in menstrual flow, possible infertility after coming off the Pill, breast tenderness, weight change, headaches, rash, vaginal itching and burning, general vaginal infection, nervousness, dizziness, formation of eye cataract, changes in sex drive, changes in appetite, loss of hair.

Possible Adverse Drug Effects

Women who take oral contraceptives are more likely to develop several serious conditions including the formation of blood clots in the deep veins, stroke, heart attack, liver cancer, gallbladder disease, and high blood pressure. Women who smoke cigarettes are much more likely to develop some of these adverse effects.

Drug Interactions

Interaction with Rifampin decreases the effectiveness of oral contraceptives. The same may be true of barbiturates, Phenylbutazone, Phenytoin, Ampicillin, Neomycin, Penicillin

V, Tetracycline, Chloramphenicol, sulfa drugs, Nitrofurantoin, and tranquilizers.

Another interaction reduces the effect of anticoagulant (blood-thinning) drugs. Discuss this with your doctor.

The Pill can also increase blood cholesterol (fat), and can interfere with blood tests for thyroid function and blood sugar.

Usual Dose

The first day of bleeding is the first day of the menstrual cycle. At the start, 1 tablet, beginning on the fifth day of the menstrual cycle, is taken every day for 20 to 21 days according to the number of contraceptive tablets supplied by the manufacturer. If 7 days after taking the last tablet menstrual flow has not begun, begin the next month's cycle of pills.

Overdosage

Overdosage may cause nausea and withdrawal bleeding in adult females. Accidental overdosage in children who take their mother's pills has not shown serious adverse effects.

Special Information

Some manufacturers have included 7 blank or 7 iron pills in their packages, to be taken on days when the Pill is not taken. These pills have the number 28 as part of the brand name and a pill should be taken every day.

If you forget to take the Pill for 1 day, take 2 pills the following day. If you miss 2 consecutive days, take 2 pills for the next 2 days. Then continue to take 1 pill daily. If you miss 3 consecutive days, don't take any more pills for the next 7 days; then start a new cycle.

Forgetting to take the Pill reduces your protection: if you keep forgetting to take it, you should consider other means of birth control.

All oral contraceptive prescriptions must come with a "patient package insert" for you to read. It gives detailed information about the drug and is required by federal law.

Brand Name

Ornade

Ingredients

Chlorpheniramine Maleate
Isopropamide Iodide
Phenylpropanolamine

Other Brand Names

Orahist Capsules
Rhinolar-Ex 12 Capsules

Type of Drug

Long-acting combination antihistamine-decongestant.

Prescribed for

Relief of sneezing, runny nose, and nasal congestion associated with the common cold, allergy, or other upper respiratory condition.

General Information

Ornade is one of many products marketed to relieve the symptoms of the common cold. Most of these products contain ingredients to relieve nasal congestion or to dry up runny noses or relieve a scratchy throat; and several of them may contain ingredients to suppress cough, or to help eliminate unwanted mucus. All these products are good only for the relief of symptoms and do not treat the underlying problem, such as a cold virus or other infections.

Cautions and Warnings

If you are pregnant you should not take this drug.

Possible Side Effects

Mild drowsiness has been seen in patients taking Ornade.

Possible Adverse Drug Effects

Infrequent: restlessness, tension, nervousness, tremor, weakness, inability to sleep, headache, palpitations, elevation of blood pressure, sweating, sleeplessness, loss of appetite, nausea, vomiting, dizziness, constipation.

Drug Interactions

One of the ingredients in Ornade may cause drowsiness and/or sleepiness and other signs of central nervous system depression. Do not take this drug with alcohol, sedatives, tranquilizers, antihistamines, sleeping pills, thyroid medicine, or antihypertensive drugs such as Reserpine or Guanethidine.

Do not self-medicate with over-the-counter drugs for the relief of cold symptoms along with Ornade, as this may aggravate high blood pressure.

Usual Dose

Adult and child (age 12 and over): 1 tablet every 12 hours.
Child (under age 12): not recommended.

Special Information

Since drowsiness may occur during use of Ornade, be cautious while performing mechanical tasks requiring alertness.

If this drug upsets your stomach it should be taken with food.

Brand Name

Os-Cal

Ingredients

Calcium
Copper
Iron
Magnesium
Manganese
Silica
Vitamin D
Zinc

Type of Drug

Calcium and mineral supplement.

Prescribed for

Calcium deficiency.

General Information

This drug is used as an aid in the treatment of any disorder associated with calcium deficiency. The Vitamin D helps promote more efficient absorption of the calcium.

Usual Dose

1 tablet 3 times per day with meals.

Generic Name

Oxacillin Sodium

Brand Names

Bactocill
Prostaphlin

Type of Drug

Broad-spectrum antibiotic.

Prescribed for

Gram-positive bacterial infections. Gram-positive bacteria (pneumococci, streptococci, and staphylococci) are organisms which usually cause diseases such as pneumonia, infections of the tonsils and throat, venereal disease, meningitis (infection of the spinal column), and septicemia (infection of the bloodstream). This drug is best used to treat infections resistant to Penicillin, although it may be used as initial treatment for some patients.

General Information

Oxacillin Sodium is manufactured in the laboratory by fermentation and by general chemical reaction, and is classified as a semisynthetic antibiotic. Because the effectiveness of the antibiotic is determined by the drug's ability to affect the cell wall of the invading bacteria, it is very important that the patient completely follow the doctor's prescribing directions. These directions include spacing of doses as well as the number of days the patient should continue taking the medicine. If they are not followed, the effect of the antibiotic is severely reduced. To ensure the maximum effect, you should take the medication on an empty stomach, either 1 hour before or 2 hours after meals.

Cautions and Warnings

If you have a known history of allergy to Penicillin you should avoid taking Oxacillin Sodium, since the drugs are chemically similar. The most common allergic reaction to Oxacillin Sodium, as well as to the other penicillins, is a hivelike rash over the body with itching and redness. It is important to tell your doctor if you have ever taken Oxacillin Sodium or penicillins before and if you have experienced any adverse reaction to the drug such as rash, itching, or difficulty in breathing.

Possible Side Effects

Common: stomach upset, nausea, vomiting, diarrhea, possible rash. Less common: hairy tongue, itching or irritation around the anus and/or vagina. If these symptoms occur, contact your doctor immediately.

Drug Interactions

The effect of Oxacillin Sodium can be significantly reduced when it is taken with other antibiotics. Consult your doctor if you are taking both during the same course of therapy. Otherwise, Oxacillin Sodium is generally free of interactions with other medications.

Usual Dose

Adult and child (88 pounds or more): 500 to 1000 milligrams every 4 to 6 hours.

Child (less than 88 pounds): 20 to 40 milligrams per pound of body weight per day in divided doses.

This drug is frequently used in higher doses when given intravenously. It must be given intravenously for serious infections because of the unusually high doses required.

Storage

Oxacillin Sodium can be stored at room temperature.

Special Information

Do not take Oxacillin Sodium after the expiration date on the label.

The safety of the drug in pregnancy has not been established.

Generic Name

Oxazepam

Brand Name

Serax

Type of Drug

Tranquilizer.

Prescribed for

Relief of symptoms of anxiety, tension, fatigue, or agitation.

General Information

Oxazepam is a member of the chemical group of drugs known as benzodiazepines. These drugs are used as either antianxiety agents, anticonvulsants, or sedatives (sleeping pills). They exert their effects by relaxing the large skeletal muscles and by a direct effect on the brain. In doing so, they can relax you and make you either more tranquil or sleepier, depending on the drug and how much you use. Many doctors prefer Oxazepam and the other members of this class to other drugs that can be used for the same effect. Their reason is that the benzodiazepines tend to be safer, have fewer side effects, and are usually as, if not more, effective.

These drugs are generally used in any situation where they can be a useful adjunct.

Benzodiazepine tranquilizing drugs can be abused if taken for long periods of time and it is possible to develop withdrawal symptoms if you discontinue the therapy abruptly. Withdrawal symptoms include convulsions, tremor, muscle cramps, stomach cramps, vomiting, and sweating.

Cautions and Warnings

Do not take Oxazepam if you know you are sensitive or

allergic to this drug or other benzodiazepines such as Chlordiazepoxide, Prazepam, Clorazepate, Diazepam, Lorazepam, Flurazepam, and Clonazepam.

Oxazepam and other members of this drug group may aggravate narrow angle glaucoma, but if you have open angle glaucoma you may take the drugs. In any case, check this information with your doctor. Oxazepam can cause tiredness, drowsiness, inability to concentrate, or similar symptoms. Be careful if you are driving, operating machinery, or performing other activities which require concentration. Avoid taking this drug during the first 3 months of pregnancy except under strict supervision of your doctor.

Possible Side Effects

Most common: mild drowsiness during the first few days of therapy, especially in the elderly or debilitated. If drowsiness persists, contact your doctor.

Possible Adverse Drug Effects

Major adverse reactions: confusion, depression, lethargy, disorientation, headache, lack of activity, slurred speech, stupor, dizziness, tremor, constipation, dry mouth, nausea, inability to control urination, changes in sex drive, irregular menstrual cycle, changes in heart rhythm, lowered blood pressure, retention of fluids, blurred or double vision, itching, rash, hiccups, nervousness, inability to fall asleep, (occasional) liver dysfunction. If you experience any of these reactions stop taking the medicine and contact your doctor immediately.

Drug Interactions

Oxazepam is a central nervous system depressant. Avoid alcohol, tranquilizers, narcotics, sleeping pills, barbiturates, MAO inhibitors, antihistamines, and other medicines used to relieve depression.

Usual Dose

Adult: 10 to 120 milligrams per day as individualized for maximum benefit, depending on symptoms and response to treatment, which may call for a dose outside the range given.

Elderly: usually require less of the drug to control anxiety and tension.

Overdosage

Symptoms are confusion, sleep or sleepiness, lack of response to pain such as a pin stick, shallow breathing, lowered blood pressure, and coma. The patient should be taken to a hospital emergency room immediately. ALWAYS bring the medicine bottle.

Generic Name

Oxtriphylline

Brand Name

Choledyl

Type of Drug

Xanthine bronchodilator.

Prescribed for

Relief of bronchial asthma and spasms of bronchial muscles associated with emphysema, bronchitis, and other diseases.

General Information

Oxtriphylline is one of several drugs known as xanthine derivatives which are the mainstay of therapy for bronchial asthma and similar diseases. Other members of this group are Aminophylline, Dyphylline, and Theophylline. Although the dosage for each of these drugs is different, they all work by relaxing bronchial muscles and helping reverse spasms in these muscles.

Cautions and Warnings

Do not use this drug if you are allergic or sensitive to it or to any related drug, such as Aminophylline. If you have a stomach ulcer or heart disease, you should use this drug with caution. If you are pregnant or think that you may be pregnant you should carefully discuss the use of this drug with your doctor, since Oxtriphylline may induce an adverse effect in the unborn child.

Possible Side Effects

Possible side effects from Oxtriphylline or other xanthine derivatives are nausea, vomiting, stomach pain, diarrhea, irritability, restlessness, difficulty sleeping, excitability, muscle twitching or spasms, heart palpitations, other unusual heart rates, low blood pressure, rapid breathing, and local irritation (particularly if a suppository is used).

Possible Adverse Drug Effects

Infrequent: vomiting blood, fever, headache, dehydration.

Drug Interactions

Taking Oxtriphylline at the same time as another xanthine derivative may increase side effects. Don't do it except under the direct care of a doctor.

Oxtriphylline is often given in combination with a stimulant drug such as Ephedrine. Such combinations can cause excessive stimulation and should be used only as specifically directed by your doctor.

Some reports have indicated that combining Erythromycin and Oxtriphylline will give you higher blood levels of Oxtriphylline. Remember that higher blood levels mean the possibility of more side effects.

Usual Dose

Adult: 200 milligrams 4 times per day.

Child (age 2 to 12): 6⅔ milligrams per pound of body weight per day in 4 divided doses.

Note: Each 100 milligrams of Oxtriphylline is equal to 64 milligrams of Theophylline in potency.

Overdosage

The first symptoms are loss of appetite, nausea, vomiting, difficulty sleeping, and restlessness, followed by unusual behavior patterns, frequent vomiting, and extreme thirst, with delirium, convulsions, very high temperature, and collapse. These serious toxic symptoms are rarely experienced after overdose by mouth, which produces loss of appetite, nausea, vomiting, and stimulation. The overdosed patient should be taken to a hospital emergency room where proper treatment can be given.

Special Information

Take on an empty stomach, at least 1 hour before or 2 hours after meals; but occasional mild stomach upset can be minimized by taking the dose with some food (note if you do this a reduced amount of drug will be absorbed into your bloodstream).

Generic Name

Oxymetazoline Hydrochloride

Brand names

Afrin (nose drops and spray)
Duration (nose drops and spray)
St. Josephs Decongestant for Children (nose drops and spray)

Type of Drug

Nasal decongestant.

Prescribed for

Relief of stuffed nose secondary to allergy, the common cold, or any other cause.

Cautions and Warnings

Do not use Oxymetazoline Hydrochloride if you are taking an MAO inhibitor or antidepressant, if you are allergic to Oxymetazoline or any similar preparations, or if you have glaucoma, high blood pressure, heart disease, chest pains, thyroid disease, or diabetes.

Possible Side Effects

Common side effects are burning, stinging, dryness of the mucosa inside the nose, and sneezing.

Possible Adverse Drug Effects

Oxymetazoline Hydrochloride may produce abnormal heart rhythms, increase in blood pressure, headache, feeling of light-headedness, nervousness, difficulty in sleeping, blurred vision, and some drowsiness or lethargy.

Drug Interactions

Oxymetazoline Hydrochloride is a stimulant drug which will increase the effect of any other stimulant. It may block some of the effect of depressant drugs such as tranquilizers or sleeping medications, but this is unusual if recommended doses are observed.

Interaction with MAO inhibitor drugs may cause severe stimulation.

Usual Dose

Adult and child (age 6 and over): 2 to 3 drops or sprays of the (generally 0.5 percent) solution in each nostril no more than twice a day.

Child (age 2 to 5): 2 to 3 drops of half-strength solution in each nostril no more than twice a day.

Overdosage

Symptoms are sedation, desire to go to sleep, possible coma—or with extreme overdosage, high blood pressure, low heart rate, other effects on the heart, with even collapse of the cardiovascular system, and depressed breathing. The patient should be taken to a hospital emergency room immediately, where proper care can be provided. ALWAYS bring the medicine bottle.

Special Information

Use this drug exactly as directed—not more frequently. If Oxymetazoline Hydrochloride is used more than twice a day or in excessive quantities, "rebound congestion" will occur. The nose will produce excessive amounts of mucus in reaction to the medication.

Generic Name

Oxyphenbutazone

Brand Names

Oxalid
Tandearil

Type of Drug

Anti-inflammatory agent.

Prescribed for

Local inflammation related to gout, rheumatoid arthritis, osteoarthritis, painful shoulder such as bursitis or arthritis of a joint, or other inflammatory diseases which cause pain that cannot be controlled by Aspirin, and when severe disability, because of the inflammation, is not relieved by usual treatment.

General Information

This drug should never be taken without strict medical supervision. Oxyphenbutazone should be used only for the short-term relief of pain due to inflammation of muscles, tendons, and joint area.

Oxyphenbutazone and its sister drug Phenylbutazone are toxic and dangerous and should only be used when absolutely necessary. The list of potential side effects is long. Therefore, any change in habits or unusual effect which may be even remotely connected with the use of these drugs should be reported immediately to your doctor.

Cautions and Warnings

You should not take Oxyphenbutazone if you have a history or symptoms associated with gastrointestinal inflammation or ulcer, including severe, recurrent, or persistent upset stomach. This drug is not a simple pain reliever and should never be taken casually. It should not be prescribed before a careful and detailed history, plus physical and laboratory tests, have been completed by the doctor. If your problem can be treated by a less toxic drug such as Aspirin, use that first and try to stay away from Oxyphenbutazone. Never take more than the recommended dosage: this would lead to toxic effects. If you have blurred vision, fever, rash, sore throat, sores in the mouth, upset stomach or pain in the stomach, feeling of weakness, bloody, black, or tarry stool, water retention, or a significant or sudden weight gain, report this to the doctor immediately. In addition, stop taking the drug. If the drug is not effective after 1 week, stop taking it.

Possible Side Effects

Most common: stomach upset, drowsiness, water retention.

Possible Adverse Drug Effects

Infrequent: acute gastric or duodenal ulcer, ulceration or perforation of the large bowel, bleeding from the stomach, anemia, stomach pain, vomiting, vomiting of blood, nausea, diarrhea, changes in the components of the blood, water retention, disruption of normal chemical balance of the body. This drug can cause fatal or nonfatal hepatitis, black-and-blue marks on the skin, serum sickness, drug allergy serious enough to cause shock, itching, serious rashes, fever, and signs of arthritis. It has been known to cause kidney effects including bleeding and kidney stones. Oxyphenbutazone may be a cause of heart disease, high blood pressure, blurred vision, bleeding in the back of the eye, detachment of a retina, hearing loss, high blood sugar, thyroid disease, agitation, confusion, or lethargy.

Drug Interactions

Oxyphenbutazone increases the effects of blood-thinning drugs, Phenytoin, Insulin, and oral antidiabetic agents. If you are taking any of these drugs, discuss this matter with your doctor immediately.

Usual Dose

Adult and child (age 14 years or over): depending upon the condition being treated, 300 to 600 milligrams per day in 3 to 4 equal doses for 7 days. If dose is effective it can then be reduced to 100 to 400 milligrams per day, depending on the condition being treated.

Elderly: drug to be given only for 7 days because of high risk of severe reactions. Not to be given to senile patients.

Child (under age 14): not recommended.

Overdosage

Symptoms are convulsions, euphoria, depression, headache, hallucinations, giddiness, dizziness, coma, rapid breathing rate, and insomnia or sleeplessness. Contact your doctor immediately.

Special Information

Oxyphenbutazone is a central nervous system depressant that can cause drowsiness and tiredness: be careful when driving or operating other equipment, and avoid large quantities of alcoholic beverages, which will aggravate the situation.

Oxyphenbutazone causes stomach upset in many patients; take your dose with food, and if stomach pain continues, notify your doctor.

This drug should be avoided by pregnant women.

Generic Name

Papaverine

Brand Names

Cerespan	Pavakey
Delapav	Pava-Mead
Dilart	Pava-Par
Dipav	Pava-Rx
Kavrin	Pavased
Lapav	Pavasule
Myobid	Pavatym
Orapav Timecelles	Paverine-Spancaps
Pavabid HP	Paverolan
Pavabid Plateau Caps	Therapan
Pavacap Unicelles	Tri-Pavasule
Pavacen Cenules	Vasal Granucaps
Pavadur	Vasocap
Pavadyl	Vasospan
Pavagen	

Type of Drug

Vasodilator.

Prescribed for

Relief of spasms of arteries in the heart, brain, arms, and legs.

General Information

Papaverine relaxes various smooth muscles: it slows their

normal degree of responsiveness but does not paralyze them. Papaverine may directly widen blood vessels in the brain and other areas, increasing the flow of blood and oxygen to those areas.

Cautions and Warnings

Papaverine may aggravate glaucoma. If you develop stomach upset, yellowing of the skin, and/or the whites of the eyes, call your doctor immediately.

Possible Side Effects

Most frequent: nausea, stomach upset, loss of appetite, sweating, flushing of the face, not feeling well, dizziness, drowsiness, headache, skin rash, constipation, diarrhea. In general, few side effects are experienced by people taking Papaverine.

Usual Dose

Plain tablet, 100 to 300 milligrams 3 to 5 times per day. Time-release tablets or capsules, 150 milligrams every 12 hours; if patients do not respond to this, medication may be increased to 150 milligrams every 8 hours, or 300 milligrams every 12 hours.

Brand Name

Parafon Forte

Ingredients

Acetaminophen
Chlorzoxazone

Other Brand Names

Chlorofon-F	Parachlor
Chlorzone Forte	Tuzon
Lobac	

Type of Drug

Skeletal muscle relaxant.

Prescribed for

Relief of pain and spasm of muscular conditions, including lower back pain, strains, sprains, or muscle bruises.

General Information

Parafon Forte is one of several drugs used to treat the aches and pains associated with muscle aches, strains, or a bad back. It gives only temporary relief and is not a substitute for other types of therapy such as rest or surgery.

Cautions and Warnings

Do not take Parafon Forte if you are allergic to either of its ingredients. Do not take more than the exact amount of medication prescribed.

Possible Side Effects

The major side effects are stomach upset and other gastrointestinal problems. Parafon Forte has been associated with bleeding from the stomach, drowsiness, dizziness, lightheadedness, not feeling well, and overstimulation.

Possible Adverse Drug Effects

Both ingredients in Parafon Forte have been associated with liver disease: this is especially true when the medicine is taken in large doses for a long time. If you have been taking it for several weeks, your doctor should perform routine tests to be sure that your liver is functioning properly; but if you take Parafon Forte for a short time (several days or less), the problem should not bother you.

Usual Dose

2 tablets 4 times per day.

Overdosage

Symptoms of massive overdosage are sleepiness, weakness, tiredness, turning blue of lips, fingertips, or other areas, and signs of liver damage such as nausea, vomiting, diarrhea, and severe abdominal pain. Contact your doctor immediately or go to a hospital emergency room where appropriate therapy can be provided. ALWAYS bring the medicine bottle.

Special Information

Parafon Forte can make you sleepy, dull your senses, or disturb your concentration, so be extremely careful while driving or operating equipment or machinery. Drinking alcoholic beverages further complicates this problem and enhances the sedative effects of Parafon Forte.

A breakdown product of the Chlorzoxazone ingredient in Parafon Forte can turn your urine orange to purple-red: this is not dangerous.

Generic Name

Paregoric

Type of Drug

Antidiarrheal.

Prescribed for

Symptomatic treatment of diarrhea.

General Information

Paregoric and other antidiarrheal agents should only be used for short periods: they will relieve the diarrhea, but not its underlying causes. Sometimes these drugs should not be used even though there is diarrhea present: people with some kinds of bowel, stomach, or other disease may be harmed by taking antidiarrheal drugs. Obviously, the decision to use Paregoric must be made by your doctor. Do not use Paregoric without his advice.

Cautions and Warnings

Paregoric is a derivative of Morphine; the cautions and warnings that go with the use of narcotics also go with the use of Paregoric. When taken in the prescribed dose, however, there should be no serious problems.

Possible Side Effects

Most people do not experience side effects from Paregoric, but some may experience nausea, upset stomach, and other forms of gastrointestinal disturbance.

Possible Adverse Drug Effects

Most adverse drug effects associated with narcotic drugs are not experienced with Paregoric because of the limited amount of narcotic contained in the medication and the unappealing taste of the drug. Prolonged use of Paregoric may produce some of the narcotic effects such as difficulty in breathing, light-headedness, dizziness, sedation, nausea, and vomiting.

Drug Interactions

Paregoric, a depressant on the central nervous system, may cause tiredness or inability to concentrate, and may thus increase the effect of sleeping pills, tranquilizers, and alcohol. Avoid large amounts of alcoholic beverages.

Usual Dose

Adult: for diarrhea, 1 to 2 teaspoons 4 times per day.
Infant: for diarrhea, 2 to 10 drops 4 times per day.
Paregoric is only a symptomatic treatment: it should be accompanied by fluids and other therapy prescribed by your doctor.

Overdosage

A patient with Paregoric overdose should be taken to a hospital emergency room immediately. ALWAYS bring the medicine bottle.

Special Information

To help mask the taste, Paregoric can be mixed with a small amount of water or juice immediately before it is taken. The milky color of the mixture is of no consequence.
Take care while driving, or operating any appliance or machine.

Generic Name

Pemoline

Brand Name

Cylert

Type of Drug

Psychotherapeutic.

Prescribed for

Children with attention deficit syndrome who are also in a program that includes social, psychological, and educational counseling.

General Information

This drug stimulates the central nervous system, although its mechanism of action is not known in children with attention deficit disorder (formerly called hyperactivity). It should always be used as part of a total therapeutic program and only when prescribed by a qualified pediatrician.

Cautions and Warnings

Do not use if the patient is allergic or sensitive to Pemoline. Children under age 6 should not receive this medication. Psychotic children may experience worsening of symptoms while taking Pemoline. Patients taking this drug should have periodic blood tests for the liver. Pregnant women and nursing mothers should not use this drug.

Possible Side Effects

Sleeplessness, appetite loss, stomachache, rash, irritability, depression, nausea, dizziness, headache, drowsiness, hallucination. Drug hypersensitivity may occur.

Possible Adverse Drug Effects

Uncontrolled movements of lips, face, tongue, and the extremities; wandering eye may also occur.

Usual Dose

37.5 to 75 milligrams per day. Do not take more than 112.5 milligrams per day.

Overdosage

Symptoms are rapid heartbeat, hallucinations, agitation, uncontrolled muscle movements, and restlessness. Patients suspected of taking an overdose of Pemoline must be taken to a hospital. ALWAYS bring the medicine bottle with you.

Special Information

Take the daily dose at the same time each morning. Call your doctor if sleeplessness develops.

Generic Name

Penicillin G

Brand Names

M-Cillin B-400
Pentids
Pfizerpen G
SK-Penicillin G

Type of Drug

Antibiotic.

Prescribed for

Bacterial infections susceptible to this drug.

General Information

Because the effectiveness of the antibiotic is determined by the drug's ability to destroy the cell wall of the invading bacteria, it is very important that the patient completely follow the doctor's prescribing directions. These directions include spacing of doses as well as the number of days the patient should continue taking the medicine. If they are not followed, the effect of the antibiotic is severely reduced.

Cautions and Warnings

Serious and occasionally fatal hypersensitivity reaction has been reported to Penicillin G. Although this is more common following injection of the drug, it has occurred with oral use. It is more likely to occur in individuals with a history of sensitivity to this drug or sensitivity in general as indicated by multiple allergies.

Possible Side Effects

The most important side effect seen with Penicillin G is sensitivity or allergic reaction.

Possible Adverse Drug Effects

Occasional: stomach upset, nausea, vomiting, diarrhea, coating of the tongue, rash, itching, various types of anemia, other effects on the blood system, oral or rectal infestation with fungal diseases.

Drug Interactions

Penicillin G should not be given at the same time as one of the bacteriostatic antibiotics such as Erythromycin, Tetracycline, or Neomycin, which may diminish the effectiveness of Penicillin G.

Aspirin or Phenylbutazone will increase the level of free Penicillin G in the blood by making more of it available from blood proteins.

Usual Dose

200,000 to 500,000 units every 6 to 8 hours for 10 days.

Storage

Oral Penicillin G may have to be stored in a refrigerator. The bottle should be labeled to that effect and the information should be available on the prescription label.

Special Information

It takes 7 to 10 days for Penicillin G to be effective against most susceptible organisms; be sure to take all the medicine prescribed for the full period prescribed.

Penicillin G is best absorbed on an empty stomach. It can be taken 1 hour before or 2 hours after meals, or first thing in the morning and last thing at night with the other doses spaced evenly through the day.

Generic Name

Penicillin V (Phenoxymethyl Penicillin)

Brand Names

Beepen-VK	Pfizerpen VK
Betapen-VK	Repen-VK
Cocillin-V-K	Robicillin VK
Deltapen-VK	SK-Penicillin VK
Ledercillin VK	Suspen
LV Penicillin	Uticillin VK
Penapar VK	V-Cillin K
Pen-Vee K	Veetids
Penicillin VK	

Type of Drug

Antibiotic.

Prescribed for

Bacterial infections susceptible to this drug.

General Information

General use of Penicillin V is identical to that of Penicillin G, the difference being that Penicillin V is not destroyed by the acids of the stomach, and thus is more effective when taken by mouth than Penicillin G.

Cautions and Warnings

Serious and occasionally fatal hypersensitivity reaction has been reported to Penicillin V. Although it is more common following injection of the drug, it has occurred with oral use. It is more likely to occur in individuals with a history of sensitivity to this drug or sensitivity in general as indicated by multiple allergies.

Possible Side Effects

The most important side effect seen with Penicillin V is sensitivity or allergic reaction.

Possible Adverse Drug Effects

Occasional: stomach upset, nausea, vomiting, diarrhea, coating of the tongue, rash, itching, various types of anemia, other effects on the blood system, oral or rectal infestation with fungal diseases.

Drug Interactions

Penicillin V should not be given at the same time as one of the bacteriostatic antibiotics such as Erythromycin, Tetracycline, or Neomycin, which may diminish the effectiveness of Penicillin V.

Aspirin or Phenylbutazone will increase the level of free Penicillin V in the blood by making more of it available from blood proteins.

Usual Dose

125 to 250 milligrams every 6 to 8 hours for 10 days.

Storage

Oral Penicillin V may have to be stored in a refrigerator. The bottle should be labeled to that effect and the information should be available on the prescription label.

Special Information

It takes 7 to 10 days for Penicillin V to be effective against most susceptible organisms; be sure to take all the medicine prescribed for the full period prescribed.

Penicillin V is best absorbed on an empty stomach. It can be taken 1 hour before or 2 hours after meals, or first thing in the morning and last thing at night with the other doses spaced evenly through the day.

Generic Name

Pentazocine

Brand Name

Talwin

Type of Drug

Nonnarcotic analgesic.

Prescribed for

Relief of moderate to severe pain.

General Information

Pentazocine is used for mild to moderate pain. Fifty to 100 milligrams of Pentazocine is approximately equal in pain-relieving effect to 2 Aspirin tablets (650 milligrams). Pentazocine may be less active than Aspirin for types of pain associated with inflammation, since Aspirin reduces inflammation but Pentazocine does not.

Cautions and Warnings

Do not use Pentazocine if you believe that you are allergic to it. It is possible to develop addiction to or dependence on Pentazocine but addiction is much more likely to occur with people who have a history of abusing narcotics or other drugs. Abrupt stoppage of Pentazocine after extended periods of therapy has produced withdrawal symptoms such as stomach cramps, fever, stuffed or runny nose, restlessness, anxiety, and tearing of the eyes. The drug may cause visual hallucinations or make you disoriented and confused; if this happens, stop taking the drug immediately and contact your physician. Never give this drug or any other potent painkillers to a patient with a head injury.

Possible Side Effects

Nausea, vomiting, constipation, cramps, stomach upset, loss of appetite, diarrhea, dry mouth, alteration of taste, dizziness, light-headedness, sedation, euphoria, headache, difficulty sleeping, disturbed dreams, hallucinations, muscle spasms, irritability, excitement, nervousness, apprehension and depression, feeling of being disoriented and detached from your body.

Possible Adverse Drug Effects

Blurred vision, difficulty in focusing the eyes, double vision, sweating, flushing chills, rash, itching, swelling of the face, flushing and reddening of the skin, changes in blood pressure, abnormal heart rate, difficulty in breathing, effects on components of the blood, difficult urination, tingling in the arms and legs.

Drug Interactions

Avoid interaction with drugs that have a sedative or depressive effect, such as alcohol, barbiturates, sleeping pills, and some pain-relieving medications. The combination will produce extreme sedation, sleepiness, and difficulty concentrating.

Pentazocine has the unusual effect of being a mild narcotic antagonist. If you must take narcotics for pain relief, do not take Pentazocine, because it will reverse the effect of the narcotic drug. This can be a special problem for patients in Methadone treatment programs. If one of these patients takes Pentazocine, he will experience narcotic withdrawal effects.

Usual Dose

50 milligrams every 3 to 4 hours. Maximum dose, 600 milligrams per day to control pain.

This drug is not recommended for children.

Overdosage

Symptoms resemble those of narcotic overdose: decreased breathing, sleepiness, lassitude, low blood pressure, and even coma. The patient should be taken to a hospital emergency room immediately. ALWAYS bring the medicine bottle.

Generic Name

Pentobarbital

Brand Names

Carbrital
Nembutal

Type of Drug

Hypnotic; sedative.

Prescribed for

Daytime sedation; sleeping medication.

General Information

Pentobarbital, like the other barbiturates, appears to act by interfering with nerve impulses to the brain.

Cautions and Warnings

Pentobarbital may slow down your physical and mental reflexes, so you must be extremely careful when operating machinery, driving an automobile, or performing other potentially dangerous tasks. Pentobarbital is classified as a barbiturate; long-term or unsupervised use may cause addiction. Elderly people taking Pentobarbital may exhibit nervousness and confusion at times. Barbiturates are neutralized in the liver and eliminated from the body through the kidneys; consequently, people who have liver or kidney disorders—namely, difficulty in forming or excreting urine—should be carefully monitored by their doctor when taking Pentobarbital.

If you have known sensitivities or allergies to barbiturates, or if you have previously been addicted to sedatives or hypnotics, or if you have a disease affecting the respiratory system, you should not take Pentobarbital.

Possible Side Effects

Difficulty in breathing, rash, and general allergic reaction such as running nose, watering eyes, and scratchy throat.

Possible Adverse Drug Effects

Drowsiness, lethargy, dizziness, hangover, nausea, vomiting, diarrhea. More severe adverse reactions may include anemia and yellowing of the skin and eyes.

Drug Interactions

Interaction with alcohol, tranquilizers, or other sedatives increases the effect of Pentobarbital.

Interaction with anticoagulants (blood-thinning agents) can reduce their effect. This is also true of muscle relaxants and painkillers.

Usual Dose

Daytime sedative: 30 milligrams 3 to 4 times per day.

Hypnotic for sleep: 100 milligrams at bedtime; this may

be repeated once if necessary (occasionally) to induce sleep.

Overdosage

Symptoms are difficulty in breathing, decrease in size of the pupils of the eyes, lowered body temperature progressing to fever as time passes, fluid in the lungs, and eventually coma.

Anyone suspected of having taken an overdose must be taken to the hospital for immediate care. ALWAYS bring the medicine bottle to the emergency room physician so he can quickly and correctly identify the medicine and start treatment. Severe overdosage of this medication can kill; the drug has been used many times in suicide attempts.

Brand Name

Percocet

Ingredients

Acetaminophen
Oxycodone Hydrochloride

Type of Drug

Narcotic analgesic combination.

Prescribed for

Relief of mild to moderate pain.

General Information

Percocet is generally prescribed for the patient who is in pain but is allergic to Aspirin. Percocet is probably not effective for arthritis or other pain associated with inflammation because the Acetaminophen ingredient does not produce an anti-inflammatory effect.

Cautions and Warnings

Do not take Percocet if you know you are allergic or sensitive to any of its components. Use this drug with extreme caution if you suffer from asthma or other breathing problems. Long-term use of this drug may cause drug dependence or addiction. The Oxycodone Hydrochloride component of Percocet is a respiratory depressant, and affects the central nervous system, producing sleepiness, tiredness, and/or inability to concentrate. Be careful if you are driving, operating machinery, or performing other functions requiring concentration. If you are pregnant or suspect that you are pregnant do not take this drug.

Possible Side Effects

Most frequent: light-headedness, dizziness, sleepiness, nausea, vomiting, loss of appetite, sweating. If these effects occur, consider calling your doctor and asking him about lowering your dose of Percocet. Usually the side effects disappear if you simply lie down.

More serious side effects of Percocet are shallow breathing or difficulty in breathing.

Possible Adverse Drug Effects

Adverse effects of Percocet include euphoria (feeling high), weakness, sleepiness, headache, agitation, uncoordinated muscle movement, minor hallucinations, disorientation and visual disturbances, dry mouth, loss of appetite, constipation, flushing of the face, rapid heartbeat, palpitations, faintness, urinary difficulties or hesitancy, reduced sex drive and/or potency, itching, rashes, anemia, lowered blood sugar, and a yellowing of the skin and/or whites of the eyes. Narcotic analgesics may aggravate convulsions in those who have had convulsions in the past.

Drug Interactions

Because of its depressant effect and potential effect on breathing, Percocet should be taken with extreme care in combination with alcohol, sleeping medicine, tranquilizers, or other depressant drugs.

Usual Dose

Adult: 1 to 2 tablets every 4 hours.
Child: not recommended for children.

Overdosage

Symptoms are depression of respiration (breathing), extreme tiredness progressing to stupor and then coma, pinpointed pupils of the eyes, no response to stimulation such as a pin stick, cold and clammy skin, slowing down of the heart rate, lowering of blood pressure, yellowing of the skin and/or whites of the eyes, bluish color in skin of hands and feet, fever, excitement, delirium, convulsions, cardiac arrest, and liver toxicity (shown by nausea, vomiting, pain in the abdomen, and diarrhea). The patient should be taken to a hospital emergency room immediately. ALWAYS bring the medicine bottle.

Special Information

Percocet is best taken with food or at least ½ glass of water to prevent stomach upset.

Brand Name

Percodan

Ingredients

Aspirin
Caffeine
Oxycodone
Phenacetin

Type of Drug

Narcotic analgesic combination.

Prescribed for

Relief of mild to moderate pain.

General Information

Percodan is one of many combination products containing narcotics and analgesics. These products often also contain barbiturates or tranquilizers, and Acetaminophen may be substituted for Aspirin, or Phenacetin and/or Caffeine may be omitted.

Cautions and Warnings

Do not take Percodan if you know you are allergic or sensitive to any of its components. Use this drug with extreme caution if you suffer from asthma or other breathing problems. Long-term use of this drug may cause drug dependence or addiction. The Oxycodone component of Percodan is a respiratory depressant and affects the central nervous system, producing sleepiness, tiredness, and/or inability to concentrate. If you are pregnant or suspect that you are pregnant do not take this drug.

Possible Side Effects

Most frequent: light-headedness, dizziness, sleepiness, nausea, vomiting, loss of appetite, sweating. If these effects occur, consider calling your doctor and asking him about lowering the dose of Percodan you are taking. Usually the side effects disappear if you simply lie down.

More serious side effects of Percodan are shallow breathing or difficulty in breathing.

Possible Adverse Drug Effects

Euphoria (feeling high), weakness, sleepiness, headache, agitation, uncoordinated muscle movement, minor hallucinations, disorientation and visual disturbances, dry mouth, loss of appetite, constipation, flushing of the face, rapid heartbeat, palpitations, faintness, urinary difficulties or hesitancy, reduced sex drive and/or potency, itching, skin rashes, anemia, lowered blood sugar, yellowing of the skin and/or whites of the eyes. Narcotic analgesics may aggravate convulsions in those who have have convulsions in the past.

Drug Interactions

Interaction with alcohol, tranquilizers, barbiturates, or sleeping pills produces tiredness, sleepiness, or inability to concentrate, and seriously increases the depressive effect of Percodan.

The Aspirin component of Percodan can affect anticoagulant (blood-thinning) therapy. Be sure to discuss this with your doctor so that the proper dosage adjustment can be made.

Interaction with adrenal cortical steroids, Phenylbutazone, or alcohol can cause severe stomach irritation with possible bleeding.

Usual Dose

1 tablet every 6 hours as needed for relief of pain.

Overdosage

Symptoms are depression of respiration (breathing), extreme tiredness progressing to stupor and then coma, pinpointed pupils of the eyes, no response to stimulation such as a pin stick, cold and clammy skin, slowing down of the heartbeat, lowering of blood pressure, convulsions, and cardiac arrest. The patient should be taken to a hospital emergency room immediately. ALWAYS bring the medicine bottle.

Special Information

Drowsiness may occur: be careful when driving or operating hazardous machinery.

Take with food or ½ glass of water to prevent stomach upset.

The Phenacetin ingredient of Percodan may be toxic to your kidneys; do not take this medication for longer than 10 days unless so directed by your doctor.

Brand Name

Peri-Colace

Ingredients

Casanthranol
Docusate Sodium

Other Brand Names

Afko-Lube Lax	Diothron
Bu-Lax Plus	Disanthrol
Comfolax-plus	D-S-S plus
Constiban	Molatoc-CST

Type of Drug

Laxative.

Prescribed for

Treatment or prevention of constipation. Also used to clear intestines before X-ray procedures.

General Information

This is one of many laxative combinations available without a prescription. Composed of a stool softener and a stimulant which makes the stool easier to pass by acting directly on the intestine to move the stool through it, such laxatives should be used for short periods only when necessary. Long-term use of a stimulant laxative can produce laxative dependency, where normal bowel function is lost and the stimulant is required to pass any stool.

Cautions and Warnings

Patients with abdominal pain, nausea, vomiting, or symptoms of appendicitis should not take a laxative.

Possible Side Effects

Severely constipated patients may experience stomach cramps. Nausea, vomiting, and diarrhea may occur after excessive amounts have been taken.

Usual Dose

1 to 2 capsules at bedtime.

Special Information

If this laxative is not effective after 7 days, stop taking it and call your doctor.

Generic Name

Phenazopyridine Hydrochloride

Brand Names

Azodine	Phenazodine
Azo-100	Pyridiate
Azo-Standard	Pyridium
Di-Azo	Pyrodine
Phen-Azo	

Type of Drug

Urinary analgesic.

Prescribed for

Relief of pain and discomfort associated with urinary tract infection.

General Information

Phenazopyridine Hydrochloride is used only to relieve the pain associated with urinary infections. It has little antibacterial action and cannot be used, therefore, to cure a urinary infection. It is usually used in combination with an antibacterial sulfa drug.

Cautions and Warnings

This drug should not be used if you have kidney disease or are experiencing decrease in urination.

Possible Side Effect

Occasional stomach upset.

Usual Dose

200 milligrams 3 times per day.

Special Information

Phenazopyridine Hydrochloride may produce an orange-red color in the urine. This is normal, but the color change may interfere with urine tests to monitor diabetes.

Generic Name

Phendimetrazine

Brand Names

Adphen	DI-AP-PROL
Anorex	Dietaps
Aptrol	Ex-Obese
Bacarate	Limit
Bontril PDM	Melfiat

Metra	Phenzine
Obelan	Plegine
Obepar	Prelu-2
Obestrol	Reton
Obepal	Sperx
Obezine	Statobex
Omnibese	Stim-35
PDM	Trimstat
PE-DE-EM	Trimtabs
Phenazine	Weh-less
Phendimead	Weightrol

Type of Drug

Nonamphetamine appetite suppressant.

Prescribed for

Suppression of appetite and treatment of obesity.

General Information

Although Phendimetrazine is not an amphetamine, it can produce the same adverse effects as the amphetamine appetite suppressants. There are several other nonamphetamine appetite suppressants. One, Phenmetrazine (Preludin) is closely related to Phendimetrazine and has similar actions and effects.

Cautions and Warnings

Do not use Phendimetrazine if you have heart disease, high blood pressure, thyroid disease, or glaucoma, or if you are sensitive or allergic to this or similar drugs. Prolonged use of this drug may be habit-forming.

Possible Side Effects

Palpitations, high blood pressure, overstimulation, nervousness, restlessness, drowsiness, sedation, weakness, dizziness, inability to sleep, tremor, headache, dry mouth, nausea, vomiting, diarrhea and other intestinal disturbances, rash, itching, changes in sex drive, hair loss, muscle pain, difficulty in passing urine, sweating, chills, blurred vision, fever.

Drug Interactions

Do not take Phendimetrazine if you take other stimulants or antidepressants.

This drug may reduce the effectiveness of antihypertensive drugs.

Usual Dose

Tablets: 35-milligram tablet 1 hour before meals.
Sustained-release capsules: 105 miligrams once per day.

Overdosage

Symptoms are restlessness, tremor, shallow breathing, confusion, hallucinations, and fever, followed by fatigue and depression, with additional symptoms such as high or possibly low blood pressure, cold and clammy skin, nausea, vomiting, diarrhea, and stomach cramps. The patient should be taken to a hospital emergency room immediately. ALWAYS bring the medicine bottle.

Special Information

Use only for a few weeks as an adjunct to diet, under strict supervision of your doctor.
    Medicine alone will not take off weight. You must limit and modify your food intake, preferably under medical supervision.

Brand Name

Phenergan Expectorant Plain

Ingredients

Alcohol
Citric Acid
Potassium Guaiacolsulfonate
Promethazine Hydrochloride
Sodium Citrate

Other Brand Names

Mallergan Expectorant Plain
Pentazine Expectorant Plain
Promethazine HCL Expectorant Plain
Prothazine Expectorant

Type of Drug

Expectorant combination.

Prescribed for

Relief of coughs and symptoms associated with the common cold.

General Information

Phenergan Expectorant Plain is one of many products marketed for the relief of coughs. The major active ingredient contained in Phenergan Expectorant Plain is an antihistamine. Therefore, the drug is most effective in relieving the symptoms of excess histamine production. It cannot help you recover more quickly, only more comfortably.

Cautions and Warnings

Phenergan Expectorant Plain may cause drowsiness or sleepiness. Do not use this product with similar products such as sedatives, tranquilizers, sleeping pills, antihistamines, or other drugs which can cause sleepiness or drowsiness.

Possible Side Effects

Dryness of the mouth, blurred vision, occasional dizziness.

Drug Interactions

Avoid alcohol, which increases central nervous system depression and leads to drowsiness, sleepiness, or similar problems.

Usual Dose

1 teaspoon every 4 to 6 hours.

Special Information

Take with a full glass of water to help the expectorant effect and reduce any stomach upset caused by the drug.

Brand Name

Phenergan Expectorant with Codeine

Ingredients

Alcohol
Citric Acid

Codeine Phosphate
Potassium Guaiacolsulfonate
Promethazine Hydrochloride
Sodium Citrate

Other Brand Names

K-Phen Expectorant with Codeine
Mallergan Expectorant with Codeine
Pentazine Expectorant with Codeine
Promethazine Hydrochloride Expectorant with Codeine
Prothazine with Codeine Expectorant

Type of Drug

Cough suppressant and expectorant combination.

Prescribed for

Coughs, symptoms of the common cold.

General Information

Phenergan Expectorant with Codeine is one of almost 100 products marketed to treat symptoms of the common cold or other upper respiratory problems. It is useful in helping to relieve symptoms but does not treat the basic problem.

Cautions and Warnings

Do not take this medicine if you are allergic to any of its ingredients.

Possible Side Effects

Drowsiness, dry mouth, blurred vision, difficulty in urination, constipation.

Possible Adverse Drug Effect

Palpitations—pounding of the heart.

Drug Interactions

Avoid alcohol, sedatives, tranquilizers, antihistamines, or other medication which can cause tiredness and/or drowsiness.

Taking Phenergan Expectorant with Codeine with Isocarboxazid (Marplan), Tranylcypromine Sulfate (Parnate), Phenelzine Sulfate (Nardil), or other MAO inhibitor drugs can produce a severe interaction. Consult your doctor first.

Usual Dose

Adult: 2 teaspoons 4 times per day.
Child (over age 1): ½ to 1 teaspoon 3 to 4 times per day.
Take with a full glass of water. This will help the expectorant effect of the drug and may reduce stomach upset.

Special Information

Be aware of the potential depressive effects of Phenergan Expectorant with Codeine; be careful when driving, or operating heavy or dangerous machinery.

Brand Name

Phenergan VC Expectorant Plain

Ingredients

Alcohol
Citric Acid
Phenylephrine
Potassium Guaiacolsulfonate
Promethazine Hydrochloride
Sodium Citrate

Type of Drug

Expectorant combination.

Prescribed for

Coughs.

General Information

Phenergan VC Expectorant Plain is one of many products marketed to relieve the symptoms of the common cold or other upper respiratory infections. These products relieve runny nose, eliminate unwanted mucus, and unclog nasal and sinus passages.

Cautions and Warnings

Drowsiness, dry mouth, blurred vision, difficulty in urination, and/or constipation can occur.

Possible Side Effects

The drug may cause mild stimulation and you may experience nervousness, restlessness, or even inability to sleep.

Drug Interactions

Avoid alcohol, sedatives, tranquilizers, antihistamines, or other medication which can cause tiredness and/or drowsiness. Taking Phenergan VC Expectorant Plain with MAO inhibitor drugs can produce severe interaction. Consult your doctor first.

Usual Dose

1 teaspoon every 4 to 6 hours as needed for the relief of cough or the expectoration of undesired mucus.

Special Information

Be aware of the potential depressive effects of this drug; take care when driving, or operating heavy or dangerous machinery.

Brand Name

Phenergan VC Expectorant with Codeine

Ingredients

Alcohol
Citric Acid
Codeine Phosphate
Phenylephrine
Potassium Guaiacolsulfonate
Promethazine Hydrochloride
Sodium Citrate

Other Brand Names

Mallergan-VC Expectorant with Codeine
Pentazine VC Expectorant with Codeine
Promethazine HCL VC Expectorant with Codeine

Type of Drug

Decongestant; expectorant.

Prescribed for

Relief of cough, nasal congestion, runny nose, and other symptoms associated with the common cold, viruses, or other upper respiratory diseases. The drug may also be used to treat allergies, asthma, ear infections, or sinus infections.

General Information

Phenergan VC Expectorant with Codeine is one of almost 100 products marketed to relieve the symptoms of the common cold and other respiratory infections. These products contain medicine to relieve congestion, act as an antihistamine, relieve or suppress cough, and help you to cough up mucus. They may contain medicine for each purpose, or may contain a combination of medicines. Some combinations leave out the antihistamine, the decongestant, or the expectorant. You must realize while taking Phenergan VC Expectorant with Codeine or similar products that these drugs are good only for the relief of symptoms and will not treat the underlying problem, such as a cold virus or other infections.

Cautions and Warnings

Can cause excessive tiredness or drowsiness.

Possible Side Effects

Dry mouth, blurred vision, difficulty passing urine, (possibly) constipation, nervousness, restlessness, or even inability to sleep.

Drug Interactions

Taking Phenergan VC Expectorant with Codeine with MAO inhibitor drugs can produce severe interaction. Consult with your doctor first.

Drinking alcoholic beverages while taking Codeine may produce excessive drowsiness and/or sleepiness, or inability to concentrate.

Usual Dose

1 to 2 teaspoons 4 times per day.

Special Information

Take with a full glass of water to reduce stomach upset and help remove excessive mucus.

Generic Name

Phenobarbital

Brand Names

Barbita	PBR/12
Barbipil	Pheno-Squar
Henotal	Sedadrops
Infadorm Drops	SK-Phenobarbital
Luminal	Solfoton

Type of Drug

Hypnotic; sedative; anticonvulsive.

Prescribed for

Epileptic seizures, convulsions, as an anticonvulsive or a daytime sedative; as a mild hypnotic (sleeping medication); for eclampsia (toxemia in pregnancy).

General Information

Phenobarbital, like the other barbiturates, appears to act by interfering with nerve impulses to the brain. When used as an anticonvulsive, Phenobarbital is not very effective by itself, but when used with anticonvulsive agents such as Phenytoin, the combined action of Phenobarbital and Phenytoin is dramatic. This combination has been used very successfully to control epileptic seizures.

Cautions and Warnings

Phenobarbital may slow down your physical and mental reflexes, so you must be extremely careful when operating machinery, driving an automobile, or performing other potentially dangerous tasks. Phenobarbital is classified as a barbiturate; long-term or unsupervised use may cause addiction. Elderly patients on Phenobarbital exhibit nervousness and confusion at times. Barbiturates are neutralized in the liver and eliminated from the body through the kidneys: consequently, people who have liver or kidney disorders—namely, difficulty in forming or excreting urine—should be carefully monitored by their doctor when taking Phenobarbital.

If you have known sensitivities or allergies to barbiturates, or have previously been addicted to sedatives or hypnotics, or if you have a disease affecting the respiratory system, you should not take Phenobarbital.

Possible Side Effects

Difficulty in breathing, skin rash, and general allergic reaction such as running nose, watering eyes, and scratchy throat.

Possible Adverse Drug Effects

Drowsiness, lethargy, dizziness, hangover, nausea, vomiting, diarrhea. More severe adverse reactions may include anemia and yellowing of the skin and eyes.

Drug Interactions

Interaction with alcohol, tranquilizers, the antibiotic Chloramphenicol, or other sedatives increases the sedative effect of Phenobarbital.

Interaction with anticoagulants (blood-thinning agents) can reduce their effect. This is also true of muscle relaxants and painkillers. Phenobarbital has been shown to reduce the potency of the antibiotic Doxycycline.

Usual Dose

Anticonvulsant: 15 to 30 milligrams 3 times per day. Hypnotic (for sleep): 30 milligrams at bedtime. Sedative: 15 to 30 milligrams 3 times per day.

Specific dose is determined by patient's size, weight, and physical condition.

Overdosage

Symptoms are difficulty in breathing, decrease in size of the pupils of the eyes, lowered body temperature progressing to fever as time passes, fluid in the lungs, and eventually coma.

Anyone suspected of having taken an overdose must be taken to the hospital for immediate care. ALWAYS bring the medicine bottle to the emergency room physician so he can quickly and correctly identify the medicine and start treatment. Severe overdosage of this medication can kill; the drug has been used many times in suicide attempts.

Generic Name

Phentermine Hydrochloride

Brand Names

Adipex	Parmine
Delcophen	Phentrol
Fastin	Tora
Ionamin	Unifast Unicelles
Obephen	Wilpowr

Type of Drug

Nonamphetamine appetite suppressant.

Prescribed for

Suppression of appetite and treatment of obesity.

General Information

Although Phentermine Hydrochloride is not an amphetamine, it can produce the same adverse effects as the amphetamine appetite suppressants.

Cautions and Warnings

Do not use Phentermine Hydrochloride if you have heart disease, high blood pressure, thyroid disease, or glaucoma, or if you are sensitive or allergic to this or similar drugs. Prolonged use of this drug may be habit-forming.

Possible Side Effects

Palpitations, high blood pressure, overstimulation, nervousness, restlessness, drowsiness, sedation, weakness, dizziness, inability to sleep, tremor, headache, dry mouth, nausea, vomiting, diarrhea and other intestinal disturbances, rash, itching, changes in sex drive, hair loss, muscle pain, difficulty in passing urine, sweating, chills, blurred vision, and fever.

Drug Interactions

Do not take Phentermine Hydrochloride if you take other stimulants or antidepressants.

Phentermine Hydrochloride may reduce the effectiveness of antihypertensive drugs.

Usual Dose

Adult: 8 milligrams ½ hour before meals, or 15 to 37 milligrams once a day before breakfast.

Overdosage

Symptoms are restlessness, tremor, shallow breathing, confusion, hallucinations, and fever followed by fatigue and depression, with additional symptoms such as high or possibly low blood pressure, cold and clammy skin, nausea, vomiting, diarrhea, and stomach cramps. The patient should be taken to a hospital emergency room immediately. ALWAYS bring the medicine bottle.

Special Information

Use only for a few weeks as an adjunct to diet, under strict supervision of your doctor.

Medicine alone will not take off weight. You must limit and modify your food intake, preferably under medical supervision.

Generic Name

Phenylbutazone

Brand Names

Azolid
Butazolidin

Type of Drug

Anti-inflammatory agent.

Prescribed for

Local inflammation of bone joints such as gout, rheumatoid

arthritis, osteoarthritis, painful shoulder such as bursitis or arthritis of a joint, or other inflammatory diseases that cause pain which cannot be controlled by Aspirin, and when severe disability, because of the inflammation, is not relieved by usual treatment.

General Information

This drug should never be taken without strict medical supervision. Phenylbutazone should be used only for the short-term relief of pain due to inflammation of muscles, tendons, and joint area. It has anti-inflammatory, analgesic, and fever-reducing properties. This drug is quite useful but is limited by its side effects and adverse drug reactions.

Phenylbutazone and its sister drug Oxyphenbutazone are toxic and dangerous and should only be used when absolutely necessary. The list of potential side effects is long. Therefore, any change in habits or unusual effect which may be even remotely connected with the use of these drugs should be reported immediately to your doctor.

Cautions and Warnings

You should not take Phenylbutazone if you have a history or symptoms associated with gastrointestinal inflammation or ulcer, including severe, recurrent, or persistent upset stomach. This drug is not a simple pain reliever and should never be taken casually. It should not be prescribed before a careful and detailed history, plus physical and laboratory tests, have been completed by the doctor. Always discuss your state of health and medical history with your doctor completely before taking this medicine. If your problem can be treated by a less toxic drug such as Aspirin, use that first and try to avoid taking Phenylbutazone. Never take more than the recommended dosage: this would lead to toxic effects. If you have blurred vision, fever, rash, sore throat, sores in the mouth, upset stomach or pain in the stomach, feeling of weakness, bloody, black, or tarry stool, water retention, or a significant or sudden weight gain, report this to the doctor immediately. In addition, stop taking the drug. If the drug is not effective after 1 week, stop taking it.

Possible Side Effects

Most common: stomach upset, drowsiness, water retention.

Possible Adverse Drug Effects

Gastric or duodenal ulcer, ulceration or perforation of the large bowel, bleeding from the stomach, anemia, stomach pain, vomiting, vomiting of blood, nausea, diarrhea, changes in the components of the blood, water retention, disruption of normal chemical balance of the body. This drug can cause fatal or nonfatal hepatitis, black-and-blue marks on the skin, serum sickness, drug allergy serious enough to cause shock, itching, serious rashes, fever, and signs of arthritis. It has been known to cause kidney effects including bleeding and kidney stones. Phenylbutazone may be a cause of heart disease, high blood pressure, blurred vision, bleeding in the back of the eye, detachment of a retina, hearing loss, high blood sugar, thyroid disease, agitation, confusion, or lethargy.

Drug Interactions

Phenylbutazone increases the effects of blood-thinning drugs, Phenytoin, Insulin, and oral antidiabetic agents. If you are taking any of these drugs, discuss this matter with your doctor immediately.

Usual Dose

Adult and child (age 14 or over): 300 to 600 milligrams per day in 3 to 4 equal doses for 7 days. If dose is effective it can then be reduced to 100 to 400 milligrams per day, depending on the condition being treated.

Elderly: drug to be given only for 7 days because of high risk of severe reactions. Not to be given to senile patients.

Child (under age 14): not recommended.

Overdosage

If symptoms of convulsions, euphoria, depression, headache, hallucinations, giddiness, dizziness, coma, rapid breathing rate, continued stomach pain, and insomnia or sleeplessness appear, contact your doctor immediately.

Special Information

This drug can make you drowsy and/or tired: be careful when driving or operating equipment. Avoid alcoholic beverages.

Phenylbutazone causes stomach upset in many patients;

take your dose with food, and if stomach pain continues, notify your doctor.

This drug should be avoided by pregnant women.

Generic Name

Phenytoin

Brand Names

Dilantin (extended)
Diphenylan Sodium (prompt)
Ditan (prompt)

Type of Drug

Anticonvulsant.

Prescribed for

Control of epileptic seizures.

General Information

Phenytoin is one of several drugs of the same chemical group used to control convulsions. All these drugs act by the same mechanism, although some patients may respond to some and not another.

Cautions and Warnings

If you have been taking Phenytoin for a long time and no longer need it, the dosage should be reduced gradually over a period of about a week. Stopping abruptly may bring on severe epileptic seizures. Pregnant women who use anticonvulsive medicine are said to tend to give birth to children with birth defects, but the data available are somewhat questionable. If you become pregnant and you are taking this medicine, consult your doctor immediately.

Possible Side Effects

Most common: slurred speech, mental confusion, nystagmus (a rhythmic, uncontrolled movement of the eyeballs), dizziness, insomnia, nervousness, uncontrollable twitching, double vision, tiredness, irritability, depression, tremors, head-

aches. These side effects will generally disappear as therapy
continues and the dosage is reduced.

Possible Adverse Drug Effects

Nausea, vomiting, diarrhea, constipation, fever, rashes, bald-
ing, weight gain, numbness of the hands and feet, chest
pains, retention of water, sensitivity to bright lights, especially sunlight, conjunctivitis, changes of the blood system
including anemia, swollen glands. Phenytoin can cause an
abnormal growth of the gums surrounding the teeth, so
good oral hygiene including gum massage, frequent brushing, and appropriate dental care is very important. Occasionally Phenytoin produces unusual hair growth over the
body, and liver damage, including hepatitis.

Drug Interactions

A barbiturate taken with Phenytoin may increase the rate at
which Phenytoin is excreted from the body; then if the
barbiturate is discontinued the patient may show an increased
response to Phenytoin, and the dose may have to be reduced
slightly.

Warfarin, Isoniazid, Chloramphenicol, Disulfiram, Phenylbutazone, and Oxyphenbutazone can cause Phenytoin to
remain in the body for a longer time, increasing the incidence of Phenytoin side effects. Folic acid or high doses of
tricyclic antidepressant drugs may increase seizures. The
dose of Phenytoin may have to be adjusted by your doctor.

Usual Dose

Adult: initial dose, 300 milligrams per day. If this does not
result in satisfactory control, gradually increase to 600 milligrams per day. (The most frequent maintenance dose is 300
to 400 milligrams per day.) Only Dilantin may be taken once
daily. The other brands of Phenytoin must be taken throughout the day, as convenient.

Child: initial dose, 2½ milligrams per pound of body weight
per day in 2 to 3 equally divided doses; then adjust according to needs and response of child (normal maintenance
dose, 2 to 4 milligrams per pound of body weight per day).
Children over age 6 may require the same dose as an adult,
but no child should be given more than 300 milligrams per
day.

Overdosage

Symptoms are listed in "Possible Side Effects" and "Possible Adverse Drug Effects" above. The patient should be taken to a hospital emergency room immediately. ALWAYS bring the medicine bottle.

Special Information

If you get upset stomach after taking Phenytoin, take the medicine with meals. If you develop a rash, sore throat, fever, unusual bleeding, or bruising, contact your doctor immediately. Phenytoin sometimes produces a pink-brown color in the urine; don't worry about it. Do not change brands of Phenytoin without notifying your doctor.

Generic Name

Pilocarpine Ophthalmic Solution

Brand Names

Adsorbocarpine	Pilocar
Akarpine	Pilocel
Almocarpine	Pilomiotin
Isopto Carpine	Piloptic
Ocusert Pilo	P.V. Carpine Liquifilm

Type of Drug

Miotic agent.

Prescribed for

Management of open angle glaucoma (increased pressure in the eye).

General Information

Pilocarpine Ophthalmic Solution is the drug of choice in the treatment of open angle glaucoma. It works on muscles in the eye to open passages so that fluid can flow normally out of the eye chamber, reducing fluid pressure inside the eye. Pilocarpine Ophthalmic Solution may also help reduce the amount of fluid produced within the eye.

Although used as eyedrops, the drug can affect other parts of the body, especially after long use. When this drug is prescribed, it is usually given for long periods of time, as long as eye pressure does not increase or eyesight does not worsen. The concentration of Pilocarpine Ophthalmic Solution is determined by the physician, and is based on the severity of the disease. This drug is also marketed in a special form called Pilo-Ocusert—a thin football-shaped wafer designed to continuously release the drug for 1 week. This eliminates the need for putting drops in your eyes 3 to 4 times a day. The wafer is placed under the eyelid similarly to the way contact lenses are placed.

If you use the conventional eyedrops, be very careful not to touch the eyelids or surrounding area with the dropper tip; otherwise you will contaminate the dropper and cause the medicine to become unsterile. Be sure you recap the bottle tightly in order to preserve the sterility of the medicine.

Cautions and Warnings

Pilocarpine Ophthalmic Solution should only be used when prescribed by an eye specialist (ophthalmologist). This drug should not be used if you are allergic to it.

Possible Side Effects

This drug may produce spasms of the eye muscles resulting in an aching feeling over the brow. You may also find it hard to focus your eyes. These effects are seen in younger people and will disappear with continued use. Some people may complain of decreased vision in low light.

Possible Adverse Drug Effects

Allergy or itching and tearing of the eye may develop after prolonged use.

Usual Dose

Initial dose, 1 to 2 drops in the affected eye up to 6 times per day, then according to severity of disease.

Ocusert Pilo: insert into eye sac and replace weekly.

At first Pilocarpine Ophthalmic Solution is also placed in the healthy eye to keep it from becoming diseased.

The usual concentration of the drug is 0.5 to 4 percent. Concentrations above 4 percent are used less often. The most frequently used concentrations are 1 and 2 percent.

Overdosage

After long-term use, small amounts of Pilocarpine Ophthalmic Solution may be absorbed by the drainage systems of the eye. If symptoms of stomach upset, nausea, vomiting, diarrhea, and cramps appear, contact your doctor immediately.

Generic Name

Piroxicam

Brand Name

Feldene

Type of Drug

Non-steroidal anti-inflammatory

Prescribed for

Arthritis and other forms of bone and joint inflammation.

General Information

This new non-steroidal anti-inflammatory agent represents an entirely different chemical class than any of its predecessors. It is long-acting and given only once a day. Like other non-steroidal anti-inflammatories, it is thought to work by preventing the body from manufacturing hormones called prostaglandins, thus reducing pain, inflammation and fever.

Cautions and Warnings

Do not take this drug if you are allergic to it, to aspirin or to other non-steroidal anti-inflammatory drugs. It may cause stomach ulcers. Piroxicam should not be taken by pregnant women or nursing mothers. All patients taking this drug should have regular eye examinations since it may cause blurred vision or other problems.

Possible Side Effects

Most Common: Upset stomach, nausea, iron deficiency, and blood loss through the gastrointestinal tract.

Piroxicam may also cause loss of appetite, abdominal dis-

comfort, constipation, diarrhea, stomach gas or pains, indigestion, adverse effects on the blood system, reduced
kidney function, dizziness, sleepiness, ringing or buzzing in
the ears, headache, a sickly feeling, fluid in the arms or
legs, itching, and rash.

Possible Adverse Drug Effects

Piroxicam may cause reduced liver function, vomiting with
or without blood, blood in the urine or stool, bleeding from
the stomach, dry mouth, sweating, unusual bruising, loss of
patches of skin, swollen eyes, blurred vision, eye irritations,
high blood pressure, lowered blood sugar, body weight
changes (either up or down), depression, nervousness, sleeplessness, heart palpitations, difficulty breathing and difficulty
in urination.

Drug Interactions

Avoid alcohol, since this may increase upset stomach associated with Piroxicam or aggravate any problems with drowsiness or lack of alertness.

Piroxicam may interact with anticoagulant (blood-thinning)
drugs. Although you will probably not experience a serious
interaction, your doctor should monitor your anticoagulant
therapy during the first few weeks of Piroxicam therapy in
case any adjustment is needed.

Aspirin, in doses of 12 tablets per day or more, will reduce
the effect of Piroxicam by reducing its level in the blood.
These drugs should not be taken together since there is
no special benefit from the combination and it may cause
unwanted side effects.

Since Piroxicam may cause lowered blood sugar levels,
diabetics taking Piroxicam may need to have the dose of
their antidiabetic drug reduced.

Usual Dose

10 to 20 milligrams per day.

Special Information

You will not feel the maximum effects of Piroxicam until you
have taken the drug for 2 to 3 months, although you may
begin to experience some relief as early as 2 weeks after
beginning treatment.

If you get an upset stomach after taking Piroxicam, take the medicine with meals. If you develop swollen hands or feet, itching, rash, black tarry stools, vomiting, blurred vision or other visual disturbances, or unusual bruises, contact your doctor immediately.

Brand Name

Poly-Vi-Flor Chewable Tablets

Ingredients

Folic Acid	Vitamin B_6
Sodium Fluoride	Vitamin B_{12}
Vitamin A	Vitamin C
Vitamin B_1	Vitamin D
Vitamin B_2	Vitamin E
Vitamin B_3	

Type of Drug

Multivitamin supplement with a fluoride.

Prescribed for

Vitamin deficiencies and prevention of dental cavities in infants and children.

General Information

Fluorides taken in small daily doses have been effective in preventing cavities in children by strengthening their teeth and making them resistant to cavity formation. Too much fluoride can damage the teeth. Because of this, vitamins with a fluoride should only be used in areas where the water supply is not fluoridated.

Cautions and Warnings

Poly-Vi-Flor Chewable Tablets should not be used in areas where the fluoride content exceeds 0.7 ppm (part per million). Your pediatrician or local water company can tell you the fluoride content of the water you drink.

Possible Side Effects

Occasional skin rash, itching, stomach upset, headache, weakness.

Usual Dose

1 tablet per day.

Generic Name

Potassium Chloride

Brand Names

Liquids
  Cena-K
  Kaochlor 10%
  Kay Ciel
  KK-10,20
  Klorvess 10%
  Klorvess Granules
  Kloride
  Kolyum
  Pan-Kloride
  Pfiklor
  Potasalan
  Rum-K
  S.K. Potassium Chloride
Powders
  Kato
  K-Lor
  KLOR-CON
  K-Lyte/Cl
  Kolyum

Effervescent tablets
  Kaochlor-Eff
  K-Lyte/Cl
  KEFF
  Klorvess
  K-Lyte DS

Oral tablets
  Kaon-Cl (wax matrix)
  Klotrix (wax matrix)
  K-Tab (wax matrix)
  Potassium CL Coated
  Slow-K (wax matrix)

Type of Drug

Potassium supplement.

Prescribed for

Replacement of potassium in the body.

General Information

Potassium Chloride is a very important component of the body which has a major effect on maintaining the proper tone of all body cells. Potassium Chloride is also important for the maintenance of normal kidney function. Potassium Chloride is required for the passage of electrical impulses in the nervous system, and has a major effect on the heart and all other muscles of the body.

Cautions and Warnings

Potassium replacement should always be monitored and controlled by your physician. Potassium Chloride tablets have produced ulceration in some patients with compression of the esophagus. Potassium Chloride supplements for these patients should be given in liquid form. Potassium Chloride tablets have been reported to cause ulcers of the small bowel, leading to hemorrhage, obstruction, and/or perforation.

Do not take Potassium Chloride supplements if you are dehydrated or experiencing muscle cramps due to excessive sun exposure. The drug should be used with caution in patients who have kidney and/or heart disease.

Possible Side Effects

Potassium Chloride toxicity, or overdose, is extremely rare. Toxicity can occur when high doses of Potassium Chloride supplements are taken in combination with foods high in Potassium Chloride. Common side effects are nausea, vomiting, diarrhea, and abdominal discomfort. Less common side effects are tingling of hands and feet, listlessness, mental confusion, weakness and heaviness of legs, decreased blood pressure, and/or heart rhythm changes.

Drug Interactions

Potassium Chloride supplements should not be taken with Spironolactone, Triamterene, or combinations of these drugs, as Potassium Chloride toxicity may occur.

Usual Dose

As regulated by physician; generally 20 to 60 milliequivalents per day.

Special Information

Directions for taking Potassium Chloride supplements should be followed closely. Liquid Potassium Chloride supplement should be diluted properly. Effervescent tablets and Potassium Chloride supplement powders should be dissolved completely.

Generic Name

Prazepam

Brand Name

Centrax

Type of Drug

Tranquilizer.

Prescribed for

Relief of symptoms of anxiety, tension, fatigue, or agitation.

General Information

Prazepam is a member of the chemical group of drugs known as benzodiazepines. These drugs are used as either antianxiety agents, anticonvulsants, or sedatives (sleeping pills). They exert their effects by relaxing the large skeletal muscles and by a direct effect on the brain. In doing so, they can relax you and make you either more tranquil or sleepier, depending on the drug and how much you use. Many doctors prefer Prazepam and the other members of this class to other drugs that can be used for the same effect. Their reason is that the benzodiazepines tend to be safer, have fewer side effects, and are usually as, if not more, effective.

These drugs are generally used in any situation where they can be a useful adjunct.

Benzodiazepine tranquilizing drugs can be abused if taken for long periods of time and it is possible to develop withdrawal symptoms if you discontinue the therapy abruptly. Withdrawal symptoms include convulsions, tremor, muscle cramps, stomach cramps, vomiting, and sweating.

Cautions and Warnings

Do not take Prazepam if you know you are sensitive or allergic to this drug or other benzodiazepines such as Chlordiazepoxide, Oxazepam, Clorazepate, Diazepam, Lorazepam, Flurazepam, and Clonazepam.

Prazepam and other members of this drug group may aggravate narrow angle glaucoma, but if you have open angle glaucoma you may take the drugs. In any case, check this information with your doctor. Prazepam can cause tiredness, drowsiness, inability to concentrate, or similar symptoms. Be careful if you are driving, operating machinery, or performing other activities which require concentration. Avoid taking this drug during the first 3 months of pregnancy except under strict supervision of your doctor.

Possible Side Effects

Most common: mild drowsiness during the first few days of therapy, especially in the elderly or debilitated. If drowsiness persists, contact your doctor.

Possible Adverse Drug Effects

Major adverse reactions: confusion, depression, lethargy, disorientation, headache, lack of activity, slurred speech, stupor, dizziness, tremor, constipation, dry mouth, nausea, inability to control urination, changes in sex drive, irregular menstrual cycle, changes in heart rhythm, lowered blood pressure, retention of fluids, blurred or double vision, itching, rash, hiccups, nervousness, inability to fall asleep, (occasional) liver dysfunction. If you experience any of these reactions stop taking the medicine and contact your doctor immediately.

Drug Interactions

Prazepam is a central nervous system depressant. Avoid alcohol, tranquilizers, narcotics, sleeping pills, barbiturates, MAO inhibitors, antihistamines, and other medicines used to relieve depression.

Usual Dose

Adult: 20 to 60 milligrams per day as individualized for maximum benefit, depending on symptoms and response to treatment, which may call for a dose outside the range given. 20 milligrams may be taken at bedtime for sleep.

Elderly: usually require less of the drug to control anxiety and tension.

Overdosage

Symptoms are confusion, sleep or sleepiness, lack of response to pain such as a pin stick, shallow breathing, lowered blood pressure, and coma. The patient should be taken to a hospital emergency room immediately. ALWAYS bring the medicine bottle.

Generic Name

Prazosin

Brand Name

Minipress

Type of Drug

Antihypertensive.

Prescribed for

High blood pressure.

General Information

Prazosin works by dilating and reducing pressure in blood vessels. It is quite effective when used in combination with a thiazide diuretic and/or beta-adrenergic blocker. It is much safer than other drugs which work in the same way because it does not affect the heart.

Cautions and Warnings

This drug can cause dizziness and fainting, most often due to an effect called "postural hypotension" where blood supply to the brain is reduced when rising suddenly from a sitting or lying-down position. This often occurs after taking first dose of 2 milligrams or more of Prazosin.

Pregnant women and nursing mothers should avoid Prazosin unless taking it is absolutely necessary.

Possible Side Effects

The most common side effects of Prazosin are dizziness, headache, drowsiness, lack of energy, weakness, heart palpitations, and nausea. Usually these side effects subside and people become more tolerant to the drug.

Possible Adverse Drug Effects

Vomiting, diarrhea, constipation, stomach upset or pain, unusual swelling in the arms or legs, shortness of breath, passing out, rapid heart rate, increased chest pain (angina), nervousness, depression, tingling in the hands or feet, rash, itching, frequent urination, poor urinary control, sexual impotence, blurred vision, redness of the eyes, ringing or buzzing in the ears, dry mouth, stuffed nose, sweating.

Usual Dose

1 milligram 2 to 3 times per day to start; the dose may be increased to 20 milligrams a day, and 40 milligrams has been used in some cases. The daily dose of Prazosin must be tailored to patient's needs.

Overdosage

Overdosage may lead to very low blood pressure. Call your doctor or poison control center for advice. If you go to a hospital emergency room, remember to BRING THE MEDICINE BOTTLE.

Special Information

Take this drug exactly as prescribed. Do not stop taking Prazosin unless directed to do so by your doctor. Do not take over-the-counter medicines containing stimulants. If you are unsure which ones to avoid, ask your pharmacist.

Prazosin can cause dizziness, drowsiness, or headache, especially when you begin taking the drug. Avoid driving or operating any equipment 4 hours after the first dose and take care for the first few days. You may want to take the first dose before you go to bed. If you experience severe dizziness, lie down and wait for the episode to pass.

Generic Name

Prednisone

Brand Names

Cortan   Panasol
Deltasone   Prednicen-M
Fernisone   SK-Prednisone
Meticorten   Sterapred
Orasone

Type of Drug

Adrenal cortical steroid.

Prescribed for

Reduction of inflammation. The variety of disorders for which
Prednisone is prescribed is almost endless, from skin rash to
cancer. The drug may be used as a treatment for adrenal
gland disease, since one of the hormones produced by the
adrenal gland is very similar to Prednisone. If patients are
not producing sufficient adrenal hormones, Prednisone may
be used as replacement therapy. It may also be prescribed
for the treatment of bursitis, arthritis, severe skin reactions
such as psoriasis or other rashes, severe allergic conditions,
asthma, drug or serum sickness, severe, acute, or chronic
allergic inflammation of the eye and surrounding areas such
as conjunctivitis, respiratory diseases including pneumonitis,
blood disorders, gastrointestinal diseases including ulcerative colitis, and inflammation of the nerves, heart, or other
organs.

General Information

Prednisone is one of many adrenal cortical steroids used in
medical practice today. The major differences between
Prednisone and other adrenal cortical steroids are potency
of medication and variation in some secondary effects. Choice
of an adrenal cortical steroid to be used for a specific disease is usually a matter of doctor preference and past experience. Other adrenal cortical steroids include Cortisone,
Hydrocortisone, Prednisolone, Triamcinolone, Methylprednisolone, Meprednisone, Paramethasone, Fluprednisolone, Dexamethasone, Betamethasone, and Fludrocortisone.

Cautions and Warnings

Because of the effect of Prednisone on your adrenal gland, it is essential that the dose be tapered from a large dose down to a small dose over a period of time. Do not stop taking this medication suddenly or without the advice of your doctor. If you do, you may cause a failure of the adrenal gland with extremely serious consequences.

Prednisone has a strong anti-inflammatory effect, and may mask some signs of infections. If new infections appear during the use of Prednisone therapy, they may be difficult to discover and may grow more rapidly due to your decreased resistance. If you think you are getting an infection during the time that you are taking Prednisone, you should contact your doctor, who will prescribe appropriate therapy.

If you are taking Prednisone, you should not be vaccinated against any infectious diseases, because of inability of the body to produce the normal reaction to vaccination. Discuss this with your doctor before he administers any vaccination.

If you suspect that you are pregnant and are taking Prednisone, report it immediately to your doctor. If you are taking Prednisone and have just given birth, do not nurse; used prepared formulas instead.

Possible Side Effects

Stomach upset is one of the more common side effects of Prednisone, which may in some cases cause gastric or duodenal ulcers. If you notice a slight stomach upset when you take your dose of Prednisone, take this medication with food or a small amount of antacid. If stomach upset continues or bothers you, notify your doctor. Other side effects: retention of water, heart failure, potassium loss, muscle weakness, loss of muscle mass, loss of calcium which may result in bone fractures and a condition known as aseptic necrosis of the femoral and humoral heads (this means the ends of the large bones in the hip may degenerate from loss of calcium), slowing down of wound healing, black-and-blue marks on the skin, increased sweating, allergic skin rash, itching, convulsions, dizziness, headache.

Possible Adverse Drug Effects

May cause irregular menstrual cycles, slowing down of growth in children, particularly after the medication has been taken for long periods of time, depression of the adrenal and/or pituitary glands, development of diabetes, increased pressure of the fluid inside the eye, hypersensitivity or allergic reactions, blood clots, insomnia, weight gain, increased appetite, nausea, and feeling of ill health. Psychic derangements may appear which range from euphoria to mood swings, personality changes, and severe depression. Prednisone may also aggravate existing emotional instability.

Drug Interactions

Prednisone and other adrenal corticosteroids may interact with Insulin and oral antidiabetic drugs, causing an increased requirement of the antidiabetic drugs.

Interaction with Phenobarbital, Ephedrine, and Phenytoin may reduce the effect of Prednisone by increasing its removal from the body.

If a doctor prescribes Prednisone you should discuss any oral coagulant (blood-thinning) drugs you are taking: the dose of them may have to be changed.

Interaction with diuretics such as Hydrochlorothiazide may cause you to lose blood potassium. Be aware of signs of lowered potassium level such as weakness, muscle cramps, and tiredness, and report them to your physician. Eat high potassium foods such as bananas, citrus fruits, melons, and tomatoes.

Usual Dose

Initial dose, 5 to 60 or even more milligrams; maintenance dose, 5 to 60 milligrams depending on patient's response. Dose also varies according to disease being treated. The lowest effective dose is desirable. Stressful situations may cause a need for a temporary increase in your Prednisone dose.

This drug must be tapered off slowly, not stopped abruptly. Prednisone may be given in alternate day therapy; twice the usual daily dose is given every other day.

Overdosage

There is no specific treatment for overdosage of adrenal cortical steroids. Symptoms are anxiety, depression and/or stimulation, stomach bleeding, increased blood sugar, high blood pressure, and retention of fluid. The patient should be taken to a hospital emergency room immediately, where stomach pumping, oxygen, intravenous fluids, and other supportive treatments are available.

Generic Name

Primidone

Brand Name

Mysoline

Type of Drug

Anticonvulsive.

Prescribed for

Control of epileptic and other seizures.

General Information

Although this drug is not a barbiturate, it is a close chemical cousin to the barbiturates and possesses many of their characteristics. It acts on a portion of the brain that inhibits the unusual nerve transmissions that are present in seizure disorders.

Cautions and Warnings

If you have been taking Primidone for a long time and no longer need it do not stop abruptly, but reduce the dosage gradually over a period of about a week. Stopping abruptly may bring on severe epileptic seizures. Pregnant women who use anticonvulsive medicine are said to tend to give birth to children with birth defects, but the data available are somewhat questionable. If you become pregnant while you are taking this medicine, consult your doctor immediately.

Possible Side Effects

Dizziness and some loss of muscle coordination. Side effects tend to disappear with time.

Possible Adverse Drug Effects

Fatigue, loss of appetite, nystagmus (a rhythmic, uncontrolled movement of the eyeballs), irritability, emotional upset, sexual impotence, double vision, rash. If side effects are persistent or severe, your doctor may have to discontinue treatment or use a different medication.

Drug Interactions

This drug, because of its relation to barbiturates, may affect oral anticoagulants, Doxycycline, corticosteroids, or Griseofulvin. Special care should be taken if you need any sedative, sleeping pill, antidepressant, or strong analgesic, because of the possibility of drug interaction. Consult your physician or pharmacist for more information. Avoid alcoholic beverages, which may enhance the side effects of fatigue and dizziness normally experienced with Primidone.

Usual Dose

Adult (and child age 8 and over): 250 milligrams per day to start. Dose may be increased in steps of 250 milligrams per day up to 1500 milligrams per day, according to patient's need.

Child (under age 8): 125 milligrams per day to start. Dose may be increased in steps of 125 milligrams per day up to 750 milligrams per day, according to patient's need.

Overdosage

Symptoms are listed in "Possible Side Effects" and "Possible Adverse Drug Effects" above. The patient should be taken to a hospital emergency room immediately. ALWAYS bring the medicine bottle.

Special Information

If you get an upset stomach after taking Primidone, take the medicine with meals. If you develop a rash, sore throat, fever, or unusual bleeding or bruising, contact your doctor immediately. Primidone sometimes produces a pink-brown color in the urine; this is normal, and not a cause for worry.

Brand Name

Pro-Banthine with Phenobarbital

Ingredients

Phenobarbital
Propantheline

Type of Drug

Gastrointestinal anticholinergic agent.

Prescribed for

Symptomatic relief of stomach upset and spasms.

General Information

Pro-Banthine with Phenobarbital works by reducing spasms in muscles of the stomach and other parts of the gastrointestinal tract. In doing so, it helps relieve some of the uncomfortable symptoms associated with peptic ulcer, irritable bowel and/or colon, spastic colon, and other gastrointestinal disorders. It only relieves symptoms. It does not cure the underlying disease. There are many other combinations of anticholinergics and tranquilizers used to treat stomach ulcers and similar disorders. One such combination product is Pathibamate.

Cautions and Warnings

Pro-Banthine with Phenobarbital should not be used if you know you are sensitive or allergic to Propantheline. Do not use this medicine if you have glaucoma, asthma, obstructive disease of the gastrointestinal tract, or other serious gastrointestinal disease. Because this drug reduces your ability to sweat, its use in hot climates may cause heat exhaustion. The safety of this drug for pregnant or nursing women has not been established.

Possible Side Effects

Occasional: difficulty in urination, blurred vision, rapid heartbeat, palpitations, sensitivity to light, headache, flushing of the skin, nervousness, dizziness, weakness, drowsiness, nausea, vomiting, fever, nasal congestion, heartburn, constipation, loss of taste, feeling of being bloated; also a drug allergy or a drug idiosyncratic reaction, which may include itching or other skin manifestations.

Possible Adverse Drug Effects

Elderly patients taking this drug may develop mental confusion or excitement.

Drug Interactions

Interaction with antihistamines, phenothiazines, long-term use of corticosteroids, tranquilizers, antidepressants, and some narcotic painkillers may cause blurred vision, dry mouth, or drowsiness. Antacids should not be taken together with Pro-Banthine with Phenobarbital, or they will reduce the absorption of the Pro-Banthine with Phenobarbital.

Do not use with MAO inhibitor drugs, which will tend to prevent excretion of Pro-Banthine with Phenobarbital from the body and thus potentiate it (increase its effect).

Usual Dose

1 to 2 tablets 3 to 4 times per day.

Special Information

Dry mouth from Pro-Banthine with Phenobarbital can be relieved by chewing gum or sucking hard candy; constipation can be treated by using a stool-softening laxative (rather than a harsh cathartic).

Generic Name

Procainamide Hydrochloride

Brand Names

Procan	Sub-Quin
Procan SR	Pronestyl

Type of Drug

Antiarrhythmic.

Prescribed for

Abnormal heart rhythms.

General Information

Procainamide Hydrochloride is frequently used as the primary treatment for arrythmias (unusual heart rhythms), which it controls by affecting the response of heart muscle to nervous system stimulation. It also slows the rate at which nervous system impulses are carried through the heart. It may be given to patients who do not respond to or cannot tolerate other antiarrhythmic drugs.

Cautions and Warnings

Tell your doctor if you have the disease myasthenia gravis. If you do, you should be taking a drug other than Procainamide Hydrochloride. Tell your doctor if you are allergic to Procainamide Hydrochloride or to the local anesthetic Procaine. Patients taking this drug should be under strict medical supervision.

This drug is eliminated from the body through the kidney and liver. Therefore, if you have either kidney or liver disease your dose of Procainamide Hydrochloride may have to be adjusted.

Possible Side Effects

Large oral doses of Procainamide Hydrochloride may produce loss of appetite, nausea, or itching. A group of symptoms resembling the disease lupus erythematosus has been reported in patients taking the drug: fever and chills, nausea, vomiting, and abdominal pains. Your doctor may detect enlargement of your liver and changes in blood tests indicating a change in the liver. Soreness of the mouth or throat, unusual bleeding, rash, or fever may also occur. If any of these symptoms occur while you are taking Procainamide Hydrochloride, tell your doctor immediately.

Possible Adverse Drug Effects

Bitter taste in the mouth, diarrhea, weakness, mental depression, giddiness, hallucinations, drug allergy (such as rash and drug fever).

Drug Interactions

Avoid over-the-counter cough, cold, or allergy remedies containing drugs which have a direct stimulating effect on your heart. Ask your pharmacist to tell you about the ingredients in over-the-counter remedies.

Usual Dose

Adult: Initial dose, 1000 milligrams; maintenance dose, 25 milligrams per pound per day in divided doses every 3 hours, adjusted according to individual needs.

Storage

Store capsules in a place protected from excessive moisture; do not keep them in a bathroom medicine chest where they will be exposed to high concentrations of moisture.

Generic Name

Prochlorperazine

Brand Name

Compazine

Other Brand Name

Compa-Z

Type of Drug

Phenothiazine antipsychotic, antinauseant.

Prescribed for

Severe nausea, vomiting, psychotic disorders, excessive anxiety, tension, and agitation.

General Information

Prochlorperazine and other members of the phenothiazine group act on a portion of the brain called the hypothalamus. They affect parts of the hypothalamus that control metabolism, body temperature, alertness, muscle tone, hormone balance, and vomiting, and may be used to treat problems related to any of these functions.

Cautions and Warnings

Sudden death has occurred in patients who have taken this drug, because of its effect on the cough reflex. In some cases the patients choked to death because of failure of the cough reflex to protect them. Prochlorperazine, because of its effect in reducing vomiting, can obscure signs of toxicity due to overdose of other drugs or symptoms of disease.

Prochlorperazine should not be taken if you are allergic to one of the drugs in the broad classification known as phenothiazine drugs. Do not take Prochlorperazine if you have any blood, liver, kidney, or heart disease, very low blood pressure, or Parkinson's disease. This medication is a tranquilizer and can have a depressive effect, especially during the first few days of therapy. Care should be taken when performing activities requiring a high degree of concentration, such as driving. If you are taking this medication and become pregnant contact your doctor immediately.

This drug should be used with caution and under strict supervision of your doctor if you have glaucoma, epilepsy, ulcers, or difficulty passing urine.

Avoid insecticides and extreme exposure to heat.

Possible Side Effects

Most common: drowsiness, especially during the first or second week of therapy. If the drowsiness becomes troublesome, contact your doctor.

Possible Adverse Drug Effects

Prochlorperazine can cause jaundice (yellowing of the whites of the eyes or skin), usually in 2 to 4 weeks. The jaundice usually goes away when the drug is discontinued, but there have been cases when it did not. If you notice this effect or if you develop symptoms such as fever and generally not feeling well, contact your doctor immediately. Less frequent: changes in components of the blood including anemias, raised or lowered blood pressure, abnormal heart rates, heart attack, feeling faint or dizzy.

Phenothiazines can produce "extrapyramidal effects," such as spasm of the neck muscles, rolling back of the eyes, convulsions, difficulty in swallowing, and symptoms associated with Parkinson's disease. These effects look very serious but disappear after the drug has been withdrawn; however, symptoms of the face, tongue, and jaw may persist for as long as several years, especially in the elderly with a history of brain damage. If you experience extrapyramidal effects contact your doctor immediately.

Prochlorperazine may cause an unusual increase in psychotic symptoms or may cause paranoid reactions, tiredness, lethargy, restlessness, hyperactivity, confusion at night, bizarre dreams, inability to sleep, depression, and euphoria. Other reactions are itching, swelling, unusual sensitivity to bright lights, red skin, and rash. There have been cases of breast enlargement, false positive pregnancy tests, changes in menstrual flow, impotence and changes in sex drive in males, as well as stuffy nose, headache, nausea, vomiting, loss of appetite, change in body temperature, pallor, excessive salivation, excessive perspiration, constipation, diarrhea, changes in urine and stool habits, worsening of glaucoma, blurred vision, weakening of eyelid muscles, and spasms in bronchial and other muscles, increased appetite, fatigue, excessive thirst, and changes in the coloration of skin, particularly in exposed areas.

Drug Interactions

Prochlorperazine should be taken with caution in combination with barbiturates, sleeping pills, narcotics, other tranquilizers, or any other medication which may produce a depressive effect. Avoid alcohol.

Usual Dose

Adult: 15 to 150 milligrams per day, depending on disease and patient's response. For nausea and vomiting, 15 to 40 milligrams per day by mouth, 25 milligrams twice per day in rectal suppositories.

Child (40 to 85 pounds): 10 to 15 milligrams per day; (30 to 40 pounds), 2½ milligrams 2 to 3 times per day; (20 to 30 pounds), 2½ milligrams 1 to 2 times per day; not recommended for children under age 2 or weight 20 pounds, except to save life. Usually only 1 to 2 days of therapy is needed for nausea and vomiting. For psychosis, doses of 25 milligrams or more per day may be required.

This drug may turn the color of your urine pink or reddish brown.

Overdosage

Symptoms are depression, extreme weakness, tiredness, desire to go to sleep, coma, lowered blood pressure, uncontrolled muscle spasms, agitation, restlessness, convulsions, fever, dry mouth, and abnormal heart rhythms. The patient should be taken to a hospital emergency room immediately. ALWAYS bring the medicine bottle.

Generic Name

Propantheline Bromide

Brand Names

Norpanth
Pro-Banthine
Ropanth

Type of Drug

Gastrointestinal anticholinergic agent.

Prescribed for

Relief of stomach upset and spasms. This medication is sometimes prescribed to treat morning sickness during the early months of pregnancy.

General Information

Propantheline Bromide works by reducing spasms in muscles of the stomach and other parts of the gastrointestinal tract. In doing so, it helps relieve some of the uncomfortable symptoms associated with peptic ulcer, irritable bowel and/or colon, spastic colon, and other gastrointestinal disorders. It only relieves symptoms, but does not cure the underlying disease.

Cautions and Warnings

Propantheline Bromide should not be used if you know you are sensitive or allergic to it. Do not use this medicine if you have glaucoma, asthma, obstructive disease of the gastrointestinal tract, or other serious gastrointestinal disease. Because this drug reduces your ability to sweat, its use in hot climates may cause heat exhaustion. The safety of this drug for pregnant or nursing women has not been established.

Possible Side Effects

Difficulty in urination, blurred vision, rapid heartbeat, skin rash, sensitivity to light, headache, flushing of the skin, nervousness, dizziness, weakness, drowsiness, nausea, vomiting, fever, nasal congestion, heartburn, constipation, loss of taste.

Possible Adverse Drug Effects

Elderly patients taking this drug may develop mental confusion or excitement.

Drug Interactions

Interaction with antihistamines, phenothiazines, long-term use of corticosteroids, tranquilizers, antidepressants, and some narcotic painkillers may cause blurred vision, dry mouth, or drowsiness. Antacids should not be taken together with Propantheline Bromide, or they will reduce the absorption of the Propantheline Bromide.

Do not use with Tranylcypromine Sulfate (Parnate), Isocarboxazid (Marplan), Phenelzine Sulfate (Nardil), or other MAO inhibitor drugs, which will tend to prevent excretion of Propantheline Bromide from the body and thus potentiate it (increase its effect).

Usual Dose

30 milligrams at bedtime or 7½ to 15 milligrams 3 times per day; or 7½ milligrams 3 times per day for mild symptoms.

Special Information

Dry mouth from Propantheline Bromide can be relieved by chewing gum or sucking hard candy; constipation can be treated by using a stool-softening laxative.

Generic Name

Propoxyphene Hydrochloride

Brand Names

Darvon
Dolene
Pargesic 65
Proxagesic
Proxene
SK-65
Wygesic

Type of Drug

Analgesic.

Prescribed for

Relief of pain.

General Information

Propoxyphene Hydrochloride is a chemical derivative of Methadone, a narcotic used for pain relief. It is estimated that Propoxyphene Hydrochloride is about half to two-thirds as strong a pain reliever as Codeine and about as effective as Aspirin. Propoxyphene Hydrochloride is widely used for mild pain; it can produce drug dependence when used for extended periods of time.

Propoxyphene Hydrochloride may interfere with your ability to concentrate. Therefore, be very careful when driving an automobile or operating complicated or dangerous machinery. Do not drink alcohol when taking this medicine. As there is a possibility that Propoxyphene Hydrochloride may affect the development of unborn children, do not take this medicine, except under your doctor's advice, if you are pregnant or suspect that you may be pregnant. Never take more medicine than is prescribed by your doctor.

Cautions and Warnings

Do not take Propoxyphene Hydrochloride if you are allergic to this or similar drugs. This drug can produce psychological or physical drug dependence (addiction). The major sign of dependence is anxiety when the drug is suddenly stopped. Propoxyphene Hydrochloride can be abused to the same degree as Codeine.

Possible Side Effects

Dizziness, sedation, nausea, vomiting. These effects usually disappear if you lie down and relax for a few moments.

Possible Adverse Drug Effects

Infrequent: constipation, stomach pain, skin rashes, light-headedness, headache, weakness, euphoria, minor visual disturbances. Taking Propoxyphene Hydrochloride over long periods of time and in very high doses has caused psychotic reactions and convulsions.

Drug Interactions

Propoxyphene Hydrochloride may cause drowsiness. Therefore, avoid other drugs which also cause drowsiness, such as tranquilizers, sedatives, hypnotics, narcotics, alcohol, and possibly antihistamines.

There may be an interaction between Propoxyphene Hydrochloride and Orphenadrine. However, this reaction is only a probability and only for patients who have a tendency toward low blood sugar.

Usual Dose

65 milligrams every 4 hours as needed.

Take with a full glass of water or with food to reduce the possibility of stomach upset.

Overdosage

Symptoms resemble those of a narcotic overdose: decrease in rate of breathing (in some people breathing rate is so low that the heart stops), changes in breathing pattern, extreme sleepiness leading to stupor or coma, pinpointed pupils, convulsions, abnormal heart rhythms, and development of fluid in the lungs. The patient should be taken to a hospital emergency room immediately. ALWAYS bring the medicine bottle.

Generic Name

Propranolol Hydrochloride

Brand Name

Inderal

Type of Drug

Beta-adrenergic blocking agent.

Prescribed for

High blood pressure, angina pectoris (a specified type of

chest pain), abnormal heart rhythm, thyroid disease, and pheochromocytoma, a tumor associated with hypertension. In addition, Propranolol Hydrochloride has been studied for its ability to reduce the possibility of a second heart attack, its effect on migraine headaches, diarrhea, and other applications which may or may not be generally accepted by the medical profession.

General Information

Propranolol Hydrochloride was the first beta-adrenergic blocking agent available in the United States. The drug acts to block a major chemical reaction of the nervous system in our bodies. For this reason, it can exert a broad range of effects, as is evident from the wide variety of diseases in which it can be used effectively. Because of this spectrum of effects, it is impossible to say specifically what you will be taking this drug for. Therefore, this information must be discussed with your doctor. This drug has been used, for example, in low (5-10 milligrams) doses by musicians and others to treat nervousness and "butterflies" experienced before going on stage.

Cautions and Warnings

Propranolol Hydrochloride should be used with care if you have a history of asthma, upper respiratory disease, or seasonal allergy, which may be made worse by the effects of this drug.

Possible Side Effects

Propranolol Hydrochloride may decrease the heart rate; may aggravate a condition of congestive heart failure; and may produce lowered blood pressure, tingling in the extremities, light-headedness, mental depression including inability to sleep, weakness, and tiredness. It may also produce a mental depression which is reversible when the drug is withdrawn, visual disturbances, hallucinations, disorientation, and short-term memory loss. Patients taking Propranolol Hydrochloride may experience nausea, vomiting, stomach upset, abdominal cramps and diarrhea, or constipation. If you are allergic to this drug, you may show typical reactions associated with drug allergies, including sore throat, fever, difficulty in breathing, and various effects on the blood system. Propranolol Hydrochloride may induce bronchospasms (spasms of muscles in the bronchi), which will aggravate any existing asthmatic condition or any severe upper respiratory disease.

Possible Adverse Drug Effects

Occasionally, patients taking Propranolol Hydrochloride may experience emotional instability, may appear to be somewhat detached or show other unusual personality changes, or the drug may produce unusual effects on the blood system.

Drug Interactions

This drug will interact with any psychotropic drug, including the MAO inhibitors, which stimulates one of the adrenergic segments of the nervous system. Since this information is not generally known, you should discuss the potential problem of using Propranolol Hydrochloride with your doctor if you are taking any psychotropic or psychiatric drug.

Propranolol Hydrochloride may cause increased effectiveness of Insulin or oral antidiabetic drugs. If you are diabetic, discuss the situation with your doctor, who will probably reduce the dose of antidiabetic medication.

Propranolol Hydrochloride may reduce the effectiveness of Digitalis on your heart. Any dose of Digitalis medication will have to be altered. If you are taking Digitalis for a purpose other than congestive heart failure, the effectiveness of the Digitalis may be increased by Propranolol Hydrochloride, and the dose of Digitalis may have to be reduced.

Propranolol Hydrochloride may interact with certain other drugs to produce lowering of blood pressure. This interaction often has positive results in the treatment of patients with high blood pressure.

Do not self-medicate with over-the-counter cold, cough, or allergy remedies which may contain stimulant drugs that will aggravate certain types of heart disease and high blood pressure, or other ingredients that may antagonize the effects of Propranolol Hydrochloride. Double-check with your doctor or pharmacist before taking any over-the-counter medication.

Usual Dose

30 to 700 milligrams per day, depending on disease treated and patient's response. The drug is given in the smallest effective dose, that is, the smallest dose which will produce the desired therapeutic effect.

Overdosage

Symptoms are slowed heart rate, heart failure, lowered blood pressure, and spasms of the bronchial muscles which make it difficult to breathe. The patient should be taken to a hospital emergency room where proper therapy can be given. ALWAYS bring the medicine bottle with you.

Special Information

Take Propranolol Hydrochloride before meals for maximum effectiveness.

There have been reports of serious effects on the heart when this drug is stopped abruptly. Instead, the dose should be lowered gradually from what you are taking to nothing over a period of 2 weeks.

Generic Name

Protriptyline Hydrochloride

Brand Name

Vivactil

Type of Drug

Antidepressant.

Prescribed for

Depression with or without symptoms of anxiety.

General Information

Protriptyline Hydrochloride and other members of this group are effective in treating symptoms of depression. They can elevate your mood, increase physical activity and mental alertness, improve appetite and sleep patterns. These drugs are mild sedatives and therefore useful in treating mild forms of depression associated with anxiety. You should not expect instant results with this medicine: benefits are usually seen after 1 to 4 weeks. If symptoms are not affected after 6 to 8 weeks, contact your doctor. Occasionally this drug and other members of the group of drugs have been used in treating night-time bed-wetting in the young child, but they do not produce long-lasting relief and therapy with one of them for night-time bed-wetting is of questionable value.

Cautions and Warnings

Do not take Protriptyline Hydrochloride if you are allergic or sensitive to this or other members of this class of drug: Doxepin, Nortriptyline, Imipramine, Desipramine, and Amitriptyline. The drugs should not be used if you are recovering from a heart attack. Protriptyline Hydrochloride may be taken with caution if you have a history of epilepsy or other convulsive disorders, difficulty in urination, glaucoma, heart disease, or thyroid disease. Protriptyline Hydrochloride can interfere with your ability to perform tasks which require concentration, such as driving or operating machinery. Protriptyline Hydrochloride will pass from mother to unborn child: consult your doctor before taking this medicine if you are pregnant.

Possible Side Effects

Changes in blood pressure (both high and low), abnormal heart rates, heart attack, confusion, especially in elderly patients, hallucinations, disorientation, delusions, anxiety, restlessness, excitement, numbness and tingling in the extremities, lack of coordination, muscle spasms or tremors, seizures and/or convulsions, dry mouth, blurred vision, constipation, inability to urinate, rash, itching, sensitivity to bright light or sunlight, retention of fluids, fever, allergy, changes in composition of blood, nausea, vomiting, loss of appetite, stomach upset, diarrhea, enlargement of the breasts in males and females, increased or decreased sex drive, increased or decreased blood sugar.

Possible Adverse Drug Effects

Infrequent: agitation, inability to sleep, nightmares, feeling of panic, a peculiar taste in the mouth, stomach cramps, black coloration of the tongue, yellowing eyes and/or skin, changes in liver function, increased or decreased weight, perspiration, flushing, frequent urination, drowsiness, dizziness, weakness, headache, loss of hair, nausea, not feeling well.

Drug Interactions

Interaction with monoamine oxidase (MAO) inhibitors can cause high fevers, convulsions, and occasionally death. Don't take MAO inhibitors until at least 2 weeks after Protriptyline Hydrochloride has been discontinued.

Protriptyline Hydrochloride interacts with Guanethidine, a drug used to treat high blood pressure: if your doctor prescribes Protriptyline Hydrochloride and you are taking medicine for high blood pressure, be sure to discuss this with him.

Protriptyline Hydrochloride increases the effects of barbiturates, tranquilizers, other depressive drugs, and alcohol. Don't drink alcoholic beverages if you take this medicine.

Taking Protriptyline Hydrochloride and thyroid medicine will enhance the effects of the thyroid medicine. The combination can cause abnormal heart rhythms.

Large doses of Vitamin C (Ascorbic Acid) can reduce the effect of Protriptyline Hydrochloride. Drugs such as Bicarbonate of Soda or Acetazolamide will increase the effect of Protriptyline Hydrochloride.

Usual Dose

Adult: 15 to 60 milligrams per day in divided doses. The dose of this drug must be tailored to patient's need.

Adolescent and elderly: lower doses are recommended, usually up to 20 milligrams per day. An elderly patient taking more than 20 milligrams per day should have regular heart examinations.

Overdosage

Symptoms are confusion, inability to concentrate, hallucinations, drowsiness, lowered body temperature, abnormal heart rate, heart failure, large pupils of the eyes, convulsions, severely lowered blood pressure, stupor, and coma (as well as agitation, stiffening of body muscles, vomiting, and high fever). The patient should be taken to a hospital emergency room immediately. ALWAYS bring the medicine bottle.

Generic Name

Pseudoephedrine

Brand Names

Afrinol	Novafed
Cenafed	Sinufed
D-Feda	Sudafed
First Sign	Sudrin
NeoFed	Symptom 2

Type of Drug

Bronchodilator-decongestant.

Prescribed for

Symptomatic relief of stuffy nose, upper respiratory congestion, or bronchospasm associated with asthma, asthmatic bronchitis, or a similar disorder.

General Information

This drug will produce central nervous system stimulation, and it should not be taken by people with heart disease or high blood pressure. Elderly people are more likely to experience adverse effects from this and other stimulant drugs; overdosage of stimulants in this age group may cause hallucinations, convulsions, depression, and even death.

Pseudoephedrine should be used with caution if you are pregnant or nursing a newborn child. It is possible to transfer a small amount of this drug to the unborn child through the placenta, or to the newborn child through the mother's milk.

Cautions and Warnings

Do not take Pseudoephedrine if you are allergic or sensitive to this or similar drugs or if you have severe high blood pressure, coronary artery disease (angina pectoris), abnormal heart rhythms, or closed angle glaucoma.

This drug should be used with caution and only under medical supervision if you have chest pain, stroke, high blood pressure, diabetes, overactive thyroid, glaucoma, or history of convulsions.

Possible Side Effects

Excessive tiredness or drowsiness, restlessness, nervousness with an inability to sleep. Less frequent: tremor, headache, palpitations, elevation of blood pressure, sweating, sleeplessness, loss of appetite, nausea, vomiting, dizziness, constipation.

Drug Interactions

Interaction with alcoholic beverages may produce excessive drowsiness and/or sleepiness, and/or inability to concentrate. Pseudoephedrine may increase the effect of antidepressant drugs and antihistamines, and reduce the effect of some high blood pressure medicine like Reserpine or Guanethidine.

Do not self-medicate with additional over-the-counter drugs for the relief of cold symptoms: taking Pseudoephedrine with such drugs may result in aggravation of high blood pressure, heart disease, diabetes, or thyroid disease.

Do not take Pseudoephedrine if you are taking or suspect you may be taking a monoamine oxidase (MAO) inhibitor: severe elevation in blood pressure may result.

Usual Dose

Adult: 60 milligrams every 4 hours.
Child (age 6 to 12): 30 milligrams every 4 hours.
Child (age 2 to 6): 15 milligrams every 4 hours.

Liquid form contains 30 milligrams per teaspoon; tablets contain 30 or 60 milligrams depending on strength prescribed; time-release dosage contains 60 to 120 milligrams (taken twice per day).

Brand Name

Quibron

Ingredients

Guaifenesin
Theophylline

Other Brand Names

Bronchial Capsules

Cerylin
Glyceryl T
Lanophyllin GG
Slo-Phyllin GG

Type of Drug

Antiasthmatic combination product.

Prescribed for

Relief of asthma symptoms or other upper respiratory disorders.

General Information

Quibron is one of several antiasthmatic combination products prescribed for the relief of asthmatic symptoms and other breathing problems. These products contain drugs which help relax the bronchial muscles, drugs which increase the diameter of the breathing passages, and a mild tranquilizer to help relax the patient. Other products in this class may contain similar ingredients along with other medicine to help eliminate mucus from the breathing passages.

Cautions and Warnings

Do not use this drug if you are allergic or sensitive to it or to any related drug, such as Aminophylline. If you have stomach ulcer or heart disease, you should use this drug with caution. If you are pregnant or think that you may be pregnant you should carefully discuss the use of this drug with your doctor, since Quibron may induce an adverse effect in the unborn child.

This drug should not be taken if you have severe kidney or liver disease.

Possible Side Effects

Large doses of Quibron can produce excitation, shakiness, sleeplessness, nervousness, rapid heartbeat, chest pains, or irregular heartbeat, Occasionally people have been known to develop hesitation or difficulty in urination.

Possible Adverse Drug Effects

Excessive urination, heart stimulation, drowsiness, muscle

weakness, muscle twitching, unsteady walk. These effects can usually be controlled by having your doctor adjust the dose.

Drug Interactions

Quibron may cause sleeplessness and/or drowsiness. Do not take this drug with alcoholic beverages.

Taking Quibron or similar medicines with an MAO inhibitor can produce severe interaction. Consult your doctor first.

Quibron or similar products taken together with Lithium Carbonate will increase the excretion of lithium; they have neutralized the effect of Propranalol. Erythromycin and similar antibiotics cause the body to hold Theophylline, leading to possible side effects.

Usual Dose

Capsules: 1 to 2 every 6 to 8 hours.
Elixir: 1 to 2 tablespoons every 6 to 8 hours.

Special Information

Take this drug with food to avoid upset stomach.

Brand Name

Quibron Plus

Ingredients

Butabarbital
Ephedrine
Guaifenesin
Theophylline

Type of Drug

Antiasthmatic combination product.

Prescribed for

Relief of asthma symptoms or other upper respiratory disorders.

General Information

Quibron Plus is one of several antiasthmatic combination products prescribed for the relief of asthmatic symptoms and other breathing problems. These products contain drugs which help relax the bronchial muscles, drugs which increase the diameter of the breathing passages, and a mild tranquilizer to help relax the patient. Other products in this class may contain similar ingredients along with other medicine to help eliminate mucus from the breathing passages.

Cautions and Warnings

Do not use this drug if you are allergic or sensitive to it or to any related drug, such as Aminophylline. If you have stomach ulcer or heart disease, you should use this drug with caution. If you are pregnant or think that you may be pregnant you should carefully discuss the use of this drug with your doctor, since Quibron Plus may induce an adverse effect in the unborn child.

This drug should not be taken if you have severe kidney or liver disease.

Possible Side Effects

Large doses of Quibron Plus can produce excitation, shakiness, sleeplessness, nervousness, rapid heartbeat, chest pains, irregular heartbeat, dizziness, dryness of the nose and throat, headache, and sweating. Occasionally people have been known to develop hesitation or difficulty in urination.

Possible Adverse Drug Effects

Excessive urination, heart stimulation, drowsiness, muscle weakness, muscle twitching, unsteady walk. These effects can usually be controlled by having your doctor adjust the dose.

Drug Interactions

Quibron Plus may cause sleeplessness and/or drowsiness. Do not take this drug with alcoholic beverages.

Taking Quibron Plus or similar medicines with an MAO inhibitor can produce severe interaction. Consult your doctor first.

Quibron Plus or similar products taken together with Lithium Carbonate will increase the excretion of lithium; they have neutralized the effect of Propranolol. Erythromycin and similar antibiotics cause the body to hold Theophylline, leading to possible side effects.

Usual Dose

Capsules: 1 to 2 every 6 to 8 hours.
  Elixir: 1 to 2 tablespoons every 6 to 8 hours.

Special Information

Take this drug with food to avoid upset stomach.

Generic Name

Quinidine Sulfate

Brand Names

Cin-Quin
Quinidex Extentabs
Quinora
SK-Quinidine Sulfate

Type of Drug

Antiarrhythmic.

Prescribed for

Abnormal heart rhythms.

General Information

Derived from the bark of the cinchona tree (which gives us Quinine), the drug works by affecting the flow of potassium into and out of cells of the heart muscle (myocardium). Its basic action is to slow down the pulse. Its action allows normal control mechanisms in the heart to take over and keep the heart beating at a normal rate and rhythm.

Cautions and Warnings

Do not take Quinidine Sulfate if you are allergic to it or a related drug. If you are pregnant use this drug only after a careful review of your state of health with your doctor.

Possible Side Effects

High doses of Quinidine Sulfate can give you rash, changes in hearing, dizziness, ringing in the ears, headache, nausea, or disturbed vision: this group of symptoms, called cinchonism, is due to ingestion of large amounts of Quinidine Sulfate and is not necessarily a toxic reaction. However, report signs of cinchonism to your doctor immediately. Do not stop taking this drug unless instructed to do so by your doctor.

Possible Adverse Drug Effects

Quinidine Sulfate may cause unusual heart rhythms, but such effects are generally found by your doctor during routine examination or electrocardiogram. It can cause nausea, vomiting, stomach pain, and diarrhea. It may affect components of the blood system and can cause headache, fever, dizziness, feeling of apprehension or excitement, confusion, delirium, disturbed hearing, blurred vision, changes in color perception, sensitivity to bright lights, double vision, difficulty seeing at night, flushing of the skin, itching, nausea, vomiting, cramps, unusual urge to defecate or urinate, and cold sweat.

Drug Interactions

If you are taking an oral anticoagulant (blood-thinning medicine) and have been given a new prescription for Quinidine Sulfate, be sure your doctor knows about the blood-thinning medication, because Quinidine Sulfate may affect the ability of the anticoagulant to do its job. The anticoagulant dose may have to be adjusted for the effect of Quinidine Sulfate.

Either Phenobarbital or Phenytoin may reduce the time that Quinidine Sulfate is effective in your body, and may increase your need for it. Quinidine Sulfate in combination with Digoxin can increase the effects of the Digoxin causing possible Digoxin toxicity. This combination should be monitored closely by your doctor.

Avoid over-the-counter cough, cold, allergy, or diet preparations. These medications may contain drugs which will stimulate your heart; this can be dangerous while you are taking Quinidine Sulfate. Ask your pharmacist, if you have any questions about the contents of a particular cough, cold, or allergy remedy.

Usual Dose

Extremely variable, depending on disease and patient's response. Most doses are 800 to 1200 milligrams per day.

Overdosage

Produces abnormal effects on the heart and symptoms of cinchonism. Patient should be taken to a hospital emergency room where proper therapy can be given. ALWAYS bring the medicine bottle.

Special Information

If Quinidine Sulfate gives you stomach upset, take it with food. If this does not solve the problem, contact your doctor.

Brand Name

Regroton

Ingredients

Chlorthalidone
Reserpine

Other Brand Name

Demi-Regroton

Type of Drug

Antihypertensive.

Prescribed for

High blood pressure.

General Information

Regroton is a good example of a drug taking advantage of a drug interaction. Each of the drug ingredients works by different mechanisms to lower your blood pressure. The Chlorthalidone relaxes the muscles in your veins and arteries and also helps reduce the volume of blood flowing through those blood vessels. Reserpine works on the nervous system to reduce the efficiency of nerve transmissions which are contributing to the increased pressure. These drugs complement each other so that their combined effect is better than the effect of either one alone.

It is essential that you take your medicine exactly as prescribed, for maximum benefit.

An ingredient in this drug may cause excessive loss of potassium, which may lead to a condition called hypokalemia. Warning signs are dryness of mouth, excessive thirst, weakness, drowsiness, restlessness, muscle pains or cramps, muscular fatigue, lack of urination, abnormal heart rhythms, and upset stomach. If warning signs occur, call your doctor. You may need potassium from some outside source. This may be done by taking a potassium supplement or by eating foods such as bananas, citrus fruits, melons, and tomatoes, which have high concentrations of potassium.

This drug should be stopped at the first sign of despondency, early morning insomnia, loss of appetite, or sexual impotence. Drug-induced depression may persist for several months after the drug has been discontinued; it has been known to be severe enough to result in suicide attempts. This drug should be used with care by women of childbearing age.

Cautions and Warnings

Do not take this drug if you are sensitive or allergic to either of its ingredients or if you have a history of mental depression, active peptic ulcer, or ulcerative colitis.

Possible Side Effects

Loss of appetite, stomach irritation, nausea, vomiting, cramps, diarrhea, constipation, dizziness, headache, tingling in the arms and legs, restlessness, chest pains, abnormal heart rhythms, drowsiness, depression, nervousness, anxiety, nightmares, glaucoma, blood disorders, itching, fever, difficulty in breathing, muscle spasms, weakness, high blood sugar, sugar in the urine, blurred vision, stuffed nose, dryness of the mouth, rash. Occasional: impotence or decreased sex drive.

Drug Interactions

Interaction with Digitalis or Quinidine may cause abnormal heart rhythms.

Caution must be taken if this drug is given with other antihypertensive agents such as Guanethidine, Veratrum,

Methyldopa, Chlorthalidone or Hydralazine: the dose of these drugs must be monitored carefully by your physician. It is strongly advised not to take MAO antidepressant drugs while taking Regroton.

Interaction with drugs containing lithium may lead to toxic effects of lithium.

Avoid over-the-counter cough, cold, or allergy remedies containing stimulant drugs which may raise your blood pressure.

Usual Dose

Must be individualized to patient's response.

Generic Name

Rifampin

Brand Names

Rifadin
Rimactane

Type of Drug

Antitubercular.

Prescribed for

Tuberculosis. Also used to treat people who are carriers of certain infections rather than infected patients.

General Information

This is an important drug for the treatment of tuberculosis. It is always used together with Isoniazid or another antitubercular drug because it is not effective by itself. It also eradicates an organism which causes meningitis in people who are carriers: although they are not infected, they carry the organism and spread it to others.

Cautions and Warnings

Do not take this drug if you are allergic to it. It may cause liver damage and should not be used by people with liver disease or those taking other drugs which may cause liver damage. This drug should only be used by pregnant women or nursing mothers if absolutely necessary.

Possible Side Effects

Flulike symptoms, heartburn, upset stomach, loss of appetite, nausea, vomiting, stomach gas cramps, diarrhea, headache, drowsiness, tiredness, menstrual disturbances, dizziness, fever, pains in the arms and legs, confusion, visual disturbances, numbness, hypersensitivity to the drug.

Possible Adverse Drug Effects

Adverse effects on the blood, kidneys, or liver.

Drug Interactions

When this is taken with other drugs that cause liver toxicity, severe liver damage may develop.

Rifampin will increase patient requirements for oral anticoagulant drugs and may affect Methadone, oral antidiabetic drugs, digitalis drugs, or adrenal corticosteroids. Women taking oral contraceptives and Rifampin should supplement with other contraceptive methods while taking the two drugs together.

Usual Dose

Adult: 600 milligrams once daily.

Child: 1 to 2 milligrams per pound, or up to 600 milligrams per day.

Overdosage

Signs are nausea, vomiting, and tiredness. Unconsciousness may develop, with severe liver damage. A brown-red or orange discoloration of the skin may develop. Patients suspected of taking a Rifampin overdose must be taken to the hospital at once. ALWAYS take the medicine bottle with you.

Special Information

Take this medicine 1 hour before or 2 hours after a meal, at the same time every day. This drug may cause a red-brown or orange coloration of the urine, stool, saliva, sweat, and tears. Call your doctor if you develop the flu, fever, chills, muscle pains, headache, tiredness or weakness, loss of appetite, nausea, vomiting, sore throat, unusual bleeding or bruising or yellow discoloration of the skin or eyes, rash, or itching.

Generic Name

Ritodrine

Brand Name

Yutopar

Type of Drug

Uterine relaxant.

Prescribed for

Controlling preterm labor to prevent premature delivery.

General Information

This drug stimulates the beta nerve receptors in muscles in the uterus and prevents them from contracting. This drug must be used only under the direction of your doctor and only after the fifth month of pregnancy. It should be started with intravenous dosage and then continued as pills.

Cautions and Warnings

This drug should not be used until after the twentieth week of pregnancy or if the mother has any complicating factors.

Possible Side Effects

Increased heart rate and blood pressure in both mother and child, palpitations, tremor, nausea, vomiting, headache, swelling of the extremities.

Possible Adverse Drug Effects

Nervousness, jitteriness, restlessness, emotional anxiety, upset, feeling of ill health, chest pains, abnormal heart rates, rash, heart murmur, upset stomach, bloating, constipation, diarrhea, sweating, chills, drowsiness, weakness, difficulty breathing, sugar in the urine.

Drug Interactions

Adrenal corticosteroids may lead to fluid in the lungs when given together with Ritodrine.

All beta-adrenergic blocking drugs will directly inhibit the effect of Ritodrine.

Usual Dose

After intravenous therapy, tablets are taken in a dose of 10 milligrams every 2 hours on the first day, then 10 to 20 milligrams every 4 to 6 hours. The drug may be used as long as it is desirable to prolong the pregnancy.

Overdosage

Signs are rapid heart rate, palpitation, abnormal heartbeats, low blood pressure, nervousness, tremor, nausea, and vomiting. Take the patient to a hospital emergency room. ALWAYS bring the medicine bottle.

Special Information

Take only as directed by your doctor. Report any unusual effect immediately.

Brand Name

Salutensin

Ingredients

Hydroflumethiazide
Reserpine

Type of Drug

Antihypertensive.

Prescribed for

High blood pressure.

General Information

Salutensin is a good example of a drug taking advantage of a drug interaction. Each of the drug ingredients works by different mechanisms to lower your blood pressure. The Hydroflumethiazide relaxes the muscles in your veins and arteries and also helps reduce the volume of blood flowing through those blood vessels. Reserpine works on the nervous system to reduce the efficiency of nerve transmissions which are contributing to the increased pressure. These drugs complement each other so that their combined effect is better than the effect of either one alone.

It is essential that you take your medicine exactly as prescribed, for maximum benefit.

An ingredient in this drug may cause excessive loss of potassium, which may lead to a condition called hypokalemia. Warning signs are dryness of mouth, excessive thirst, weakness, drowsiness, restlessness, muscle pains or cramps, muscular fatigue, lack of urination, abnormal heart rhythms, and upset stomach. If warning signs occur, call your doctor. You may need potassium from some outside source. This may be done by taking a potassium supplement or by eating foods such as bananas, citrus fruits, melons, and tomatoes, which have high concentrations of potassium.

This drug should be stopped at the first sign of despondency, early morning insomnia, loss of appetite, or sexual impotence. Drug-induced depression may persist for several months after the drug has been discontinued; it has been known to be severe enough to result in suicide attempts. This drug should be used with care by women of childbearing age.

Cautions and Warnings

Do not take this drug if you are sensitive or allergic to either of its ingredients or if you have a history of mental depression, active peptic ulcer, or ulcerative colitis.

Possible Side Effects

Loss of appetite, stomach irritation, nausea, vomiting, cramps, diarrhea, constipation, dizziness, headache, tingling in the arms and legs, restlessness, chest pains, abnormal heart rhythms, drowsiness, depression, nervousness, anxiety, nightmares, glaucoma, blood disorders, itching, fever, difficulty in breathing, muscle spasms, weakness, high blood sugar, sugar in the urine, blurred vision, stuffed nose, dry-

ness of the mouth, rash. Occasional: impotence or decreased
sex drive.

Drug Interactions

Interaction with Digitalis or Quinidine may cause abnormal
heart rhythms.

Caution must be taken if this drug is given with other
antihypertensive agents such as Guanethidine, Veratrum,
Methyldopa, Chlorthalidone, or Hydralazine: the dose of
these drugs must be monitored carefully by your physician.
It is strongly advised not to take MAO antidepressant drugs
while taking Salutensin.

Interaction with drugs containing lithium may lead to toxic
effects of lithium.

Avoid over-the-counter cough, cold, or allergy remedies
containing stimulant drugs which may raise your blood
pressure.

Usual Dose

Must be individualized to patient's response.

Generic Name

Secobarbital

Brand Name

Seconal

Type of Drug

Hypnotic; sedative.

Prescribed for

Daytime sedation, sleeplessness, sedation before surgery.

General Information

Secobarbital, like the other barbiturates, works by interfering
with the passage of certain nerve impulses to the brain. It is
useful in any situation where a fast-acting sedative or hypnotic (sleep-producing) effect is needed. This drug can be

addicting if taken for a period of time in large enough doses, especially if more than 400 milligrams a day is taken for 3 months. Larger doses will produce barbiturate addiction in a shorter time.

Cautions and Warnings

Secobarbital may slow down your physical and mental reflexes; be extremely careful when operating machinery, driving an automobile, or performing other potentially dangerous tasks. Secobarbital is classified as a barbiturate; long-term or unsupervised use may cause addiction. Elderly people on Secobarbital may exhibit nervousness and confusion at times. Barbiturates are neutralized in the liver and eliminated from the body through the kidneys; consequently, people who have liver or kidney disorders—namely, difficulty in forming or excreting urine—should be carefully monitored by their doctor when taking Secobarbital.

If you have known sensitivities or allergies to barbiturates, or if you have previously been addicted to sedatives or hypnotics, or if you have a disease affecting the respiratory system, you should not take Secobarbital.

Possible Side Effects

Difficulty in breathing, rash, and general allergic reaction such as running nose, watery eyes, and scratchy throat.

Possible Adverse Drug Effects

Drowsiness, lethargy, dizziness, hangover, nausea, vomiting, diarrhea. More severe adverse reactions may include anemia and yellowing of the skin and eyes.

Drug Interactions

Interaction with alcohol, tranquilizers, or other sedatives increases the effect of Secobarbital.

Interaction with anticoagulants (blood-thinning agents) can reduce their effect. This is also true of muscle relaxants and painkillers.

Usual Dose

Daytime sedative: 30 to 50 milligrams.
  Hypnotic for sleep: 100 to 200 milligrams.

Sedation before surgery: 200 to 500 milligrams 1 to 2 hours before surgery.

Child: sedative, 2.7 milligrams per pound per day; sedation before surgery, 50 to 100 milligrams.

Overdosage

Symptoms are difficulty in breathing, decrease in size of the pupils of the eyes, lowered body temperature progressing to fever as time passes, fluid in the lungs, and eventually coma.

Anyone suspected of having taken an overdose must be taken to the hospital for immediate care. ALWAYS bring the medicine bottle to the emergency room physician so he can quickly and correctly identify the medicine and start treatment. Severe overdosage of this medication can kill; the drug has been used many times in suicide attempts.

Brand Name

Septra

Ingredients

Sulfamethoxazole
Trimethoprim

Other Brand Name

Bactrim

Type of Drug

Urinary anti-infective.

Prescribed for

Urinary tract infections. Septra can also be used to treat bronchitis caused by susceptible organisms.

General Information

Septra is one of many combination products used to treat urinary tract infections. This is a unique combination because it attacks the infecting organism in two ways; it is effective in many situations where other drugs are not.

Cautions and Warnings

Do not take this medication if you have a folic acid deficiency, are allergic or sensitive to either ingredient or to any sulfa drug, or are pregnant or nursing. Infants under age 2 months should not be given this combination product. Symptoms such as unusual bleeding or bruising, extreme tiredness, rash, sore throat, fever, pallor, or yellowing of the skin or whites of the eyes may be early indications of serious blood disorders. If any of these effects occur, contact your doctor immediately and stop taking the drug.

Possible Side Effects

Effects on components of the blood system, allergic reactions including itching, rash, drug fever, swelling around the eyes, arthritislike pains. Septra can also cause nausea, stomach upset, vomiting, abdominal pain, diarrhea, coating on the tongue, headache, tingling in the arms and/or legs, depression, convulsions, hallucinations, ringing in the ears, dizziness, difficulty sleeping, feeling of apathy, tiredness, weakness, and nervousness. Septra may affect your kidneys and cause you to produce less urine.

Drug Interactions

This drug may prolong the effects of blood-thinning agents (such as Warfarin) and antidiabetic oral drugs.

Usual Dose

1 to 2 tablets every 12 hours for 10 to 14 days. Oral suspension, 2 to 4 teaspoons every 12 hours for 10 to 14 days.

Special Information

Take Septra in the exact dosage and for the exact period of time prescribed. Do not stop taking it just because you are beginning to feel better.

You may develop unusual sensitivity to sun or bright light. If you have a history of light sensitivity or if you have sensitive skin, avoid prolonged exposure to sunlight while using Septra.

Drink lots of fluid to help decrease the chances of crystals forming in your kidneys. Take each dose with a full glass of water.

Brand Name

Ser-Ap-Es Tablets

Ingredients

Hydralazine
Hydrochlorothiazide
Reserpine

Other Brand Names

Cam-ap-es	Ser-A-Gen
HHR	Seralazide
HRH	Ser Hydra Zine
Hyserp	Tri-Hydroserpine
R-HCTZ-H	Unipres Tablets

Type of Drug

Antihypertensive combination.

Prescribed for

High blood pressure.

General Information

Be sure to take this medicine exactly as prescribed: if you don't, the medicine will not be able to work best for you.

An ingredient in this drug may cause you to lose an excessive amount of potassium, which may lead to a condition known as hypokalemia. Warning signs of hypokalemia are dryness of the mouth, excessive thirst, weakness, drowsiness, restlessness, muscle pain or cramps, muscular fatigue, lack of urination, abnormal heart rhythms, and upset stomach. If you notice these warning signs, call your doctor. You may need to take extra potassium to replace the loss caused by the drug. You may do this either by taking a potassium supplement (liquid, powder, or tablet), or by increasing the amounts of foods in your diet which are high in potassium. Some of these foods are bananas, citrus fruits, melons, and tomatoes.

One of the ingredients in Ser-Ap-Es Tablets may cause mental depression. If you have a history of depressive problems, make sure your doctor knows, so that the appropriate changes can be made. Stop taking this drug at the first sign of despondency, early morning insomnia, loss of appetite, or sexual impotence. Drug-induced depression may persist for several months after the drug has been stopped; it has been known to be severe enough to result in suicide attempts. This drug should be used with care by women of childbearing age.

Cautions and Warnings

Do not take Ser-Ap-Es Tablets if you are sensitive or allergic to any of its ingredients or if you have a history of mental depression, active peptic ulcer, or ulcerative colitis. Long-term administration in large doses may produce symptoms similar to arthritis in a few patients. This usually resolves itself when you stop taking the drug. The recurrence of fever, chest pains, not feeling well, or other unexplained problems should be investigated further by your doctor.

Possible Side Effects

Common: headache, loss of appetite, vomiting, nausea, diarrhea, abnormal heart rate, chest pains, stomach upset, cramps, tingling in the arms and legs, restlessness, drowsiness, depression, nervousness, anxiety, nightmares, glaucoma, blood disorders, rash, itching, fever, difficulty in breathing, muscle spasms, weakness, high blood sugar, sugar in the urine, blurred vision, stuffed nose, dry mouth, rash. Impotence and decreased sex drive have also been reported.

Possible Adverse Drug Effects

Flushing of the skin, tearing of the eyes, conjunctivitis, disorientation, and anxiety are infrequent. Rarely, long-term users have developed symptoms of hepatitis.

Drug Interactions

Ser-Ap-Es Tablets may interact with MAO inhibitor drugs, Digitalis, or Quinidine.

Ser-Ap-Es Tablets will interact with drugs containing lithium, producing a higher incidence of adverse effects from the lithium products.

Avoid over-the-counter cough, cold, or allergy remedies which contain stimulant drugs, as these can counteract the antihypertensive medication.

Usual Dose

Must be individualized to patient's response.

Overdosage

Symptoms are extreme lowering of blood pressure, rapid heartbeat, headache, generalized skin flushing, chest pains, and poor heart rhythms. The patient should be treated in a hospital where proper facilities and procedures are available. ALWAYS bring the medicine bottle to the emergency room.

Special Information

It is important to eat a well-balanced diet or follow the special diet given to you by your doctor. You must take your medicine exactly as prescribed.

Slight stomach upset from Ser-Ap-Es Tablets can be overcome by taking each dose with some food. If stomach pain continues or becomes severe, call your doctor.

Brand Name

Sinemet

Ingredients

Carbidopa
Levodopa

Type of Drug

Anti-Parkinsonian.

Prescribed for

Parkinson's disease.

General Information

This is another good example of how medical science takes advantage of a drug interaction. Levodopa is the active ingredient that helps against Parkinson's disease. Carbidopa prevents the destruction of Levodopa so that more can get into the brain, where Levodopa does its work. This combination is so effective that the amount of Levodopa needed is reduced by about 75 percent, which results in fewer side effects and, generally, safer drug treatment. Carbidopa prevents the destruction of Levodopa by Vitamin B_6. Consequently, people using the combination can take extra vitamins without having to worry about the presence of B_6.

Cautions and Warnings

Do not take this drug if you are allergic to either of the ingredients. Patients being switched from Levodopa to Sinemet should stop taking Levodopa 8 hours before their first dose of Sinemet. It can be increased gradually, as needed. Side effects with Sinemet can occur at much lower dosages than with Levodopa, because of the effect of Carbidopa.

These drugs are known to cause birth defects in laboratory animals. The effect in humans is not known. However, women who are pregnant or breast-feeding should use this drug only if it is absolutely necessary.

Possible Side Effects

Uncontrolled muscle movements, loss of appetite, nausea, vomiting, stomach pain, dry mouth, difficulty swallowing, dribbling saliva from the side of the mouth, shaking of the hands, headache, dizziness, numbness, weakness, feeling faint, grinding of the teeth, confusion, sleeplessness, nightmares, hallucinations, anxiety, agitation, tiredness, lack of feeling well, feeling of euphoria (high).

Possible Adverse Drug Effects

Adverse effects on the heart including palpitations, dizziness when rising quickly from a sitting or lying position, and sudden extreme slowness of movement (on-off phenomenon); mental changes including paranoia, psychosis and depression, and slowdown of mental functioning; also difficult urination, muscle twitching, spasms of the eyelids, lockjaw, burning sensation on the tongue, bitter taste, diarrhea, constipation, stomach gas, flushing of the skin, rash, sweating, unusual breathing, double or blurred vision, dilation of the pupils of the eyes, hot flashes, changes in body weight, darkening of the urine or sweat.

Occasionally Sinemet may cause bleeding of the stomach or development of an ulcer, high blood pressure, adverse effects on components of the blood, irritation of blood vessels, convulsions, inability to control movements of the eye muscles, hiccups, feeling of being stimulated, retention of body fluid, hair loss, hoarseness of the voice, or persistent penile erection. The drug may affect blood tests for kidney and liver function.

Drug Interactions

The effectiveness of Sinemet may be increased by taking drugs with an anticholinergic effect, such as Trihexyphenidyl. Methyldopa, an antihypertensive drug, has the same effect on Levodopa as Carbidopa. It can increase the amount of Levodopa available in the central nervous system, and it may have a slight effect on Sinemet as well.

Patients taking Guanethidine or a diuretic to treat high blood pressure may find they need less medication to control their pressure.

Reserpine, benzodiazepine tranquilizers, major tranquilizers, Phenytoin, and Papaverine may interfere with the effects of Sinemet. Vitamin B_6 will interfere with Levodopa but not with Sinemet.

Diabetics who start taking Sinemet may need adjustments in their antidiabetic drugs.

Patients taking Sinemet together with an MAO inhibitor drug may experience a rapid increase in blood pressure. MAO inhibitors should be stopped 2 weeks before Sinemet.

Sinemet may increase the effects of Ephedrine, amphetamines, Epinephrine, and Isoproterenol. This interaction can result in adverse effects on the heart. This reaction may also occur with some of the antidepressants.

Usual Dose

Dose must be tailored to individual need. For patients who have been taking Levodopa, the starting dose of Sinemet should contain 20 to 25 percent of the amount of Levodopa that was taken previously.

For patients who have not been taking Levodopa 3 times per day, the dose is 1 10/100 tablet a day. Dosage may be adjusted slowly thereafter.

Overdosage

Patients taking an overdose of Sinemet should be taken to a

hospital emergency room. ALWAYS bring the medicine bottle. The most worrisome effect of an overdosage with Sinemet is the development of abnormal heart rhythms.

Special Information

This drug may be taken with food to reduce upset stomach. Take care while driving or operating machinery; Sinemet can cause tiredness or lack of concentration. Call your doctor if you experience dizziness, light-headedness or fainting spells, uncontrollable movements of the face, eyelids, mouth, tongue, neck, arms, hands, or legs, mood changes, mental changes, abnormal heartbeats or heart palpitations, difficult urination, or persistent nausea or vomiting.

This drug may cause darkening of the urine or sweat. This effect is not harmful, but may interfere with urine tests for diabetes.

Call your doctor before making any adjustments in your treatment.

Brand Name

Singlet Tablets

Ingredients

Acetaminophen
Chlorpheniramine Maleate
Phenylephrine Hydrochloride

Type of Drug

Decongestant; antihistamine.

Prescribed for

Relief of congestion, runny nose, and other general symptoms associated with the common cold, influenza, or other upper respiratory diseases.

General Information

Singlet Tablets is one of many products marketed to alleviate the symptoms of the common cold. These products contain medicine to relieve nasal congestion or to dry up runny noses or soothe a scratchy throat; and several of them may contain ingredients to suppress cough, or to help eliminate unwanted mucus. All these products are good only for the relief of symptoms and will not treat the underlying problem, such as a cold virus or other infections.

Cautions and Warnings

Can cause excessive tiredness or drowsiness.

This product should not be used for newborn infants or taken by pregnant or nursing women. People with glaucoma or difficulty in urinating should avoid this drug and other drugs containing antihistamines.

Possible Side Effects

Excessive tiredness or drowsiness, restlessness, tension, nervousness, tremor, weakness, inability to sleep, headache, palpitations, elevation of blood pressure, sweating, sleeplessness, loss of appetite, nausea, vomiting, dizziness, constipation.

Drug Interactions

Interaction with alcoholic beverages may produce excessive drowsiness and/or sleepiness, or inability to concentrate. Also avoid sedatives, tranquilizers, antihistamines, and sleeping pills.

Do not self-medicate with additional over-the-counter drugs for the relief of cold symptoms; taking Singlet Tablets with such drugs may result in aggravation of high blood pressure, heart disease, diabetes, or thyroid disease.

Do not take Singlet Tablets if you are taking or suspect you may be taking a monoamine oxidase (MAO) inhibitor: severe elevation in blood pressure may result.

Usual Dose

1 tablet morning and night.

Special Information

Since drowsiness may occur during use of Singlet Tablets, be cautious while performing mechanical tasks requiring alertness.

Brand Name

Sinubid

Ingredients

Acetaminophen
Phenylproloxamine
Phenylpropanolamine

Type of Drug

Decongestant; antihistamine.

Prescribed for

Relief of congestion, runny nose, and other general symptoms associated with the common cold, influenza, or other upper respiratory diseases.

General Information

Sinubid is one of many products marketed to relieve the symptoms of the common cold. These products contain medicine to relieve nasal congestion or dry up runny noses or relieve a scratchy throat, and several of them may contain ingredients to suppress cough, or to help eliminate unwanted mucus. All these products are good only for the relief of symptoms and will not treat the underlying problem, such as cold virus, or other infections.

Cautions and Warnings

This drug can cause excessive tiredness or drowsiness. Sinubid should not be used for newborn infants or taken by pregnant or nursing mothers. People with glaucoma or difficulty in urinating should avoid this drug and other drugs containing antihistamines.

Possible Side Effects

Excessive tiredness or drowsiness, restlessness, tension, nervousness, tremor, weakness, inability to sleep, headache, palpitations, elevation of blood pressure, sweating, loss of appetite, nausea, vomiting, dizziness, constipation.

Drug Interactions

Interaction with alcoholic beverages may produce excessive drowsiness and/or sleepiness, or inability to concentrate. Also avoid sedatives, tranquilizers, other antihistamines, and sleeping pills.

Do not self-medicate with over-the-counter drugs for the relief of cold symptoms; taking Sinubid with such drugs may result in aggravation of high blood pressure, heart disease, diabetes, or thyroid disease.

Do not take Sinubid if you are taking or suspect you may be taking a monoamine oxidase (MAO) inhibitor: severe elevation in blood pressure may result.

Usual Dose

1 tablet morning and night.

Special Information

Since drowsiness may occur during use of Sinubid, be cautious while performing mechanical tasks requiring alertness.

Generic Name

Spironolactone

Brand Name

Aldactone

Other Brand Name

Spiractone

Type of Drug

Diuretic.

Prescribed for

High blood pressure; fluid in the body due to other diseases.

General Information

Spironolactone is a specific physiologic antagonist of aldosterone. Therefore, it is extremely useful for the treatment of excess fluid in the body related to the presence of high levels of aldosterone (hyperaldosteronism) when used alone or in combination with other diuretics.

Cautions and Warnings

Do not use this drug if you know you have kidney failure or high blood levels of potassium. Patients taking Spironolactone should not take potassium or foods rich in potassium. This drug has been shown to cause tumors when given in very high doses to experimental rats. If at all possible this drug should not be given to pregnant or nursing women.

Possible Side Effects

Drowsiness, lethargy, headache, gastrointestinal upset, cramps and diarrhea, rash, mental confusion, fever, feeling of ill health, enlargement of the breasts, inability to achieve or maintain erection in males, irregular menstrual cycles or deepening of the voice in females. These side effects are generally reversible.

Drug Interactions

Spironolactone will potentiate (increase the action of) other antihypertensive drugs; frequently it is used for this effect. The dosage of other antihypertensive drugs may be reduced as much as 50 percent when Spironolactone is added to the regimen.

Patients taking Spironolactone for the treatment of high blood pressure should not self-medicate with over-the-counter cough, cold, or allergy remedies containing stimulant drugs which may counteract its effectiveness and have an adverse effect on their hearts.

Usual Dose

Adult: for high blood pressure, initial dose is 2 to 4 tablets per day in divided doses; for excess fluids related to other diseases, 4 tablets per day in divided doses.

Child: 1 to 1.5 milligrams per pound of body weight, if deemed necessary.

Special Information

Take the drug exactly as it has been prescribed for maximum therapeutic effect. High blood levels of potassium associated with use of Spironolactone may cause weakness, lethargy, drowsiness, muscle pains or cramps, and muscular fatigue. Patients should be careful when driving.

Generic Name

Sucralfate

Brand Name

Carafate

Type of Drug

Nonsystemic anti-ulcer therapy.

Prescribed for

Duodenal ulcer.

General Information

Sucralfate is not absorbed into the body from the gastrointestinal tract, but instead works within it by exerting a soothing local effect. After the drug binds to proteins in the damaged mucous tissue within the ulcer, it forms a barrier to acids and enzymes normally found in the gastrointestinal tract, protecting the ulcerated tissue from further damage and allowing it to begin to heal naturally. Although its mechanism of action is completely different from Cimetidine, Sucralfate is equally effective in treating ulcer disease.

Cautions and Warnings

This drug should not be used by pregnant women or nursing mothers unless absolutely necessary. The use of Sucralfate in children is not recommended because the drug has only been studied in adults.

Possible Side Effects

Most frequent: constipation. Others are: diarrhea, nausea, upset stomach, indigestion, dry mouth, rash, itching, back pain, dizziness, sleepiness. The incidence of reported side effects to Sucralfate is only about 5%.

Drug Interactions

No drug interactions have been reported with Sucralfate. However, like all other relatively new drugs, the experience of a year or two of use will probably show previously unknown interactions. Since Sucralfate stays in the gastrointestinal tract, the interactions likely to be reported are those related to interference with the normal passage of other drugs in the bloodstream.

Usual Dose

One tablet before meals and at bedtime.

Overdosage

There have been no reports of human overdoses of Sucralfate. Animals given the equivalent of 5½ grams per pound of body weight did not experience any unusual effects, and therefore the risk associated with Sucralfate overdose is thought to be minimal.

Special Information

Take each dose 1 hour before meals and before bedtime. Be sure to take the medicine for a full 6 to 8 week course of treatment. Notify your doctor if you develop constipation, diarrhea, or other gastrointestinal side effects. If you are taking antacids as part of your ulcer therapy, separate antacid doses from Sucralfate by at least half an hour.

Generic Name

Sulfamethazole

Brand Names

Microsul
Proklar
Thiosulfil
Urifon

Type of Drug

Urinary anti-infective.

Prescribed for

Urinary tract infections.

General Information

Sulfamethazole is one of the sulfa drugs, some of which are used for the treatment of urinary tract infections. Others may be used for high blood pressure, diabetes mellitus, or as diuretic (urine-producing) drugs. When taking Sulfamethazole for urinary tract infections, it is essential that you take your medicine for the full course prescribed by your doctor. If you don't, your infection will not be cured and may actually become more difficult to treat. Sulfa drugs are usually the best choice for urinary infections.

Cautions and Warnings

Do not take Sulfamethazole if you know you are allergic to sulfa drugs, salicylates, or similar agents. Do not take this drug if you are pregnant or nursing, since the drug can pass from the mother into the child. Sulfamethazole should not be considered if you have advanced kidney disease, or intestinal or urinary obstruction.

Possible Side Effects

Headache, itching, rash, sensitivity to strong sunlight, nausea, vomiting, abdominal pains, feeling of tiredness or lassitude, hallucinations, dizziness, ringing in the ears, chills, feeling of ill health.

Possible Adverse Drug Effects

Blood diseases or alterations of normal blood components, itching of the eyes, arthritic pain, diarrhea, loss of appetite, stomach cramps or pains, hearing loss, drowsiness, fever, chills, loss of hair, yellowing of the skin and/or eyes, reduction in sperm count.

Drug Interactions

When Sulfamethazole is taken with an anticoagulant (blood-thinning) drug, any drug used to treat diabetes, or Methotrexate, it will cause unusually large amounts of these drugs to be released into the bloodstream, producing symptoms of overdosage. If you are going to take Sulfamethazole for an extended period, your physician should reduce the dosage of these interactive drugs. Also avoid large doses of Vitamin C.

Usual Dose

Adult: ½ to 1 gram 3 to 4 times per day.

Child and infant (age over 2 months): 3 to 5 milligrams per pound 4 times per day.

Overdosage

Induce vomiting and give a rectal enema; then take the patient to a hospital emergency room. ALWAYS bring the medicine bottle.

Special Information

Avoid prolonged exposure to strong sunlight while you are taking Sulfamethazole, which can cause photosensitivity—a severe reaction to strong sunlight.

Sore throat, fever, unusual bleeding or bruising, rash, and feeling tired are early signs of serious blood disorders and should be reported to your doctor immediately.

Take each dose with a full glass of water.

Therapy should continue 1 to 2 days after symptoms have subsided. Take the medicine for the time prescribed by your doctor; do not stop just because you have begun to feel better.

Generic Name

Sulfamethoxazole

Brand Names

Gantanol
Gantanol DS
Methoxal
Methoxanol

Type of Drug

Urinary anti-infective.

Prescribed for

Urinary tract infections.

General Information

Sulfamethoxazole is a member of the group called sulfa drugs. Some sulfa drugs are used for the treatment of urinary tract infections. Others may be used for high blood pressure or diabetes mellitus, or as diuretic (water-losing) drugs. When taking Sulfamethoxazole for urinary tract infections it is essential that you take your medicine for the full course prescribed by your doctor. If you don't, your infection will not be cured and may become more difficult to treat. Sulfa drugs are usually the best choice for urinary infections, and may also be used to treat other infections.

Cautions and Warnings

Do not take Sulfamethoxazole if you know you are allergic to sulfa drugs, salicylates, or similar agents. Do not take this drug if you are pregnant or nursing a young child, since the drug can pass from the mother into the child. Sulfamethoxazole should not be considered if you have advanced kidney disease or intestinal or urinary obstruction.

Possible Side Effects

Headache, itching, rash, sensitivity to strong sunlight, nausea, vomiting, abdominal pains, feeling of tiredness or lassitude, hallucinations, dizziness, ringing in the ears, chills, feeling of ill health.

Possible Adverse Drug Effects

Blood diseases or alterations of normal blood components, itching of the eyes, arthritic pain, diarrhea, loss of appetite, stomach cramps or pains, hearing loss, drowsiness, fever, chills, loss of hair, yellowing of the skin and/or eyes, reduction in sperm count.

Drug Interactions

When Sulfamethoxazole is taken with an anticoagulant (blood-thinning) drug, any drug used to treat diabetes, or Methotrexate, it will cause unusually large amounts of these drugs to be released into the bloodstream, producing symptoms of overdosage. If you have to take Sulfamethoxazole for an extended period, your physician should reduce the dosage of these interactive drugs. Also avoid large doses of Vitamin C.

Usual Dose

Adult: first dose, 4 tablets; then 2 tablets 2 to 3 times per day.

Child (suspension): first dose, 25 to 30 milligrams per pound of body weight; then 12.5 to 15 milligrams per pound morning and evening. No more than 34 milligrams per pound per day.

Take each dose with a full glass of water.

Therapy should continue 1 to 2 days after symptoms have subsided. Take the medicine for the time prescribed by your doctor; do not stop just because you have begun to feel better.

Overdosage

Induce vomiting and give a rectal enema; then take the patient to a hospital emergency room. ALWAYS bring the medicine bottle.

Special Information

Sulfamethoxazole can cause photosensitivity—a severe reaction to strong sunlight. Avoid prolonged exposure to strong sunlight while you are taking it.

Sore throat, fever, unusual bleeding or bruising, rash, and feeling tired are early signs of serious blood disorders and should be reported to your doctor immediately.

Generic Name

Sulfasalazine

Brand Names

Azulfidine	S.A.S.-500
Azulfidine EN-tabs	Sulfadyne

Type of Drug

Sulfonamide.

Prescribed for

Treatment of ulcerative colitis.

General Information

Sulfasalazine is a member of the group called sulfa drugs. Some sulfa drugs are used for their effects as anti-infectives, others are diuretics or can be used to treat diabetes mellitus. Sulfasalazine has a unique effect in that it reduces the intestinal inflammation of ulcerative colitis.

Cautions and Warnings

Do not take Sulfasalazine if you know you are allergic to sulfa drugs, salicylates, or similar agents. Do not take this drug if you are pregnant or nursing a young child, since the drug can pass from the mother into the child. Sulfasalazine should not be considered if you have advanced kidney disease.

Possible Side Effects

Headache, itching, skin rash, sensitivity to strong sunlight, nausea, vomiting, abdominal pains, feeling of tiredness or lassitude, hallucinations, dizziness, ringing in the ears, chills, feeling of ill health.

Possible Adverse Drug Effects

Blood diseases or changes in normal blood components, itching of the eyes, arthritis-type pain, diarrhea, loss of appetite, stomach cramps or pains, hearing loss, drowsiness, fever, chills, loss of hair, yellowing of the skin and/or eyes, reduction in sperm count.

Drug Interactions

When Sulfasalazine is taken with an anticoagulant (blood-thinning) drug, any drug used to treat diabetes, or Methotrexate, it will cause unusually large amounts of these drugs to be released into the bloodstream, producing symptoms of overdosage. If you are going to take Sulfasalazine for an extended period, your physician should reduce the dosage of these interactive drugs. Also avoid large doses of Vitamin C.

Usual Dose

Adult: 6 to 8 tablets per day to start. Adjust dose as needed. Usual maintenance dose is 4 tablets per day.

Child: 20 to 40 milligrams per pound of body weight per day to start. Adjust dose as needed. Usual maintenance dose is 15 milligrams per pound per day.

Overdosage

Induce vomiting and give a rectal enema; then take the patient to a hospital emergency room. ALWAYS bring the medicine bottle.

Special Information

Sulfasalazine can cause photosensitivity—a severe reaction to strong sunlight. Avoid prolonged exposure to strong sunlight while you are taking it.

Sore throat, fever, unusual bleeding or bruising, rash, and feeling tired are early signs of serious blood disorders and should be reported to your doctor immediately.

Generic Name

Sulfisoxazole

Brand Names

Gantrisin   Sulfasox
Lipo Gantrisin   Sulfizin
SK-Soxazole

Type of Drug

Urinary anti-infective.

Prescribed for

Urinary tract infections.

General Information

Sulfisoxazole is a member of the group called sulfa drugs. Some sulfa drugs are used for the treatment of urinary tract infections. Others may be used for high blood pressure or

diabetes mellitus, or as diuretic (water-losing) drugs. When
taking Sulfisoxazole for urinary tract infections it is essential
that you take your medicine for the full course prescribed by
your doctor. If you don't, your infection will not be cured and
may become more difficult to treat. Sulfa drugs are usually
the best choice for urinary infections, and may also be used
to treat other infections.

Cautions and Warnings

Do not take Sulfisoxazole if you know you are allergic to
sulfa drugs, salicylates, or similar agents. Do not take this
drug if you are pregnant or nursing a young child, since the
drug can pass from the mother into the child. Sulfisoxazole
should not be considered if you have advanced kidney disease.

Possible Side Effects

Headache, itching, rash, sensitivity to strong sunlight, nausea, vomiting, abdominal pains, feeling of tiredness or lassitude, hallucinations, dizziness, ringing in the ears, chills,
feeling of ill health.

Possible Adverse Drug Effects

Blood diseases or alterations of normal blood components,
itching of the eyes, arthritis-type pain, diarrhea, loss of appetite, stomach cramps or pains, hearing loss, drowsiness,
fever, chills, loss of hair, yellowing of the skin and/or eyes,
reduction in sperm count.

Drug Interactions

When Sulfisoxazole is taken with an anticoagulant (blood-
thinning) drug, any drug used to treat diabetes, or Methotrexate, it will cause unusually large amounts of these drugs
to be released into the bloodstream, producing symptoms of
overdosage. If you are going to take Sulfisoxazole for an
extended period, your physician should reduce the dosage
of these interactive drugs. Also avoid large doses of Vitamin C.

Usual Dose

Adult: first dose, 4 to 8 tablets; then 2 to 3 tablets 4 times
per day (not to exceed 12 tablets daily).

Child (over 50 pounds): liquid suspension (Lipo Gantrisin),

1 teaspoon 4 times per day; liquid syrup (Gantrisin Syrup), 2 teaspoons 4 times per day.

Overdosage

Induce vomiting and give a rectal enema; then take the patient to a hospital emergency room. ALWAYS bring the medicine bottle.

Special Information

Sulfisoxazole can cause photosensitivity—a severe reaction to strong sunlight. Avoid prolonged exposure to strong sunlight while you are taking it.

Sore throat, fever, unusual bleeding or bruising, rash, and feeling tired are early signs of serious blood disorders and should be reported to your doctor immediately.

Generic Name

Sulindac

Brand Name

Clinoril

Type of Drug

Nonsteroid anti-inflammatory.

Prescribed for

Arthritis, bursitis and other forms of inflammation of joints and muscles.

General Information

Sulindac is a relatively recent addition to the list of drugs effective against arthritis and joint pain. As with the other members of this group, patient response to Sulindac is individual. For some, this drug will work wonders; for others, it will do nothing. We do not know how Sulindac works.

Cautions and Warnings

Use Sulindac with extra caution if you have a history of

ulcers, bleeding diseases, or allergic reaction to Aspirin. Sulindac should be avoided by pregnant women, nursing mothers, children under age 14, and those who have nasal polyps. It is not a simple pain reliever; it should be used only under the strict supervision of your doctor.

Possible Side Effects

Upset stomach, nausea, vomiting, constipation, loss of appetite, gas, stomach cramps and pain, itching and rash, dizziness, headache, nervousness, buzzing or ringing in the ears, swelling of the feet, legs, hands, or arms.

Possible Adverse Drug Effects

Stomach bleeding, irritation, and ulcer, as well as abnormal liver function, jaundice, and hepatitis have been reported. Heart failure in patients with already weak hearts, palpitations, blurred vision, and allergic reactions have occurred.

Drug Interactions

May increase the effect of anticoagulant (blood-thinning) drugs. Probenecid (Benemid) may increase the amount of Sulindac in your blood by reducing its elimination from the body.

Usual Dose

Adult: up to 400 milligrams twice per day.

Overdosage

Patients taking an overdose of Sulindac must be made to vomit to remove any remaining drug from the stomach. Call your doctor or poison control center before doing this. If you must go to a hospital emergency room, ALWAYS bring the medicine bottle.

Special Information

If you are allergic to Aspirin, you may be allergic to Sulindac. Since this drug can irritate the stomach, take each dose with food. While taking Sulindac, avoid taking Aspirin or alcoholic beverages. Sulindac may cause blurred vision or dizziness. Take care while driving or performing any task requiring alertness.

Call your doctor if you develop rash, itching, hives, yellowing of the skin or whites of the eyes, black or tarry stools, swelling of hands or feet, sore throat, mouth sores, unusual bleeding or bruising, or shortness of breath.

Brand Name

Synalgos-DC

Ingredients

Aspirin
Caffeine
Dihydrocodeine Bitartrate
Phenacetin
Promethazine Hydrochloride

Type of Drug

Narcotic analgesic combination.

Prescribed for

Relief of mild to moderate pain.

General Information

Synalgos-DC is one of many combination products containing narcotics and analgesics. These products often also contain barbiturates or tranquilizers, and Acetaminophen may be substituted for Aspirin, or Phenacetin and/or Caffeine may be omitted.

Cautions and Warnings

Do not take Synalgos-DC if you know you are allergic or sensitive to it. Use this drug with extreme caution if you suffer from asthma or other breathing problems. Long-term use of Synalgos-DC may cause drug dependence or addiction. Synalgos-DC is a respiratory depressant and affects the central nervous system, producing sleepiness, tiredness, and/or inability to concentrate. If you are pregnant or suspect that you are pregnant do not take this drug.

Possible Side Effects

Most frequent: light-headedness, dizziness, sleepiness, nausea, vomiting, loss of appetite, sweating. If these effects occur, consider asking your doctor about lowering your dose. Usually the side effects disappear if you simply lie down.

More serious side effects of Synalgos-DC are shallow breathing or difficulty in breathing.

Possible Adverse Drug Effects

Euphoria (feeling high), weakness, sleepiness, headache, agitation, uncoordinated muscle movement, minor hallucinations, disorientation and visual disturbances, dry mouth, loss of appetite, constipation, flushing of the face, rapid heartbeat, palpitations, faintness, urinary difficulties or hesitancy, reduced sex drive and/or potency, itching, rashes, anemia, lowered blood sugar, yellowing of the skin and/or whites of the eyes. Narcotic analgesics may aggravate convulsions in those who have had convulsions in the past.

Drug Interactions

Interaction with alcohol, tranquilizers, barbiturates, or sleeping pills produces tiredness, sleepiness, or inability to concentrate and seriously increases the depressive effect of Synalgos-DC.

The Aspirin component of Synalgos-DC can affect anticoagulant (blood-thinning) therapy. Be sure to discuss this with your doctor so that the proper dosage adjustment can be made.

Interaction with adrenal cortical steroids, Phenylbutazone, or alcohol can cause severe stomach irritation with possible bleeding.

Usual Dose

2 capsules every 4 hours.

Overdosage

Symptoms are depression of respiration (breathing), extreme tiredness progressing to stupor and then coma, pinpointed pupils of the eyes, no response to stimulation such as a pin stick, cold and clammy skin, slowing down of heartbeat,

lowering of blood pressure, convulsions, and cardiac arrest.
The patient should be taken to a hospital emergency room
immediately. ALWAYS bring the medicine bottle.

Special Information

Drowsiness may occur: be careful when driving or operating
hazardous machinery.

Take with food or ½ glass of water to prevent stomach upset.

The Phenacetin ingredient of Synalgos-DC may be toxic to
your kidneys; do not take this medication for longer than 10
days unless so directed by your doctor.

Brand Name
Tedral

Ingredients
Ephedrine
Phenobarbital
Theophylline

Other Brand Names

Lardet	Theodrine
Phedral C.T.	Theofedral
Primatene "P" Formula	Theofenal
Respirol	Theophenyllin
T.E.P. Tablets	Theoral
T-E-P Compound	

Type of Drug
Antiasthmatic combination product.

Prescribed for
Relief of asthma symptoms or other upper respiratory
disorders.

General Information
Tedral is one of several antiasthmatic combination products
prescribed for the relief of asthmatic symptoms and other

breathing problems. These products contain drugs which help relax the bronchial muscles, drugs which increase the diameter of the breathing passages, and a mild tranquilizer to help relax the patient. Other products in this class may contain similar ingredients along with other medicine to help eliminate mucus from the breathing passages.

Cautions and Warnings

Take the drug with food to help prevent stomach upset.

This drug should not be taken if you have severe kidney or liver disease.

Possible Side Effects

Large doses of Tedral can produce excitation, shakiness, sleeplessness, nervousness, rapid heartbeat, chest pains, irregular heartbeat, dizziness, dryness of the nose and throat, headache, and sweating. Occasionally people have been known to develop hesitation or difficulty in urination.

Possible Adverse Drug Effects

Excessive urination, heart stimulation, drowsiness, muscle weakness, muscle twitching, unsteady walk. These effects can usually be controlled by having your doctor adjust the dose.

Drug Interactions

Tedral may cause sleeplessness and/or drowsiness. Do not take this drug with alcoholic beverages.

Taking Tedral or similar medicines with an MAO inhibitor can produce severe interaction. Consult your doctor first.

Tedral or similar products taken together with Lithium Carbonate will increase the excretion of lithium; they have neutralized the effect of Propranolol. Erythromycin and similar antibiotics cause the body to hold Theophylline, leading to possible side effects.

Usual Dose

1 to 2 tablets every 4 hours.

Sustained-action tablet: 1 tablet every 12 hours.

Expectorant or suspension: 1 teaspoon per 60 pounds of body weight every 4 hours.

Generic Name

Temazepam

Brand Name

Restoril

Type of Drug

Sedative-sleeping medicine.

Prescribed for

Insomnia or sleeplessness, frequent nighttime awakening, or waking up too early in the morning.

General Information

Temazepam is a member of the chemical group of drugs known as benzodiazepines. These drugs are used as antianxiety agents, anticonvulsants, or sedatives (sleeping pills). They exert their effects by relaxing the large skeletal muscles and by a direct effect on the brain. In doing so, they can relax you and make you either more tranquil or sleepier, depending on the drug and how much you use. Many doctors prefer Temazepam and the other members of this class to other drugs that can be used for the same effect. Their reason is that the benzodiazepines tend to be safer, have fewer side effects, and are usually as, if not more, effective.

These drugs are generally used in any situation where they can be a useful adjunct.

Benzodiazepine tranquilizing drugs can be abused if taken for long periods of time and it is possible to develop withdrawal symptoms if you discontinue the therapy abruptly. Withdrawal symptoms include convulsions, tremor, muscle cramps, stomach cramps, insomnia, agitation, diarrhea, vomiting, sweating, and convulsions.

Cautions and Warnings

Do not take Temazepam if you know you are sensitive or allergic to this drug or other benzodiazepines such as Chlordiazepoxide, Oxazepam, Chlorazepate, Diazepam, Lorazepam, Prazepam, and Clonazepam.

Temazepam and other members of this drug group may aggravate narrow angle glaucoma, but if you have open angle glaucoma you may take the drugs. In any case, check this information with your doctor. Temazepam can cause tiredness, drowsiness, inability to concentrate, and similar symptoms. Be careful if you are driving, operating machinery, or performing other activities which require concentration. Avoid taking this drug during the first 3 months of pregnancy except under strict supervision of your doctor.

Possible Side Effects

Most common: mild drowsiness during the first few days of therapy, especially in the elderly or debilitated. If drowsiness persists, contact your doctor.

Possible Adverse Drug Effects

Major adverse reactions: confusion, depression, lethargy, disorientation, headache, tiredness, slurred speech, stupor, dizziness, tremor, constipation, dry mouth, nausea, inability to control urination, changes in sex drive, irregular menstrual cycle, changes in heart rhythm, lowered blood pressure, retention of fluids, blurred or double vision, itching, rash, hiccups, nervousness, inability to fall asleep, (occasional) liver dysfunction. If you experience any of these reactions, stop taking the medicine and contact your doctor immediately.

Drug Interactions

Temazepam is a central nervous system depressant. Avoid alcohol, tranquilizers, narcotics, sleeping pills, barbiturates, MAO inhibitors, antihistamines, and other medicines used to relieve depression.

Usual Dose

15 to 30 milligrams at bedtime. Must be individualized for maximum benefit.

Overdosage

Symptoms are confusion, sleep or sleepiness, lack of response to pain such as a pin stick, shallow breathing, lowered blood pressure, and coma. The patient should be taken to a hospital emergency room immediately. ALWAYS bring the medicine bottle.

Generic Name

Terbutaline Sulfate

Brand Names

Brethine
Bricanyl

Type of Drug

Bronchodilator.

Prescribed for

Asthma and spasm of the bronchial muscles. This drug has been used experimentally to prevent or slow down premature labor in pregnant women.

General Information

This is one of the newer bronchodilator drugs in use in the United States. It has a more specific effect than some of the older drugs and so can cause a somewhat lower incidence of side effects on the heart. Often Terbutaline Sulfate is used with other drugs to produce a beneficial effect. The tablet takes effect 30 minutes after it has been taken and continues working for 4 to 8 hours.

Cautions and Warnings

This drug should be used with caution by patients who have angina, heart disease, high blood pressure, a history of stroke or seizures, diabetes, thyroid disease, prostate disease, or glaucoma. It should be used by women who are pregnant or breast-feeding only when absolutely necessary. The potential hazard to the unborn child or nursing infant is not known at this time.

Older patients, over age 60, are more likely to experience the adverse effects of this drug.

Possible Side Effects

Restlessness, anxiety, fear, tension, sleeplessness, tremors, convulsions, weakness, dizziness, headache, flushing, pallor, sweating, nausea and vomiting, loss of appetite, muscle cramps, urinary difficulties.

Possible Adverse Drug Effects

Terbutaline Sulfate can cause some side effects on the heart and cardiovascular system, including high blood pressure, abnormal heart rhythms, and angina. It is less likely to cause these effects than some of the older drugs.

Drug Interactions

The effect of this drug may be increased by antidepressant drugs, some antihistamines, and Levothyroxine. It may antagonize the effects of Reserpine or Guanethidine.

Usual Dose

Adult: 5 milligrams every 6 hours. No more than 15 milligrams per day.

Child (age 12 to 15): 2½ milligrams every 6 hours. No more than 7½ milligrams per day.

Child (under age 12): not recommended.

Overdosage

Symptoms include palpitation, abnormal heart rhythms, rapid heartbeat, slow heartbeat, chest pain, high blood pressure, fever, chills, cold sweat, blanching of the skin, nausea, vomiting, sleeplessness, delirium, tremor, pinpoint pupils, convulsions, coma, and collapse. If you or someone you know has taken an overdose of this drug call your doctor or bring the patient to a hospital emergency room. ALWAYS remember to bring the prescription bottle with you.

Special Information

Do not take more than the amount prescribed for you. If the drug causes upset stomach, take each dose with food.

Generic Name

Terpin Hydrate with Codeine

Brand Names

Cotussis Cough Syrup
Prunicodeine Liquid
SK-Terpin Hydrate & Codeine

Type of Drug

Cough suppressant.

Prescribed for

Relief of coughs due to colds or other respiratory infections.

General Information

Terpin Hydrate with Codeine may make you tired or drowsy. Avoid other drugs which may have the same effect, since they will increase the drowsiness.

Cautions and Warnings

Terpin Hydrate is supposed to decrease the production of mucus and other bronchial secretions which can cause cough, but the usual dose of Terpin Hydrate with Codeine does not contain enough Terpin Hydrate to achieve this effect in most patients. The cough suppressant effect of Terpin Hydrate with Codeine is primarily due to the Codeine.

Do not take Codeine if you know you are allergic or sensitive to this drug. Use this drug with extreme caution if you suffer from asthma or other breathing problems. Long-term use of Codeine may cause drug dependence or addiction. Codeine is a respiratory depressant and affects the central nervous system, producing sleepiness, tiredness, and/or inability to concentrate. Be careful if you are driving, operating machinery, or performing other functions requiring concentration. If you are pregnant or suspect that you are pregnant do not take this drug.

Possible Side Effects

Most frequent: light-headedness, dizziness, sedation or sleepiness, nausea, vomiting, sweating. Because Terpin Hydrate with Codeine liquid contains 42 percent alcohol (84 proof), it is an easily abused drug product.

Possible Adverse Drug Effects

Euphoria (feeling high), weakness, sleepiness, headache, agitation, uncoordinated muscle movement, minor hallucinations, disorientation and visual disturbances, dry mouth, loss of appetite, constipation, flushing of the face, rapid heartbeat, palpitations, faintness, urinary difficulties or hesitancy, reduced sex drive and/or potency, itching, rashes, anemia, lowered blood sugar, yellowing of the skin and/or whites of the eyes. Narcotic analgesics may aggravate convulsions in those who have had convulsions in the past.

Drug Interactions

Because of its depressant effect and potential effect on breathing, Codeine should be taken with extreme care in combination with alcohol, sedatives, tranquilizers, antihistamines, or other depressant drugs.

Usual Dose

1 to 2 teaspoons 3 or 4 times per day as needed for relief of cough.

Special Information

Try to cough up as much mucus as possible while taking this medication. This will help reduce the cough and help you get better more quickly.

Brand Name

Terrastatin

Ingredients

Nystatin
Oxytetracycline

Type of Drug

Broad-spectrum antibiotic effective against gram-positive and some gram-negative organisms.

Prescribed for

Bacterial infections such as gonorrhea, infections of the mouth, gums, and teeth, Rocky Mountain spotted fever and other fevers caused by ticks and lice from a variety of carriers, urinary tract infections, and respiratory system infections such as pneumonia and bronchitis.

These diseases may be produced by gram-positive or gram-negative organisms such as diplococci, staphylococci, streptococci, gonococci, *E. coli*, and *Shigella*.

Terrastatin has also been successfully used to treat some skin infections, but is not considered the first-choice antibiotic for the treatment of general skin infections or wounds.

General Information

Terrastatin works by interfering with the normal growth cycle of the invading bacteria, preventing them from reproducing and thus allowing the body's normal growth defenses to fight off the infection. This process is called bacteriostatic action. Terrastatin has been used along with other medicines to treat amoebic infections of the intestinal tract, known as amoebic dysentery. It is also prescribed for diseases caused by ticks, fleas, and lice.

Terrastatin has been successfully used in the treatment of adolescent acne, using small doses over a long period of time. Adverse effects or toxicity in this type of therapy are almost unheard-of.

Since the action of this antibiotic depends on its concentration within the invading bacteria, it is imperative that the patient completely follow the doctor's directions.

Cautions and Warnings

Do not use Terrastatin if you are pregnant. Terrastatin, when used in children, has been shown to interfere with the development of the long bones and may retard growth. Exceptions would be when Terrastatin is the only effective antibiotic available and all risk factors have been made known to the patient.

Terrastatin should not be given to people with known liver disease or to people with kidney or urine excretion problems. You should avoid taking high doses of Terrastatin or undergoing extended Terrastatin therapy if you will be exposed to sunlight for a long period, because this antibiotic can interfere with your body's normal sun-screening mechanism, possibly resulting in a severe sunburn. If you have a known history of allergy to Terrastatin, you should avoid taking this drug or other drugs within this category such as Aureomycin, Terramycin, Rondomycin, Vibramycin, Declomycin, and Minocin.

Possible Side Effects

Nystatin, when given by mouth, is not absorbed into the blood system. For this reason, there are few side effects associated with Nystatin in this combination.

As with other antibiotics, the common side effects of Terrastatin are stomach upset, nausea, vomiting, diarrhea, and rash. Less common side effects include hairy tongue and itching and irritation of the anal and/or vaginal region. If these symptoms appear, consult your physician immediately. Periodic physical examinations and laboratory tests should be given to patients who are receiving long-term Terrastatin treatment.

Possible Adverse Drug Effects

Loss of appetite, peeling of the skin, sensitivity to the sun, fever, chills, anemia, possible brown spotting of the skin, decrease in kidney function, damage to the liver.

Drug Interactions

Terrastatin (a bacteriostatic drug) may interfere with the action of bactericidal agents such as Penicillin. It is not advisable to take both together.

The antibacterial effect of Terrastatin is neutralized if with taken with food, some dairy products (such as milk and cheese), or antacids.

Don't take multivitamin products containing minerals at the same time as Terrastatin, or you will reduce the antibiotic's effectiveness. Space the taking of the two medicines at least 2 hours apart.

If you are receiving anticoagulants (blood-thinning agents), consult your doctor, since Terrastatin will interfere with this form of therapy. An adjustment in the anticoagulant dosage may be required.

Usual Dose

Adult: 250 to 500 milligrams 4 times per day.

Child (age 9 and over): 10 to 20 milligrams per pound of body weight per day in divided doses taken 1 hour before or 2 hours after meals.

Child (up to age 8): not recommended, since Terrastatin has been shown to produce serious discoloration of the permanent teeth.

Special Information

Like other Tetracyclines, this drug is always dated. Do not take outdated Terrastatin under any circumstances. Its decomposition produces a highly toxic substance which can cause serious kidney damage. The only difference between Terrastatin and Tetracycline is that Terrastatin contains a small amount of Nystatin to prevent the growth of fungal organisms in the intestine. Since the Nystatin in Terrastatin is often ineffective in reducing the incidence of fungal infections, you may be better off taking plain Tetracycline. Discuss it with your doctor.

Generic Name

Tetracycline

Brand Names

Achromycin	SK-Tetracycline
Achromycin V	Sumycin
Bristacycline	Tetra-Bid
Centet-250	Tetra-C
Cycline-250	Tetracap
Cyclopar 500	Tetrachel
Deltamycin	Tetra-Co
M-Tetra 250	Tetracyn
Nor-Tet	Tetralan-250
Paltet	Tetram
Panmycin	Tetrex bidCAPS
Partrex	Tet-250
Retet	T-250
Robitet	

Type of Drug

Broad-spectrum antibiotic effective against gram-positive and gram-negative organisms.

Prescribed for

Bacterial infections such as gonorrhea, infections of the mouth, gums, teeth, Rocky Mountain spotted fever and other fevers caused by ticks and lice from a variety of carriers, urinary tract infections, and respiratory system infections such as pneumonia and bronchitis.

These diseases are produced by gram-positive and gram-negative organisms such as diplococci, staphylococci, streptococci, gonococci, *E. coli*, and *Shigella*.

Tetracycline has also been successfully used to treat some skin infections, but it is not considered the first-choice antibiotic for the treatment of general skin infections or wounds.

General Information

Tetracycline works by interfering with the normal growth cycle of the invading bacteria, preventing them from reproducing and thus allowing the body's normal defenses to fight off the infection. This process is referred to as bacteriostatic action. Tetracycline has also been used along with other medicines to treat amoebic infections of the intestinal tract, known as amoebic dysentery. It is also prescribed for diseases caused by ticks, fleas, and lice.

Tetracycline has been successfully used for the treatment of adolescent acne, in small doses over a long period of time. Adverse effects or toxicity in this type of therapy are almost unheard of.

Since the action of this antibiotic depends on its concentration within the invading bacteria, it is imperative that you completely follow the doctor's directions. Another form of tetracycline is Oxytetracycline (Terramycin) which is given in the same dose and has the same effects as Tetracycline.

Cautions and Warnings

You should not use Tetracycline if you are pregnant. Tetracycline when used in children has been shown to interfere with the development of the long bones and may retard growth.

Exceptions would be when Tetracycline is the only effective antibiotic available and all risk factors have been made known to the patient.

Tetracycline should not be given to people with known liver disease or kidney or urine excretion problems. You should avoid taking high doses of Tetracycline or undergoing extended Tetracycline therapy if you will be exposed to sunlight for a long period because this antibiotic can interfere with your body's normal sun-screening mechanism, possibly causing a severe sunburn. If you have a known history of allergy to Tetracycline you should avoid taking this drug or other drugs within this category such as Aureomycin, Terramycin, Rondomycin, Vibramycin, Demeclocycline, and Minocycline.

Possible Side Effects

As with other antibiotics, the common side effects of Tetracycline are stomach upset, nausea, vomiting, diarrhea, and rash. Less common side effects include hairy tongue and itching and irritation of the anal and/or vaginal region. If these symptoms appear, consult your physician immediately. Periodic physical examinations and laboratory tests should be given to patients who are on long-term Tetracycline.

Possible Adverse Drug Effects

Loss of appetite, peeling of the skin, sensitivity to the sun, fever, chills, anemia, possible brown spotting of the skin, decrease in kidney function, damage to the liver.

Drug Interactions

Tetracycline (a bacteriostatic drug) may interfere with the action of bactericidal agents such as Penicillin. It is not advisable to take both during the same course of therapy.

The antibacterial effect of Tetracycline is neutralized when taken with food, some dairy products (such as milk and cheese), or antacids.

Don't take multivitamin products containing minerals at the same time as Tetracycline, or you may reduce the antibiotic's effectiveness. Space the taking of these two medicines at least 2 hours apart.

People receiving anticoagulation therapy (blood-thinning agents) should consult their doctor, since Tetracycline will interfere with this form of therapy. An adjustment in the anticoagulant dosage may be required.

Usual Dose

Adult: 250-500 milligrams 4 times per day.
Child (age 9 and over): 50 to 100 milligrams 4 times per day.

Child (up to age 8): should avoid Tetracycline, as it has been shown to produce serious discoloration of the permanent teeth.

Take on an empty stomach 1 hour before or 2 hours after meals.

Storage

Tetracyline can be stored at room temperature.

Special Information

Do not take after the expiration date on the label. The decomposition of Tetracycline produces a highly toxic substance which can cause serious kidney damage.

Generic Name

Theophylline

Brand Names

Accurbron	Slo-Phyllin Gyrocaps
Aerolate	Somophyllin-T
Aquaphyllin	Sustaire
Asmalix	Theobid
Bronkodyl	Theocap
Elixicon	Theoclear
Elixophyllin	Theo-dur
Elixophyllin SR	Theolair
LāBid	Theolixir
Lanophyllin	Theon
Liquophylline	Theophyl
Norophylline	Theophyl-SR
Oralphyllin	Theospan SR
Physpan	Theostat
Slo-Phyllin	Theovent

Other Theophylline Products:
Aminophylline (86% Theophylline)
Aminodur Dura-Tabs (86% Theophylline)

Type of Drug

Xanthine bronchodilator.

Prescribed for

Relief of bronchial asthma and spasms of bronchial muscles associated with emphysema, bronchitis, and other diseases.

General Information

Theophylline is one of several drugs known as xanthine derivatives which are the mainstay of therapy for bronchial asthma and similar diseases. Other members of this group are Aminophylline, Dyphylline, and Oxtriphylline. Although the dosage for each of these drugs is different, they all work by relaxing bronchial muscles and helping reverse spasms in these muscles.

Cautions and Warnings

Do not use this drug if you are allergic or sensitive to it or to any related drug, such as Aminophylline. If you have a stomach ulcer or heart disease, you should use this drug with caution. If you are pregnant or think that you may be pregnant you should carefully discuss the use of this drug with your doctor, since Theophylline may induce an adverse effect in the unborn child.

Possible Side Effects

Possible side effects from Theophylline or other xanthine derivatives are nausea, vomiting, stomach pain, diarrhea, irritability, restlessness, difficulty sleeping, excitability, muscle twitching or spasms, heart palpitations, other unusual heart rates, low blood pressure, rapid breathing, and local irritation (particularly if a suppository is used).

Possible Adverse Drug Effects

Infrequent: vomiting blood, fever, headache, dehydration.

Drug Interactions

Taking Theophylline at the same time as another xanthine derivative may increase side effects. Don't do it except under the direct care of a doctor.

Theophylline is often given in combination with a stimulant drug such as Ephedrine. Such combinations can cause excessive stimulation and should be used only as specifically directed by your doctor.

Reports have indicated that combining Erythromycin, Cimetidine, and Theophylline will give you higher blood levels of Theophylline. Remember that higher blood levels mean the possibility of more side effects.

Usual Dose

Adult: 100 to 200 milligrams every 6 hours.

Child: 50 to 100 milligrams every 6 hours. On the basis of body weight, 1 to 2½ milligrams per pound every 6 hours.

The best dose of Theophylline is tailored to your needs and the severity of your disease: it is the lowest dose that will produce maximum control of your symptoms.

Overdosage

The first symptoms are loss of appetite, nausea, vomiting, difficulty sleeping, and restlessness, followed by unusual behavior patterns, frequent vomiting, and extreme thirst, with delirium, convulsions, very high temperature, and collapse. These serious toxic symptoms are rarely experienced after overdose by mouth, which produces loss of appetite, nausea, vomiting, and stimulation. The overdosed patient should be taken to a hospital emergency room where proper treatment can be given.

Special Information

Take on an empty stomach, at least 1 hour before or 2 hours after meals; but occasional mild stomach upset can be minimized by taking the dose with some food (note if you do this a reduced amount of drug will be absorbed into your bloodstream).

Generic Name

Thioguanine

Brand Name

Tabloid Brand Thioguanine

Type of Drug

Antimetabolite, antineoplastic.

Prescribed for

Treatment of leukemia.

General Information

Thioguanine is a member of the antimetabolite group of drugs used to treat neoplastic diseases. These drugs work by interfering with the metabolism of the cancerous cells. In doing so, they disrupt the cell division cycle of the disease and slow its progress.

Cautions and Warnings

Blood counts should be taken once a week while on Thioguanine to avoid excessive lowering of white-cell counts. It should be used with extreme care by pregnant women (and then only after the first 3 months of pregnancy) and patients with kidney or liver disease.

Possible Side Effects

Nausea, vomiting, loss of appetite, stomach irritation or pains.

Usual Dose

1 to 1½ milligrams per pound of body weight per day given in a single dose; adjusted to patient's response.

Overdosage

Overdosage with Thioguanine leads to an excessive drop in white-blood-cell counts. In case of overdosage, bring the patient to a hospital emergency room immediately. ALWAYS bring the medicine bottle.

Special Information

Because of the nature of the disease treated with this drug, it is absolutely essential that you remain in close contact with the doctor providing your treatment, to obtain maximum benefit with minimum side effect.

Generic Name

Thioridazine Hydrochloride

Brand Name

Mellaril

Type of Drug

Phenothiazine antipsychotic.

Prescribed for

Psychotic disorders, moderate to severe depression with anxiety, control of agitation or aggressiveness of disturbed children, alcohol withdrawal symptoms, intractable pain, and senility.

General Information

Thioridazine Hydrochloride and other members of the phenothiazine group act on a portion of the brain called the hypothalamus. They affect parts of the hypothalamus that control metabolism, body temperature, alertness, muscle tone, hormone balance, and vomiting, and may be used to treat problems related to any of these functions.

Cautions and Warnings

Thioridazine Hydrochloride should not be taken if you are allergic to one of the drugs in the broad classification known as phenothiazine drugs. Do not take Thioridazine Hydrochloride if you have any blood, liver, kidney, or heart disease, very low blood pressure, or Parkinson's disease. This medication is a tranquilizer and can have a depressive effect, especially during the first few days of therapy. Care should be taken when performing activities requiring a high degree of concentration, such as driving. If you are taking this medication and become pregnant contact your doctor immediately.

This drug should be used with caution and under strict supervision of your doctor if you have glaucoma, epilepsy, ulcers, or difficulty passing urine.

Avoid insecticides and extreme exposure to heat.

Possible Side Effects

Most common: drowsiness, especially during the first or second week of therapy. If the drowsiness becomes troublesome, contact your doctor.

Possible Adverse Drug Effects

Thioridazine Hydrochloride can cause jaundice (yellowing of the whites of the eyes or skin), usually in 2 to 4 weeks. The jaundice usually goes away when the drug is discontinued, but there have been cases when it did not. If you notice this effect or if you develop symptoms such as fever and generally not feeling well, contact your doctor immediately. Less frequent: changes in components of the blood including anemias, raised or lowered blood pressure, abnormal heart rates, heart attack, feeling faint or dizzy.

Phenothiazines can produce "extrapyramidal effects," such as spasm of the neck muscles, rolling back of the eyes, convulsions, difficulty in swallowing, and symptoms associated with Parkinson's disease. These effects look very serious but disappear after the drug has been withdrawn; however, symptoms of the face, tongue, and jaw may persist for as long as several years, especially in the elderly with a history of brain damage. If you experience extrapyramidal effects contact your doctor immediately.

Thioridazine Hydrochloride may cause an unusual increase in psychotic symptoms or may cause paranoid reactions, tiredness, lethargy, restlessness, hyperactivity, confusion at night, bizarre dreams, inability to sleep, depression, and euphoria. Other reactions are itching, swelling, unusual sensitivity to bright lights, red skin, and rash. There have been cases of breast enlargement, false positive pregnancy tests, changes in menstrual flow in females, and impotence and changes in sex drive in males, as well as stuffy nose, headache, nausea, vomiting, loss of appetite, change in body temperature, loss of facial color, excessive salivation, excessive perspiration, constipation, diarrhea, changes in urine and stool habits, worsening of glaucoma, blurred vision, weakening of eyelid muscles, spasms in bronchial and other muscles, increased appetite, fatigue, excessive thirst, and changes in the coloration of skin, particularly in exposed areas.

Drug Interactions

Thioridazine Hydrochloride should be taken with caution in combination with barbiturates, sleeping pills, narcotics, other tranquilizers, or any other medication which may produce a depressive effect. Avoid alcohol.

Usual Dose

Adult: for treatment of psychosis, 50 to 100 milligrams per day at first, then 50 to 800 milligrams per day as required to control symptoms effectively without overly sedating the patient.

Child: 0.5 to 1.5 milligrams per pound of body weight per day.

This drug may turn the color of your urine pink or reddish brown.

Overdosage

Symptoms are depression, extreme weakness, tiredness, desire to go to sleep, coma, lowered blood pressure, uncontrolled muscle spasms, agitation, restlessness, convulsions, fever, dry mouth, and abnormal heart rhythms. The patient should be taken to a hospital emergency room immediately. ALWAYS bring the medicine bottle.

Generic Name

Thiothixene

Brand Name

Navane

Type of Drug

Thioxanthene antipsychotic.

Prescribed for

Psychotic disorders.

General Information

Thiothixene is one of many nonphenothiazine agents used

in the treatment of psychosis. The drugs in this group are usually about equally effective when given in therapeutically equivalent doses. The major differences are in type and severity of side effects. Some patients may respond well to one and not at all to another: this variability is not easily explained and is thought to relate to inborn biochemical differences.

Cautions and Warnings

Thiothixene should not be used by patients who are allergic to it. Patients with blood, liver, kidney or heart disease, very low blood pressure, or Parkinson's disease should avoid this drug.

Possible Side Effects

Most common: drowsiness, especially during the first or second week of therapy. If the drowsiness becomes troublesome, contact your doctor.

Possible Adverse Drug Effects

Thiothixene can cause jaundice (yellowing of the whites of the eyes or skin), usually in 2 to 4 weeks. The jaundice usually goes away when the drug is discontinued, but there have been cases when it did not. If you notice this effect or if you develop symptoms such as fever and generally do not feel well, contact your doctor immediately. Less frequent: changes in components of the blood including anemias, raised or lowered blood pressure, abnormal heartbeat, heart attack, feeling faint or dizzy.

Thioxanthene drugs can produce "extrapyramidal effects," such as spasms of the neck muscles, severe stiffness of the back muscles, rolling back of the eyes, convulsions, difficulty in swallowing, and symptoms associated with Parkinson's disease. These effects look very serious but disappear after the drug has been withdrawn; however, symptoms of the face, tongue, and jaw may persist for several years, especially in the elderly with a long history of brain damage. If you experience extrapyramidal effects contact your doctor immediately.

Thiothixene may cause an unusual increase in psychotic symptoms or may cause paranoid reactions, tiredness, lethargy, restlessness, hyperactivity, confusion at night, bizarre dreams, inability to sleep, depression, or euphoria. Other reactions are itching, swelling, unusual sensitivity to bright lights, red skin, and rash. There have been cases of breast enlargement, false positive pregnancy tests, changes in menstrual flow in females, and impotence and changes in sex drive in males.

Thiothixene may also cause dry mouth, stuffy nose, headache, nausea, vomiting, loss of appetite, change in body temperature, loss of facial color, excessive salivation, excessive perspiration, constipation, diarrhea, changes in urine and stool habits, worsening of glaucoma, blurred vision, weakening of eyelid muscles, and spasms in bronchial and other muscles, as well as increased appetite, fatigue, excessive thirst, and changes in the coloration of skin, particularly in exposed areas.

Drug Interactions

Thiothixene should be taken with caution in combination with barbiturates, sleeping pills, narcotics, other tranquilizers, or any other medication which produces a depressive effect. Avoid alcohol.

Usual Dose

Adult and child (age 12 and over): 2 milligrams 3 times per day, to start. Dose is increased according to patient's need and may go to 60 milligrams per day.

Child (under age 12): not recommended.

Overdosage

Symptoms are depression, extreme weakness, tiredness, desire to go to sleep, coma, lowered blood pressure, uncontrolled muscle spasms, agitation, restlessness, convulsions, fever, dry mouth, and abnormal heart rhythms. The patient should be taken to a hospital emergency room immediately. ALWAYS bring the medicine bottle.

Generic Name

Thyroglobulin

Brand Name

Proloid

Type of Drug

Thyroid replacement.

Prescribed for

Replacement of thyroid hormone or low output of hormone from the thyroid gland.

General Information

Thyroglobulin is used to replace the normal output of the thyroid gland when it is unusually low. The drug is obtained from purified extract of frozen hog thyroid and is chemically standardized according to its iodine content. Thyroglobulin, or other forms of thyroid therapy, may be used for short periods in some people or for long periods in others. Some people take a thyroid replacement drug for their entire lives. It is important for your doctor to check periodically that you are receiving the correct dose. Occasionally a person's need for thyroid replacement changes, in which case, the dose should also be changed: your doctor can do this only by checking certain blood tests.

   Thyroglobulin is one of several thyroid replacement products available. The major difference between these products is in effectiveness in treating certain phases of thyroid disease.

Cautions and Warnings

If you have hyperthyroid disease or high output of thyroid hormone you should not use Thyroglobulin. Symptoms of hyperthyroid disease include headache, nervousness, sweating, rapid heartbeat, chest pains, and other signs of central nervous system stimulation. If you have heart disease or high blood pressure, thyroid replacement therapy should not be used unless it is clearly indicated and supervised by your doctor. If you develop chest pains or other signs of heart disease while you are taking thyroid medication, contact your doctor immediately.

Possible Side Effects

Most common: palpitations of the heart, rapid heartbeat, abnormal heart rhythms, weight loss, chest pains, menstrual irregularity, shaking hands, headache, diarrhea, nervousness, inability to sleep, heat discomfort, and sweating. These symptoms may be controlled by adjusting the dose of the medication. If you are suffering from one or more side effects, you must contact your physician immediately so that the proper dose adjustment can be made.

Drug Interactions

Interaction of Thyroglobulin with Cholestyramine (Questran) can be avoided by spacing the two doses at least 4 hours apart.

Avoid over-the-counter products containing stimulant drugs, such as many drugs used to treat coughs, colds, or allergies, which will affect your heart and may cause symptoms of overdosage.

Thyroid replacement therapy may increase the effect of anticoagulant (blood-thinning) drugs such as Warfarin or Bishydroxycoumarin. Be sure you report this to your physician as it will be necessary to reduce the dose of your anticoagulant drug by approximately one-third at the beginning of thyroid therapy (to avoid hemorrhage). Further adjustments may be made later, after your doctor reviews your blood tests.

Diabetics may have to increase their dose of Insulin or oral antidiabetic drugs. Changes in dose must be made by a physician.

Usual Dose

Initial dose, 16 milligrams (¼ grain) per day, then increase at intervals of 1 to 2 weeks until response is satisfactory. Maintenance dose, 32 to 190 milligrams per day or even higher.

Overdosage

Symptoms are headache, irritability, nervousness, sweating, rapid heartbeat with unusual stomach rumbling and with or without cramps, chest pains, heart failure, and shock. The patient should be taken to a hospital emergency room immediately. ALWAYS bring the medicine bottle.

Generic Name

Thyroid Hormone

Brand Names

Armour Thyroid	Thyrocrine
S-P-T	Thyro-Teric
Thermoloid	Tuloidin
Thyrar	

Type of Drug

Thyroid replacement.

Prescribed for

Replacement of thyroid hormone or low output of hormone from the thyroid gland.

General Information

Thyroid Hormone is one of several thyroid replacement products available. The major difference between them is in effectiveness in treating certain phases of thyroid disease.

Other drugs, such as Methimazole (Tapazole) and Propylthiouracil (PTU) are given to people whose thyroid gland is *Overactive*. Their effect on the thyroid gland is exactly the opposite of Thyroid Hormones. Check with your doctor if you are uncertain about why you have been given drugs which affect the thyroid gland.

Cautions and Warnings

If you have hyperthyroid disease or high output of thyroid hormone you should not use Thyroid Hormone. Symptoms of hyperthyroid disease include headache, nervousness, sweating, rapid heartbeat, chest pains, and other signs of central nervous system stimulation. If you have heart disease or high blood pressure, thyroid therapy should not be used unless it is clearly indicated and supervised by your physician. If you develop chest pains or other signs of heart disease while you are taking thyroid medication, contact your doctor immediately.

Possible Side Effects

Most common: palpitations of the heart, rapid heartbeat,

abnormal heart rhythms, weight loss, chest pains, shaking hands, headache, diarrhea, nervousness, menstrual irregularity, inability to sleep, sweating, inability to stand heat. These symptoms may be controlled by adjusting the dose of the medication. If you are suffering from one or more side effects, you must contact your doctor immediately so that the proper dose adjustment can be made.

Drug Interactions

Interaction of Thyroid Hormone with Cholestyramine (Questran) can be avoided by spacing the two doses at least 4 hours apart.

Avoid over-the-counter products containing stimulant drugs, such as many drugs used to treat coughs, colds, or allergies, which will affect your heart and may cause symptoms of overdosage.

Thyroid replacement therapy may increase the affect of anticoagulant (blood-thinning) drugs such as Warfarin or Bishydroxycoumarin. Be sure you report this to your physician as it will be necessary to reduce the dose of your anticoagulant drug by approximately one-third at the beginning of thyroid therapy (to avoid hemorrhage). Further adjustments may be made later, after your doctor reviews your blood tests.

Diabetics may have to increase their dose of Insulin or oral antidiabetic drugs. Changes in dose must be made by a doctor.

Usual Dose

The dose is tailored to the individual.

Adult: Initial dose, 15 to 30 milligrams per day, depending on severity of disease; then increase gradually to 180 milligrams per day.

Child: Initial dose, same as adult; but children may require greater maintenance doses because they are growing.

Take in 1 dose before breakfast.

Overdosage

Symptoms are headache, irritability, nervousness, sweating, rapid heartbeat with unusual stomach rumbling and with or without cramps, chest pains, heart failure, and shock. The patient should be taken to a hospital emergency room immediately. ALWAYS bring the medicine bottle.

Generic Name

Timolol

Brand Name

Timoptic Eye Drops
Blocadren Tablets

Type of Drug

Beta-adrenergic blocking agent.

Prescribed for

High blood pressure; reducing the possibility of a second
heart attack. Open angle glaucoma, increased fluid pressure
inside the eye.

General Information

When applied directly to the eye, Timolol reduces fluid pressure inside the eye by reducing the production of eye fluids
and increasing slightly the rate at which eye fluids leave the
eye. Studies have shown Timolol to produce a greater reduction in eye fluid pressure than either Pilocarpine or Epinephrine eyedrops. Women who are pregnant or breast-feeding
should not use this drug unless it is absolutely necessary.
Timolol eyedrops should not be used by people who cannot
take oral beta-blocking drugs, such as Propranolol.

Recent studies have shown Timolol to be very effective,
when taken in doses of 10 to 45 milligrams per day, in
treating a special type of heart pain called angina. It has also
been used, in doses of 60 milligrams per day, to treat high
blood pressure.

The most famous Timolol study was published in April
1981 in the prestigious *New England Journal of Medicine*.
This study showed that people who had a heart attack and
took 20 milligrams of Timolol per day by mouth had fewer
additional heart attacks and fewer additional heart problems,
and survived longer. The death rate in non-Timolol patients
was 1.6 times that in the Timolol group. The American manufacturer of this drug (Merck, Sharpe and Dohme) sells the
oral form of Timolol under the name Blocadren. Other beta-

adrenergic blockers currently available may also have this effect on heart attack patients.

Cautions and Warnings

Timolol should be used with care if you have a history of asthma or upper respiratory disease, seasonal allergy, which may become worsened by the effects of this drug. Do not use Timolol if you are allergic to it.

Possible Side Effects

Timolol may decrease the heart rate, aggravate or worsen a condition of congestive heart failure, and may produce lowered blood pressure, tingling in the extremities, light-headedness, mental depression, inability to sleep, weakness, and tiredness. It can also produce visual disturbances, hallucinations, disorientation, and loss of short-term memory. People taking Timolol may experience nausea, vomiting, upset stomach, abdominal cramps and diarrhea, or constipation. If you are allergic to Timolol, you may show typical reactions associated with drug allergies including sore throat, fever, difficulty breathing, and various effects on the blood system. Timolol Maleate may induce spasm of muscles in the bronchi, which will aggravate any existing asthma or respiratory disease.

Possible Adverse Drug Effects

Occasionally, people taking Timolol may experience emotional instability, become detached, or show unusual personality change. Timolol may cause adverse effects on the blood system.

Drug Interactions

Timolol will interact with any psychotropic drug, including the MAO inhibitors, which stimulates one of the segments of the central nervous system. Since this information is not often available to doctors, you should discuss this potential problem with your doctor if you are taking any psychotropic or psychiatric drug.

   Timolol may cause increased effectiveness of Insulin or oral antidiabetic drugs. If you are diabetic, discuss the situation with your doctor. A reduction in dosage of your antidiabetic drug may be required.

Timolol may reduce the effectiveness of Digitalis on your heart. Any dose of Digitalis will have to be altered if you are taking Timolol. If you are taking Digitalis for a purpose other than heart failure, the effectiveness of the Digitalis may be increased by Timolol, and the dose of Digitalis reduced.

Timolol may interact with other drugs to cause lowering of blood pressure. This interaction often has positive effects in the treatment of patients with high blood pressure.

Do not self-medicate with over-the-counter drugs for colds, coughs, or allergy which may contain stimulants that will aggravate certain types of heart disease and high blood pressure, or other ingredients that may antagonize the effects of Timolol. Check with your doctor or pharmacist before taking any over-the-counter medication.

Usual Dose

Eyedrops: One drop twice a day.
Tablets: 20 to 60 milligrams per day.

Overdosage

Symptoms are slowed heart rate, heart failure, lowered blood pressure, and spasms of the bronchial muscles which make it difficult to breathe. The patient should be taken to a hospital emergency room where proper therapy can be given. ALWAYS bring the medicine bottle with you.

Special Information

Take Timolol before meals for maximum effect. There have been reports of serious effects when Timolol is stopped abruptly. The dose should be lowered gradually over a period of two weeks.

If you are using Timolol eyedrops, press your finger lightly just below the eye for one minute following the instillation of the eyedrop.

Generic Name

Tolazamide

Brand Name

Tolinase

Type of Drug

Oral antidiabetic.

Prescribed for

Diabetes mellitus (sugar in the urine).

General Information

Tolazamide is one of several oral antidiabetic drugs that work by stimulating the production and release of insulin from the pancreas. The primary difference between these drugs lies in their duration of action. Because these drugs do not lower blood sugar directly, they require some function of pancreas cells.

Cautions and Warnings

Mild stress such as infection, minor surgery, or emotional upset reduces the effectiveness of Tolazamide. Remember that while you are taking this drug you should be under your doctor's continuous care.

Tolazamide is an aide to, not a substitute for, a diet. Diet remains of primary importance in the treatment of your diabetes. Follow the diet plan your doctor has prescribed for you.

Tolazamide and similar drugs are not oral Insulin, nor are they a substitute for Insulin. They do not lower blood sugar by themselves.

The treatment of diabetes is your responsibility. You should follow all instructions about diet, body weight, exercise, personal hygiene, and all measures to avoid infection. If you are not feeling well, or if you have symptoms such as itching, rash, yellowing of the skin or eyes, abnormally light-colored stools, a low-grade fever, sore throat, or diarrhea—contact your doctor immediately.

This drug should not be used if you have serious liver, kidney, or endocrine disease.

The safety of this drug during pregnancy has not been established.

Possible Side Effects

Common: loss of appetite, nausea, vomiting, stomach upset. At times you may experience weakness or tingling in the hands and feet. These effects can be eliminated by reducing the daily dose of Tolazamide or, if necessary, by switching to a different oral antidiabetic drug. This decision must be made by your doctor.

Possible Adverse Drug Effects

Tolazamide may produce abnormally low levels of blood sugar when too much is taken for your immediate requirements. (Other factors which may cause lowering of blood sugar are liver or kidney disease, malnutrition, age, drinking alcohol, and diseases of the glands.)

Tolazamide may cause a yellowing of the whites of the eyes or skin, itching, rash, or changes in the results of laboratory tests made by your doctor. Usually these reactions will disappear in time. If they persist, you should contact your doctor.

Drug Interactions

Thiazide diuretics may call for a higher dose of Tolazamide, while Insulin, sulfa drugs, Oxyphenbutazone, Phenylbutazone, Aspirin and other salicylates, Probenecid, Dicoumarol, Bis-hydroxycoumarin, Warfarin, Phenyramidol, and MAO inhibitor drugs prolong and enhance the action of Tolazamide, possibly requiring dose reduction.

Interaction with alcoholic beverages will cause flushing of the face and body, throbbing pain in the head and neck, difficult breathing, nausea, vomiting, sweating, thirst, chest pains, palpitations, lowered blood pressure, weakness, dizziness, blurred vision, and confusion. If you experience these reactions, contact your doctor immediately.

Because of the stimulant ingredients in many over-the-counter drug products for the relief of coughs, colds, and allergies, avoid them unless your doctor advises otherwise.

Usual Dose

Moderate diabetes, 100 to 250 milligrams daily. Severe diabetes, 500 to 100 milligrams daily.

Overdosage

A mild overdose of Tolazamide lowers the blood sugar, which can be treated by consuming sugar in such forms as candy and orange juice. A patient with a more serious overdose should be taken to a hospital emergency room immediately. ALWAYS bring the medicine bottle.

Generic Name

Tolbutamide

Brand Name

Orinase

Type of Drug

Oral antidiabetic.

Prescribed for

Diabetes mellitus (sugar in the urine).

General Information

Tolbutamide is one of several oral antidiabetic drugs that work by stimulating the production and release of insulin from the pancreas. The primary difference between these drugs lies in their duration of action. Because they do not lower blood sugar directly, they require some function of pancreas cells.

Cautions and Warnings

Mild stress such as infection, minor surgery, or emotional upset reduces the effectiveness of Tolbutamide. Remember that while taking this drug you should be under your doctor's continuous care.

Tolbutamide is an aide to, not a substitute for, a diet. Diet remains of primary importance in the treatment of your diabetes. Follow the diet plan your doctor has prescribed for you.

Tolbutamide and similar drugs are not oral Insulin, nor are they a substitute for Insulin. They do not lower blood sugar by themselves.

The treatment of diabetes is your responsibility. You should follow all instructions about diet, body weight, exercise, personal hygiene, and all measures to avoid infection. If you are not feeling well, or if you have symptoms such as itching, rash, yellowing of the skin or eyes, abnormally light-colored stools, a low-grade fever, sore throat, or diarrhea—contact your doctor immediately.

This drug should be used with caution and under strict supervision of your doctor if you have glaucoma, epilepsy, ulcers, or difficulty passing urine. Avoid insecticides and extreme exposure to heat.

Possible Side Effects

Common: loss of appetite, nausea, vomiting, stomach upset. At times you may experience weakness or tingling in the hands and feet. These effects can be eliminated by reducing the daily dose of Tolbutamide or, if necessary, by switching to a different oral antidiabetic drug. This decision must be made by your doctor.

Possible Adverse Drug Effects

Tolbutamide may produce abnormally low levels of blood sugar when too much is taken for your immediate requirements. (Other factors which may cause lowering of blood sugar are liver or kidney disease, malnutrition, age, drinking alcohol, and diseases of the glands.)

Tolbutamide may cause a yellowing of the whites of the eyes or skin, itching, rash, or changes in the results of laboratory tests made by your doctor. Usually these reactions will disappear in time. If they persist you should contact your doctor.

Drug Interactions

Thiazide diuretics may call for a higher dose of Tolbutamide, while Insulin, sulfa drugs, Oxyphenbutazone, Phenylbutazone, Aspirin and other salicylates, Probenecid, Dicoumarol, Bishydroxycoumarin, Warfarin, Phenyramidol, and MAO inhibitor drugs prolong and enhance the action of Tolbutamide, possibly requiring dose reduction.

Interaction with alcoholic beverages will cause flushing of the face and body, throbbing pain in the head and neck, difficult breathing, nausea, vomiting, sweating, thirst, chest pains, palpitations, lowered blood pressure, weakness, dizziness, blurred vision, and confusion. If you experience these reactions contact your doctor immediately.

Because of the stimulant ingredients in many over-the-counter drug products for the relief of coughs, colds, and allergies, avoid them unless your doctor advises otherwise.

Usual Dose

Begin with 1 to 2 grams per day; then increase or decrease according to patient's response. Maintenance dose, 250 milligrams to 2 (or, rarely, 3) grams per day.

Overdosage

A mild overdose of Tolbutamide lowers the blood sugar, which can be treated by consuming sugar in such forms as candy and orange juice. A patient with a more serious overdose should be taken to a hospital emergency room immediately. ALWAYS bring the medicine bottle.

Generic Name

Tolmetin Sodium

Brand Name

Tolectin

Type of Drug

Nonsteroid anti-inflammatory.

Prescribed for

Relief of pain and inflammation of joints and muscles; arthritis.

General Information

Tolmetin Sodium is one of several new drugs used to treat various types of arthritis. These drugs reduce inflammation and share side effects, the most common of which is possible formation of ulcers and upset stomach. The drugs are roughly comparable to Aspirin in controlling the symptoms of arthritis, and are used by some people who cannot tolerate Aspirin.

Cautions and Warnings

Do not take Tolmetin Sodium if you are allergic or sensitive to this drug, Aspirin, or other nonsteroid anti-inflammatory drugs. Tolmetin Sodium may cause stomach ulcers.

Possible Side Effects

Stomach upset, blurred vision, darkening of stool, changes in color vision, rash, weight gain, retention of fluids.

Possible Adverse Drug Effects

Most frequent: stomach upset, dizziness, headache, drowsiness, ringing in the ears. Others: heartburn, nausea, vomiting, bloating, gas in the stomach, stomach pain, diarrhea, constipation, dark stool, nervousness, insomnia, depression, confusion, tremor, lack of appetite, fatigue, itching, rash, double vision, abnormal heart rhythm, anemia or other changes in the composition of the blood, changes in liver function, loss of hair, tingling in the hands and feet, fever, breast enlargement, lowered blood sugar, occasional effects on the kidneys. If symptoms appear, stop taking the medicine and see your doctor immediately.

Drug Interactions

Tolmetin Sodium increases the action of Phenytoin, sulfa drugs, drugs used to control diabetes, and drugs used to thin the blood. If you are taking one of these drugs, be sure you discuss it with your doctor, who will probably change the dose of the drug whose action is increased.

Usual Dose

Adult: 400 milligrams 3 times per day, to start. Dosage must then be adjusted to individual need. Do not take more than 2000 milligrams per day. If upset stomach occurs, take each dose with food, milk, or antacid.

Child (age 2 and over): 9 milligrams per pound of body weight given in divided doses 3 to 4 times per day, to start. Adjust dose to individual need. Do not give more than 13.5 milligrams per pound of body weight to a child.

Child (under age 2): not recommended.

Generic Name

Tretinoin

Brand Name

Retin-A

Type of Drug

Antiacne.

Prescribed for

The early stages of acne. This drug is usually not effective in treating severe acne.

General Information

This drug works by acting as an irritant to the skin, causing the skin to peel, which is helpful in acne treatment. Because it is an irritant, any other skin irritant, such as extreme weather or wind, cosmetics, and some soaps, can cause severe irritation. Excessive application of Tretinoin will cause a lot of peeling but will not give better results.

Cautions and Warnings

Do not use this drug if you are allergic to it or any of its components. This drug may increase the skin-cancer-causing effects of ultraviolet light. Therefore, people using this drug must avoid exposure to the sun. If you can't avoid exposure to the sun, use sunscreen products and protective covering. Do not apply to areas around the eyes, corner of the mouth, or sides of the nose.

Possible Side Effects

Redness, swelling, blistering, or formation of crusts on the skin near the areas to which the drug has been applied. Overcoloration of the skin, greater sensitivity to the sun.

All side effects disappear after the drug has been stopped.

Drug Interactions

Other skin irritants will cause excessive sensitivity, irritation, and side effects. Among the substances that cause this inter-action are medication and abrasive soaps or skin cleansers, cosmetics or other creams, ointments, etc., with a severe drying effect, products with a high alcohol, astringent, spice, or lime content.

Usual Dose

Apply a small amount to the affected area when you go to bed.

Special Information

You may experience an increase in acne lesions during the first couple of weeks of treatment, because the drug is acting on deeper lesions which you had not seen before. This is beneficial and is not a reason to stop using the drug.

Results should be seen in 2 to 6 weeks.

Keep this drug away from your eyes, nose, mouth, and mucous membranes.

Avoid exposure to sunlight or sunlamp.

You may feel warmth and slight stinging when you apply Tretinoin. If you develop an excessive skin reaction or are uncomfortable, stop using this product for a short time.

Generic Name

Triamcinolone Acetonide Ointment/Cream/Gel

Brand Names

Aristocort	Kenalog
Aristogel	Spencort
Flutex	Triacet

Type of Drug

Corticosteroid.

Prescribed for

Relief of inflammation in a local area, itching, or some other dermatological (skin) problem.

General Information

Triamcinolone Acetonide is used to relieve the symptom of

any itching, rash, or inflammation of the skin. It does not treat the underlying cause of the skin problem, only the symptoms. It exerts this effect by interfering with natural body mechanisms that produced the rash, itching, etc., in the first place. If you use this drug without finding the cause of the problem, the condition may return after you stop using the drug. Triamcinolone Acetonide should not be used without your doctor's consent because it could cover an important reaction, one that may be valuable to him in treating you.

Cautions and Warnings

Triamcinolone Acetonide should not be used if you have viral diseases of the skin (herpes), fungal infections of the skin (athlete's foot), or tuberculosis of the skin, nor should it be used in the ear if the eardrum has been perforated. People with a history of allergies to any of the components of the ointment, cream, or gel should not use this drug.

Possible Side Effects

After topically applying this drug, some people may experience burning sensations, itching, irritation, dryness, and secondary infection.

Special Information

Clean the skin before applying Triamcinolone Acetonide, to prevent secondary infection. Apply in a very thin film (effectiveness is based on contact area and not on the thickness of the layer applied).

Brand Name
Triavil

Ingredients

Amitriptyline Hydrochloride
Perphenazine

Other Brand Names

Etrafon

Perphenyline
Triptazine

Type of Drug

Antidepressant-tranquilizer combination.

Prescribed for

Relief of symptoms of anxiety and/or depression associated
with chronic physical or psychiatric disease.

General Information

Triavil and other psychotherapeutic agents are effective in
treating various symptoms of psychological or psychiatric
disorders, which may result from organic disease or may be
signs of psychiatric illness. Triavil must be used only under
the supervision of a doctor. It will take a minimum of 2
weeks to 1 month for this medication to show beneficial
effect, so don't expect instant results. If you feel there has
been no change in symptoms after 6 to 8 weeks, contact
your doctor and discuss it with him. He may tell you to
continue taking the medicine and give it more time, or he
may give you another drug which he feels will be more
effective.

Cautions and Warnings

Do not take Triavil if you are allergic to it or to any related
compound. For more information on drugs related to the
ingredients found in Triavil, consult the entries for Amitriptyline and Chlorpromazine. Do not take Triavil if you have
glaucoma or difficulty pasing urine, unless you are specifically directed to by your physician. This drug is usually not
recommended for patients who are recovering from heart
attacks. Triavil may make you sleepy or tired and it may also
cause difficulty in concentration. Be extremely careful when
driving a car or operating machinery while taking this drug,
especially during the first couple of weeks of therapy. If you
are pregnant and are taking this medication, consider asking
your doctor to change drug therapy, since the ingredients
found in Triavil will pass into the unborn child.

Possible Side Effects

Most frequent: dry mouth, difficulty in urination, constipation, blurred vision, rapid heartbeat, numbness and tingling sensation in the arms and legs, yellowing of the skin and/or whites of the eyes, unusually low blood pressure, drowsiness, sleepiness.

Possible Adverse Drug Effects

Infrequent: dizziness, nausea, excitement, fainting, slight twitching of the muscles, jittery feeling, weakness, headache, heartburn, loss of appetite, stomach cramps, increased perspiration, loss of coordination, skin rash with unusual sensitivity to bright lights, itching, redness, peeling away of large sections of skin. You may experience an allergic reaction: difficulty in breathing, retention of fluids in arms and legs, drug fever, swelling of the face and tongue.

Also infrequent: effects on the hormone and blood system, convulsions, development of unusual skin colorations and spots, effect on sex drive and sexual performance.

Drug Interactions

Quinidine or Procainamide, drugs which are used to control heart rhythm, will strongly increase the effects of this drug. Avoid depressive drugs such as other tranquilizers, sleeping pills, antihistamines, barbiturates, or alcohol. Interaction will cause excessive drowsiness, inability to concentrate, and/or sleepiness. Some patients may experience changes in heart rhythm when taking this drug along with thyroid medication.

One of the ingredients in Triavil may increase your response to common stimulant drugs found in over-the-counter cough and cold preparations, causing stimulation, nervousness, and difficulty in sleeping.

Avoid large amounts of Vitamin C, which may cause you to release larger than normal amounts of Triavil from your body.

Both of the ingredients in Triavil may neutralize drugs used to treat high blood pressure. If you have high blood pressure and are taking Triavil, discuss this potential difficulty with your doctor or pharmacist to be sure that you are taking adequate doses of blood pressure medicine.

If you are taking a drug which is an MAO inhibitor, discuss this matter with your doctor, because there have been severe interactions.

Usual Dose

1 or 2 tablets 3 to 4 times per day. Milligrams in dose to be specified by physician.

Overdosage

Symptoms are central nervous system depression to the point of possible coma, low blood pressure, agitation, restlessness, convulsions, fever, dry mouth, abnormal heart rhythms, confusion, hallucinations, drowsiness, unusually low body temperature, dilated eye pupils, and abnormally rigid muscles. The patient should be taken to a hospital emergency room immediately. ALWAYS bring the medicine bottle.

Generic Name

Trifluoperazine

Brand Name

Stelazine

Type of Drug

Phenothiazine antipsychotic.

Prescribed for

Psychotic disorders, moderate to severe depression with anxiety, control of agitation or aggressiveness of disturbed children, alcohol withdrawal symptoms, intractable pain, and senility.

General Information

Trifluoperazine and other members of the phenothiazine group act on a portion of the brain called the hypothalamus. They affect parts of the hypothalamus that control metabolism, body temperature, alertness, muscle tone, hormone balance, and vomiting, and may be used to treat problems related to any of these functions.

Cautions and Warnings

Trifluoperazine should not be taken if you are allergic to one

of the drugs in the broad classification known as phenothiazine drugs. Do not take Trifluoperazine if you have any
blood, liver, kidney, or heart disease, very low blood pressure, or Parkinson's disease. This medication is a tranquilizer
and can have a depressive effect, especially during the first
few days of therapy. Care should be taken when performing
activities requiring a high degree of concentration, such as
driving. If you are taking this medication and become pregnant contact your doctor immediately.

This drug should be used with caution and under strict
supervision of your doctor if you have glaucoma, epilepsy,
ulcers, or difficulty passing urine.

Avoid insecticides and extreme exposure to heat.

Possible Side Effects

Most common: drowsiness, especially during the first or
second week of therapy. If the drowsiness becomes troublesome, contact your doctor.

Possible Adverse Drug Effects

Trifluoperazine can cause jaundice (yellowing of the whites
of the eyes or skin), usually in 2 to 4 weeks. The jaundice
usually goes away when the drug is discontinued, but there
have been cases when it did not. If you notice this effect or if
you develop symptoms such as fever and generally not
feeling well, contact your doctor immediately. Less frequent:
changes in components of the blood including anemias,
raised or lowered blood pressure, abnormal heart rates, heart
attack, feeling faint or dizzy.

Phenothiazines can produce "extrapyramidal effects," such
as spasm of the neck muscles, rolling back of the eyes,
convulsions, difficulty in swallowing, and symptoms associated with Parkinson's disease. These effects look very serious but disappear after the drug has been withdrawn;
however, symptoms of the face, tongue, and jaw may persist for as long as several years, especially in the elderly with
a history of brain damage. If you experience extrapyramidal
effects contact your doctor immediately.

Trifluoperazine may cause an unusual increase in psychotic
symptoms or may cause paranoid reactions, tiredness, lethargy, restlessness, hyperactivity, confusion at night, bizarre
dreams, inability to sleep, depression, and euphoria. Other

reactions are itching, swelling, unusual sensitivity to bright lights, red skin, and rash. There have been cases of breast enlargement, false positive pregnancy tests, changes in menstrual flow in females, and impotence and changes in sex drive in males, as well as stuffy nose, headache, nausea, vomiting, loss of appetite, change in body temperature, loss of facial color, excessive salivation, excessive perspiration, constipation, diarrhea, changes in urine and stool habits, worsening of glaucoma, blurred vision, weakening of eyelid muscles, spasms in bronchial and other muscles, increased appetite, fatigue, excessive thirst, and changes in the coloration of skin, particularly in exposed areas.

Drug Interactions

Trifluoperazine should be taken with caution in combination with barbiturates, sleeping pills, narcotics, other tranquilizers, or any other medication which may produce a depressive effect. Avoid alcohol.

Usual Dose

Adult: 2 to 4 milligrams per day (the lowest effective dose should be used). This long-acting drug will then be taken once or twice per day.

Elderly: lower dose, because of greater sensitivity to phenothiazines.

Child (age 6 to 12): 1 to 2 milligrams per day, slowly increased (to as much as 15 milligrams per day) until satisfactory control is achieved.

Overdosage

Symptoms are depression, extreme weakness, tiredness, desire to go to sleep, coma, lowered blood pressure, uncontrolled muscle spasms, agitation, restlessness, convulsions, fever, dry mouth, and abnormal heart rhythms. The patient should be taken to a hospital emergency room immediately. ALWAYS bring the medicine bottle.

Special Information

This drug may turn the color of your urine to pink or reddish brown.

Generic Name

Trihexyphenidyl Hydrochloride

Brand Names

Artane
Artane Sequels
T.H.P.
Tremin
Tri Hexane
Trihexidyl
Tri Hexy

Type of Drug

Anticholinergic.

Prescribed for

Treatment of Parkinson's disease or prevention or control of muscle spasms caused by other drugs, particularly the phenothiazine drugs.

General Information

The drug has an action on the body similar to that of Atropine Sulfate. As an anticholinergic it has the ability to reduce muscle spasm, which makes the drug useful in treating Parkinson's disease and other diseases associated with spasm of skeletal muscles.

Cautions and Warnings

Trihexyphenidyl Hydrochloride should be used with caution if you have narrow angle glaucoma, stomach ulcers, obstructions in the gastrointestinal tract, prostatitis, or myasthenia gravis.

Possible Side Effects

The same as with any other anticholinergic drug: dry mouth, difficulty in urination, constipation, blurred vision, rapid or pounding heartbeat, possible mental confusion, and increased sensitivity to strong light. The effects may increase if Trihexyphenidyl Hydrochloride is taken with antihistamines, phenothiazines, antidepressants, or other anticholinergic drugs.

Side effects are less frequent and severe than those seen with Atropine Sulfate, to which this drug is therapeutically similar.

Drug Interactions

Interaction with other anticholinergic drugs, including tricyclic antidepressants, may cause severe stomach upset or unusual abdominal pain. If this happens, contact your doctor.

Avoid over-the-counter remedies which contain Atropine or similar drugs. Your pharmacist can tell you the ingredients of over-the-counter drugs.

This drug should not be taken with alcohol.

Usual Dose

1 to 15 milligrams per day, depending on disease and patient's response. Can be taken with food.

Special Information

Side effects of dry mouth, constipation, and increased sensitivity to strong light may be relieved by, respectively, chewing gum or sucking on hard candy, taking a stool softener, and wearing sunglasses. Such side effects are easily tolerated in the absence of undesirable drug interaction.

Generic Name

Trimethobenzamide Hydrochloride

Brand Name

Tigan

Type of Drug

Antiemetic.

Prescribed for

Control of nausea and vomiting.

General Information

Trimethobenzamide Hydrochloride works on the "chemore-ceptor trigger zone" of the brain through which impulses are carried to the vomiting center. It can help control nausea and vomiting.

Cautions and Warnings

Do not use this drug if you are allergic or sensitive to it. Trimethobenzamide Hydrochloride rectal suppositories contain a local anesthetic and should not be used for newborn infants or patients who are allergic to local anesthetics. Some drugs, when taken by children with a viral illness that causes vomiting, may contribute to the development of Reye's syndrome, a potentially fatal, acute childhood disease. Although this relationship has not been confirmed, caution must be exercised. Reye's syndrome is characterized by a rapid onset of persistent severe vomiting, tiredness, and irrational behavior. It can progress to coma, convulsions, and death—usually following a nonspecific illness associated with a high fever. It has been suspected that Trimethobenzamide Hydrochloride and other drugs which can be toxic to the liver may unfavorably alter the course of Reye's syndrome; such drugs should be avoided in children exhibiting signs and symptoms associated with Reye's syndrome.

Trimethobenzamide Hydrochloride can obscure the signs of overdosage by other drugs or signs of disease because of its effect of controlling nausea and vomiting.

Possible Side Effects

Muscle cramps and tremors, low blood pressure (especially after an injection of this medication), effects on components of the blood, blurred vision, drowsiness, headache, jaundice (yellowing of skin or whites of the eyes). If you experience one of these side effects report it to your doctor. If you develop a rash or other allergic effects from Trimethobenzamide Hydrochloride, stop taking the drug and tell your doctor. Usually these symptoms will disappear by themselves, but additional treatment may be necessary.

Drug Interactions

Trimethobenzamide Hydrochloride may make you sleepy or

cause you to lose concentration. Avoid alcoholic beverages, antihistamines, sleeping pills, tranquilizers, and other depressant drugs which may aggravate these effects.

Usual Dose

Adult: 250-milligram capsule 3 to 4 times per day. Rectal suppository form, 200 milligrams 3 to 4 times per day.

Child (30 to 90 pounds): 100 to 200 milligrams 3 to 4 times per day. Rectal suppository form, 100 to 200 milligrams 3 to 4 times per day.

Child (under 30 pounds): Rectal suppository form, 100 milligrams 3 to 4 times per day.

Dose must be adjusted according to disease severity and patient's response.

Special Information

Severe vomiting should not be treated with an antiemetic drug alone: the cause of vomiting should be established and treated. Overuse of antiemetic drugs may delay diagnosis of the underlying condition or problem and obscure the signs of toxic effects from other drugs. Primary emphasis in the treatment of vomiting is on reestablishment of body fluid and electrolyte balance, relief of fever, and treatment of the causative disease process.

If you have taken Trimethobenzamide Hydrochloride, use special care when driving.

Generic Name

Trimipramine Maleate

Brand Name

Surmontil

Type of Drug

Antidepressant.

Prescribed for

Depression with or without symptoms of anxiety.

General Information

Trimipramine Maleate and other members of this group are effective in treating symptoms of depression. They can elevate your mood, increase physical activity and mental alertness, improve appetite and sleep patterns. These drugs are mild sedatives and therefore useful in treating mild forms of depression associated with anxiety. You should not expect instant results with this medicine: benefits are usually seen after 1 to 4 weeks. If symptoms are not affected after 6 to 8 weeks, contact your doctor. Occasionally other members of this group of drugs have been used in treating nighttime bed-wetting in the young child, but they do not produce long-lasting relief and therapy with one of them for nighttime bed-wetting is of questionable value.

Cautions and Warnings

Do not take Trimipramine Maleate if you are allergic or sensitive to this or other members of this class of drug: Doxepin, Nortriptyline, Imipramine, Desipramine, Protriptyline, and Amitriptyline. The drugs should not be used if you are recovering from a heart attack. Trimipramine Maleate may be taken with caution if you have a history of epilepsy or other convulsive disorders, difficulty in urination, glaucoma, heart disease, or thyroid disease. Trimipramine Maleate can interfere with your ability to perform tasks which require concentration, such as driving or operating machinery. Trimipramine Maleate will pass from mother to unborn child: consult your doctor before taking this medicine if you are pregnant.

Possible Side Effects

Changes in blood pressure (both high and low), abnormal heart rates, heart attack, confusion, especially in elderly patients, hallucinations, disorientation, delusions, anxiety, restlessness, excitement, numbness and tingling in the extremities, lack of coordination, muscle spasms or tremors, seizures and/or convulsions, dry mouth, blurred vision, constipation, inability to urinate, rash, itching, sensitivity to bright light or sunlight, retention of fluids, fever, allergy, changes in composition of blood, nausea, vomiting, loss of appetite, stomach upset, diarrhea, enlargement of the breasts in males and females, increased or decreased sex drive, increased or decreased blood sugar.

Possible Adverse Drug Effects

Infrequent: agitation, inability to sleep, nightmares, feeling of panic, peculiar taste in the mouth, stomach cramps, black coloration of the tongue, yellowing eyes and/or skin, changes in liver function, increased or decreased weight, perspiration, flushing, frequent urination, drowsiness, dizziness, weakness, headache, loss of hair, nausea, not feeling well.

Drug Interactions

Interaction with monoamine oxidase (MAO) inhibitors can cause high fevers, convulsions, and occasionally death. Don't take MAO inhibitors until at least 2 weeks after Trimipramine has been discontinued.

Trimipramine Maleate interacts with Guanethidine, a drug used to treat high blood pressure: if your doctor prescribes Trimipramine Maleate and you are taking medicine for high blood pressure, be sure to discuss this with him.

Trimipramine Maleate increases the effects of barbiturates, tranquilizers, other depressive drugs, and alcohol. Don't drink alcoholic beverages if you take this medicine.

Taking Trimipramine Maleate and thyroid medicine will enhance the effects of the thyroid medicine. The combination can cause abnormal heart rhythms.

Large doses of Vitamin C (Ascorbic Acid) can reduce the effect of Trimipramine Maleate. Drugs such as Bicarbonate of Soda or Acetazolamide will increase the effect of Trimipramine.

Usual Dose

Adult: 150 to 200 milligrams per day in divided doses or as a single bedtime dose. Hospitalized patients may need up to 300 milligrams per day. The dose of this drug must be tailored to patient's need.

Adolescent or elderly: lower doses are recommended; for people over 60 years of age, usually 50 to 100 milligrams per day.

Overdosage

Symptoms are confusion, inability to concentrate, hallucinations, drowsiness, lowered body temperature, abnormal heart rate, heart failure, large pupils of the eyes, convulsions, severely lowered blood pressure, stupor, and coma (as well as agitation, stiffening of body muscles, vomiting, and high fever). The patient should be taken to a hospital emergency room immediately. ALWAYS bring the medicine bottle.

Generic Name

Trimethoprim

Brand Names

Proloprim
Trimpex

Type of Drug

Anti-infective.

Prescribed for

Urinary tract infections.

General Information

This drug works by blocking the effects of folic acid in micro-organisms which may infect the urinary tract. It is often used in combination with a sulfa drug and was first made available in the United States only as a combination. However, it is effective by itself.

Cautions and Warnings

Do not take Trimethoprim if you are allgeric to it. This drug should not be used by pregnant women. It may be used by nursing mothers, if necesary. Patients with a possible folic acid deficiency should not take this drug.

Possible Side Effects

Itching, rash, peeling of the skin.

Possible Adverse Drug Effects

Stomach upset, nausea, vomiting, fever, adverse effects on the blood, elevation of blood enzymes.

Usual Dose

100 milligrams every 12 hours for 10 days. Patients with kidney disease will take less medication.

Overdosage

Signs may appear after taking 10 or more tablets. They are nausea, vomiting, dizziness, headache, depression, confusion, and adverse effects on the blood system. People taking high doses of this drug or those taking it for long periods of time may develop adverse effects on the blood system.

Special Information

Take exactly as directed. Call your doctor if you develop sore throat, fever, blood clots, black-and-blue marks, or a very pale sickly skin coloration.

Generic Name

Tripelennamine

Brand Names

PBZ
PBZ-SR
Pyribenzamine

Type of Drug

Antihistamine.

Prescribed for

Seasonal allergy, stuffed and runny nose, itching of the eyes, scratching of the throat caused by allergy, and other allergic symptoms such as itching, rash, or hives.

General Information

Antihistamines generally, and Tripelennamine specifically, act by blocking the release of the chemical substance histamine from the cell. Antihistamines work by drying up the secretions of the nose, throat, and eyes.

Cautions and Warnings

Tripelennamine should not be used if you are allergic to this drug. It should be avoided or used with extreme care if you have narrow angle glaucoma (pressure in the eye), stomach ulcer or other stomach problems, enlarged prostate, or problems passing urine. It should not be used by people who have deep-breathing problems such as asthma.

Tripelennamine can cause dizziness, drowsiness, and lowering of blood pressure, particularly in the elderly patient. Young children can show signs of nervousness, increased tension, and anxiety.

Possible Side Effects

Occasional: itching, rash, sensitivity to light, perspiration, chills, dryness of the mouth, nose and throat, lowered blood pressure, headache, rapid heartbeat, sleeplessness, dizziness, disturbed coordination, confusion, restlessness, nervousness, irritability, euphoria (feeling high), tingling of the hands and feet, blurred vision, double vision, ringing in the ears, stomach upset, loss of appetite, nausea, vomiting, constipation, diarrhea, difficulty in urination, tightness of the chest, wheezing, nasal stuffiness.

Possible Adverse Drug Effects

Use with care if you have a history of asthma, glaucoma, thyroid disease, heart disease, high blood pressure, or diabetes.

Drug Interactions

Tripelennamine should not be taken with MAO inhibitors.

Interaction with tranquilizers, sedatives, and sleeping medication will increase the effects of these drugs; it is extremely important that you discuss this with your doctor so that doses of these drugs can be properly adjusted.

Be extremely cautious when drinking while taking Tripelennamine, which will enhance the intoxicating effect of alcohol. Alcohol also has a sedative effect.

Usual Dose

Adult: 25 to 50 milligrams every 4 to 6 hours. Up to 600 milligrams per day may be used. Adult patient may take up to 3 of the 100-milligram long-acting (PBZ-SR) tablets per day, although this much is not usually needed.

Infant and child: 2 milligrams per pound of body weight

per day in divided doses. No more than 300 milligrams should be given per day. Older children may take up to 3 of the extended-release (long-acting) tablets per day, if needed.

Overdosage

Symptoms are depression or stimulation (especially in children), fixed or dilated pupils, flushing of the skin, and stomach upset. Take the patient to a hospital emergency room immediately, if you cannot make him vomit. ALWAYS bring the medicine bottle.

Special Information

Antihistamines produce a depressing effect: be extremely cautious when driving or operating heavy equipment.

The safety of Tripelennamine in pregnancy has not been established. A breast-feeding mother should avoid taking this medication, since it is known to pass from the mother to the baby through the milk.

Brand Name

Tri-Vi-Flor Drops

Ingredients

Sodium Fluoride
Vitamin A
Vitamin C
Vitamin D

Type of Drug

Multivitamin supplement with a fluoride.

Prescribed for

Vitamin deficiencies and prevention of dental cavities in infants and children.

General Information

Tri-Vi-Flor Drops is a vitamin supplement containing a fluoride. Fluorides taken in small daily doses have been effective in preventing cavities in children by strengthening their teeth and making them resistant to cavity formation. Too much of a fluoride can cause damage to the teeth. Because of this, vitamins with a fluoride should only be used in areas where the water supply is not fluoridated.

Cautions and Warnings

Tri-Vi-Flor Drops should not be used in areas where the fluoride content exceeds 0.7 ppm (part per million). Your pediatrician or local water company can tell you the fluoride content of the water you drink.

Possible Side Effects

Occasional skin rash, itching, stomach upset, headache, weakness.

Usual Dose

1 milliliter per day.

Brand Name

Tuinal

Ingredients

Amobarbital
Secobarbital

Other Brand Name

Twinbarbital

Type of Drug

Hypnotic.

Prescribed for

Daytime sedation, or sleeping medication.

General Information

This drug is a combination of a short- and intermediate-acting barbiturate. The combination takes advantage of the fast-acting nature of Secobarbital and the longer duration of action of Amobarbital (about 8 hours). Although the combination works well, it can be addicting if taken daily for 3 months in sufficient doses (about 100 milligrams). Larger doses will result in addiction in a shorter period of time.

Cautions and Warnings

Tuinal may slow down your physical and mental reflexes, so you must be extremely careful when operating machinery, driving an automobile, or performing other potentially dangerous tasks. Tuinal is classified as a barbiturate; long-term or unsupervised use may cause addiction. Elderly people taking Tuinal may exhibit nervousness and confusion at times. Barbiturates are neutralized in the liver and eliminated from the body through the kidneys; consequently, people who have liver or kidney disorders—namely, difficulty in forming or excreting urine—should be carefully monitored by their doctor when taking Tuinal.

If you have known sensitivities or allergies to barbiturates, or if you have previously been addicted to sedatives or hypnotics, or if you have a disease affecting the respiratory system, you should not take Tuinal.

Possible Side Effects

Difficulty in breathing, skin rash, and general allergic reaction such as running nose, watery eyes, and scratchy throat.

Possible Adverse Drug Effects

Drowsiness, lethargy, dizziness, hangover, nausea, vomiting, diarrhea. More severe adverse reactions may include anemia and yellowing of the skin and eyes.

Drug Interactions

Interaction with alcohol, tranquilizers, or other sedatives increases the effect of Tuinal.

Interaction with anticoagulants (blood-thinning agents) can reduce their effect. This is also true of muscle relaxants and painkillers.

Usual Dose

Up to 200 milligrams.

Overdosage

Symptoms are difficulty in breathing, decrease in size of the pupils of the eyes, lowered body temperature progressing to fever as time passes, fluid in the lungs, and eventually coma.

Anyone suspected of having taken an overdose must be taken to the hospital for immediate care. ALWAYS bring the medicine bottle to the emergency room physician so he can quickly and correctly identify the medicine and start treatment. Severe overdosage of this medication can kill; the drug has been used many times in suicide attempts.

Brand Name

Tussionex

Ingredients

Hydrocodone
Phenyltoloxamine

Type of Drug

Cough suppressant, antihistamine.

Prescribed for

Relief of cough and other symptoms of a cold or other respiratory condition.

General Information

This drug may be prescribed to treat a cough or congestion that has not responded to other medication. The suppressant ingredient (Hydrocodone) in this combination is more potent than Codeine.

Cautions and Warnings

Do not use Tussionex if you are allergic to any of the ingredients. Patients allergic to Codeine may also be allergic to Tussionex. Long-term use of this or any other narcotic-containing drug can lead to drug dependence or addiction. Both ingredients in Tussionex can cause drowsiness, tiredness, or loss of concentration. Use with caution if you have a history of convulsions, glaucoma, stomach ulcer, high blood pressure, thyroid disease, heart disease, or diabetes.

Possible Side Effects

Light-headedness, dizziness, sleepiness, nausea, vomiting, sweating, itching, rash, sensitivity to light, excessive perspiration, chills, dryness of the mouth, nose, and throat.

Possible Adverse Drug Effects

Euphoria (feeling high), weakness, agitation, uncoordinated muscle movement, minor hallucinations, disorientation and visual disturbances, loss of appetite, constipation, flushing of the face, rapid heartbeat, palpitations, faintness, difficult urination, reduced sexual potency, low blood sugar, anemia, yellowing of the skin or whites of the eyes, blurred or double vision, ringing or buzzing in the ears, wheezing, nasal stuffiness.

Drug Interaction

Do not use alcohol or other depressant drugs because they will increase the depressant effect of the Tussionex. This drug should not be taken in combination with MAO inhibitor drugs.

Usual Dose

Tablet or capsule: 1 every 3 to 12 hours.
  Suspension: 1 teaspoon every 8 to 12 hours.

Overdosage

Signs of overdose are depression, slowed breathing, flushing of the skin, upset stomach. In case of overdose, bring the patient to a hospital emergency room. ALWAYS bring the medicine bottle.

Special Information

Be careful while driving or operating any equipment.
  The liquid form of Tussionex does not contain any sugar.

Brand Name

Tuss-Ornade Spansules/Liquid

Ingredients

Caramiphen Edisylate
Chlorpheniramine Maleate
Isopropamide Iodide
Phenylpropanolamine Hydrochloride

Type of Drug

Decongestant; expectorant.

Prescribed for

Relief of cough, nasal congestion, runny nose, and other symptoms associated with the common cold, viruses, or other upper respiratory diseases. The drug may also be used to treat allergies, asthma, ear infections, or sinus infections.

General Information

Tuss-Ornade is one of almost 100 products marketed to relieve the symptoms of the common cold and other respiratory infections. These products contain ingredients to relieve congestion, act as an antihistamine, relieve or suppress cough, and help you to cough up mucus. They may contain medicine for each purpose, or may contain a combination of medicines. Some combinations leave out the antihistamine, the decongestant, or the expectorant. You must realize while taking Tuss-Ornade or similar products that these drugs are good only for the relief of symptoms and do not treat the underlying problem such as a cold virus or other infections.

Cautions and Warnings

Can cause excessive tiredness or drowsiness.

Possible Side Effects

Dry mouth, blurred vision, difficulty passing urine, (possibly) constipation, nervousness, restlessness or even inability to sleep.

Drug Interactions

Taking Tuss-Ornade with an MAO inhibitor can produce severe interaction, so consult your doctor before combining them.

Do not take this drug with sedatives, tranquilizers, antihistamines, sleeping pills, thyroid medicine, or antihypertensive drugs such as Reserpine or Guanethidine.

Since Tuss-Ornade contains ingredients which may cause sleepiness or difficulty in concentration, do not drink alcoholic beverages while taking this drug. The combination can cause excessive drowsiness or sleepiness, and result in inability to concentrate and carry out activities requiring extra concentration and coordination.

Usual Dose

Spansules: 1 every 12 hours.

Liquid: 1 to 2 teaspoons 3 to 4 times per day as needed for relief of cough, nasal congestion, runny nose, or other symptoms associated with the common cold or other upper respiratory diseases.

Special Information

Take with a full glass of water to remove excessive mucus from the throat and reduce stomach upset.

Brand Name

Tylox

Ingredients

Acetaminophen
Oxycodone Hydrochloride
Oxycodone Terephthalate

Type of Drug

Narcotic analgesic combination.

Prescribed for

Relief of mild to moderate pain.

General Information

Tylox is generally prescribed for the patient who is in pain but is allergic to Aspirin. Tylox is probably not effective for arthritis or other pain associated with inflammation because the ingredient Acetaminophen does not produce an anti-inflammatory effect.

Cautions and Warnings

Do not take Tylox if you know you are allergic or sensitive to it. Use this drug with extreme caution if you suffer from asthma or other breathing problems. Long-term use of Tylox may cause drug dependence or addiction. Codeine is a respiratory depressant and affects the central nervous system, producing sleepiness, tiredness, and/or inability to concentrate. Be careful if you are driving, operating machinery, or performing other functions requiring concentration. If you are pregnant or suspect that you are pregnant do not take this drug.

Possible Side Effects

Most frequent: light-headedness, dizziness, sleepiness, nausea, vomiting, loss of appetite, sweating. If these effects occur, consider calling your doctor and asking him about lowering the dose of Tylox you are taking. Usually the side effects disappear if you simply lie down.

More serious side effects of Tylox are shallow breathing or difficulty in breathing.

Possible Adverse Drug Effects

Euphoria (feeling high), weakness, sleepiness, headache, agitation, uncoordinated muscle movement, minor hallucinations, disorientation and visual disturbances, dry mouth, loss of appetite, constipation, flushing of the face, rapid heartbeat, palpitations, faintness, urinary difficulties or hesitancy, reduced sex drive and/or potency, itching, rashes, anemia, lowered blood sugar, yellowing of the skin and/or whites of the eyes. Narcotic analgesics may aggravate convulsions in those who have had convulsions in the past.

Drug Interactions

Because of its depressant effect and potential effect on breathing, Tylox should be taken with extreme care in combination with alcohol, sleeping medicine, tranquilizers, or other depressant drugs.

Usual Dose

Adult: 1 to 2 tablets every 4 hours.
Child: not recommended for children.

Overdosage

Symptoms are depression of respiration (breathing), extreme tiredness progressing to stupor and then coma, pinpointed pupils of the eyes, no response to stimulation such as a pin stick, cold and clammy skin, slowing down of the heart rate, lowering of blood pressure, yellowing of the skin and/or whites of the eyes, bluish color in skin of hands and feet, fever, excitement, delirium, convulsions, cardiac arrest, and liver toxicity (shown by nausea, vomiting, pain in the abdomen, and diarrhea). The patient should be taken to a hospital emergency room immediately. ALWAYS bring the medicine bottle.

Special Information

Tylox is best taken with food or at least ½ glass of water to prevent stomach upset.

Generic Name

Valproic Acid

Brand Name

Depakene

Type of Drug

Anticonvulsant.

Prescribed for

Various kinds of seizures.

General Information

Valproic Acid is used to treat the special kind of seizures

called petit-mal. It can also be used to treat absence sei-zures, where the patient loses memory of the seizure but does not lose consciousness.

Cautions and Warnings

Do not take Valproic Acid if you are allergic to it. Take this drug with caution if you have a history of liver problems. Some cases of liver failure have occurred in people taking Valproic Acid.

Pregnant women should avoid this drug. Although no cases of adverse effect on the human fetus have been reported, studies in animals strongly suggest that Valproic Acid has such effects.

Possible Side Effects

Nausea, vomiting and indigestion, sedation or sleepiness, weakness, skin rash, emotional upset, depression, psycho-sis, aggression, hyperactive behavoir. Valproic Acid can cause adverse effects on the blood system. The frequency of side effects increases as your dose of Valproic Acid increases.

Possible Adverse Drug Effects

Diarrhea, stomach cramps, constipation, appetite changes (either increase or decrease), headache, loss of control of eye muscles, drooping eyelids, double vision, spots before the eyes, loss of muscle control and coordination, tremors.

Drug Interactions

Valproic Acid may increase the depressive effects of alcohol, sleeping pills, tranquilizers, or other depressant drugs.

If you begin taking Valproic Acid while taking Phenytoin, your Phenytoin dosage may have to be adjusted. Use of Valproic Acid together with Clonazepam may produce a cer-tain kind of seizure. This combination should be used with extreme caution.

Valproic Acid may affect oral anticoagulant (blood-thinning) drugs. If you begin taking Valproic Acid and have been taking an anticoagulant, your anticoagulant dose may have to be changed.

Valproic Acid may cause a false positive interpretation of the test for ketones in the urine (used by diabetics).

Usual Dose

7 to 27 milligrams per pound per day.

Overdosage

Call your doctor or take the patient to a hospital emergency room immediately. ALWAYS bring the medicine bottle.

Special Information

This medicine may cause drowsiness; be careful while driving or operating machinery. It may be taken with food to reduce upset stomach. Do not chew Valproic Acid capsules or empty their contents.

Volproic Acid can cause mouth and throat irritation. All seizure patients should carry special identification indicating their disease and the medicine being taken for it.

Generic Name

Verapamil

Brand Names

Calan
Isoptin

Type of Drug

Calcium channel blocker.

Prescribed for

Angina pectoris and prinzmetal angina.

General Information

Verapamil is a member of a new drug class to be marketed in the United States. It works by blocking the passage of calcium into heart and smooth muscle. Since calcium is an essential ingredient in muscle contraction, blocking calcium reduces both muscle contraction and oxygen use by the muscle. This is why Verapamil is used in the treatment of angina, a kind of heart pain related to poor oxygen supply to the heart muscles. Verapamil also dilates the vessels that supply blood to the heart muscles and prevents spasm of these arteries. Verapamil only affects the movement of calcium into muscle cells. It does not have any effect on calcium in the blood.

Cautions and Warnings

Verapamil may cause lowered blood pressure in some patients. Patients taking a beta-blocking drug who begin taking Verapamil may develop heart failure or increased angina pain. Do not take this drug if you have had an allergic reaction to it. Pregnant women or nursing mothers should only use this drug if absolutely necessary.

Possible Side Effects

Low blood pressure, swelling of the arms or legs, heart failure, slowed heartbeat, dizziness, light-headedness, weakness, fatigue, headache, constipation, nausea, liver damage, especially in patients with previous liver damage.

Possible Adverse Drug Effects

Confusion, tingling in the arms or legs, difficulty sleeping, blurred vision, muscle cramps, shakiness, leg pains, difficulty maintaining balance, hair loss, spotty menstruation. In addition, some patients taking Verapamil have experienced heart attack and abnormal heart rhythms, but the occurrence of these effects has not been directly linked to Verapamil.

Drug Interactions

Long-term Verapamil use will cause the blood levels of digitalis drugs to increase by 50 to 70 percent. The dose of digitalis drugs will have to be drastically lowered. Disopyramide should not be given within 48 hours of taking Verapamil because of possible interaction. Patients taking Verapamil together with Quinidine may experience very low blood pressure.

Usual Dose

240 to 480 milligrams per day. The dose must be individualized to patient's need.

Overdosage

Overdosage of Verapamil can cause low blood pressure. Symptoms are dizziness, weakness, and (possibly) slowed heartbeat. If you have taken an overdose of Verapamil, call your doctor or go to a hospital emergency room. ALWAYS bring the medicine bottle.

Special Information

Take this drug 1 hour before or 2 hours after meals. Call your doctor if you develop swelling in the arms or legs, difficulty breathing, increased heart pains, dizziness, lightheadedness, or low blood pressure.

Brand Name

Vioform-Hydrocortisone Cream/Lotion/Ointment

Ingredients

Hydrocortisone
Iodochlorhydroxyquin

Other Brand Names

Bafil	Hysone
Caquin	Iodocort
Cortin	Lanvisone
Cort-Quin	Mity-Quin
Domeform-HC	Pedi-Cort
Epiform-HC	Racet
HC-Form	Vio-Hydrosone
Hexaderm I.Q.	Vioquin HC
Hydrocortisone with	Viotag
Iodochlorhydroxyquin	Vytone

Type of Drug

Topical corticosteroid combination.

Prescribed for

Inflamed conditions of the skin such as eczema, athlete's foot, and other fungal infections.

General Information

Hydrocortisone is used to relieve the symptom of any itching, rash, or inflammation of the skin. It does not treat the underlying cause of the skin problem, only the symptom. It exerts this effect by interfering with natural body mechanisms that produced the rash, itching, etc., in the first place. If you use this drug without finding the cause of the problem, the condition may return after you stop using the drug. Hydrocortisone should not be used without your doctor's consent because it could cover an important reaction, one that may be valuable to him in treating you. Iodochlorhydroxyquin is used because of its antifungal, antibacterial, and antieczema effects.

Cautions and Warnings

Keep this medication away from the eyes. Because there is some question about the safety of topical Hydrocortisone in pregnant females, these products should not be used extensively or in large amounts for a long time if you are pregnant. If local irritation worsens, or develops where there was none, stop using the drug and contact your physician immediately.

Possible Side Effects

Burning sensation, itching, irritation, dryness, secondary infection, pimples similar to acne.

Usual Dose

Apply to affected area only, 2 to 3 times per day.

Generic Name

Warfarin

Brand Names

Athrombin-K
Coumadin Sodium
Panwarfin

Type of Drug

Oral anticoagulant.

Prescribed for

Anticoagulation (thinning of the blood). This is generally a secondary form of treatment for other diseases—such as blood clots in the arms and legs, pulmonary embolism, heart attack, or abnormal heart rhythms—in which the formation of blood clots may cause serious problems.

General Information

Anticoagulants act by depressing the body's normal production of various factors which are known to take part in the coagulation mechanism. If you are taking Warfarin it is absolutely essential that you take the exact dose in the exact way prescribed by your doctor. Notify your doctor at the earliest sign of unusual bleeding or bruising (that is, the formation of black-and-blue marks), if you pass blood in your urine or stool, and/or if you pass a black tarry stool. The interactions of this class of drugs are extremely important and are discussed in detail below.

   Warfarin can be extremely dangerous if not used properly. Periodic blood tests of the time it takes your blood or various factors in your blood to begin to coagulate are required for proper control of oral anticoagulant therapy.

   If you are pregnant or think that you may be pregnant, you must discuss this with your doctor immediately: Warfarin can cause problems with the mother and will also pass into the fetus. It can cause and has caused bleeding and death of the fetus. A nursing mother should be careful, since the Warfarin will appear in the mother's milk. There are situations where the potential benefits to be gained from the use of Warfarin or one of the other anticoagulants may outweigh possible negative effects of these drugs in the pregnant patient: the decision to use one of these drugs is an important one which should be made cooperatively by you and your doctor.

Cautions and Warnings

Warfarin must be taken with care if you have a preexisting blood disease associated with coagulation or lack of coagulation. Other conditions in which the use of Warfarin should be discussed with your doctor are threatened abortion, Vitamin C deficiency, stomach ulcers or bleeding from the genital or urinary areas, severe high blood pressure, disease of the large bowel such as diverticulitis or ulcerative colitis, and subacute bacterial endocarditis.

People taking Warfarin should be extremely cautious about being exposed to cuts, bruises, or other types of injury which might cause bleeding.

Possible Side Effects

The principal side effect experienced by patients taking Warfarin or other oral anticoagulant drugs is bleeding, which may occur within therapeutic dosage ranges and even when blood tests normally used to monitor anticoagulant therapy are within normal limits. If you bleed abnormally while you are taking anticoagulants and have eliminated the possibility of drug interactions, you should discuss this matter immediately with your doctor: it may indicate the presence of an underlying problem.

Possible Adverse Drug Effects

People taking oral anticoagulant drugs have reported bleeding from peptic ulcers, nausea, vomiting, diarrhea, blood in the urine, anemia, adverse effects on components of the blood, hepatitis, jaundice or yellowing of the skin and whites of the eyes, itching, rash, loss of hair, sore throat and mouth, and fever.

Drug Interactions

Warfarin and other oral anticoagulant (blood-thinning) drugs are probably involved in more drug interactions than any other kind of drug. Contact your pharmacist or doctor to discuss any other medications which you may be taking in order to avoid serious adverse interactions, which may increase the effectiveness of Warfarin to the point of causing severe bleeding or hemorrhage, or decrease its effectiveness to the point of causing formation of blood clots. Your doctor and your pharmacist should have records of all medications which you are taking.

Drugs that may increase the effect of Warfarin include broad-spectrum antibiotics such as Neomycin or others which will act on the normal bacterial contents of the stomach and intestines to eliminate Vitamin K, the body's natural antidote to Warfarin; mineral oil; Cholestyramine; Phenylbutazone; Oxyphenbutazone; Clofibrate; Indomethacin; sulfa drugs; Chloral Hydrate; Ethacrynic Acid; Mefenamic Acid; Nalidixic Acid; Aspirin; oral antidiabetic drugs (Tolbutamide, Chlorpropamide, Tolazamide); Chloramphenicol; Allopurinol; Nortriptyline; Methylphenidate; alcohol; Cimetidine, Disulfiram; Chlortetracycline; Quinidine; Haloperidol; Ascorbic Acid in large quantities; MAO inhibitors; Meperidine; and Thyroid Hormone and antithyroid drugs such as Propylthiouracil and Methylthiouracil will also increase the effects of oral anticoagulants.

There are fewer drugs that will decrease the effect of Warfarin, but the potential interaction can be just as dangerous with barbiturates, Glutethimide, Ethchlorvynol, Meprobamate, Griseofulvin, estrogens, oral contraceptive drugs, Chlorthalidone, corticosteroids, Phenytoin (see p. 394 for interaction resulting in Phenytoin toxicity), Carbamazepine, Vitamin K, and Rifampin.

No matter what the interaction, it is essential that you discuss all medications you are taking with your doctor or pharmacist, including not only prescription drugs but over-the-counter drugs containing Aspirin or other ingredients which may interact with Warfarin. Consult your physician or pharmacist before buying any over-the-counter drugs.

Usual Dose

2 to 10 or more milligrams daily; but dose is extremely variable and must be individualized for maximum effect.

Overdosage

The primary symptom is bleeding. A laboratory test will show longer blood-clotting time, and bleeding can make itself known by appearance of blood in the urine or stool, an unusual number of black-and-blue marks, oozing of blood from small cuts made while shaving or from other trivial nicks or cuts, or bleeding from the gums after brushing the teeth. If bleeding does not stop within 10 to 15 minutes, your doctor should be called. He may tell you to skip a dose of anticoagulant and continue normal activities, or to go to a local hospital or doctor's office where blood evaluations can be made; or he may give you a prescription for Vitamin K, which antagonizes the effect of Warfarin. The latter has dangers because it can complicate subsequent anticoagulant therapy, but this is a decision that your doctor must make.

Generic Name

Zomepirac

Brand Name

Zomax

Type of Drug

Nonnarcotic analgesic antipeptic.

Prescribed for

Relief of mild to severe pain and fever.

General Information

Zomepirac is a new drug which is very effective when taken

by mouth. It is more effective than Codeine or Aspirin alone and is about as effective as analgesic combinations of Codeine and another drug. This drug is important because it can be used by people who need more pain relief than Aspirin can give but do not want to take narcotic analgesics. Zomepirac works well in relieving mild pain following dental or other minor surgery. In the body, Zomepirac works much like Aspirin.

Cautions and Warnings

Do not take Zomepirac if you are allergic or sensitive to it. Do not take more than has been prescribed for you. Patients with ulcers or a history of stomach bleeding, high blood pressure, swelling of the arms or legs, or heart failure and those who are sensitive to Aspirin or the nonsteroid anti-inflammatory drugs should be cautious about using this drug.

Possible Side Effects

The most frequent side effects of Zomepirac are nausea, stomach upset and pain, constipation, diarrhea, and vomiting. Drowsiness, dizziness, sleeplessness, rash, itching, excessive sweating, and swelling of the arms or legs can also be caused by Zomepirac. Zomepirac can raise the blood pressure.

Possible Adverse Drug Effects

Zomepirac can cause ringing in the ears and hearing loss, although this happens less frequently than with Aspirin. It can cause stomach irritation and bleeding.

Drug Interactions

Zomepirac should be used with caution by people taking drugs with anticoagulant (blood-thinning) properties especially those that work on the platelets (Aspirin, Dipyridamole).

Usual Dose

50 to 100 milligrams every 4 to 6 hours as needed.

Overdosage

If an overdose has been taken, call the nearest poison control center for instructions. If you are told to bring the patient to the emergency room, ALWAYS bring the medicine bottle.

1981
The Top 200
Prescription Drugs
Dispensed in U.S. Community Pharmacies
Brand Name As Dispensed
New and Refill Prescriptions—All Strengths

Rank 1981	Rank 1980	Drug Product	Manufacturer
1	1	Valium	Roche
2	2	Inderal	Ayerst
3	4	Lanoxin	BW
4	3	Dyazide	SKF
5	6	Lasix	Hoechst
6	5	Tylenol w/Codeine	McNeil
7	9	Tagamet	SKF
8	8	Motrin	Upjohn
9	13	Ortho-Novum	Ortho
10	11	Dalmane	Roche
11	12	Aldomet	MSD
12	7	Dimetapp	Robins
13	16	Slow-K	CIBA
14	10	Darvocet-N	Lilly
15	15	Keflex	Dista
16	26	Amoxil	Beecham
17	20	Dilantin	Parke-Davis
18	14	Actifed	BW
19	21	E.E.S.	Abbott
20	18	Premarin	Ayerst

*Not in top 200 in 1980

Rank 1981	Rank 1980	Drug Product	Manufacturer
21	19	Benadryl	Parke-Davis
22	17	Empirin w/Codeine	BW
23	24	Synthroid	Flint
24	25	Hygroton	USV
25	23	Indocin	MSD
26	28	Isordil	Ives
27	31	Naprosyn	Syntex
28	22	Clinoril	MSD
29	27	Hydrodiuril	MSD
30	35	Diabinese	Pfizer
31	*	Zomax	McNeil
32	29	V-Cillin K	Lilly
33	53	Lopressor	Geigy
34	30	Tranxene	Abbott
35	42	Lo/Ovral	Wyeth
36	51	Ativan	Wyeth
37	32	Donnatal	Robins
38	33	Mellaril	Sandoz
39	44	Zyloprim	BW
40	34	Percodan	Endo
41	46	Persantine	Boehringer
42	38	Drixoral	Schering
43	41	Aldoril	MSD
44	47	E-Mycin	Upjohn
45	39	Elavil	MSD
46	40	Ovral	Wyeth
47	43	Thyroid	Armour
48	37	Fiorinal	Sandoz
49	54	Omnipen	Wyeth
50	36	Amcill	Parke-Davis
51	56	Norinyl	Syntex
52	97	Theo-Dur	Key
53	55	Monistat	Ortho
54	70	Timoptic	MSD
55	62	Atarax	Roerig
56	45	Achromycin V	Lederle
57	49	Mycolog	Squibb
58	50	Aldactazide	Searle
59	60	Antivert	Roerig

Rank 1981	Rank 1980	Drug Product	Manufacturer
60	76	Minipress	Pfizer
61	69	Naldecon	Bristol
62	57	Triavil	MSD
63	72	Phenobarbital	Lilly
64	65	Bactrim DS	Roche
65	48	Vibramycin	Pfizer
66	52	Librium	Roche
67	59	Lomotil	Searle
68	92	Haldol	McNeil
69	58	Librax	Roche
70	71	Sinequan	Roerig
71	84	Septra DS	BW
72	78	Nitro-Bid	Marion
73	77	Larotid	Roche
74	61	Ornade	SKF
75	67	Tetracycline	Parke-Davis
76	131	Ceclor	Lilly
77	65	Ser-Ap-Es	CIBA
78	63	Ilosone	Dista
79	66	Principen	Squibb
80	86	Apresoline	CIBA
81	95	Nalfon	Dista
82	94	Brethine	Geigy
83	88	Coumadin	Endo
84	81	Pen-Vee K	Wyeth
85	64	Sumycin	Squibb
86	80	Macrodantin	Norwich
87	85	Phenergan w/Codeine	Wyeth
88	87	Synalgos-DC	Ives
89	82	Cortisoporin	BW
90	73	Pfizerpen VK	Pfipharmecs
91	113	Hydergine	Sandoz
92	79	Parafon Forte	McNeil
93	107	Catapres	Boehringer
94	109	Nitrostat	Parke-Davis
95	102	Deltasone	Upjohn
96	68	Butazolidin Alka	Geigy
97	*	Corgard	Squibb
98	90	Erythromycin	Abbott

Rank 1981	Rank 1980	Drug Product	Manufacturer
99	105	Serax	Wyeth
100	128	Tolinase	Upjohn
101	119	Septra	BW
102	91	Diuril	MSD
103	98	Valisone	Schering
104	74	Darvon Compound-65	Lilly
105	118	Esidrix	CIBA
106	116	Flagyl	Searle
107	104	Orinase	Upjohn
108	96	Pfizerpen-A	Pfipharmecs
109	115	Thorazine	SKF
110	140	Flexeril	MSD
111	108	Tolectin	McNeil
112	123	Sorbitrate	Stuart
113	106	Fiorinal w/Codeine	Sandoz
114	120	Amoxicillin	Parke-Davis
115	125	Compazine	SKF
116	101	Hydropres	MSD
117	147	Bactrim	Roche
118	111	Bentyl	Merrell
119	100	Tuss-Ornade	SKF
120	137	Vistaril	Pfizer
121	89	Phenaphen w/Codeine	Robins
122	93	Demulen	Searle
123	83	Gyne-Lotrimin	Schering
124	99	Pavabid	Marion
125	114	Ledercillin VK	Lederle
126	127	Enduron	Abbot
127	121	Kenalog	Squibb
128	126	Neosporin	BW
129	132	K-Lyte	Mead Johnson
130	*	Meclomen	Parke-Davis
131	129	Penicillin VK	Parke-Davis
132	143	Trimox	Squibb
133	138	Slo-Phyllin	Rorer
134	117	Talwin	Winthrop
135	103	Ovulen	Searle
136	136	Hydrochlorothiazide	Lederle
137	130	Phenergan VC w/Codeine	Wyeth

Rank 1981	Rank 1980	Drug Product	Manufacturer
138	135	Kwell	Reed & Carnrick
139	141	Limbitrol	Roche
140	133	Vanceril	Schering
141	148	Norpace	Searle
142	*	Wymox	Wyeth
143	177	Pyridium	Parke-Davis
144	151	Tigan	Beecham
145	134	Actifed-C	BW
146	142	Minocin	Lederle
147	176	Zaroxolyn	Pennwalt
148	122	Tenuate	Merrell
149	139	Alupent	Boehringer
150	*	Centrax	Parke-Davis
151	145	Combid	SKF
152	150	Periactin	MSD
153	152	Erythromycin Stearate	Abbott
154	153	Aldactone	Searle
155	156	Stelazine	SKF
156	112	Modicon	Ortho
157	162	Lidex	Syntex
158	149	Nitroglycerin	Lilly
159	110	Bendectin	Merrell
160	*	Vibra-Tab	Pfizer
161	154	Choledyl	Parke-Davis
162	164	Cogentin	MSD
163	167	Sinemet	MSD
164	158	Poly-Vi-Flor	Mead Johnson
165	*	Adapin	Pennwalt
166	188	Navane	Roerig
167	172	Medrol	Upjohn
168	155	Butisol Sodium	McNeil
169	*	Nitrol	Kremers-Urban
170	185	Provera	Upjohn
171	166	Benylin	Parke-Davis
172	124	Atromid-S	Ayerst
173	173	Phenergan Syrup	Wyeth
174	195	Imodium	Ortho
175	174	Isopto Carpine	Alcon
176	163	Ritalin	CIBA

Rank 1981	Rank 1980	Drug Product	Manufacturer
177	*	Stuartnatal 1 + 1	Stuart
178	147	Gantrisin	Roche
179	175	Sodium Sulamyd	Schering
180	170	Phenobarbital	Parke-Davis
181	171	Tofranil	Geigy
182	157	Ionamin	Pennwalt
183	182	Apresazide	CIBA
184	179	Veetids	Squibb
185	*	Percocet-5	Endo
186	178	Sudafed	BW
187	144	Equagesic	Wyeth
188	187	Tussionex	Pennwalt
189	160	Robaxin	Robins
190	*	K-Lor	Abbott
191	183	Decadron	MSD
192	*	Chronulac	Merrell
193	159	Norgesic Forte	Riker
194	*	K-Tab	Abbott
195	161	AVC Cream	Merrell
196	*	Tegretol	Geigy
197	192	SK-Ampicillin	SKF
198	184	Quinidine Sulfate	Parke-Davis
199	*	Topicort	Hoechst
200	168	Vasodil	Mead Johnson

Source:
All data supplied by Pharmaceutical Data Services, Phoenix, AZ., a subsidiary of Foremost-McKesson, Inc. PDS provides various marketing research and sales analyses to the pharmaceutical industry, government, and academia.

141 Drugs Considered Less Than Effective by the U.S. Food and Drug Administration

The federal government wants to halt reimbursement to state Medicaid systems for the following drugs, which the Food and Drug Administration classifies as "lacking substantial evidence of effectiveness for all labelled indications." Although some of these drugs are no longer widely prescribed, and others have been taken off the market, some doctors may still be writing prescriptions for them. If you receive a prescription for one of these drugs, check with your physician and your pharmacist to see if any other medicine will suit your needs. The list below may change without notice, and other drugs may be added at any time. Check with your doctor and/or pharmacist for the latest F.D.A. classifications.

Brand Name (Ingredients)	Dosage Form
Adrenosem Salicylate (Carbazochrome Salicylate)	Tablet/Oral; Solution/Intramuscular
Alevaire (Tyloxapol)	Solution/Inhaler
Amesec (Aminophylline—Amobarbital—Ephedrine HCl)	Enteric Coated Tablets, Capsule/Oral
Aminophylline & Amytal (Aminophylline—Amobarbital)	Capsule/Oral

Brand Name (Ingredients)	Dosage Form
Amphocortrin (Calcium Amphomycin—Hydrocortisone Acetate—Neomycin Sulfate)	Cream/Topical
Ananase (Bromelains)	Enteric Coated Tablets/Oral
Antora-B.T.D. (Pentaerythritol Tetranitrate—Secobarbital)	Capsule/Oral
Arlidin (Nylidrin HCl)	Tablet/Oral
Avazyme (Chymotrypsin)	Enteric Coated Tablets/Oral
Azo Gantanol (Phenazopyridine HCl—Sulfamethoxazole)	Tablet/Oral
Bentyl/Phenobarbital[1] (Dicyclomine HCl—Phenobarbital)	Capsule, Tablet/Oral
Betadine Vaginal Gel (Providone—Iodine)	Gel form/Vaginal
Brophed (Ephedrine Sulfate-Hydroxyzine HCl-Theophylline)	Tablet/Oral
Butazolidin Alka (Aluminum Hydroxide Gel [dried]-Magnesium Trisilicate-Phenylbutazone)	Capsule/Oral
Cantil with Phenobarbital (Mepenzolate Bromide-Phenobarbital)	Tablet/Oral
Caldecort (Calcium Undecylenate—Hydrocortisone Acetate or Calcium Undecylenate—Hydrocortisone Acetate-Neomycin Sulfate)	Ointment/Topical
Carbital (Carbromal-Sodium Pentobarbital)	Capsule, Elixir/Oral

Brand Name (Ingredients)	Dosage Form
Cartax (Hydroxyzine HCl—Pentaerythritol Tetranitrate)	Tablet/Oral
Celestone with Neomycin (Betamethasone-Neomycin Sulfate)	Cream/Topical
Cetacaine (Benzocaine-Tetracaine HCl)	Aerosol, Ointment, Gel, Liquid/Topical
Chymoral (Chymotrypsin-Trypsin)	Enteric Coated Tablets/Oral
Combid (Isopropamide Iodide—Prochlorperazine Maleate)	Sustained Release Capsule/Oral
Cordran-N (Flurandrenolide—Neomycin Sulfate)	Sustained Release Capsule/Oral
Corovas (Pentaerythritol Tetranitrate-Secobarbital)	Sustained Release Capsule/Oral
Cor-Tar-Quin (Coal Tar Solution—Diiodohydroxyquin-Hydrocortisone)	Cream, Lotion/Topical
Cortisporin (Gramicidin-Hydrocortisone-Neomycin Sulfate—Polymyxin B Sulfate)	Cream/Topical
Cortomycin (Hydrocortisone—Neomycin Sulfate)	Ointment/Topical
Cyclandelate (Cyclandelate)	Tablet/Oral
Cyclospasmol (Cyclandelate)	Capsule, Tablet/Oral
Dainite (Aluminum Hydroxide Gel [dried]-Aminophylline—Benzocaine-Ephedrine HCl-Phenobarbital)	Tablet/Oral
Dainite-KI (Aluminum Hydroxide Gel [dried]-Aminophylline—Benzocaine-Ephedrine HCl—Phenobarbital-Potassium Iodide)	Tablet/Oral

Brand Name (Ingredients)	Dosage Form
Daricon PB (Oxyphency-clidine HCl-Phenobarbital)	Tablet/Oral
Deaner (Deanol Acetamido-Benzoate)	Tablet/Oral
Deprol (Benactyzine HCl—Meprobamate)	Tablet/Oral
Di-Ademil-K (Hydro-flumethiazide—Potassium Chloride)	Tablet/Oral
Dibenzyline[2] (Phenoxy-benzamine HCl)	Capsule/Oral
Diutensen (Methy-clothiazide—Cryptenamine Tannates)	Tablet/Oral
Donnatal Extentabs[3] (Atropine Sulfate-Hyoscine Hydrobromide-Hyoscya-mine Sulfate—Pheno-barbital)	Sustained Release Tablet/Oral
Equagesic (Aspirin-Meprobamate-Ethohepta-zine Citrate)	Tablet/Oral
Equanitrate (Meproba-mate—Pentaerythritol Tetranitrate)	Tablet/Oral
Erythrocin (Erythromycin)	Ointment/Topical
Erythromycin (Erythro-mycin)	Ointment/Topical
Florinef (Fludrocortisone Acetate—Gramicidin-Neomycin Sulfate)	Lotion/Topical
Hydrocortisone-Neomycin (Hydrocortisone Acetate-Neomycin Sulfate)	Cream/Topical

Brand Name (Ingredients)	Dosage Form
Hydromet (Hydrocortisone—Neomycin Sulfate)	Lotion/Topical
Ilotycin (Erythromycin)	Ointment/Topical
Iodochlorhydroxyquin with Hydrocortisone (Hydrocortisone—Iodochlorhydroxyquin)	Cream/Topical
Isordil with Phenobarbital (Isosorbide Dinitrate-Phenobarbital)	Tablet/Oral
Isoxsuprine HCl (Isoxsuprine HCl)	Tablet/Oral
Kenalog-S (Gramicidin-Neomycin Sulfate-Triamcinolone Acetonide)	Ointment, Cream, Lotion/Topical
Librax (Chlordiazepoxide HCl—Clidinium Bromide)	Capsule/Oral
Luftodil (Ephedrine HCl-Guaifenesin-Phenobarbital-Theophylline)	Tablet/Oral
Lufyllin-EPG (Dyphlline-Ephedrine HCl-Guaifenesin-Phenobarbital)	Tablet, Elixir/Oral
Marax (Theophylline—Ephedrine Sulfate-Hydroxyzine HCl)	Tablet, Syrup/Oral
Mepergan Fortis (Meperidine HCl-Promethazine HCl)	Capsule/Oral
Meti-Derm with Neomycin (Neomycin Sulfate-Prednisolone)	Ointment, Aerosol/Topical
Midrin (Acetaminophen-Dichloralphenazone-Isometheptene)	Capsule/Oral

Brand Name (Ingredients)	Dosage Form
Migral (Caffeine-Cyclizine HCl—Ergotamine Tartrate)	Tablet/Oral
Milpath (Meprobamate-Tridihexethyl Chloride)	Tablet/Oral
Miltrate (Meprobamate-Pentaerythritol Tetranitrate)	Tablet/Oral
Myco Triacet (Gramicidin-Neomycin Sulfate-Nystatin-Triamcinolone Acetonide)	Ointment/Topical
Mycolog (Gramicidin-Neomycin Sulfate-Nystatin-Triamcinolone Acetonide)	Ointment, Cream/Topical
Myconef (Fludrocortisone Acetate—Gramicidin-neomycin Sulfate-Nystatin)	Ointment/Topical
Naturetin with K (Bendroflumethiazide-Potassium Chloride)	Tablet/Oral
Neo-Aristocort (Neomycin Sulfate-Triamcinolone Acetonide)	Cream, Ointment/Topical
Neo-Aristoderm (Neomycin Sulfate-Triamcinolone Acetonide)	Aerosol/Topical
Neo-Cort-Dome (Hydrocortisone—Neomycin Sulfate)	Lotion, Cream/Topical
Neo-Cortef (Hydrocortisone Acetate-Neomycin Sulfate)	Ointment, Lotion, Cream/Topical
Neo-Decadron (Dexamethasone Sodium-Neomycin Sulfate)	Cream/Topical

Brand Name (Ingredients)	Dosage Form
Neo-Decaspray (Dexa-methasone—Neomycin Sulfate)	Aerosol/Topical
Neo-Delta-Cortef (Neomycin Sulfate-Prednisolone Acetate)	Ointment, Lotion/Topical
Neo-Diloderm (Dichlorisone—Neomycin Sulfate)	Cream/Topical
Neo-Domeform-HC (Hydrocortisone-Iodochlor-hydroxyquin—Neomycin Sulfate)	Cream/Topical
Neo-Hydeltrasol (Neomycin Sulfate-Prednisolone Sodium Phosphate)	Lotion, Ointment/Topical
Neo-Hytone (Hydro-cortisone—Neomycin Sulfate)	Cream/Topical
Neo-Magnacort (Hydro-cortamate HCl-Neomycin Sulfate)	Ointment/Topical
Neo-Medrol Acetate (Methyl-Prednisolone Acetate—Neomycin Sulfate)	Cream/Topical
Neo-Nysta-Cort (Hydrocortisone—Neomycin Sulfate-Nystatin)	Ointment/Topical
Neo-Oxylone (Fluorometholone—Neomycin Sulfate)	Ointment/Topical
Neo-Resulin-F (Hydrocortisone—Neomycin Sulfate-Resorcinol Monoacetate Sulfur)	Cream/Topical

Brand Name (Ingredients)	Dosage Form
Neo-Synalar (Fluocinolone Acetonide-Neomycin Sulfate)	Cream/Topical
Neo-Tarcortin (Coal Tar Extract—Hydrocortisone-Neomycin Sulfate	Ointment/Topical
Neomycin Sulfate-Hydrocortamate HCl (Hydrocortamate HCl-Neomycin Sulfate)	Ointment/Topical
Neomycin Sulfate-Hydrocortisone (Hydrocortisone-Neomycin Sulfate)	Ointment/Topical
Neomycin Sulfate-Hydrocortisone Acetate (Hydrocortisone Acetate-Neomycin Sulfate)	Ointment/Topical
Neosporin (Neomycin Sulfate—Polymyxin B Sulfate)	Lotion/Topical
Neosporin-G (Gramicidin-Neomycin Sulfate-Polymyxin B Sulfate)	Cream/Topical
Nycin-HC (Hydrocortisone-Neomycin Sulfate)	Ointment/Topical
Nylidrin HCl (Nylidrin HCl)	Tablet/Oral
Nysta-Cort (Hydro-cortisone—Nystatin)	Lotion/Topical
Nystaform-HC (Hydro-cortisone-Iodochlor-hydroxyquin-Nystatin)	Ointment, Lotion/Topical
Nystatin-Neomycin Sulfate-Gramicidin-Triamcinolone Acetonide (Gramicidin-Neomycin Sulfate-Nystatin-Triamcinolone Acetonide)	Cream, Ointment/Topical

Brand Name (Ingredients)	Dosage Form
Onycho-Phytex (Alcohol—Boric Acid-Salicylic Acid-Tannic Acid)	Solution/Topical
Orenzyme (Trypsin-Chymotrypsin)	Enteric Coated Tablet/Oral
Oxaine M (Alumina Gel-Magnesium Hydroxide-Oxethazine)	Suspension form/Oral
Papase (Proteolytic Enzymes from Carica Papaya)	Chewable Tablet/Oral or Buccal
Pathibamate (Meprobamate-Tridihexethyl Chloride)	Tablet/Oral
Pathilon/Phenobarbital (Phenobarbital-Tridihexethyl Chloride)	Tablet, Sustained Release Capsule/Oral
Pathilon Sequels[4] (Tridihexethyl Chloride)	Sustained Release Capsule/Oral
Peritrate with Phenobarbital (Phenobarbital—Pentaerythritol Tetranitrate)	Sustained Release Tablet, Tablet/Oral
Potaba (Aminobenzoate Potassium)	Tablet, Capsule, Powder/Oral
Priscoline (Tolazoline HCl)	Solution/Intramuscular-Intravenous-Subcutaneous
Pro-Banthine/Phenobarbital (Phenobarbital-Propantheline Bromide)	Tablet/Oral
Propazine (Isopropamide Iodide—Prochlorperazine)	Capsule/Oral
Propion Gel (Propionate Calcium-Propionate Sodium)	Gel form/Vaginal

Brand Name (Ingredients)	Dosage Form
Quadrinal (Ephedrine HCl-Phenobarbital—Potassium Iodide—Theophylline Calcium Salicylate)	Tablet/Oral
Quibron Plus (Buta-barbital—Ephedrine HCl-Guaifenesin—Theophylline)	Capsule, Elixir/Oral
Racet (Hydrocortisone—Iodochlorhydroxyquin)	Cream/Topical
Rautrax (Flumethiazide-Potassium Chloride-Rauwolfia Serpentina)	Tablet/Oral
Rautrax-N (Bendroflu-methiazide—Potassium Chloride-Rauwolfia Serpentina)	Tablet/Oral
Rautrax-N Modified (Ben-droflumethiazide-Potassium Chloride-Rauwolfia Serpentina)	Tablet/Oral
Roniacol (Nicotinyl Alcohol or Nicotinyl Alcohol Tartrate)	Tablet, Elixir/Oral
Ruhexatal Pb (Mannitol Hexanitrate-Pheno-barbital)	Tablet/Oral
Ruhexatal and Reserpine (Mannitol Hexanitrate-Reserpine)	Tablet/Oral
Sterazolidin (Aluminum Hydroxide Gel [dried]-Mag-nesium Trisilicate-Phenyl-butazone—Prednisone)	Capsule/Oral
Supertah H-C (Coal Tar-Hydrocortisone)	Ointment/Topical

Brand Name (Ingredients)	Dosage Form
Synalgos (Aspirin-Caffeine-Promethazine HCl)	Capsule/Oral
Synalgos DC (Aspirin-Caffeine—Dihydrocodeine Bitartrate—Promethazine HCl)	Capsule/Oral
T.C.M. (Meprobamate-Tridi-hexethylchloride)	Tablet/Oral
Terra-Cortril (Hydro-cortisone—Oxytetracycline HCl or Hydrocortisone—Oxytetracycline HCl—Poly-myxin B Sulfate)	Ointment or Aerosol/Topical
Tigan[5] (Trimethobenzamide HCl)	Capsule/Oral & Suppository/Rectal
Tri-Statin (Gramicidin-Neomycin Sulfate-Nys-tatin-Triamcinolone Acetonide)	Cream/Topical
Trocinate (Thiphenamil HCl)	Tablet/Oral
Valpin PB (Anisotropine Methylbromide-Phenobar-bital)	Tablet/Oral
Vasocon-A (Antazoline Phosphate-Naphazoline HCl)	Solution/Opthalmic
Vasodilan (Isoxsuprine HCl)	Tablet/Oral; Solution/Intramuscular
Vioform-Hydrocortisone (Hydrocortisone-Iodochlor-hydroxyquin)	Cream, Ointment/Topical
Vytone (Diiodohy-droxyquin—Hydro-cortisone)	Cream/Topical

Brand Name (Ingredients)	Dosage Form
Wyanoids HC (Belladonna Extract-Bismuth Sub-carbonate—Bismuth Oxyiodide-Boric Acid—Ephedrine Sulfate-Hydro-cortisone Acetate-Peruvian Balsam—Zinc Oxide)	Suppository/Rectal
Zactane (Ethoheptazine Citrate)	Tablet/Oral
Zactirin (Aspirin-Etho-heptazine Citrate)	Tablet/Oral
Zactirin Compound 100 (Aspirin—Caffeine-Ethoheptazine—Phena-cetin)	Tablet/Oral
Ze-Tar-Quin (Coal Tar-Diiodohydroxyquin-Hydrocortisone)	Cream/Topical
Zetone (Coal Tar-Hydrocortisone)	Cream/Topical

1. Does not apply to syrup.
2. Does not apply to "pheochromocytoma" indication.
3. Applies only to controlled release product.
4. Does not apply to conventional dosage forms of *Pathlion*.
5. Does not apply to capsules in 200 or 400 mg strengths.

How Different Drug Types Work in the Body

During the last 50 years there have been dramatic advances in medicine, particularly in the development of new drugs which have improved our overall health and extended our life expectancy. Many of the recent drugs, like antibiotics, oral contraceptives, psychotropic drugs, and the new heart medicines, have changed our life-styles. Today there are thousands of brand-name and generic drugs available; they dry up runny noses, curb pain, and, very often, arrest serious disease.

Although some drugs are "synthetic" products, concocted in the laboratory, others are derived from plants, herbs, roots, and other naturally occurring minerals and substances which have been known and used for centuries. Digoxin, for example, was derived from digitalis which has been used for over 200 years to treat heart disease and other ailments such as "fits" and comes from the foxglove family; Quinine is derived from tree bark; Insulin and other hormones are produced from animal glands; and, of course, Penicillin originally came from simple bread mold. In some ways, today's giant pharmaceutical companies are direct descendants of the medicine men of earlier times who mixed exotic "potions."

The difference between drugs we use today and the potions of past eras is standardization. Except for certain combinations that your pharmacist will make up for you, today all pills are made in modern manufacturing facilities which are strictly supervised. Because of stringent regulations and laws which have come into force in the U.S. since the early part of this century, all drugs are carefully made. Each new drug is required to pass through many testing levels before it is

557

marketed. By the time a drug reaches your mouth, it has been proved *both* safe and effective. The Food and Drug Administration (FDA), which supervises new-drug introduction, requires that drugs be tested on lab animals and humans before they can be marketed. Some drugs are studied after their introduction to see if they can be used to treat other diseases— or if they will produce previously unreported side effects.

Two examples of this follow-up or postmarketing surveillance are oral contraceptives (the Pill) and the beta blocker Propranolol (Inderal). The serious potential side effects of the Pill were not revealed until millions of women had used the drug for 10 to 20 years. Only after its long-term effects on the body became known could scientists fully evaluate it. On the other hand, Propranolol had already been shown to be very effective in the treatment of abnormal heart rhythms, angina, high blood pressure, and other diseases. Recent tests demonstrated its effectiveness in preventing second heart attacks and were so successful that a long-range study was stopped at midpoint to allow those in the control group (who were getting placebos) to benefit from the drug's newly uncovered properties.

The drug introduction process can take 3 to 10 years and may cost millions of dollars. Even drugs available outside the U.S. are required to undergo retesting to meet FDA standards. Many critics have suggested that the U.S. drug laws are too tough; however, the United States has yet to have a drug tragedy of the scale of the Thalidomide scandal of the 1960s in Europe. At that time, many women were given the sedative during the first months of pregnancy. The drug caused many horrible birth defects and led directly to stronger FDA regulations in the 1960s.

Each year hundreds of drugs are tested, but only a small percentage will reach the market. Some drugs which are in the various stages of testing can be used for special medical cases, as can drugs that are never introduced because they may not have great commercial value. These drugs are called "orphan drugs" but can be obtained through the FDA under a "compassionate IND," a special application procedure, which is undertaken by physicians; it's wise to check with your doctor before taking any medication not regularly prescribed in the United States.

HOW DO PILLS WORK?

Drugs work by altering a normal function in the body or by correcting an abnormal function. Generally they are taken by mouth in either solid (capsule or tablet) or liquid form, depending on their chemical makeup. Some drugs are injected directly into the bloodstream for quicker action or are not made in oral form.

When a pill is taken, it is first broken down in the stomach by the gastric juices. The drug passes through the walls of the stomach and the rest of the digestive system into the bloodstream. (Food already in the stomach may slow this absorption process, so it's important to ask your doctor or pharmacist if your drug should be taken with or before meals.) Once in the bloodstream, drugs, along with foods and other substances, are sent to and metabolized by the liver. When the liver has done its work it may have turned the drug into its most useful form, or it may have deactivated the drug. In either case, the drug is then sent back out into the bloodstream and then to its site of action.

Once the drug has exerted its effect it returns to the bloodstream and is excreted. Because drugs work for only a certain period of time, we have to take them in repeated doses. Therefore, it's important to take all drugs exactly as prescribed to avoid overloading or overdosing your body.

The following information will give you a brief idea of how various drug types work in the body.

ANTIBIOTICS

Antibiotics are used to treat infections which may be caused by any of hundreds of microorganisms. You must take an antibiotic specific for the organism causing your problem; otherwise, your infection cannot be cured.

How do we identify the trouble-making organism? By running specific tests called "cultures." Your doctor, a nurse, or a trained technician takes a small sample from the infected area and puts it in a medium where it can multiply and grow, from which it can draw appropriate nutrients. The culture is placed in an environment which promotes growth. Within 2 days the organisms multiply to form a colony; samples of the colony can be examined under a microscope and identified.

The organisms may be tested against various antibiotics to see which is the best choice for treatment. This is called testing for sensitivity.

Your doctor often has a good idea of what the infecting organisms are as soon as he evaluates the location and appearance of the infection and correlates this information with your symptoms. However, he must confirm his hypothesis by taking a culture.

If you are already taking an antibiotic, there is one difficulty about taking a culture: the culture may give a false negative by not growing even if you have an infection. Even small amounts of antibiotic in your body can grossly interfere with this test.

Many infections, including the common cold, the flu, and some other upper respiratory (lung) infections, are caused by viruses. Viruses are simpler organisms than bacteria; for the most part, they are not affected by antibiotics, so taking an antibiotic will not cure your disease. You must depend upon your doctor to distinguish between bacterial and virus infections, which often present the same general symptoms. Often the only way to tell them apart is through a culture.

Can taking an antibiotic when you don't need one hurt you? Yes. Taking any drug unnecessarily exposes you to potential side effects and adverse reactions. Also, unwarranted use of an antibiotic can sensitize you to it, so that the next time you use it, perhaps in a situation where you badly need it, you may develop an allergic reaction. Self-medication with antibiotics is unwise for other reasons: you may take too much or too little, or you may have an infection caused by an organism not affected by the antibiotic. Do not take any antibiotic unless specifically directed to do so by your doctor.

In general, antibiotics are considered either bactericidal or bacteriostatic. Batericidal antibiotics kill the microorganisms they affect by interfering with natural processes such as development of the cell wall or normal chemical reactions. Bactericidal antibiotics include Penicillin, Ampicillin, Amoxicillin, Cefadroxil (Duricef), Cephalexin, Carbenicillin (Geocillin), Polymyxin, Bacitracin, Amphotericin, and Nystatin.

Bacteriostatic antibiotics interfere with microorganisms by disturbing chemical processes (usually, stages of protein production) necessary to their reproduction. Bacteriostatic antibiotics include Tetracycline, Doxycycline, Minocycline,

Erythromycin, Griseofulvin, and Chloramphenicol. (Chloramphenicol may be bacteriostatic in some situations.)

ANTIHYPERTENSIVE DRUGS

High blood pressure is a major problem in the United States, since many people have it and there are problems associated with treating it. Twelve percent of Americans have high blood pressure but don't know it. Of those who know they have high blood pressure, only half have achieved constant pressure readings in the acceptable range.

High blood pressure can cause heart attack, heart failure, stroke, aneurysm (ballooning out of a major blood vessel—death can result if the blood vessel wall bursts like a balloon), and kidney failure.

How do you know if you have high blood pressure?

For diagnosis a series of blood pressure readings, on at least three visits, are taken to be sure that the high pressure is persistent. The way your high blood pressure is treated depends upon how high the pressure is and also on an evaluation of how much damage has already been done.

Drugs usually play a major role in the treatment of high blood pressure. Four types of drugs are used to help reduce muscle tension in veins and arteries: diuretics, vasodilators, drugs that interfere with nervous system activity, and one drug that interferes with body hormone function.

Diuretics help lower blood pressure by lowering the amount of water in the body. They decrease the amount of fluid that must be handled by the circulatory system and lower the blood pressure by reducing fluid volume inside blood vessels. Diuretics alone can often control mild or moderate hypertension. Some diuretics used to treat hypertension are Hydrochlorothiazide, Chlorothiazide, Polythiazide (Renese), Chlorthalidone, Ethacrynic Acid (Edecrin), Furosemide, and Zaroxolyn (Diulo).

Vasodilators work directly on the muscles in the walls of arteries to relax them, reducing blood pressure, so they are called direct-acting vasodilators. An example is Hydralazine, an ingredient in the drug Ser-Ap-Es and available by itself in tablet form; it is always used in combination with another antihypertensive drug.

The third group of drugs act on the nervous system to help control muscle tone in blood vessels. Some of these drugs work in the brain or spinal cord (central nervous system);

some at intermediate centers for nervous system control called autonomic ganglia; some at nerve endings where control of muscle tone actually takes place; and some at points in muscle tissue (receptor sites) where chemical messages from the nervous system are received. Some of the more important drugs in this group are Reserpine, Methyldopa, Clonidine, Guanethidine, and Propranolol (also used for heart disease).

The fourth group is represented by a new drug, Captopril, which prevents the conversion of a potent hormone called angiotensin inhibitors and can drastically lower blood pressure.

More than one drug is usually prescribed in the treatment of hypertension. By mixing medications from the three major groups we can get drugs that complement one another, resulting in more efficient lowering of blood pressure.

One of the problems in the treatment of high blood pressure is that people often don't do what is best for them. They don't take their medicines as directed, they don't follow special diets given to them, and they don't follow other instructions relating to exercise and weight control. In high blood pressure, as in many other diseases, effective treatment can only be accomplished by you. The medication prescribed for your hypertension can help only if taken exactly as directed.

HEART DRUGS

This section is about drugs that have a direct effect on the heart rather than drugs that have only a secondary effect, for example, by reducing high blood pressure. We will discuss digitalis drugs, drugs used to correct abnormal heart rhythm, and drugs used to treat angina pectoris.

Digitalis Group

The members of the digitalis group are chemically similar. Originally derived from the garden plant *Digitalis purpurea* (foxglove), they are chemically synthesized today. Most commonly used are Digoxin and Digitoxin. Digitalis drugs may differ in how long it takes the drug to start working, how long the drug effect lasts, how the drug is eliminated from the body, and how well the drug is tolerated by patients.

What are the effects of digitalis on your heart? First, it makes your heart beat more forcefully, which helps people with congestive heart failure by helping the heart to work more efficiently and increase the amount of blood pumped with each contraction, or beat. The heart is essentially a pump; the more efficiently it works, the better off we are.

Second, digitalis slows the rate at which the heart beats. This is also important in helping the heart to be more efficient. When a person suffers from heart failure, the heart muscle contracts with less force and pumps less blood with each beat. The normal response of the heart is to try to work faster and keep a sufficient supply of blood flowing. But a faster heartbeat creates another problem: like any pump, the heart can only work when there is sufficient fluid (blood) inside the pump chamber. When the heart beats too rapidly, the pump chambers of the heart (ventricles) do not fill enough between beats, reducing the potential output of the heart.

Correcting Abnormal Heart Rhythms

When abnormalities in the conduction of nervous impulses through the heart muscle are present, they cause the heart to beat in uneven cycles or in an uncoordinated manner. Arrhythmias (abnormal heart rhythms) have many causes, including:

- Imbalances in body levels of potassium or sodium.
- Thyroid or other disease.
- Adverse drug effects.
- Cardiac disease directly affecting nerve pathways in the heart.

Arrhythmias, which come in many sizes, shapes, and styles, are classified according to heart area affected, cause (if one can be found), and severity. Classification aids in drug selection. Commonly used drugs include Phenytoin, Procainamide, Propranolol, and Quinidine. They slow down the rate of nerve impulse conduction and nerve response in the heart, which decreases the rate of contraction of various parts of the heart.

When drugs do not satisfactorily control abnormal heart rhythms, an electrical device called a pacemaker may be inserted. The pacemaker controls heart rate by sending out an electrical impulse of its own that overrides or counterbalances abnormal impulses being transmitted within the heart. It may be implanted permanently if use for some time does not convert the heart to a normal rhythm of its own.

Treatment of Angina

Angina pectoris is characterized by a squeezing, choking, or heavy pain or discomfort in the chest. These symptoms can also be found in or can extend to the arm, shoulder, back, neck, or lower jaw. Angina usually sets in or gets worse while or immediately after the patient has undergone physically strenuous activity. It is thought to be caused by a decrease in oxygen supply to the heart. Oxygen deficit develops when blood flow to the heart is partly blocked by deposits of cholesterol or other materials in blood vessels. Development of this kind of blockage is called atherosclerosis and the disease (such as angina) resulting from it is called atherosclerotic heart disease. Oxygen deficit can also occur if the blood vessels develop a spasm and choke off blood supply.

Drugs used to treat angina help dilate (open) the blood vessels serving the heart. Nitroglycerin, the main example of the nitrate group, is taken in tablets under the tongue and can provide almost immediate relief from angina as the tablets are absorbed directly into the bloodstream and help relax the muscles in the walls of bood vessels serving the heart. Other drugs of this group, such as Isosorbide Dinitrate (Isordil Sorbitrate), Erythrityl Tetranitrate (Cardilate), and Pentaerythrityl Tetranitrate (Peritrate, Duotrate) have different durations of activity. A long-acting drug may not give as prompt relief, but it is hoped that by keeping the blood vessels dilated, the frequency of angina attacks will be reduced. An attack that occurs while a person is taking a long-acting drug can be treated by the faster-acting Nitroglycerin.

Propranolol (Inderal) does not affect blood vessels by dilating them. It slows the activity of the heart so that the heart requires less oxygen to work; this decreases the likelihood of an angina attack. Most effective when used with one of the drugs discussed above, it can only prevent an angina attack; it cannot be used to treat an acute angina attack.

Calcium Channel Blockers

Calcium channel blockers, or calcium antagonists, are the newest class of heart drugs. They interfere with the passage of calcium from the blood vessels into the heart muscles. Since calcium is an essential ingredient in muscle contraction, any drug that affects calcium in this way will interfere with and reduce muscle contraction, thereby reducing the need for oxygen. The calcium channel blockers are used to treat several conditions, including angina (heart pains caused when too little oxygen is supplied to the muscle), abnormal heart rhythms (arrhythmia), and high blood pressure. The calcium channel blockers are also being studied for their effect on blood clotting, exercise-induced asthma, and spasms of the upper gastrointestinal tract; however, their usefulness for these conditions is not yet established. A much needed addition to the growing list of cardiac drugs, they will be used by thousands of patients in the next decade. The two currently available members of this group are Nifedipine and Verapamil.

Beta Blockers

These are another new group of drugs. They block the effect of naturally occurring stimulants (norepinephrine, or adrenaline) on the "beta" receptors found in the heart and in some blood vessels. This effect produces several important changes in body function; it slows the rate of the heartbeat, reduces the amount of work done by the heart, causes dilation of some of the major blood vessels, and antagonizes some of the usual physiologic effects of natural body stimulants. The beta blockers are used to treat abnormal heart rhythms, angina, high blood pressure, hyperthyroid disease, and some other conditions.

Recent studies of these beta blockers show that they have an important effect on patients who have had a heart attack. If patients are given a beta blocker a few days after a first heart attack, there is a significant reduction in the occurrence of second heart attacks. No one knows yet why the beta blockers produce this effect, although it is thought to be because these drugs reduce the amount of work done by the weakened heart. Members of this group include Propranolol, Timolol, Atenolol, and Nadolol.

ANTICOAGULANTS

Anticoagulants are popularly known as blood-thinning drugs: by preventing blood from clotting, they keep it "thinner." They have been in use for some 400 years and are prescribed to anyone who has a disease that increases the chance of forming a blood clot or who has had some damage from a blood clot in the brain (stroke), heart, lung, or other critical area. Those who have had a myocardial infarction (heart attack) may be given an anticoagulant to keep heart damage from causing the formation of a blood clot.

The clotting process is a complex set of chemical reactions; anything that upsets one or more of these reactions will prevent clot formation.

If you are taking an anticoagulant, its effectiveness should be carefully monitored by blood tests, which can easily and conveniently be performed in your doctor's office and are used to help decide if you need more or less medication. Anticoagulants should not be used if you have a history of severe bleeding episodes, have an active bleeding ulcer, have had a recent stroke with continued bleeding in the head, or are pregnant (especially if your doctor feels you may spontaneously lose your baby).

Most people taking anticoagulant drugs have no major problems so long as they take care of themselves, follow instructions, and avoid unnecessary medications, including over-the-counter drugs containing Aspirin. (Guidance on specific over-the-counter drugs can be obtained from your doctor or pharmacist.) Aspirin and other over-the-counter drugs can interact with oral anticoagulants to increase the action of the anticoagulant, causing bleeding, most commonly at first from the nose or gums. If you are taking an anticoagulant and begin to ooze blood from the nose or gums, contact your doctor *immediately.*

Other drug interactions may decrease the effect of the anticoagulant, which increases the risk of a blood clot—exactly what you were trying to prevent in the first place. The best policy is to avoid drugs (if possible) which can interfere with anticoagulant activity, including barbiturates, Glutethimide, oral contraceptive drugs, and Phenytoin.

Interactions with anticoagulant drugs can be compensated for by adjusting the dosage of anticoagulant. For example, if you must take Phenytoin on a long-term basis, the doctor can give you more anticoagulant drug than he otherwise would.

ANTINEOPLASTICS (Anticancer Drugs)

Drugs used to treat cancer are designed to slow or completely stop the abnormal growth of cancerous cells. Basically, cancerous cells grow uncontrollably at a much faster rate than others in surrounding tissues. The abnormal growth rate causes functional problems and interferes with normal life processes. A great deal of time, effort, and money has gone into research aimed at discovering more about the growth process of human cells so that drugs could be designed which would interfere with specific phases in the growth of the cancerous cells. Drugs which do this are called, "cell cycle specific" drugs. Other anticancer drugs work on cells that are growing or resting; they are called "cell cycle nonspecific." In other words, these drugs do not work on a specific phase of cell growth. In reviewing the antineoplastic drugs, we will only provide a brief description of the various classes of drugs used. Also, many drugs given to cancer patients are not given to treat the basic disease. Rather, they are used to relieve other symptoms which may have developed as a result of the cancer (pain, constipation, nutritional deficiency, etc.) or to relieve the stress caused by the disease (tranquilizers, antianxiety drugs, etc.).

Alkylating Agents

These drugs interfere with DNA and render it powerless to carry out its normal function in cell duplication. Members of this group include Mechlorethamine, Chlorambucil (Leukeran), Melphalan, Cyclophosphamide (Cytoxan), Lomustine, Carmustine, Uracil Mustard, Thiotepa, Busulfan, and Pipobroman. These drugs all have severe side effects and can be as dangerous as the diseases against which they are used if not taken under the strict supervision of a doctor who has been trained to use these medications. The alkylating agents are cell cycle nonspecific.

Antimetabolites

These drugs can also interfere with normal cells and cause their eventual destruction. They can accomplish this by either substituting for a normal component of the cell, thereby rendering that part of the cell nonfunctional, or by inhibiting a key enzyme directly within the cell. Members of this group include Methotrexate, Fluorouracil, Floxuridine, Cytarabine, Mercaptopurine, and Thioguanine. The antimetabolites are cell cycle specific agents and only work on the so-called "s phase" of cell growth.

Hormones

Hormone therapy has been successfully used as part of the

treatment of various cancers although the exact mechanism of action is not known. Adrenocortical steroids (Prednisone, Hydrocortisone, Dexamethasone, etc.) are used most widely. Male (androgens) and female (estrogens) hormones are used to counterbalance the overproduction of sex hormones produced by some tumors, thereby restricting their growth. For example, androgens such as Dromostanolone, Calusterone, or Testolactone are used in the treatment of breast cancer in women. Estrogens such as Diethylstilbestrol may be given to men with prostate cancer to counterbalance the overproduction of male hormone resulting from that tumor. Other hormones used in cancer treatment are the progestins (Megestrol Acetate and Medroxyprogesterone Acetate). One drug has been developed which counters the effect of estrogen. This "anti-estrogen" is Tamoxifen and can be used to neutralize excessive estrogen.

Antibiotics

Several antineoplastic drugs are derived from natural sources and have antimicrobial activity. These drugs work by disrupting cellular functions in normal tissues as well as in invading microorganisms. When used in cancer treatment, the drug is taken up by the cancerous tissue because those cells are dividing at a much more rapid pace than normal cells. These drugs are cell cycle nonspecific. They inhibit DNA-dependent cell functions and delay or inhibit the process by which cells divide. The members of this group are Bleomycin, Doxorubicin, Daunorubicin, Mitomycin, Dactinomycin, and Mithramycin.

Mitotic Inhibitors

There are only two drugs in this group: Vincristine and Vinblastine. They work by interfering with a specific phase of cell duplication, that point at which the two strands of DNA separate to form the nuclei of the two new cells. These drugs are cell cycle specific and are used frequently because of their relatively low incidence of serious toxic effects on the bone marrow.

Radioactive Drugs

Radiation is used to kill cancerous cells. Drugs tagged with a radioactive component are used when the drug is absorbed by a specific organ that is cancerous and in need of treatment. Examples of this type of drug are Iodine 131 (thyroid cancer) and Phosphorous 32 (leukemias, polycythemia vera, lung cancer).

Immunosuppressants

Azathioprine (Imuran) is a unique medicine used to suppress the body's immune response mechanism, which normally allows us to respond to infection, outside agents that cause allergies, or other foreign objects. When it is artificially suppressed with this medication, as in the case of a transplanted kidney, it permits the new kidney to continue functioning in the body of the transplant patient. Without Azathioprine the body would react to a new kidney as a foreign object and soon destroy it. People taking this drug are unusually susceptible to infection and must be constantly alert to any changes. Normal responses (fever, etc.) may not be present or may be delayed by Azathioprine treatment.

Other

Other drugs have been developed which do not fall into any of the previously discussed groups, although some of them act in the same way as those in certain groups. Hydroxyurea inhibits DNA synthesis. It is cell cycle specific. Procarbazine inhibits protein DNA and RNA synthesis. It is cell cycle specific and used only for Hodgkins disease. Dacarbazine inhibits DNA and acts very similarly to the alkylating agents. It is cell cycle nonspecific. Cisplatin also works similarly to the alkylating agents. It is used in the treatment of tumors of the ovary and testicle and is cell cycle nonspecific. Mitotane is used in cancer of the adrenal cortex (the part of the body that produces adrenal corticosteroids). Its action is very specific and, therefore, it does not have many severe side effects. Asparaginase is used in the treatment of leukemia. It is a highly toxic drug that must be used only under strict supervision in a hospital.

Newer agents are continuously being investigated for their effect against cancer. Several have shown promise but many have received more notoriety and publicity than they deserve. Two examples are Laetrile and Interferon. Laetrile was recently found to be worthless in cancer treatment. Interferon is still undergoing preliminary studies in several different types of cancer. The premise in using Interferon is that many cancers are caused by viruslike particles. Interferon, theoretically, interrupts virus activity and thus can treat cancer. It will be years before there are final results on Interferon.

DRUGS FOR THE COMMON COLD

Have you ever felt unwell and had a runny or stuffed nose, postnasal drip, muscle aches, cough, headache, or fever? If so, you probably have been told, "It's just a cold." The common cold is a catchall name given to a set of symptoms that can be caused by over 150 different viruses. Although we know what causes a cold we cannot prevent or cure it: we can only let it run its course and take medicine to make us more comfortable and help relieve the symptoms. Antibiotic drugs are not effective against cold viruses. How, then, can you make yourself more comfortable during a cold? You can take nasal decongestants, antihistamines, cough suppressants, expectorants, analgesics (pain relievers), or antipyretics (fever reducers). Usually, if you get a prescription for a cold remedy it will contain drugs in two or three of these categories. Let us consider each type of drug and how it helps relieve our suffering.

Nasal Decongestants

When your nose is stuffed or runny, tissue in the lining of the nose and blood vessels are dilated and produce more secretions (mucus) than normal. There has to be some place for the extra material to go, so it either goes out the front way (runny nose) or the back way (postnasal drip). Dilated tissues give one the feeling of nasal congestion or stuffiness. Decongestant drugs are stimulants which, when they reach the congested area, act on the swollen vessels and tissues to cause them to return to normal size by vasoconstriction, allowing nasal passages to clear. This can improve sinus drainage and help relieve sinus headache.

Decongestants can be applied topically as nose drops or sprays, or can be swallowed in tablet or liquid form. People often use the drugs in both forms—the tablet or liquid to produce a deeper, longer-lasting constriction, and the spray to produce almost immediate response by constriction of surface vessels and tissues. In tablet or liquid form, decongestants are frequently combined with antihistamines.

People with high blood pressure, diabetes, heart disease, or thyroid disease should avoid decongestants because they could worsen their disease. People taking antidepressant drugs or MAO inhibitors should not take decongestants because of possible drug interaction.

Antihistamines

Antihistamines block the effects of histamine, a naturally occurring chemical in the body which is released into the bloodstream as part of its reponse to outside challenge. This response is sometimes called the allergic response, and when we experience it we say we have an allergy, whether the challenge is from an insect bite or from pollen or some other allergenic (allergy-provoking) substance. Antihistamines can only block histamine after it is in the bloodstream; they cannot prevent histamine from being released.

People's response to any drug is variable. There are four major chemical types of antihistamines, and there is even greater variability in response to each type.

Cough Suppressants

Coughing can be good for you. It is a natural reflex designed to protect you by helping to clear the respiratory tract of any unwanted material, be it foreign matter or unusually heavy natural secretions. When you take a cough medicine it suppresses this natural reflex. The medicine cannot cure the cause of your cough.

Cough medicine is helpful when it allows you to get a restful night's sleep when you might otherwise have been kept up by a cough. It is also beneficial in reducing the amount of coughing because frequent, deep coughing tends to cause irritation of the respiratory tract. Cough suppressants act either on the cough control center (there actually is such a place) in the part of the brain called the medulla, or on the source of irritation in your throat causing the cough center to be activated. Most commercial cough suppressants (both prescription and over-the-counter) tend to combine a centrally acting drug (such as Codeine or Dextromethorphan) with an ingredient that will help reduce local irritation (such as glycerine, honey, or some other soothing syrupy medicine). Expectorants such as Terpin Hydrate, Guiafenesin, and Potassium Iodide are often used in cough formulas on the theory that by making mucus secretions in the throat thinner and perhaps easier to bring up, they will help reduce cough.

Expectorants

Expectorants stimulate the production of mucus and other respiratory secretions, helping loosen thick, tenacious secretions by diluting them with more secretory material. Once diluted, they can be removed by natural action. Expectorants work well in respiratory diseases that cause very thick secretions. Their effectiveness with coughs due to colds, however, is questionable because thickness of secretions is not a major problem. When purchasing a cough medicine, especially one sold over the counter, be sure that if there is an expectorant in it, there is also a cough suppressant. If you are not sure, consult your pharmacist.

Analgesics and Antipyretics

The two antipyretic analgesics (reducing fever, reducing pain) commonly used in cold medicines are Aspirin and Acetaminophen (Tylenol, Datril, etc.). Aspirin also reduces inflammation. Aspirin or Acetaminophen should only be used if you have fever, pain, or inflammation (Aspirin only, not Acetaminophen). Taking these drugs unnecessarily may expose you to drug-induced side effects without gaining any counterbalancing benefit. If your doctor has given you a prescription drug to relieve pain, fever, or inflammation, don't take the medicine later on for another illness unless you consult him first.

PSYCHOTROPIC DRUGS

Psychotropic drugs are used to alleviate symptoms in psychiatric disorders, from minor anxiety to major psychoses. They are extremely useful in today's stressful society and often enable people to function normally on a day-to-day basis.

Psychotropic drugs affect brain chemicals or chemical systems called neurotransmitters, which mediate such basic functions as sleep, wakefulness, and memory, by increasing or blocking their effects. There are three major classes of psychotropic drugs: antianxiety drugs, antipsychotic drugs, and antidepressants.

Antianxiety Drugs

These are the minor tranquilizers such as Diazepam (Valium), Chlordiazepoxide (Librium), Oxazepam (Serax), and related benzodiazepines, and Meprobamate, which are used to treat anxiety neurosis. People with an anxiety neurosis experience waves of anxiety characterized by apprehension, tension, sudden fatigue, and a panic reaction; these feelings may be accompanied by sweating, rapid heartbeat (palpitation), weakness, dizziness, and irritability, which are defenses set up by the brain to avoid the actual source of the anxiety. Antianxiety drugs generally direct their activity at brain centers involved with emotion.

Antipsychotic Drugs

The antipsychotic (neuroleptic) drugs alter the activity of dopamine, norepinephrine, and serotonin in the brain, with a profound effect on psychotic disorder, whether paranoid or schizophrenic. People with psychotic disorders show severe personality disintegration and distortion of the world around them, have difficulty separating reality from fantasy, and often suffer from hallucinations and delusions.

The major groups of antipsychotic drugs are the phenothiazines, such as Chlorpromazine (Thorazine), Trifluoperazine (Stelazine), and Thioridazine (Mellaril); the butyrophenones, such as Haloperidol (Haldol); and the thioxanthenes, such as Thiothixene (Navane). All of them tend to exhibit more side effects than antianxiety drugs and are reserved for more severe situations. Other groups of anti-psychotic drugs are the dibenzoxazepines: Loxipine (Loxitane); and the dihydroindolones: Molindone (Moban, Lidone).

The benzodiazapine tranquilizers can also be used as anticonvulsant drugs. In fact, one of that class, Clonazepam (Clonopin) is used solely for that purpose. Its other effects are similar to Diazepam (Valium) and other members of that group.

Special care should be used by patients with a family and/or personal history of alcohol or substance abuse when taking benzodiazapine or other anti-anxiety drugs. Recent research studies indicate that these people are at greater risk to become dependent on these drugs.

Antidepressants

Depressed people tend to be self-critical, self-deprecating, brooding; they have a feeling of extreme helplessness. Loss of self-esteem, withdrawal from personal relationships, and inhibition of normal aggressive activity may result. Those suffering from depression also frequently suffer from anxiety. Here the depression is thought to be a defense against the underlying anxiety and is accompanied by physical complaints of headache, tiredness, loss of appetite, and constipation.

The two classes of antidepressant drugs are the tricyclic antidepressants, such as Amitriptyline (Elavil and Endep) and Imipramine (Tofranil), and the MAO inhibitors, such as Isocarboxazid (Marplan), Tranylcypromine Sulfate (Parnate), and Phenelzine Sulfate (Nardil). Both classes are effective in relieving depressive symptoms, but they do not cure depression; they only help the patient to deal more effectively with his problems.

MAO INHIBITORS

MAO inhibitor drugs block a naturally occurring enzyme system called monoamine oxidase, from which the name MAO comes. One of its important functions is to break down other naturally occurring chemicals called amines. Amines are responsible for much of the stimulating effects of the central nervous system. By giving an MAO inhibitor we *increase* the amount of amines available. Too much MAO inhibitor can produce excess amine effects such as overstimulation, very high blood pressure, agitation, changes in heart rate and rhythm, muscle spasms and tremors, and sleeplessness; but taken under the supervision of a physician, MAO inhibitors can be valuable, relatively safe therapeutic agents.

Because of their high potential for drug interaction and side effects, MAO inhibitor drugs are prescribed only for patients who are severely depressed and do not respond to tricyclic therapy (Tranylcypromine [Parnate] and Isocarboxazid [Marplan]), or for people with severe high blood pressure (Pargyline [Eutonyl]), Hodgkin's disease (Procarbazine [Matulane]), and infections (Furazolidone [Furoxone]); here the beneficial effects may not be related directly to MAO inhibition, but many of the adverse effects and all the drug interactions are so related. These drugs are not included in *The Pill Book* because of their limited use.

When an MAO inhibitor is given along with a drug which

is broken down, at least in part, by the MAO enzyme system, the result is *higher concentration* of the second drug. For example, when antidepressant drugs are given with an MAO inhibitor, unusually high antidepressant levels resulting from this combination can cause fever and convulsions. Similarly, when a diabetic patient is given an MAO inhibitor drug, his blood sugar will be lowered if he is taking either an oral antidiabetic drug or Insulin.

MAO inhibitors have also been implicated in serious inter-actions with certain foods—those containing large amounts of naturally occurring amines (tyramine or dopa). The MAO inhibitor makes you lose the ability to rapidly destroy these chemicals, with possible results of headache, rapid rise in blood pressure, hemorrhaging due to bursting of small blood vessels, and general stimulation. Several deaths have been caused by this interaction.

Some foods to be avoided if you are taking an MAO inhibitor are broad beans, Chianti wine, chicken or beef liver, pickled herring, and cheddar cheese, as well as Camembert, Stilton, Brie, Emmentaler, and Grùyère cheese. Avoid large amounts of chocolate, sour cream, canned figs, raisins, soy sauce, pineapple, and bananas.

CORTICOSTEROIDS

Corticosteroid drugs are chemically related to hydrocortisone, corticosterone, aldosterone, and deoxycorticosterone (natu-rally produced hormones that are essential to normal body functions). The first two hormones control the storage of carbohydrates (sugars) in the body, affect the breakdown of body proteins, and reduce inflammation. The last two pri-marily control the regulation of sodium and potassium in the body, although they possess some activity similar to that of hydrocortisone and corticosterone.

Some of the corticosteroid drugs most commonly used in patient treatment are related to the hormones hydrocorti-sone and corticosterone: Betamethasone, Cortisone, Dexa-methasone, Fluprednisolone, Hydrocortisone, Meprednisone, Methylprednisolone, Paramethasone, Prednisolone, Predni-sone, and Triamcinolone.

Others are related to the hormone deoxycorticosterone: Deoxycorticosterone and Fludrocortisone.

Corticosteroids are used to treat a wide variety of conditions. They can be used to replace naturally produced hormones in patients who cannot make enough of their own. They can also be used to treat diseases in which it is desirable to administer a potent anti-inflammatory drug. Some of the host of diseases in which corticosteroids are used for this effect are those which affect collagen (connective) tissue such as lupus erythematosus and pemphigus vulgaris; allergic disorders including asthma, hay fever, and allergic rhinitis (nasal inflammation due to allergy); and reactions to drugs, serum, and blood transfusions. Skin rashes of various types, causes, and severities are also treated with corticosteroids. The drugs can be especially helpful in treating itchy, inflamed rashes and in psoriasis, neurodermatitis, and similar conditions. Corticosteroids are also given to treat inflammation of areas of the body including tendons, muscles, eye, brain, and liver. They are of great value in shock and are often used as part of the treatment of certain cancers.

Because of the wide variety of diseases for which corticosteroids are used, your doctor must individualize treatment for you, depending upon the drug being used and the disease being treated.

Corticosteroids can have many serious side effects. The possibility of experiencing side effects increases with the amount of drug being taken and the length of time it is taken. Some of the possible side effects of corticosteroids are irritation of the stomach (possibly leading to peptic ulcer), loss of body potassium, infection (due to temporary disabling of body defense mechanisms), behavioral and personality changes, loss of calcium from bone leading to subsequent bone weakness and increased possibility of fracture in elderly patients, increased pressure inside the eye, excessive breakdown of body proteins, change in the quality and appearance of skin to which corticosteroids are topically applied, muscle weakness, aggravation of diabetes, and unusual or excessive retention of water in the body, leading to fluid accumulation under the skin.

Corticosteroids are remarkable drugs which can be lifesaving. They should only be used under the direct supervision of your doctor because of the many serious side effects which can develop. The carefully supervised use of corticosteroids is quite safe, in most cases. If you must take one of these drugs, be sure to follow your doctor's directions explicitly: only then will you get the maximum benefit.

ANALGESICS

Analgesics are drugs used to relieve pain. They act on centers in the nervous system to affect your response to painful stimuli. They don't take the pain away, they simply reduce the response produced by the pain.

Analgesics are classified by the severity of pain they relieve. Those that relieve severe pain are called strong analgesics; those that relieve mild to moderate pain are called mild analgesics.

Strong analgesics have the additional quality of altering the psychological response to pain and alleviating the anxiety and apprehension which often accompany the painful situation. Some drugs considered to be strong analgesics are narcotics, such as Morphine, Meperidine (Demerol), Opium, Oxymorphone (Numorphan), Oxycodone (found in Percodan), Pentazocine (Talwin), and Methotrimeprazine (Levoprome). They all exert basically the same effect on the central nervous system. Their usefulness is related to the length of their effective pain relief, how fast they start working, and the type and degree of side effects and adverse reactions. The differences among them are not great and a doctor will usually choose one based on his training and experience. Patients may express a strong feeling for one of these drugs according to past experience.

Strong analgesics should not be used for mild to moderate pain because of their relative potency and the definite potential for addiction after prolonged use. Other side effects associated with these drugs are difficulty in breathing, nausea, vomiting, constipation, lowered blood pressure, slowed heart rate, and drug reaction or allergy.

Mild analgesics are divided into two categories: those which are chemical derivatives of one of the strong analgesics such as Codeine Sulfate, Mefenamic Acid (Ponstel), Propoxyphene (Darvon, Dolene, SK-65), Ethoheptazine (Zactane), and those considered also to be antipyretic (fever-reducing) such as Aspirin, Sodium Salicylate, Salicylamide, Salsalate (Disalcid), Acetaminophen, Phenacetin, Dipyrone, and Mefenamic Acid (Ponstel).

Of the mild analgesics which are derivatives of one of the strong analgesics, Codeine Sulfate is the most effective, although it can become addicting after long periods of use. It is generally considered more effective than Aspirin and is therefore held in reserve by most doctors for patients who either cannot be effectively treated by the milder drugs or who cannot take them for some reason.

The analgesic-antipyretic drugs are among the most widely used in the world, primarily because most members of this group are available without a prescription. They are used to treat any mild or moderate pain of headache or muscle ache, or from arthritis (inflammation of bone joints), sprains, strains, and so on. They may also be prescribed as part of the treatment of pain due to surgical procedures, cancer, and periodic cramps, and for the reduction of fever. The two drugs most used are Aspirin and Acetaminophen.

See page 11 for information on Acetaminophen, and page 53 for Aspirin.

Some analgesics are used for relief or prevention of severe vascular (migrane) headaches. One of these drugs, Methysergide (Sansert) blocks the effect of serotonin, a naturally occuring chemical thought to be involved in producing these headaches.

Other analgesics are reserved for a special purpose. One of these is Carbamazepine (Tegretol), a potent pain reliever used to treat trigeminal neuralgia (*tic doloreaux*). It has also been used to treat certain forms of epilepsy. This is a potent drug with some very severe side effects and must be taken with caution and only while under a doctor's direction.

Drugs and . . .

DRUGS AND FOODS

Recently, much attention has been paid to the effect of diet on drug therapy and the effect of drugs on diet and nutrition.

How Does Diet Affect Drug Therapy?

Food can interfere with the ability of drugs to be absorbed into the blood through the gastrointestinal system. For this reason, most medications are best taken at least 1 hour before or 2 hours after meals, unless you are directed otherwise by your doctor.

Among drugs which are best taken with meals because the food reduces the amount of stomach irritation caused by the drug are Indomethacin, Phenylbutazone, and Oxyphenbutazone. Other drugs, for example Amoxicillin, may not be affected at all by food. Consult the monographs for specific information about the best time to take medicines.

Some food effects interfere with a drug by reducing the amount of medication available to be absorbed. Juice or milk taken to help you swallow drugs can interfere with them. Many fruit juices, because of their acid content, break down Penicillin-G, Erythromycin, and other antibiotics. Milk or milk products (such as ice cream) can interfere with the absorption of Tetracycline antibiotics through the gastrointestinal tract.

Investigators have questioned the seriousness of such effects; it is generally difficult to prove that people don't get well as fast as a result of them. Probably there is some effect, but its extent is not known.

Some medications react with specific diets. People taking anticoagulant (blood-thinning) drugs should avoid foods rich in fats because they may cause a reduction in anticoagulant effectiveness. People taking Levodopa (L-dopa) should avoid high-protein diets rich in Vitamin B6 (Pyridoxine), which can reduce the effectiveness of Levodopa.

Raw vegetables (cabbage, okra, and some others) contain Vitamin K, which interferes with oral anticoagulant drugs. This interaction can contribute to the development of potentially fatal blood clots.

An ingredient in licorice can cause you to retain sodium and lose potassium. This can be dangerous if you have high blood pressure (increased sodium = increased water = higher blood pressure) or if you are taking a digitalis drug for your heart (less potassium = more digitalis drug side effects).

Many foods interact with MAO inhibitors (see page 574).

Foods containing potassium can be useful to people taking diuretics who need to add potassium to their diet:

Apricots (dried)	Peaches (dried)
Bananas	Prune juice
Cantaloupe	Raisins
Dates	Steak
Figs (dried)	Turkey
Milk	Watermelon
Orange juice	

How Do Drugs Affect Diet and Nutrition?

Drugs can affect your appetite. Drugs that can stimulate your appetite include tricyclic antidepressants and phenothiazine tranquilizers.

Drugs that can cause you to lose your appetite include antibiotics (especially Penicillin) and any medication with a possible side effect of nausea and vomiting.

Many drugs can interfere with the normal absorption of one or more body nutrients:

Antacids	Colchicine
Anticholinergics	Glutethimide
(Atropine, etc.)	Isoniazid
Anticonvulsants	Methotrexate
Barbiturates	Neomycin Sulfate
Cathartics (laxatives)	Oral contraceptives
Chloramphenicol	Sulfa drugs
Clofibrate	

DRUGS AND ALCOHOL

Drug interactions with alcohol, itself a potent drug, are a significant problem and can be experienced by anyone, even those who avoid drinking near the time that they take prescription pills. Many over-the-counter medicines are alcohol-based and have the potential to interact with any prescription drug: there are more than 500 pharmaceutical items that contain alcohol, some in concentrations up to 68 percent. Alcohol is used to dissolve drugs, as in vitamin tonics and antitussive-decongestant liquids, and also to enhance sedative effects. Alcohol is found in almost all decongestant cold-suppressing mixtures.

Alcohol's action in the body is simply that of a central nervous system depressant. It may either enhance or reduce the effect of a drug. The amount of alcohol consumed may not be as important, in some drug interactions, as the chemical reactions it causes in your body. Small concentrations can cause excess stomach secretions, while larger intake can inhibit stomach secretions, eroding the stomach's lining. Use of over-the-counter alcohol-based products by the elderly is especially dangerous, since their systems may be more sensitive to alcohol. People with stomach disorders such as peptic or gastric ulcer should be fully aware of the alcohol levels in products they use.

The effects of alcohol on certain classes of drugs are described below.

One drug, Disulfiram (Anatabuse) is used to treat alcoholism. Alcoholics using this medication will experience abdominal cramps, nausea, vomiting, headaches and flushing if they drink any alcohol, including beer, wine, whiskey or medication with alcohol base such as cough medications. These effects help alcoholics abstain from drinking. Some other drugs also produce this effect, but they are not used in primary treatment programs. They include the oral anti-diabetics and Metrondiazole.

Analgesics

Certain pain relievers such as Aspirin (salicylates) have been linked with intestinal bleeding. Use of alcohol with these products can aggravate an already existing condition.

Strong narcotic pain relievers have a sedative effect on the central nervous system. Adding alcohol can lead to serious central nervous system depression, respiratory arrest, and death.

Alcohol should never be used with narcotic drugs.

Anticoagulants

Alcohol may interact with blood-thinning drugs, extending coagulation time. This is especially true for heavy drinkers. Those taking anticoagulant drugs should avoid alcohol and alcohol-based products.

Antihistamines

Alcohol enhances the sedative effects of antihistamines, even in small doses. Be especially careful, when taking antihistamines, to avoid driving a car or operating machinery.

Antihypertensive Drugs

Certain antihypertensive drugs will interact with alcohol to cause orthostatic hypotension (dizziness, fainting). Be sure that the effectiveness of antihypertensive combinations is not being counteracted by alcohol-based over-the-counter products. Take all antihypertensive medication exactly as prescribed by your doctor.

Antianxiety Drugs and Antidepressants

Phenothiazines and other strong tranquilizers like Thorazine work by depressing the central nervous system. Alcohol will increase this effect, leading to severely impaired ability to drive or operate machinery. Judgment, alertness, and coordination will be diminished. In excess amounts, phenothiazines and alcohol can depress the respiratory control center, leading to death. Since phenothiazines are metabolized in the liver, they may impair livers already damaged by alcohol abuse.

Tricyclic antidepressants (Elavil, for example) have similar interactions when combined with alcohol; the central nervous system depressant effect is enhanced. Psychomotor skills—driving, etc.—are affected by alcohol combined with antidepressants; such combinations have led to serious accidents or death. Antidepressant drugs are also metabolized in the liver; they can reach toxic levels if a damaged liver cannot fully metabolize them.

MAO Inhibitors

Chianti wines, vermouth, and unpasteurized beer can cause serious drug interactions with MAO inhibitors. These drugs, which block a naturally occurring enzyme system called monoamine oxidase, are sometimes used to treat severe depression or high blood pressure. Using alcohol-based products with MAO inhibitors can result in increased blood pressure, headache, and fever; such use should be avoided.

Sedatives/Hypnotics

This is one of the most frequently prescribed classes of drugs and one of the most dangerous to mix with alcohol. Drugs like Chloral Hydrate, Methaqualone, Carbromal, Methylprylon, Glutethimide, Ethclorvynol, Ethinamate, and Flurazepam, when taken with alcohol, can cause excessive sedation and potentiate central nervous system effects. Barbiturates, Diazepam (Valium), and other sedative drugs can cause impairment of motor abilities when taken in combination with alcohol. Some studies have shown that Diazepam and alcohol abuse can lead to addiction, even at prescribed doses.

Before you use alcohol and sedative/hypnotic drugs together, check with your doctor.

Stimulants/Amphetamines

Alcohol in combination with Amphetamine or stimulant drugs can lead to a sudden, dangerous rise in blood pressure. The combination should be avoided.

Antidiabetics

Use of alcohol with antidiabetic drugs such as Insulin or oral antidiabetic pills such as Diabenese or Tolbutamide can be dangerous. The combination can cause excessive hypoglycemia, a dangerous lowering of the glucose (sugar) level in the blood, which can lead to coma.

DRUGS AND SEXUAL ACTIVITY

Sexual activity is usually not limited by drugs; however, some drugs can have an effect on libido and their side effects can lead to impotence. This is especially true in men taking certain drugs which affect the central nervous or circulatory system. It's important to discuss such effects with your doctor: a simple reduction in dosage, or a change to another drug in the same class, may solve the problem.

Many antihypertensives can impair potency and cause retrograde ejaculation in the male. Amphetamines and sedatives have similar effects on libido and can reduce potency. Oral contraceptives have been linked to reduced libido in women.

Some drugs, such as Levodopa and Methaqualone, have been reported to increase libido; note that this is age- and dose-related.

DRUGS AND PREGNANCY

Today we are acutely aware of the potential damage to a fetus from drugs of all kinds. In order for a drug to affect the fetus, it must cross the placental barrier from the mother's bloodstream to that of the fetus. Once in the baby's bloodstream, the drug may affect any of the normal growth and development processes. Because a fetus grows much more rapidly than a fully developed human, the effects of a drug on this process are exaggerated. Adverse results can range from physical disfigurement to severe mental and/or physical damage to death.

An illustration of the damage caused by drug use during pregnancy is the recent discovery of the latent effect of DES (Diethylstilbestrol). This hormone, given to many women during the 1940s and '50s to prevent miscarriage, has been linked to vaginal cancer in the daughters of the women who used it. The Thalidomide scandal of the 1960s was caused by a drug which was intended to help pregnant women but which resulted in birth defects and deformities in children. This led to a complete reevaluation of the use of drugs during pregnancy.

Many obstetricians now recommend that pregnant women avoid all unnecessary medication during pregnancy and after birth while lactating. This includes analgesics such as Aspirin. Unfortunately, potential damage to a fetus is greatest during the first three months of pregnancy, when a woman may not be aware that she is pregnant. If you are considering becoming pregnant, it is wise to curtail any drug use immediately and discuss it fully with your ob/gyn specialist.

Today, most doctors suggest that pregnant women use only vitamins or iron supplements and limit their alcohol, tobacco, and caffeine intake.

DRUGS AND CHILDREN

Medications for children should only be given on direct orders from a pediatrician or other doctor. Of course, children suffer from colds and runny noses and there are many over-the-counter medicines which parents use frequently. Parents should be aware of the ingredients of such products—for example, the alcohol content—and of possible side effects.

Children are at greater risk for drug side effects and interactions because their body systems are not fully developed. This is especially true of infants and young children. Some drugs like tetracyclines have been linked to serious side effects in children and should be avoided. It's wise to ask your doctor whether side effects such as fever or rash are to be expected when he prescribes a drug for a child.

Some drugs have opposite effects on adults and children. Ritalin, which is given to children to calm hyperactivity, acts as a stimulant in adults.

Drug doses for children are usually lower and are often determined by body weight. Be sure you know all there is to know about a drug before you give it to your child. If you can, check with your doctor about over-the-counter products unless you've used them before and are sure they can't interact with other drugs the child is taking.

DRUGS AND THE ELDERLY

Because of changes in the body system from age or disease, the elderly are three times as likely to have adverse drug reactions—nausea, dizziness, blurred vision—as younger people. The greatest danger to the elderly is from drug interactions. Since many elderly are on multiple drug regimens for more than one chronic condition, the potential for drug interaction is much greater.

Older persons often suffer from "asymptomatic drug reactions," silent undetected reactions caused by slowly building amounts of drugs that are not being properly metabolized by their older, less efficient systems.

Most people over the age of 65 take prescription drugs

regularly; in fact, 25 percent of all prescriptions are filled for elderly customers, who make up only 10 percent of the population. Many spend up to $100 a year to get an average of 13 prescriptions filled. The 1.5 million elderly in nursing homes are also at great risk for drug interactions: 54 percent of them take 6 or more pills per day, and some receive up to 23.

Studies have shown that 70 to 90 percent of the elderly take pills and over-the-counter medicines with little knowledge of their dangerous effects. Often elderly people who show speech or hearing problems, absentmindedness, and other symptoms we attribute to aging are suffering from drug reactions. This condition is called reversible dementia.

The elderly are often the victims of overdose, and not necessarily as a result of mistaken dosages. Often body weight fluctuations may lead to overdose unless the dosage of a drug is altered accordingly.

Antihistamines, phenothiazines, and tricyclic antidepressants are known to cause frequent adverse reactions in the elderly. Older people are sometimes unknowing victims of a drug reaction that causes another disease state. For example, gout can be precipitated by certain diuretics, and kidney disease can be caused by long overuse of anti-inflammatories like Aspirin.

It's important to make sure that elderly people understand their drugs completely. Follow the tips for safe drug use on pages 593 to 594 to assist an older person in managing drug intake properly. Install a drug control system which lists the pills prescribed, the sequence in which they should be taken, the time of day, how they should be taken, and a place to indicate what was taken.

Further points, classified by type of drug:

Analgesics

Pain relievers can be especially dangerous to the elderly, who tend to increase the dosages in order to manage pain. This can lead to overdose, since the drugs are excreted more slowly by aging kidneys.

Antiarthritics

Antiarthritics are widely used by the elderly and are generally effective to control pain caused by swollen or inflamed joints. Side effects are gastric upset, blurred vision, and nausea.

Mild anti-inflammatories used by the elderly to combat arthritis include Motrin, Nalfon, Indocin, Naprosyn, and Clinoril. Stronger anti-inflammatories include Oxalid, Tandearil, Azolid, and Butazolidin.

The mild analgesics most commonly used to combat the effects of arthritis are the salicylates, mainly Aspirin. There are hundreds of brand-name products which have been shown to be effective in reducing the pain of mild arthritic conditions. Main drawbacks are stomach irritation, Aspirin's link to blood thinning which may increase the effect of anticoagulants, and Aspirin's excretion through the kidneys.

Strong analgesics such as Codeine Sulfate, Talwin, and narcotics such as Demerol, are especially dangerous to the elderly and should be carefully monitored by a doctor. They can provoke serious drug interactions with glaucoma drugs, tranquilizers, antidepressants, and antihypertensives, and should only be used under a doctor's close supervision.

Oral Antidiabetics

Although most diabetic conditions in the elderly can be controlled by dietary supervision, oral antidiabetics like Diabenese, Tolinase, Orinase, and Dymelor are also used. These drugs differ in their length of effect; often a doctor will tailor the dosage to the individual. Side effects include loss of appetite, nausea, and general gastric distress. Minor infections and emotional problems can affect the actions of these drugs. They should be used carefully when taken with thiazide diuretics, sulfa drugs, Aspirin, anticoagulants, or MAO inhibitors.

Antihypertensive Drugs

Hypertension (high blood pressure) is experienced by 40 to 50 percent of those over 65. This condition, often linked to heart problems, is treated by control of diet and proper, consistent use of medication. Doctors treat hypertension with diuretics (also used to treat heart conditions), vasodilators, and more potent drugs like Reserpine, Guanethidine, Methyldopa, and Propranolol. Vasodilators, which affect the muscles of the artery wall, relaxing them to reduce blood pressure, include Apresoline, Dralzine, Unipres, and Ser-Ap-Es.

The side effects which include depression, light-headedness, and dizziness or feeling faint, are serious; a doctor should be contacted immediately if any of these occur.

Antihypertensives must be taken exactly as prescribed.

Heart Drugs

Heart disease is the leading cause of death in the United States. For many of the elderly, treatment programs for heart disease are the focus of their lives. They must use their drugs exactly as prescribed, often in combination with strict dietary restrictions and technical equipment like pacemakers.

Digitalis drugs including Lanoxin, Digoxin, and Digitoxin are commonly prescribed for congestive heart failure in the elderly. Digitalis intoxication occurs when digitalis drugs are excreted too slowly from the body and is more likely in the elderly because of reduced kidney function. Early symptoms include loss of appetite, vomiting, and nausea. They are serious and a doctor should be contacted immediately.

Diuretics eliminate excess fluid from the body and are often called water pills. The elderly should take the lowest dose possible when using these drugs, and a doctor should carefully monitor their use. They often are used in combination with other drugs; check with a doctor about potential side effects. Diuretics can cause potassium depletion which often results in dry mouth, thirst, weakness, lethargy, drowsiness, restlessness, and muscle pains or cramps.

Other Drugs

Some drugs are more often prescribed for elderly people because certain conditions are found more frequently in this group. One example is Hydergine, often used to treat the symptoms of Alzheimer-like diseases. (See page 190—Ergot Alkaloids). Another example of this would be Methandrostenolone (Dianabol), an anabolic steroid, which has been shown to be somewhat effective as secondary therapy in treating senile and post-menopausal osteoporosis (bone disease). Conditions like osteoporosis are treated primarily with diet, calcium balance, and physiotherapy.

Questions and Answers About Drug Use

Q: How many Americans die of drug overdose each year?
A: About 70,000 Americans are treated for drug overdose or poisoning each year. About 7000 cases are fatal. (Source: National Center for Health Statistics)

Q: How long have pills existed?
A: Pills have been used for thousands of years, although they weren't mass-produced until this century. Before the days of mass-produced medicines, pills were rolled substances or potions made from a mass of a root or herb or other ingredient. Sometimes they were coated with a glucose-like substance to make them easier to swallow.

Q: How long should I keep my prescription drugs?
A: Generally, prescription drugs should be kept only as long as you need to take them. Some drugs cannot be used after a year; some can be used longer. Broken tablets should not be used unless your pharmacist indicates they are all right. If you have an ongoing condition and will be taking medication daily—for example, for high blood pressure—check with your pharmacist to determine your drug's expiration dates. Do not use the drug after that date has passed.

Q: Is it illegal to give someone your prescription drugs?
A: It is not only illegal—only doctors can prescribe drugs—it is also a very bad idea. Although your friends may think they have the same symptoms as you, they can't know for sure without being examined by a doctor. A drug that works well for you may cause serious side effects in

someone who has a different weight or underlying condition. *Never take a prescription drug unless a doctor tells you to.*

Q: What is the difference between a generic and a brand-name drug?

A: In theory, there should be no difference except price. A brand-name drug is manufactured by a company under its trade name, with advertising promotion adding to the cost. You can expect it to be the same as the generic product which is sold under the "official" or chemical name of the drug by several manufacturers. Not every drug can be bought under both generic and brand name; many are available only as a specific brand. Check with your pharmacist to determine if you can save money on a prescription by substituting a generic drug.

Q: How do you store drugs?

A: All drugs should be stored in sealed, light-resistant containers. Keep your prescriptions in their original containers from the drugstore, to prevent mistakes when you take them. Certain liquids packaged by your pharmacist should be kept refrigerated. Check when you purchase the drug. Protect your medicines from excessive humidity, which can speed drug breakdown.

Q: What causes a drug interaction?

A: Drug interaction is caused when two chemical substances, from drugs or other substances like alcohol, mix in the body to cause an unexpected or undesired reaction or effect. Do not take more than one drug without checking with your doctor or pharmacist about interaction.

Q: What is the most popular prescription drug in the United States?

A: In 1980 more prescriptions were filled for Valium than for any other prescription drug. In terms of sales dollars, Tagamet, an anti-ulcer preparation introduced only in 1976, was the largest moneymaker.

Q: What is the best way to avoid side effects?

A: Take each drug exactly as prescribed and let your doctor

know about other drugs you are taking, including over-the-counter products. He will be able to tailor your dose to your body's needs.

Q: **What's a placebo?**

A: A placebo is a capsule or a tablet with no active ingredient that looks like a real pill. There is a "placebo effect" by which many patients taking placebo pills not only feel better but show medically measurable improvement. This is a good example of mind over matter.

Twenty Questions to Ask About Your Prescription

1. What is the name of this medicine?
2. What results can be expected from taking it?
3. How long should I wait before reporting if this medicine does not help me?
4. How does the medicine work?
5. What is the exact dose of the medicine?
6. What time of day should I take it?
7. Can I drink alcoholic beverages while taking this medicine?
8. Do I have to take special precautions with this medicine in combination with other prescription drugs I am taking?
9. Do I have to take special precautions with this medicine in combination with nonprescription (over-the-counter) drugs?
10. Can I take this medicine without regard to food or mealtimes?
11. Are there any special instructions I should have about how to use this medicine?
12. How long should I continue to take this medicine?
13. Is my prescription renewable?
14. For how long a period can my prescription be renewed?
15. Which side effects should I report and which can I disregard?
16. Can I save any unused portion of this medicine for future use?
17. How should I store this medicine?
18. How long can I keep this medicine without its losing strength?
19. What should I do if I forget to take a dose of this medicine?
20. Is this medicine available in a less expensive, generic form? If so, is the less expensive form of equal quality?

Other Points to Remember
for Safe Drug Use

- Make sure you tell the doctor everything that is wrong. The more information he has, the more effectively he can treat you.
- Make sure each doctor you see knows all the medicines you use regularly, including prescription and nonprescription drugs.
- Keep a record of any bad reaction you have had to a medicine.
- Fill each prescription you are given. If you don't fill a prescription, make sure the doctor knows it.
- Don't take extra medicine without consulting your doctor or pharmacist.
- Follow the label instructions *exactly*. If you have any questions, call your doctor or pharmacist.
- Report any unusual symptoms that develop after taking medicine.
- Don't save unused medicine for future use unless you have consulted your doctor. Dispose of unused medicine by flushing it down the toilet.
- Never keep medicine where children can see or reach it.
- Always read the label before taking your medicine. Don't trust your memory.
- Consult your pharmacist for guidance on the use of over-the-counter (nonprescription) drugs.
- Don't share your medicine with anyone. Your prescription was written for you and only you.

- Be sure the label stays on the container until the medicine is used or destroyed.
- Keep the label facing up when pouring liquid medicine from the bottle.
- Don't use a prescription medicine unless it has been specifically prescribed for you.
- When you travel, take your prescription with you in its original container.
- If you move to another city, ask your pharmacist to forward your prescription records to your new pharmacy.
- Carry important medical facts about you in your wallet. Such things as drug allergies, chronic diseases (diabetes, etc.), and special requirements can be very useful.
- Don't hesitate to discuss the cost of medical care with your doctor or pharmacist.
- Exercise your right to make decisions about buying medicines:

  1. If you suffer from a chronic condition, you can probably save by buying in larger quantities.

  2. Choose your pharmacist as carefully as you choose your doctor.

  3. Remember, the cost of your prescription includes the professional services offered by your pharmacy. If you want more service you will have to pay for it.

Glossary of Drug-Related Words

Addiction—Habituation to the use of a drug or other substance. Withdrawal of the addicting agent gives rise to physical symptoms and an overwhelming desire for the agent.

Adrenal corticosteroid—Drug related to hydrocortisone, corticosterone, or deoxycorticosterone used primarily for its ability to reduce inflammation. Also used to replace natural corticosteroids in deficient patients.

Allergy—Unusual response produced in some people when exposed to a drug, food, or other substance. The response can vary widely from a simple rash to life-threatening symptoms.

Amoebicide—Drug used to treat infections caused by amoebas, tiny microorganisms commonly found in nature.

Analgesic—Pain-relieving.

Androgen—Drug or hormone that stimulates activity in male sex organs or prevents changes in male sex characteristics already present.

Anemia—Condition in which the number or size of red blood cells or the amount of oxygen-carrying hemoglobin contained in red blood cells is deficient. Anemia is usually further defined according to the causative agent or disease.

Anesthetic—Drug that produces loss of sensation or of response to stimulation.

Angina pectoris—Severe chest pain, often extending down the left shoulder and arm, relieved by Nitroglycerin.

Antacid—Drug used to neutralize excess acid in the stomach.

Antianxiety drug—Drug used to treat symptoms of anxiety (feeling of apprehension or danger accompanied by restlessness).

Antiarrhythmic drug—Drug used to help regulate unusual or abnormal heart rhythms.

Antiasthmatic drug—Drug used to treat symptoms of asthma, including difficulty in breathing, with wheezing.

Antibacterial drug—Drug that is destructive to or prevents the growth of bacteria.

Antibiotic—Substance derived from a mold or bacteria which slows or stops the growth of other bacteria.

596 THE PILL BOOK

Anticholinergic drug—Drug that antagonizes or counteracts the effects of acetylcholine, a natural hormone responsible for certain nervous system activities.

Anticoagulant drug—Drug used to extend the time it normally takes for blood to clot.

Anticonvulsant drug—Drug used to prevent or treat any disease associated with violent involuntary muscle contractions.

Antidepressant—Drug used to treat the symptoms of depression (dejection, sinking of one's spirits).

Antidiabetic drug—Drug used to treat diabetes mellitus.

Antidiarrheal drug—Drug used to treat diarrhea.

Antidote—Drug used to counteract the adverse effects of a drug or chemical.

Antiemetic drug—Drug to control vomiting.

Antiflatulent drug—Drug used to relieve discomfort due to excessive gas in the stomach or intestines.

Antihelminthic drug—Drug used to treat infections caused by helminths (worms).

Antihistamine—Drug used for its ability to neutralize or antagonize the effects of histamine, a naturally occurring substance; used to relieve the symptoms of allergy.

Antihyperlipidemic drug—Drug used to help control high levels of fats (cholesterol; triglycerides) in the blood.

Anti-infective—Relating to any agent used to treat an infection.

Antineoplastic drug—Drug used to treat neoplasms (unusual growths of tissue). Cancers are neoplastic diseases. Benign (noncancerous) growths are also neoplastic.

Antipruritic drug—Drug used to relieve itching.

Antipyretic drug—Drug used to reduce fever.

Antirheumatic drug—Drug used to treat or prevent rheumatism.

Antitoxin—Drug that neutralizes the effects of toxins (poisons, usually produced by bacteria invading the body).

Antitussive drug—Drug used to relieve cough.

Arrhythmia—Unusual or irregular heartbeat.

Ataxia—Loss of ability to coordinate muscular movements.

Bacteria—Living organisms, visible only under a microscope, which may infect humans and cause disease. Bacteria are classified according to shape, chemical reactivity, and nutrients they require.

Bactericidal drug—Drug that kills bacteria.

Bacteriostatic drug—Drug that inhibits the reproduction of bacteria.

Blood count—Number of red and white blood cells found in a standard sample of blood.

Blood dyscrasia—General term for any blood disease.

Blood sugar—Sugar normally found in the blood and burned for energy. Normal level of blood sugar is approximately 100 mg of glucose in approximately 3 oz of blood.

Bradycardia—Slowing of the heartbeat, usually to less than 60 beats per minute.

Bronchodilator—Drug used to help relax the bronchial muscles and to widen the bronchial passages.

Calorie—Unit of measure used to determine the energy (heat) value of foods to the body.

Cancer—General term used to describe malignant neoplasms which tend to spread rapidly and will result in illness and death if left untreated.

Capillary—Microscopic blood vessel connecting veins with arteries.

Carcinoma—Cancer.

Cardiac—Having to do with the heart.

Cardiac arrest—Stoppage of heart activity.

Cardiac glycoside—Type of drug that has the ability to increase the strength of and help regulate the rate of the heartbeat.

Cataract—Condition in which the lens of the eye loses its transparency, so that light cannot pass through it normally.

Cerebrum—Portion of the brain that is the seat of conscious mental processes.

Cerumen—Earwax.

Chilblain—Frostbite.

Climacteric—Menopause.

Coagulant drug—Drug which causes clotting of the blood.

Coma—State of unconsciousness from which one cannot be awakened. Causes include diabetes, liver disease, and thyroid disease.

Conception—Act of becoming pregnant.

Congestion—Presence of abnormal amounts of fluids due to increased flow into the area or decreased drainage.

Corticosteroid—See **Adrenal corticosteroid**.

Decongestant—Drug that reduces congestion.

Decubitus—Bedsore.

Delirium—Condition of extreme mental excitement marked by a stream of confused, unconnected ideas.

Dementia—General mental deterioration.

Demulcent—Agent applied to the skin or mucous membranes to relieve an irritation.

Dermatologic drug—Agent applied directly to the skin.

Dextrose—See **Glucose**.

Diabetes—Disease of body metabolism in which there is an insufficient supply of natural insulin. This reduces the body's ability to store or burn glucose.

Diagnostic drug—Agent used by a physician to assist in the diagnosis of a disease.

Dilate—To enlarge a cavity, canal, blood vessel, or opening.

Disinfectant—Agent that inhibits or destroys bacteria which cause disease.

Diuretic—Drug that stimulates the production and passing of urine.

Dose—Quantity of a drug or medicine to be taken or applied all at once or over a designated period.

Drug dependence—Term used to describe drug habituation or addiction.

Drug interaction—What occurs when one drug affects (increases or decreases) the ability of a second drug to exert a therapeutic effect.

Drug sensitivity—Reaction or allergy to a drug.

Edema—Accumulation of clear watery fluid.

EEG—Electroencephalogram.

EKG—Electrocardiogram.

Electrolytes—Chemicals such as sodium, potassium, calcium, and bicarbonate found in body tissues and fluids.

Embolism—Obstruction of a blood vessel, caused by a blood clot or a large mass of bacterial or foreign material.

Emollient—Agent that softens or smooths irritated skin or mucous membranes.

Endocarditis—Inflammation of the membrane lining the heart.

Endocrine glands—Glands that produce hormones and release them directly into the bloodstream.

Enzyme—Protein, produced by body cells, which stimulates a chemical reaction in the body and remains unchanged during the reaction.

Epilepsy—Chronic disease characterized by periods of unconsciousness, convulsions, or both.

Eruption—Redness, spotting, or breaking out in a rash on the skin.

Estrogen—Drug or hormone that stimulates activity in female sex organs or prevents changes in female sex characteristics already present.

Euphoria—Feeling of exaggerated well-being.

Exfoliation—Profuse scaling of large areas of skin.

Expectorant—Drug that stimulates the production of secretions from mucous membranes.

Extrapyramidal effects—Spasm of neck muscles, rolling of the eyeballs, convulsions, difficulty swallowing, and other symptoms associated with Parkinson's disease, but also seen as an adverse drug effect.

Fever—Body temperature above 98.6°F (37°C).

Ganglia—Aggregations or groups of nerve cells.

Gastritis—Inflammation of the stomach.

Generic name—Standard name accepted for a drug. Manufacturers often use their own trade name that correspond to the generic name.

Glucose—Principal sugar used by the body for energy; also called dextrose.

Gonad—Sexual gland.

Hallucination—Perception of something which does not exist.

Hemorrhoids—Piles.

Hepatitis—Inflammation of the liver.

Histamine—Substance produced by the body as part of an allergic reaction; it causes dilation of blood vessels, lowered blood pressure, and stimulation of secretions from the stomach and other organs.

Hyperacidity—Abnormally large amounts of acid in the stomach.

Hyperglycemia—Presence of high level of sugar (glucose) in the blood.

Hyperkalemia—Presence of high potassium level in the blood.

Hyperlipidemia—High blood level of cholesterol and/or triglycerides.

Hypertension—High blood pressure.

Hypoacidity—Unusually low level of stomach acid.

Hypoglycemia—Low blood sugar (glucose) level.

Hypokalemia—Low blood potassium level.

Hypotension—Low blood pressure.

Immunity—Resistance to the effects of a specified disease or of some other abnormal condition.

Ketonuria—The passage of ketone bodies (acetone) in the urine. This condition may be present in diabetes or as a result of an unbalanced high-protein diet.

Laudanum—Tincture of opium.

Laxative—Drug that can loosen the bowels (act as a cathartic). Types of laxatives are bulk, saline, and stimulant.

Lesion—Wound or injury.

Lethargy—Drowsiness.

Malaise—Feeling of general discomfort or of being out of sorts.

Metastasis—Shifting of a disease, or its local effect, from one part of the body to another.

Migraine headache—Pain on one side of the head; complex of effects consisting of head pain, dizziness, nausea and vomiting, and extreme sensitivity to bright light.

Myopia—Nearsightedness.

Nebulizer—Atomizer or vaporizer.

Neoplasm—New or abnormal growth of tissue usually associated with a tumor.

Normotension—Blood pressure in the normal range.

Nystagmus—Rapid uncontrolled eye movement.

Obesity—Body weight at least 10 to 20 percent greater than the expected value.

Over-the-counter drug—Medication sold without a prescription. May be purchased in pharmacies and other outlets.

Palpitation—Rapid heart beat in which the patient feels throbbing in his chest.

Paralysis—Loss of power in one or more muscles because of injury or disease.

Pill—Small mass of material containing a medication and taken by swallowing.

Plasma—Fluid portion of circulating blood.

Platelet—Component of the blood whose primary role is in the clotting mechanism.

Pneumonia—Inflammation of the lungs, from any cause.

Polydipsia—Excessive thirst.

Polyuria—Excessive urination.

Prescription—Written formula for the preparation and administration of any remedy or medicine, by a qualified, licensed medical practitioner.

Progestins—Female hormones that cause changes in the uterus to prepare it for the fertilized egg. Progestins may also affect other female sex characteristics.

Pruritis—Itching.

Psychotherapeutic drug—Drug used as treatment or part of the treatment of emotional disorders.

Rash—Local or generalized eruption.

Respiration—Breathing.

Rhinorrhea—Running nose.

Somnifacient drug—Drug that produces sleep.

Sulfa drug—Drug belonging to the chemical group of sulfonamides. Members of this group can have anti-infective, diuretic, and antidiabetic properties.

Sulfonamide—See **Sulfa drug.**

Sympathomimetic drug—Drug with stimulating action, also causing relief of congestion, increase in blood pressure, and other effects.

Symptom—Any change in function, appearance, or sensation related to a disease.

Syndrome—Group of symptoms which, when taken together, indicate the presence of a specific disease.

Tablet—Solid dosage form containing medicine. Tablets from different manufacturers may vary in size, color, shape, and content.

Testosterone—Male sex hormone.

Tinnitus—Ringing or noise in the ears, often as a drug side effect.

Toxic—Poisonous or harmful.

Toxin—Substance produced by a cell or group of cells, or by bacteria during their growth, that produces a poisonous effect.

Toxoid—Toxin that has been treated with chemicals to destroy its harmful properties. After this treatment it can be injected into the human body and will provide immunity to the original toxin.

Tremor—Involuntary trembling or quivering.

Tumor—Swelling or neoplasm that grows at an unusual rate.

Ulcer—Lesion on the surface of the skin or mucous membrane.

Urticaria—Hives or itching rash.

Vaccine—Solution of modified virus or bacteria that, when injected, provides immunity to the original virus or bacteria.

Vasodilator—Drug that causes opening or widening of the blood vessels.

Vitamin—Chemical present in foods that is essential to normal body functions and to normal chemical reactions in the body.

Sources

Abramowicz, Mark, ed., *The Medical Letter on Drugs and Therapeutics,* Medical Letter, New Rochelle, N.Y., 1980, 1981.

Adams, George, *Essentials of Geriatric Medicine,* 4th ed., Oxford Medical Publications, London, 1981.

American Medical Association, Department of Drugs, *AMA Drug Evaluations,* 3d ed., Publishing Sciences Group, Acton, Mass., 1977.

American Medical Association, Department of Mental Health, *Drug Abuse, A Guide for the Primary Care Physician,* 1st ed., Chicago, 1981.

American Pharmaceutical Association, *Evaluations of Drug Interactions,* 2d ed., American Pharmaceutical Association, Washington, D.C., 1976.

American Pharmaceutical Association, *Handbook of Nonprescription Drugs,* 6th ed., American Pharmaceutical Association, Washington, D.C., 1979.

American Society of Hospital Pharmacists, *American Hospital Formulary Service,* American Society of Hospital Pharmacists, Washington, D.C., 1981.

Chilnick, L. D., *Taking Care of Mom and Pop,* Bantam Books, Inc., New York, forthcoming.

Consumer Guide, Gossel, T. A., and Stansloski, D. W., *Prescription Drugs,* Beekman House, New York, 1979.

Conn, H. F., ed., *Current Therapy 1977,* W. B. Saunders, Philadelphia.

DH. F., ed., *Current Therapy 1977,* W. B. Saunders, Philadelphia.

Deichman, W. B., and Gerarde, H. W., *Toxicology of Drugs and Chemicals,* Academic Press, New York, 1969.

Dorlands Illustrated Medical Dictionary, 24th ed., W. B. Saunders Co., Philadelphia, 1965.

Dukes, G. E., Kuhn, J. G. and Evens, R. P. "Alcohol in Pharmaceutical Products," *Family Practice,* September, 1977.

Gleason, M. N., Gosselin, R. E., Hodge, H. C., and Smith, R. P., *Clinical Toxicology of Commercial Products,* 3d ed., Williams & Wilkins, Baltimore, 1969.

602

Goldstein, A., Aronow, L., and Kalman, S., *Principles of Drug Action: The Basis of Pharmacology,* 2d ed., John Wiley & Sons, New York, 1974.

Goodman, L. S., and Gilman, A., *The Pharmacological Basis of Therapeutics,* 6th ed., Macmillan, New York, 1980.

Graedon, J., *The People's Pharmacy, A Guide to Prescription Drugs, Home Remedies and Over-the-Counter Medications,* St. Martin's Press, New York, 1976.

Graedon, J., with Graedon, T., *The People's Pharmacy-2,* Avon Books, New York, 1980.

Greenblatt, D. J., and Shader, R. I., *Benzodiazepines in Clinical Practice,* Raven Press, New York, 1974.

Hansten, P. D., *Drug Interactions,* 3d ed., Lea & Febiger, Philadelphia, 1975.

Hodkinson, H. M., *Common Symptoms of Disease in the Elderly,* 2d ed., Blackwell Scientific Publications, London, 1979.

Jones, Judith K., *Family Guide to Medications,* Hearst Books, New York, 1980.

Kastrup, E. K., and Schwach, G., eds., *Facts and Comparisons,* Facts and Comparisons, St. Louis, 1981.

Lamy, P. P., *Prescribing for the Elderly,* PSG Publishing Company, Littleton, Mass., 1980.

Langley, L., Cheraskin, F., and Sleeper, R., *Dynamic Anatomy and Physiology,* 2d ed., McGraw-Hill, New York, 1963.

Long, J. S., *The Essential Guide to Prescription Drugs,* 3d. ed. Harper & Row, New York, 1982.

Medical Economics, *Physicians' Desk Reference,* 35th ed., Medical Economics, Oradell, N.J., 1981.

Mortality Statistics Branch, Division of Vital Statistics, *Vital Statistics of the United States,* Vol. 2, Mortality, National Center for Health Services, Hyattsville, Maryland, 1982.

National Clearing House for Poison Control Centers, *Bulletin,* Vol. 25, No. 6, U.S. Department of Health and Human Services, Food and Drug Administration, August, 1981.

National Institute on Drug Abuse, *Sex and Race Differentials in Acute Drug Abuse,* (NIDA Statistical Series H #1) 1982.

Parish, P., *The Doctors and Patients Handbook of Medicines and Drugs,* Alfred A. Knopf, New York, 1977.

Silverman, H. M., "Anticoagulant Therapy," *New Environment of Pharmacy* 3:5 (Nov./Dec.) 1976.

Silverman, H. M., "Antineoplastic Therapy," *Physician Assistant* 1:23 (May/June) 1976.

Silverman, H. M., "Classification of Antibiotics," *Hospital Formulary Management* 7:26 (Feb.) 1972.

Silverman, H. M., "Fetal and Newborn Adverse Drug Reactions," *Drug Intelligence and Clinical Pharmacy* 8:690 (Dec.) 1974.

Silverman, H. M., "MAO Inhibitors," *Hospital Formulary Management* 8:14 (March) 1973.

Silverman, H. M., "The Proper Time for Taking Drugs," *Hospital Formulary Management* 9:18 (Feb.) 1974.

Strauss, S., *Your Prescription and You,* 3d ed., Medical Business Services, Ambler, Pa., 1978.

Thomas, C. L., ed., *Tabers Cyclopedic Medical Dictionary,* 12th ed., F. A. Davis, Philadelphia, 1973.

United States Department of Health, Education and Welfare, "Health Status of the Elderly."

United States Pharmacopeial Convention, Inc., *About Your Medicines,* United States Pharmacopeial Convention, Inc., Rockville, Maryland, 1981.

Wesson, Donald R., M.D., and Smith, David E., M.D., "Low Dose Benzodiazapine Withdrawal Syndrome: Receptor Site Mediated," NEWS, California Society for the Treatment of Alcoholism and Other Drug Dependencies, Vol. 9, No. 1, (Feb.) 1982.

Index of Generic and Brand Name Drugs

Generic drugs are printed in boldface type.

Index of Drug Types

618

ABOUT THE MEDICAL WRITERS

HAROLD M. SILVERMAN, PHARM.D., is Director of the Department of Pharmacy at Mount Sinai Hospital, Miami Beach, Fla. Dr. Silverman previously was associated with Lenox Hill Hospital in New York City for 14 years. He has served as president of the Westchester County and New York State Council of Hospital Pharmacists. He has contributed extensively to the professional pharmacy literature, including published articles and papers, textbook chapters and is coauthor of the *Med-File* Drug Interaction System. He has been a consultant to the State of New York and City of New York as well as to several corporations and to professional journals of pharmacy and pharmacology. Dr. Silverman holds two degrees from Columbia University, where he was elected to the Rho Chi Pharmaceutical Honor Society. He has served on the faculties of Columbia University and Long Island University. He is listed in *Outstanding Young Men of America* for 1976, 1977, and 1979. Dr. Silverman resides with his wife, Barbara, and two daughters, Melissa and Jennifer, in North Miami Beach, Fla.

GILBERT I. SIMON, SC.D., is Director of the Department of Pharmacy at Beth Israel Medical Center, New York City. From 1961 to 1982 he was Director of the Department of Pharmacy, Lenox Hill Hospital, New York City. Dr. Simon received his B.S. from Fordham University, his M.S. from Long Island University, and his Doctorate, Honoris Causa, from the College of Pharmacy Sciences, City of New York (Columbia University). He was an associate professor of pharmaceutical sciences at Columbia University from 1964 to 1976. Dr. Simon has served as president to both the New York State and the New York City societies. In 1973 he was honored with the Award of Merit from the New York City Society of Hospital Pharmacists for his contribution to the practice of institutional pharmacy. He has been a member of the Pharmacy Advisory Committee of the Greater New York Hospital Association and served on committees of the Hospital Association of the State of New York. Dr. Simon is currently a member of the New York State Medical Advisory Committee, Department of Social Services, and has served as a consultant to the pharmacy industry. He has been a principal speaker on contemporary hospital pharmacy practice throughout the United States and in Europe. In 1975, Drs. Simon and Silverman coauthored *Med-File*, a book on common non-prescription drugs and their interactions. Dr. Simon lives in Bronxville, New York.

INTRODUCING
THE
PILL POSTER

You can now have a full-color 18″ × 48″ poster featuring 600 of the drugs most commonly prescribed in the United States. Both attractive and highly useful, THE PILL POSTER is arranged by color to allow you to identify any of these 600 drugs at a glance.

And for a limited time and only with the coupon below, THE PILL POSTER (regular price $5.00) is available for only $4.00 including postage and handling. So order yours today.